I thank senior editor Barbara Ellington, who acquired the book for Westview Press, for her support of the project and for her valuable editorial work on the manuscript.

I dedicate this book to Kathi, my love and teacher in the art of positive thinking.

Menno Vellinga
Utrecht University

D0002663

1

The Changing Role of the State in Latin America

Menno Vellinga

¿Como cambiar al estado?—"how to change the state?"—was the theme of a 1993 conference organized in Lima, one of many such meetings with similar titles held in the early 1990s.[1] "State reform" was a generalized preoccupation among leading politicians, social scientists, and representatives of organizations in the field of international development cooperation, who livelily debated what should follow in the wake of the old development state. State reform was given top priority on political agendas as governments were confronted with the results of the structural reforms that multilateral funding organizations had promoted. It was presented as the issue whose successful resolution would determine the eventual success of the economic and social reforms that, from their perspective, were necessary to secure stable long-term economic growth.[2]

Economic priorities—the modernization of the production apparatus or the productive sectors and their integration into the international economy—raised less controversy. Productivity increases, competitiveness, and flexibility in adapting to changes in demand in the international market remain generally accepted key concepts. The priority of market criteria, however, requires regulating competition, consumer protection, capital markets, labor conditions, and the like. These objectives imply, in turn, a modernization of the general administrative capacity of the state, including its ability to define and execute policies in a multitude of areas that influence national economic and social development. This calls for the reorganization of the public administration apparatus as well as the institutions of the judicial, legislative, and executive branches of government and those securing the participation of regional and local government in decision making through effective programs of decentralization. These are a few, among many, themes that dominate the more recent discussions on state reform.[3] Earlier reforms in the wake of the economic shock policies of the 1980s and the structural adjustment programs that followed dealt essentially with a one-sided reduction of the state interventions in the production and social services sectors and a dismantling of the institutions identified with the state-centered, protectionist practices of the previous period.[4]

It should be emphasized that the pattern for the withdrawal of the state from major policy areas in the economic and social sphere shows considerable differences among individual countries. How state reform is handled in response to international economic pressures that emphasize the necessity of structural adjustment consistent with market reforms varies according to the interplay of domestic political and economic forces. These policies often had drastic consequences. "Reform" amounted, in practice, to a demolition of institutions involving massive dismissals of personnel, resulting in a debilitating influence on state policymaking regarding "core obligations" that will not easily be taken care of by other institutions. The technical capacity and expertise that could have been mobilized to help define policies and systems in these core areas were lost, thus hindering the search for an efficient way to alleviate *the* basic problem of Latin American society: the structural inequalities imbedded in the organization of economy and society and the social, economic, and political exclusion of the poor.[5]

The present debate emphasizes the need for reforms that will reestablish institutional strength, state authority, efficiency, and planning capacity in the various economic and social sectors. Priorities are established within those sectors that traditionally depend on normative action by the state and, more important, within those requiring the reduction of socioeconomic inequalities and the correction of patterns of allocation of resources traditionally directed to enclaves of power through clientelist mechanisms and conjunctural networks. Strong emphasis is placed on the necessity to create institutions, norms, and procedures that would reduce the possibility of corrupt practices and establish responsibility and accountability in public administration. These measures must be accompanied by a deepening of the process of democratization, an extension of democratic ground rules to state-civil society relations, and the creation of a consensus among state agencies about policy priorities and the accompanying long-term budget allocations.[6] The patrimonial-bureaucratic tradition in Latin America transforms these processes into an exceptionally complicated enterprise. In political practice what is lacking is a system of rules and procedures whose legitimate status is generally accepted and through which those who govern are selected and decisions are taken. In short, Latin America misses a tradition of legal-rational legitimacy of the democratic state in the Weberian sense.

State and Society

In recent decades economic, social, and political processes have been co-ordinated through what Cavarozzi has called a state-centred matrix (SCM).[7] This concept implies a double dependency in state–civil society relations. Social actors such as industrial workers, state bureaucrats, members of the middle class, all forming part of the urban-industrial complex, became a factor of sociopolitical importance, but they depended on the state for the realization of their demands and aspirations. The state, in turn, needed the support of these actors to give its functioning a certain basis of legitimacy. The SCM was obviously the stereotypical configuration under populist rule where those sectors associated with the model of import-substitution industrialization formed the social basis and political force of the state. However, the presence of SCM was not limited to populist rule. Populism was not the only political formula that emerged under the model of *desarrollo hacia adentro* (inward-directed development), although, admittedly, it was the most important. These political solutions to a highly complex economic and social situation shared a common emphasis on an all-encompassing trend toward state intervention in all spheres of economic, social, political, and cultural life. The trend was supported by politicians of widely differing political persuasion, although the specific content of policies depended on the composition and orientation of the supporting class alliance.[8]

The state thus became a "developmental state" that not only provided a majority of the infrastructure that supported the development process but—in the long term—extended its power and influence to all those areas that had an impact on the process. In this manner, in addition to the essential concerns with the internal order, continuity, and external relations of the social system, state action came to include an ever-increasing number of interventions in, for example:[9]

- educational, technological, and scientific development;
- social policies concerning social security and social services, wages and salaries, level of employment, functioning of the labor market, consumer purchasing power, and the composition of the labor force;
- financial policies concerning conditions of credit, monetary issues (the printing of currency, devaluation, and exchange rates), fiscal affairs (exemptions, concessions, and taxes), budgets, and public expenditures (subsidies);
- economic policies concerning budgets, public investments, the production of goods and services, the buying and selling of goods and services, nationalization, privatization, and transnationalization;

- legal policies concerning conciliation and arbitration, legal justice (penal and civil), sanctions, and law enforcement; and
- issues of cultural and ideological legitimacy.

The increase in range and reach of state policies was not always accompanied by an increase in administrative capacity. In many cases state intervention lacked bureaucratic efficiency and revealed the strong influence of clientelism, patronage, and patrimonialism. State action suffered from the combined effects of, in Schmitter's terms, "structural overbureaucratization" and "behavioral underbureaucratization," two processes that, as Schneider shows, in bureaucratic practice had become interdependent.[10] Also, the state had expanded—often beyond its financial limits—but it had not strengthened its capacity to define policies that went beyond the interests of the many narrow social groups that enjoyed established particularistic links to public agencies. Weyland describes this process with regard to Brazil.[11] He explains the paradox of an ever-expanding state apparatus, suggesting a "strong state on-the-move," which, at the same time however, undermined its own potential for coherent action as a result of its corporatist policies toward civil society. These policies produced a social fragmentation that served well the objectives of political control but made it increasingly difficult to create a sufficiently strong social basis for broad development-related policies. The continuous growth of the state apparatus was not accompanied by an equal growth in internal coordination, efficiency, and effectiveness of state action, or an increase in autonomy with regard to particularistic demands. The result is that private interests have infiltrated public institutions and have, in fact, "captured,"[12] parts of the state. The process, which has occurred in other countries of Latin America as well, increasingly weakened the state's potential to pursue overarching interests, especially macroeconomic ones. In this socially fragmented situation, corporatist and clientelist political practices acquired a new functionality, controlling social tensions in an environment characterized by extremely unequal distribution of wealth, income, and access to other resources that affect social mobility.

The analysis above underlines once more that by the "state" we do not allude to a "neutral" administrative body but to a sociopolitical entity that in the growth and differentiation of its institutional structure and in its functioning is a product of and an object of struggle among interest groups and social classes, as well as a determining force in it. In other words, the structure and functioning of the state are a product of the competition between social actors and the efforts to control it. Once this process of state formation has been consolidated, the state, through its operations and actions, develops a certain autonomy with a decisive influence on the patterns and issues of the power struggle among groups or classes. Finally, the political power of the state—its potential for control and the institutions in which that potential is concentrated—in turn becomes an object of class contention.[13]

The state represents a mechanism for the articulation of social relations within a complex structure of power relations that may, at times, be congruent with and may, at other times, contradict one another. Considerable variations in the relationship between the state and civil society are the result, a situation that is further complicated by the persistent presence of strong international constraints on Latin American states, as Peter Smith shows so convincingly in his chapter on the developmental state. In the course of the history of state–civil society relations in Latin America since independence, though, certain basic patterns can be recognized.

The Nature of the State

The state in Latin America has been characterized, as Castañeda has written, by a "lack of accountability," an "undemocratic nature," and an "inability" to perform the tasks of a responsibly functioning bureaucracy. I agree with him that the *real* problem of the state can be found on this level.[14] The nature of the state is a distinctly greater problem than its size or even the definition of its developmentalist role. It is directly associated with the historical legacy of patrimonialism and related traditional patterns that established a political practice through which particularistic interests privatized state institutions and policies.[15] During colonial times no well-defined borders were established between the colonial bureaucratic administration and private patrimony, and this lack of separation between public office and private interests continued to haunt the new Latin American nations after independence. State and government often became confused with each other. The institutions that could have supported the separation of the two were weakly developed. On the basis of historical experience in Western Europe and North America, one would have expected in the course of time the growth of a certain autonomy of the state relative to civil society, an autonomy grounded in a traditional and legal basis and supported by powerful civil and military institutions. However, this development toward autonomy stagnated in Latin America. Few countries were able to develop an independent and powerful functioning judiciary; even fewer can boast a competent, relatively honest and (more or less) permanent civil service; in most countries, the military was a continually destabilizing factor.

The colonial regime did not establish the legal order and bureaucratic structure through which power could have been delegated, a structure that could have functioned with a certain autonomy and without the need for constant personal interventions by the highest authority. On the contrary, the system of administration and control was authoritarian, centralist, and functioned through "divide and rule" strategies of the Machiavellian type. This strong central authority disappeared with the Wars of Independence, and the administrative chaos that ensued came as no surprise.

After independence, there was a strong tendency to preserve the structure and logic of the old patrimonial system in order to maintain order, stability, and continuity. The almost sacred authority of the former patrimonial ruler was transferred to the postcolonial bureaucracy, which used nationalism and constitutionalism as sources of legitimacy. In political practice, nationalism or, rather, a feeling of belonging to a nation functioned as a counterweight against centrifugal tendencies and the regional interests that saw their chance with the demise of the system of colonial domination. Constitutionalism served as a façade behind which traditional practices related to particularistic interests were continued. The constitutions contained some progressive elements taken from the U.S. Constitution as well as the French Declaration of the Rights of Man and the Citizen. The model of the Napoleonic state, however, was a more practical source of inspiration, being congruent with the authoritarian, centralist, and hierarchical tendencies of previous administrative practices. The tension between center and periphery that accompanies patrimonial-bureaucratic rule was controlled, limiting the jurisdiction of the regional and local levels of public administration and creating constitutional provisions for strong presidentialist rule. Obviously, in political practice the success of these efforts at concentration and centralization of power depended on the power of local leaders. In many countries and for a long period, regional disputes and struggles among political factions led by *caudillos* were endemic and defined the political arena. The state only existed in terms of the external recognition of its political sovereignty (and even this was not always guaranteed) and served as an instrument for repression and control.[16]

Through the years, the combination of interest groups or social classes taking control of state and government and establishing an alliance that supported a particular regime followed a similar pattern in many countries. Initially power was held by a small oligarchy of landowners, the military, and the clergy. The gradual integration of the Latin American economies into the world economy and the appearance in the political arena of new social groups that this created complicated this situation. The institutions that emerged in the process of state formation in this period were closely associated with these developments.[17] They satisfied the need for "macro controls" of economic growth and the internationalization process and served the interests of the actors involved through legislation, public organizations, administrative mechanisms, and resource allocation in the areas of capital formation, the mobilization and education of labor, high-risk ventures, infrastructure, etc. In the course of the second half of the last century state action became indispensable. This applies to countries whose industrial development was directed toward the emerging internal market as well as to those where primary production linked to the international market set the pace of the development process.[18] The actual policies adopted in each case were the obvious result of the structural imperatives and circumstances in which the state operated, the purpose of the developmental project it had defined, the relative importance of foreign and national interests in the principal productive sectors, and the influence of dominant groups and the outcome of the struggle among them. In this context, the model of development pursued was a dependent variable. This applies to the general orientation of the individual economies toward either primary export or import substitution, as well as to the amount of regulation and planning that accompanied these processes.

The process of state formation was limited by the ability to mobilize the financial resources that would enable it to build an institutional apparatus capable of defining and implementing the regulations and infrastructural arrangements supporting economic growth. In addition, the state had to guarantee its continuity, to consolidate its power on a national level, and to establish legitimacy of its rule. Initially, financial resources consisted only of customs duties levied on foreign trade, especially in the export-oriented "enclave economies," and loans contracted in the international financial markets. Later, with the growth of urban society, other sources of state revenue were developed.

Within these limits, the growth of the institutional apparatus and the increase in the number of areas to which the state extended its influence was to an important extent dependent upon the problems presented by the dynamics of economy and society and by the interests of social groups and classes. These issues and interests were often managed through corporatist structures in combination with extensive clientelist networks. The state, as we noted, is a product, a conditioning force, and an object of the struggle among interest groups and social classes. With the growing differentiation of the economy and society and the increasing influence of interest groups, the state's institutional apparatus and how it functioned became an arena of negotiation and dispute.[19]

Whether these developments—in particular those connected with the growth of an export economy, investments in infrastructure, the emergence of a national market, urbanization and massive immigration, and the rise of autocratic regimes (which in the last decades of the nineteenth century established state control over the national territory by invoking

an "order and "progress" ideology)—marked a separation from the patrimonial-bureaucratic type state of the past is an issue of debate. I tend
to agree with Wiarda who argues in his chapter that we should be careful in presuming such watersheds in political culture and practice.[20] The
forces of continuity in Latin American politics are often stronger than
one is inclined to think. Whether the state, confronted with the macro-
processes of urbanization and industrialization and with the accompanying sociopolitical changes that culminated in the demise of most of the
"oligarchical republics," was forced to take a radically different course
from its political practice of particularism, clientelism, and patrimonialism is debatable as well.[21] We recall Weyland's analysis of the present
crisis of the Brazilian state and his thesis that the expansion of its institutional apparatus and the further differentiation of its functions undermined the potential for autonomy and emphasized its traditional particularistic characteristics.[22]

State and Development

The changes that were forced on Latin American society as a result of the
1929 collapse of export economies led to a new development model, one
directed toward the internal market. In many countries the resulting economic growth lasted until the mid-1950s. Populism was used to integrate
actors and social classes in the political process, preventing radical reforms of economy and society.[23] The state apparatus expanded and entered a great number of new policy areas. Many traditional elements of
Latin American political practice were mobilized in the process. One of
them was corporatism.

Purely corporatist systems never emerged, and, in practice, corporatist
elements were combined with those originating in other traditions, including liberal-democratic ones. The basic pattern in the representation
of interest groups, however—subsidized, maintained, and controlled by
the state—is recognizable in all cases.[24] Another traditionally corporatist
element involved the heritage of patrimonial-bureaucraticism, which can
be seen in the consolidation of centralized rule by authoritarian regimes
and in the use of extensive clientelist networks as mechanisms for class
control. The expansion of the state apparatus offered ample room for the
distribution of jobs, material rewards, and other "pay-offs" to the political clientele of the populist regime.[25]

With the growth of the institutional dimensions of the state, the number of issues that were sources of conflict among classes and interest
groups increased. The populist regimes were structurally hierarchical
and authoritarian. Their rejection of class antagonisms and the fostering
of social collaboration within coalitions with a multiclass composition,

however, created a strong need for adequate management of potential and actual conflicts of interests. This implied an emphasis on negotiation and conflict resolution through the personalistic, particularistic ties existing between strong persuasive leaders and their followers.[26] The class alliance that supported the economic growth model of import-substitution industrialization and the populist regimes were dominated by urban middle and upper-middle class groups as well as important sectors of the urban working class. The latter formed a mass electoral base.

In the course of the growth process, the differentiation of the economic structure it induced, and the expansion of state apparatus, this alliance came to include a new social segment of managers, bureaucrats, professionals, and technocrats, who developed their own relationship with the national and international business communities. Together with sectors of the middle classes and the bourgeoisie—and explicitly excluding the popular classes—they formed an important part of a new alliance that, along with the military, opted for a bureaucratic-authoritarian solution to the crisis of the model of import substitution implemented by the developmental state, the collapse of populist rule, and the failure of the brief democratic interlude that some countries had experienced.[27]

Some analysts of this phenomenon interpret the bureaucratic-authoritarian regimes as a unique conjuncture of class alliances, coercive and co-optive state policies, and levels of industrial development that distinguishes it from other types of authoritarian regimes.[28] They see a break with the patrimonial-bureaucratic tradition as the outcome of a historical scenario that would lead to the emergence of a different kind of state. The public sector had to bring the politically and economically strategic sectors of society under its control in order to ensure unhindered progress of the model of capitalist industrial development. At the same time, the state apparatus had to be reorganized and its particularist, clientelist elements eliminated. This process had to result in an efficiently operating bureaucracy led by technocrats who were expected to define and execute policies on the basis of "objective" criteria, maintaining a certain autonomy with regard to the interest groups in civil society. Within the state bureaucracy rigid and hierarchical structures were to be organized under ultimate military control.

In hindsight, it appears that traditional political culture and practice were far too strong in Latin America to permit a radical break with the past. Those changes that were thought to represent a structural break with "traditional" patterns appear to have been more of a contemporary and conjunctural nature. Despite the differences among the various regimes in Latin America in their respective relations with social classes, interest groups, and the like, we note common elements in the structure and functioning of the state that go back to this shared heritage: the importance of the "aristocratic culture,"[29] generated under the former *lati-fundia* system with its emphasis on social distance, hierarchy, absolute authority, arbitrariness, and the discretionary character of decision making; the importance of personalism and *caudillismo* in politics; the weight of patron-client relationships and the significance of extensive networks of a clientelist nature as a vertically structuring mechanism in society; and the constant tendency to compartmentalize society, with an emphasis on political over social categories and intervention in processes of class formation.[30] All these obviously have a presence of varying importance and intensity in any particular political system and appear in differing combinations. Striking in most situations—for example, Mexico, Argentina, Peru, Colombia, and the Central American countries—is the combination of historical continuity with a flexibility in adapting to a changing economic and sociopolitical environment. The economic crisis of the 1980s, the demise of the authoritarian regimes, and the trend towards democratization presented such changing environments.[31]

The State's Changing Role

The response to economic downturn involved a generalized recourse to neoliberal adjustment policies, whether in regimes of a center-right persuasion, neopopulist regimes, or those with a center-left orientation like Brazil.[32] Political support was drawn from the economic elites and the middle sector, and in some instances the composition of this alliance turned out to be rather similar to the one that initially had supported the bureaucratic-authoritarian regime.[33] The macroeconomic policies of these coalitions, which supported the dynamic, export-oriented sector of the economy, have produced selective economic growth while marginalizing small producers in the countryside and certain segments of the urban poor.

In many countries, the state institutions attending to the latter's needs have been dismantled. In some cases they were replaced by social emergency funds—often financed through foreign aid—that were directed towards situations of acute poverty.[34] Their future, in the long term, is uncertain, and their contribution to structural solutions to the problem of urban and rural poverty is small. In addition, because they are mostly managed under the auspices of the Ministry of the Presidency, they tend to become an instrument of political patronage and traditional political practices.[35] This applies also to more massive programs like Solidarity in Mexico and the various programs managed by the Venezuelan state, as shown in the chapters by Rodríguez, Shefner, and Gómez Calcaño.

The new dualism in society between those participating in the processes of modernization and those excluded is the Achilles heel of the neoliberal strategy. The withdrawal of the state from social policy areas coincided with an incipient process of democratization that was encouraging marginalized segments of the population to express their demands and put pressure on state institutions that often had radically scaled down operations. Neoliberal policies generally succeeded in restoring investor confidence, at the cost, however, of accumulating a "social debt" of considerable magnitude, which, in turn, threatens the democratization process. State withdrawal has led to a "policy void" at the lower levels of society, which has been filled increasingly by the activities of social movements and nongovernment organizations. In some cases these organizations are participating in a chaotic "privatization" of services that under normal conditions are—and in order to guarantee equal access to all must be—the responsibility of the public sector.[36]

In historical perspective, the trend toward democratization since the end of the 1970s in almost all Latin American countries has been remarkable. The basic tendencies in the structure and functioning of the political process point, historically, in an undemocratic or even antidemocratic direction. Countries that called themselves "democratic" at an earlier stage often maintained very traditional political practice behind a "modern" façade.[37] Obvious examples are Mexico, Colombia, Venezuela, and more recently Peru, which has experienced the reestablishment of an extreme presidentialism with roots in a populist past.

A return to the practice of coup d'etats and authoritarian military-led regimes is not very probable. The global arena of politics would immediately exert supraregional pressures. So far, these pressures have been quite effective in encouraging the consolidation of the "democratic experiment." In the long term, free elections, pluralism in party systems and parliamentary representation, a certain decentralization of decision making and budgetary allocation to the regional and local levels, and a less central role for the military will most likely become stable elements in Latin American politics. It will mean a formal conformation to the democratic model. Till now, however, how these elements have been defined and realized in political practice has often deviated from the Western model, taking a specific Latin American "coloring" very much conditioned by the political tradition in the region, with external determinants playing a minor role. As a result, elections may be rigged, the political opposition co-opted or intimidated, parliamentary decision making overridden by presidential decrees, decentralization applied through the transfer of responsibilities without budgetary means, and the military invited to participate in political decision making. The authoritarian, organicist, corporatist, centralist, and antidemocratic features of the patrimonial-bureaucratic past continuously reappear, and in an environment of enormous socioeconomic inequalities existing behind the democratic façade, the functions of these traditional elements as instruments of co-optation and social control are being put to the test. In the short term this has led to a special variant of democracy.

A full-fledged process of democratization—à la T. H. Marshall[38]—should aim at the realization of civil, political, and social citizenship, and a certain degree of success in all these areas will be necessary to ensure success of the process as a whole. In situations of continuing extreme socioeconomic inequality, democratization proceeds on shaky ground, with serious consequences for the process of state reform. This reform cannot be successful without democratization that goes beyond the present antipoverty programs promoted by "traditional" politics.

Structural social and economic inequalities will perpetuate dependencies that offer endless possibilities for manipulation and abuse of power and equally endless problems of access by the poor to public services that fulfill basic needs. As long as they exist, the formation—in the Weberian tradition—of a "permanent, apolitical, well-paid and competent civil service with rights, duties, hierarchies and promotion ladders"[39] that would represent a break with the patrimonial past—one of the top priorities on the state reform agenda—will remain an illusion. The confusion between state and ruling government, with its supporting alliance of interest groups, will continue.

Administrative autonomy and the separation of the state from the executive powers remain as great a need as they have ever been. The success of reforms in either the social, economic, or political sector heavily depends on the consolidation of reforms in the others. Political reform—the strengthening of state institutions to protect them from changes in the political arena, to increase their accountability, to reduce the high rates of turnover of officials, to eliminate the possibilities for abuse and corruption, and to limit executive discretion[40]—depends in turn on the success of economic and social reforms.

State Reform and Its Adversities

The study of the various dimensions of the changing role of the state in this volume indicate considerable differences among individual countries in content and scope of state reform and in the redefinition of the relation between state, market, and civil society. The structural adjustment recipes that recommend state withdrawal and strengthening of market relations, as formulated by the international development establishment, however, are founded upon very similar strategies everywhere. Figure 1.1 indicates the most salient general characteristics of the structural adjustment process of the 1980s and the elements that figure with differing emphasis in the present debate on the relation between stable long-term economic growth, type of change in the structure and functioning of the state apparatus, and type of reform in state–civil society relations.[41] But the arrangements between state and market and the impact of adjustment policies on social classes and other interest groups often differ considerably across countries, as the country analyses in this volume show. Structural adjustment has its own winners and losers.[42] The privatization of public services and the reductions in subsidies, public social services, and welfare provisions tend to worsen the distribution of income, already skewed to the disadvantage of lower- and middle-income families. The recent tax reforms initiated by many countries have not yet corrected this trend. The emphasis on indirect taxes (linked to the consumption of goods and services with a low income-elasticity of demand) must shift to taxation based primarily on income and property. The reorganization of the revenue service—a priority objective of state reform—is only in its beginning stages, and the traditional regressive state revenue-raising structure is largely intact. Thus, the lower- and middle-income strata are forced to contribute comparatively more to a state that has reduced its support of the public services that primarily serve their needs.[43]

State reform also encounters resistance on other fronts. Close links between the reorganizing state agencies and sectors identified with modernization and globalization of Latin American economies create the risk of repeating the ills of the patrimonial past. While qualifying these phenomena, it is useful to be attentive to the often sharp differences between the theory and practice of state reform. A leaner state—better organized, more efficient, less politicized—is not always the immediate result of reforms. State reform has often created new institutions that continue old patterns. State agencies have remained arenas for competition, negotiation, and dispute among interest groups and social classes. Changes in the pattern of relations among state, market, and civil society have created opportunities in particular for groups and classes identified with the modernization of the economy and its integration into the international economic system, at the expense of others.

The manner in which the privatization programs have been carried out exemplifies how public and private interests continue to be intertwined.[44] The success of privatization has come to depend heavily upon the success of the strategy to disentangle these interests and, in fact, to privatize the private sector. And even then, as William Glade shows in his chapter, the tradition of rent seeking "in which business profits derive not from innovation and production efficiency but from such things as the manipulation of returns on capital by government regulations, favoritism in government spending, and preferential tax treatment" does not provide an environment in which privatization will automatically improve performance and encourage independence from state-sanctioned privilege and favor.[45]

Figure 1.1 The Structural Adjustment Process in Latin America and its Aftermath: Formal Objectives, Methods, and Actors

Phases	Objectives	Strategy	Methods	Actors	Implementation
First Phase Demolition of the old model of development	Combatting hyperinflation Restoring internal preconditions for a resumption of economic growth Restoring international creditworthiness and investor confidence	Changing the macroeconomic ground rules Reducing size and scope of state apparatus Dismantling institutions identified with the protectionist, state-led development model	Reduction of state budget General liberalization of prices Termination of state subsides for basic services, food, fuel, etc. Liberalization of the participation in international trade; elimination of tariff barriers Liberalization of the condition for foreign investment Deregulation of private sector Privatization of economically and/or politically nonstrategic state enterprises (the "easy" privitization) Organization of social emergency funds outside the social sector ministries	The president Ministers of the socioeconomic sector ministries The president of the Central Bank The multilateral financial institutions National and international financial investors	Definition and execution of adjustment policies by a small technocratic elite

Second Phase

Construction of a new model of development

Objectives	Socioeconomic sector	State reform	Political actors	Institutional reforms
Improving socioeconomic conditions of the poor sectors of the population	Restructuring institutions in the socioeconomic sector	Reform of the structure and functioning of the state bureaucracy	The president and the cabinet	Institutional reforms with participation of all interested parties
Improving the national economy's capacity to compete on an international level	Reforming the system of social services, their provision, and financing	Reformulation of responsibilities and participation in the national budgets of central, regional, and local governments	Parliament	Active involvement of the medium levels in government influenced by institutional reforms
Consolidating policies directed toward macroeconomic stability	Increasing productivity in the private sector	Reform of the judiciary and the system of law enforcement	State bureaucracy	National policy directed toward the creation of consensus and broad support in civil society for the program of reform; amplification and intensification of the democratization process
	Organizing the economic institutions of capitalism (regulation of competition, consumer protection, patent registration, etc.)	Tax reform: organization of a more progressive revenue-raising structure and reorganization of the system of tax collection	Regional and local government	
	Integrating into the world economy on the basis of the competitiveness of the national business sector	Improvement of the quality of management of the civil service	Judicial powers	
		Improvement in the functioning of parliament	Labor unions	
		Privatization of the more important state enterprises (the "difficult" privatization)	Popular organizations	
		Modernization production apparatus and integration into the international economy	Political parties	
			Private enterprise, national and international	
			The media	

New Actors?

The strengthening of the technocratic orientation of public administration in many Latin American countries is thought, as Patricio Silva's chapter explains, to contribute to the growth of a Weberian state that can resist these special interest groups and distributional coalitions. However, the decision making that is dominated by technocrats who are supposedly pursuing "politically neutral" policies based on rigidly "objective" analyses may become a façade for traditional ways of doing business and for ideologically prescribed actions that promote the interests of certain sectors while excluding others.[46] The rise of technocracy was already underway in the 1960s but it became publicly prominent because of the implementation of structural adjustment programs inspired by neoliberalism in the 1980s. The technocrats' position was fortified by the success of the neoliberal recipe in providing general guidelines for the running of any open, capitalist market economy. They became traditional politicians' favorite allies to whom the definition and implementation of unpopular economic and institutional reforms, expected to restore investor confidence, could be delegated. Schneider argues that this is the major reason for the growing power position of technocratic government officials in the last decade.[47]

Analyses of the role of technocrats focus mainly on how they function within key central government institutions and how they define the macroeconomic parameters of a new growth model, often in coordination with representatives of the major multilateral organizations: the World Bank, the International Monetary Fund, and the Inter-American Development Bank. At a macro level, considerable variations exist in the manner these new policies are adopted and integrated with traditional courses of action, depending on the domestic economic and political pressures and the conditionalities of multilateral loan programs. These variations multiply if other levels of state action are taken into consideration. In this respect, Migdal makes a useful distinction among various levels of the state, each of them experiencing pressures from other state institutions and from actors in civil society:[48]

1. the level of "the trenches" where the direct application of state rules and regulations takes place, often in face-to-face situations;
2. the level of "the dispersed field offices" where implementation of regional and state policies is mapped out;
3. the level of "the agency's central offices" in the nation's political center where national policies are defined and enacted, the sources of state revenue are mobilized, and the resource allocation takes place. The rise of technocracy has to an important extent taken place at this level;

4. the level of "the commanding heights," the top executive leadership, where pressures from within the state organization and from nonstate forces, both domestic and international, compete with each other in the effort to influence executive decision making.

At each of these levels social forces meet in situations of negotiation and dispute. In addition, conflicts of interest may arise between levels. Victoria Rodríguez, in her chapter on decentralization in Mexico, analyzes a situation in which the central government and the regional and local governments were in conflict over decisions made at "the commanding heights" level to such an extent that the original policy objectives were aborted and in some cases reversed.

Jon Shefner's chapter describes a similar situation at the local level, in which the Solidarity antipoverty programs in Mexico are often at the mercy of traditional politics, whose leaders implement programs in a way that is contrary to nationally defined objectives. Decentralization of government tasks and responsibilities to the regional and local levels, accompanied by an adequate allocation of funds, is a central issue of state reform. At the same time—and given the rachitic nature of the process of democratization—it may open a Pandora's box, creating new maneuvering room and access to resources for traditional elites and interest groups.[49].

General state reform at the regional and local levels may also meet resistance from an unexpected source. The withdrawal by the state from areas that provide services to meet basic needs has resulted in a policy void that has been filled increasingly by grass-roots movements and the activities of nongovernmental organizations (NGOs). The grass-roots movements that have proliferated since the 1980s are organized and mobilized along issue lines and do not necessarily manifest a class perspective, although they are found predominantly among the poor segments of the population.[50]

In the overcrowded cities of Latin America where city management proved completely unable to deal with the immense infrastructural problems surrounding the provision of clean water, sewage treatment, electricity, transportation, health care, education, and housing, informal movements of a self-help nature appeared. Their significance in the context of the incipient process of democratization can hardly be underestimated, as shown in the chapters by David Lehmann and Anthony Bebbington and by Joe Foweraker. However, these movements represent a privatization of basic services that—as we emphasized before—should properly be the responsibility of the public sector.

The case of NGOs is more complicated. Their mushroom-like growth in Latin American countries has led to their presence in many policy debates at the local and regional levels that concern state reform.[51] The re-lationship between the state and the NGOs depends on the degree of compatibility in ideology, development strategy, and basic policy objec-tives. During the authoritarian regimes of the 1970s they worked in favor of social justice, democratization, and respect for human rights and pro-vided a safe haven for intellectuals in the political opposition. During the period of structural adjustment, the major NGOs, with their documenta-tion centers, expertise, and international contacts, created continuity in areas that suffered the effects of state withdrawal and the destruction of institutions. In the postadjustment period the state reform program is confronted with policy areas that have been "occupied" by NGOs oper-ating with a philosophy and a purpose that does not necessarily agree with the state's. The "official" sectors in many countries complain that the uncontrolled action of NGOs sometimes contradicts state action.[52] Further democratization and progress in state reform will require a rede-finition of most NGO strategies, including their relationship to the state, assuming that a democratizing state would not only require knowledge of these organizations' activities but would wish to exert some degree of coordination and control.

Conclusion

The debate over issues related to state reform is part of a wider debate over whether the combined processes of economic restructuring and de-mocratization in Latin America can generate a new model of develop-ment that will combine economic growth with equity.[53] This requires a special role for the state and makes a further retreat in any aggregate sense unlikely, even undesirable. In the social field there remains much to be done to provide welfare to large segments of the population. And even in economic affairs, it is a fallacy to suggest that a deregulated market economy could function without the presence of a strong state, however paradoxical this may sound.

On this issue economists in favor of state intervention and those who would rely on the market are approaching a common ground.[54] They share a growing consciousness that every capitalist economy is a result of mixed market and state coordination and that governments have a pro-nounced role in providing physical and social infrastructure and in real-izing more equitable distributions of income, wealth, knowledge, and power. In these areas markets cannot be relied upon. There is an increas-ing interest in a "new interventionism"—which is distinctly different from the traditional "market-unfriendly" interventionism—and which seeks to guide, not replace, the market. In economic matters, this would channel investment away from unproductive uses through stimuli of various sorts, expand technological capacity, strengthen links with the international business community, provide a directional thrust to selected industries, and create general conditions for sustainable development.[55] Such policies would have to be based on a strategy for the development of trade and industry over time, a plan that must be open to feedback from the market; state assistance should be made conditional on performance. For the proponents of radical neoliberal strategies this form of planning would be extreme. They would prefer a state role limited to defining and enforcing the regulatory context for the operations of market actors.

In reality, both perspectives—in spite of their differences—leave little room for a "retreat" of the state in an aggregate sense and argue for a redefinition of responsibilities. This does not necessarily include a weakening of the state role. It is true that this redefinition is taking place within the constraints of a world dense with flows of trade, money and regulatory obligations. But, even then, the state continues to have considerable power in the area of economic and social policies.[56] The increasing globalization of the world economy will not emasculate the national states. They will continue to retain wide discretion over the extent in which they control resources. In contrast to the major western-industrial economies, where the average public spending ratio even has increased between 1980 and 1994 from 36 percent of GDP to 40 percent,[57] most Latin American countries have experienced substantial decreases in public spending since the beginning of the 1980s when the neoliberal offensive took effect.[58] However, in view of the immense needs in virtually all sectors of the Latin American economy and society to which the market does not necessarily respond, it is hard to imagine future development for the continent that would include a permanent contraction of public sector activity.

The first precondition for a future role for the public sector—including returning its capacity to plan and implement policy as part of a course of action combining stable growth with equity—remains a resolution to the fiscal crisis of the state.[59] The resistance by the privileged sectors against any type of tax reform that involves increasing their tax burden and improves collection cannot be underestimated; it will be furious. However, there are no alternatives. Other options—increasing public debt or printing money, both preferred choices in the past—are no longer viable courses of action. Increasing public savings and a reduction of the public deficit are equally difficult measures—but equally necessary to "bring the state back in."[60] The search is for a strategy that would not only restore general investors' confidence and revive the credit of the state—as neoliberalism has done in many countries—but also begin to resolve the problem of "the social debt": how to realize civil, political, and social citizenship for Latin Americans. Theoretically, the realization of citizenship rights would be the logical corollary to the primacy of market criteria in the organization and functioning of economy and society, as has occurred in the United States and Western Europe.[61] The conditions and possibilities for such a development, though, are very different in Latin America, as this historical argument has shown. To balance the exigencies of democratization with the implications of neoliberal macroeconomic policies in the presence of an embedded political culture and persistent traditional political practices is not an easy task.[62] The result may reaffirm the idiosyncratic nature of Latin American development.

Notes

1. Enrique Correa, Alexis Guardia, and Juan Enrique Vega, *¿Como Cambiar al Estado?* (Lima: Grupo Propuesta, 1993); "Crisis y Requerimientos de Nuevos Paradigmas en la Relación Estado Sociedad y Economía." Regional conference organized by UNDP, UNESCO, and Centro Latinoamerico de Ciencias Sociales (CLACSO), Buenos Aires, April 1990; "¿El Perú, Es Gobernable?" National conference organized by Grupo Propuesta, October 1991; "Regiones ¿Si o No?" National debate on decentralization organized by Grupo Propuesta, August 1993.

2. See *Elementos para la Modernización del Estado* (Washington, D.C.: Inter-American Development Bank, 1994); *Report on the Eighth General Increase in the Resources of the Inter-American Development Bank* (Washington, D.C.: Inter-American Development Bank, 1994).

3. Ibid.

4. Jonathan Hartlyn and Samuel A. Morley, eds. *Latin American Political Economy: Financial Crisis and Political Change* (Boulder: Westview Press, 1986); Barbara Stallings and Robert R. Kaufman, eds. *Debt and Democracy in Latin America* (Boulder: Westview Press, 1989).

5. See Luiz Carlos Bresser Pereira, "Economic Reforms and Economic Growth: Efficiency and Politics in Latin America," in Luiz Carlos Bresser Pereira, José Maria Maravall and Adam Przeworski, eds., *Economic Reforms in New Democracies: A Social Democratic Approach* (Cambridge: Cambridge University Press, 1993), pp. 15–36; Howard Handelman and Werner Baer, eds., *Paying the Costs of Austerity in Latin America* (Boulder: Westview Press, 1989).

6. Ibid. See also Jorge G. Castañeda, *Utopia Unarmed: The Latin American Left after the Cold War* (New York: Vintage Books, 1993), pp. 358–90; Ludolfo Paramío, "América Latina en los Noventas," *NEXOS*, no. 168, 1991, pp. 29–36; *Social Reform and Poverty: Towards an Integrated Development Agenda* (Washington, D.C., and New York: Inter-American Development Bank and United Nations Development Programme, 1993).

7. Marcelo Cavarozzi, "Beyond Transitions to Democracy in Latin America," *Journal of Latin American Studies*, vol. 24, no. 3, 1993, pp. 665–84; Marcelo Cavarozzi, "Politics: A Key for the Long Term in South America," in William C. Smith, Carlos H. Acuña, and Eduardo A. Gamarra, eds., *Latin American Political*

Economy in the Age of Neoliberal Reform (Boulder: Lynne Rienner, 1994), pp. 127–56.

8. On the various forms of populism, an extensive literature has been published. See Ruth Collier and David Collier, *Shaping the Political Arena* (Princeton: Princeton University Press, 1991). On populism as a political formula, see the classic article by Torcuato di Tella, "Populism and Reform in Latin America," in Claudio Veliz, ed., *Obstacles to Change in Latin America* (New York: Oxford University Press, 1964), pp. 47–74; also Steve Stein, *Populism in Peru: The Emergence of the Masses and the Politics of Social Change* (Madison: University of Wisconsin Press, 1980), pp. 3–17.

9. Pablo González Casanova, "Sobre el Estado, la Sociedad Civil y la Crisis en América Latina y el Caribe," paper presented at the conference "The State and International Linkages," The Hague, May, 1987.

10. Philippe C. Schmitter, *Interest Conflict and Political Change in Brazil* (Stanford: Stanford University Press, 1971), p. 34; Ben Ross Schneider, *Politics within the State: Elite Bureaucrats and Industrial Policy in Authoritarian Brazil* (Pittsburgh: Pittsburgh University Press, 1991), p. 35.

11. Kurt Weyland, "The Decline of the Developmental State in Brazil: A Neostatist Interpretation," paper presented at the XVIII International Congress of the Latin American Studies Association, Atlanta, March 1994.

12. Ibid., p. 1.

13. For a similar perspective, see Joel S. Migdal, "The State in Society: An Approach to Struggles for Domination," in Joel S. Migdal, Atul Kohli and Vivienne Shue, eds., *State Power and Social Forces: Domination and Transformation in the Third World* (Cambridge: Cambridge University Press, 1994), pp. 7–36.

14. Castañeda, *Utopia Unarmed*, p. 374.

15. In dealing with the implications of the historical legacy of bureaucratic-patrimonialism I was inspired by the publications of Richard Morse, Howard Wiarda, and James Malloy; see Richard M. Morse, *New World Soundings: Culture and Ideology in the Americas* (Baltimore: Johns Hopkins University Press, 1989); Howard J. Wiarda, *The Democratic Revolution in Latin America* (New York: Holmes & Meier, 1990); Howard J. Wiarda, ed., *Political and Social Change in Latin America* (Boulder: Westview Press, 1992), pp. 1–22 and 315–46; and James M. Malloy, ed., *Authoritarianism and Corporatism in Latin America* (Pittsburgh: University of Pittsburgh Press, 1977). The thesis about the importance of this legacy in explaining the present structure and functioning of the political process in Latin America is not without debate; see Larry Diamond and Juan J. Linz, "Politics, Society and Democracy in Latin America," in Larry Diamond, Juan J. Linz, and Seymour Martin Lipset, eds., *Democracy in Developing Countries*, Vol. 4: *Latin America* (Boulder: Lynne Rienner, 1989), pp. 1–58. Diamond and Linz assume a radical break with this traditional political behavior in the course of the nineteenth century as a result of the new economic, social, and political developments in that period.

16. See Oscar Oszlak, "The Historical Formation of the State in Latin America," *Latin American Research Review*, vol. XVI, no. 2, 1981, pp. 17 and 21.

17. Ibid., p. 23.

18. Mario Cerutti and Menno Vellinga, eds., *Burguesías e Industria en América Latina y Europa Meridional* (Madrid: Alianza Editorial, 1989).

19. Oscar Oszlak, "The Historical Formation of the State in Latin America," p. 23.

20. See also the discussion in Larry Diamond and Juan Linz, "Politics, Society and Democracy in Latin America," p. 4.

21. Richard M. Morse, "Claims of Political Tradition," in Howard J. Wiarda, ed., *Politics and Social Change in Latin America*, pp. 96 ff.

22. Kurt Weyland, "The Decline of the Developmental State in Brazil," passim.

23. See Steve Stein, *Populism in Peru*, pp. 3–17; also Robert E. Dix, "Populism, Authoritarian and Democratic," *Latin American Research Review*, vol. XX, no. 2, 1985, pp. 29–52.

24. See Robert R. Kaufman, "Corporatism, Clientelism, and Partisan Conflict: A Study of Seven Latin American Countries," in James M. Malloy, ed., *Authoritarianism and Corporation in Latin America*, pp. 109–43.

25. Ian Roxborough, *Theories of Development* (London: MacMillan, 1979), pp. 107–19.

26. Steve Stein, *Populism in Peru*, p. 13; In the course of this process the labor movement was incorporated into the political system and new institutions of state-labor and capital-labor relations were created; see Ruth Collier and David Collier, *Shaping the Political Arena*, p. 161. Those labor organizations that managed to operate with some degree of autonomy in relation to "official" politics were few in number and were mostly found in primary-production enclaves in mining and plantation areas; see Dirk Kruijt and Menno Vellinga, *Labor Relations and Multinational Corporations: The Cerro de Pasco Corporation in Peru* (Assen: Van Gorcum, 1980), pp. 208–16.

27. The classic study of the rise of bureaucratic-authoritarianism is, of course, Guillermo O'Donnell's *Modernization and Bureaucratic-Authoritarianism: Studies in South American Politics* (Berkeley: Institute of International Studies, University of California, 1973; see also David Collier, ed., *The New Authoritarianism in Latin America* (Princeton: Princeton University Press, 1979).

28. See William L. Canak, "The Peripheral State Debate: State Capitalist and Bureaucratic-Authoritarian Regimes in Latin America," *Latin American Research Review*, vol. XIX, no. 1, 1984, p. 18.

29. The concept of "aristocratic culture" is an insightful tool in the analysis of Latin American political practice; it was elaborated by Karl Mannheim in *Essays on the Sociology of Culture* (London: Routledge & Kegan Paul, 1956), pp. 206–39.

30. See Alain Touraine, "Latin America: From Populism to Social Democracy," in Menno Vellinga, ed., *Social Democracy in Latin America: Prospects for Change* (Boulder: Westview Press, 1993), pp. 297–309.

31. Guillermo O'Donnell, Philippe C. Schmitter, and Lawrence Whitehead, eds., *Transitions from Authoritarian Rule: Comparative Perspectives* (Baltimore: Johns Hopkins University Press, 1986); Jonathan Hartlyn and Samuel Morley, *Latin American Political Economy*, passim.

32. Luiz Carlos Bresser Pereira, "Economic Reforms and Economic Growth," passim.

33. Robert R. Kaufmann, "Liberalization and Democratization in South America: Perspectives from the 1970s," in Guillermo O'Donnell, Philippe C. Schmitter, and Lawrence Whitehead, *Transitions from Authoritarian Rule*, pp. 90–6.

34. Typical examples are the Solidarity and Social Investment Fund (FOSIS) in Chile and the Social Development and Compensation Fund (FONCODES) in Peru; see Pilar Vergara, "Market Economy, Social Welfare and Democratic Consolidation in Chile," in William C. Smith, Carlos H. Acuña, and Eduardo A. Gamarra, eds., *Democracy, Markets, and Structural Reform in Latin America* (Boulder: Lynne Rienner, 1994), p. 250; Santiago Pedraglio, "Perú: Políticas Sociales, Desarrollo y Reforma del Estado," paper presented at the conference "Democracia: Descentralización y Política Social," Lima, May 1994; see also Meine Pieter van Dijk, "Socioeconomic Development Funds to Mitigate the Social Costs of Adjustment Experiences in Three Countries," *The European Journal of Development Research*, vol. IV, 1992, pp. 97–111.

35. On the Peruvian case, see Mariano Valderrama, *Perú y América Latina en el Nuevo Panorama de la Cooperación Internacional.* (Lima: Centro Peruana de Estudios Sociales [CEPES], 1995), pp. 70–84.

36. See, for example, Marcelo Cavarozzi and Vicente Palermo, "State, Civil Society, and Popular Neighborhood Organizations in Buenos Aires: Key Players in Argentina's Transition to Democracy," in Charles A. Reilly, *New Parths to Democratic Development in Latin America: The Role of NGO-Municipal Collaboration.* (Boulder: Lynne Rienner, 1995), p. 36–9.

37. The classic study elaborating this theme is still Pablo González Casanova, *La Democracia en México* (Mexico, D.F.: Ediciones Era, 1965).

38. See T. H. Marshall, *Class, Citizenship and Social Development* (New York: Doubleday, 1964).

39. Jorge Castañeda, *Utopia Unarmed*, p. 387.

40. Ibid., p. 384.

41. Moisés Naim, "Latin America: The Second Stage of Reform," in Larry Diamond and Marc F. Plattner, eds., *Economic Reform and Democracy* (Baltimore: Johns Hopkins University Press, 1995), pp. 28–44.

42. See Carlos M. Vilas's provocative comments in "Between Adam Smith and Thomas Hobbes: State, Market, and Privatization in Latin America," paper presented at the XVIII International Congress of the Latin American Studies Association, Atlanta, March 1994.

43. Ibid., p. 4.

44. See Horatio Verbitsky, *Robo para la Corona* (Buenos Aires: Editorial Planeta, 1991). A more general analysis of this problem is offered by Robin Theobald, *Corruption, Development, and Underdevelopment* (Durham, NC: Duke University Press, 1990), p. 77–9; also Barry Ames, *Political Survival: Politicians and Public Policy in Latin America* (Berkeley: University of California Press, 1987).

45. William Glade, *Privatization of Public Enterprises in Latin America* (San Francisco: ICS Press, 1991), p. 8.

46. See Frances Hagopian, "Traditional Politics against State Transformation in Brazil," in Joel S. Migdal, Atul Kohli and Vivienne Shue, eds., *State Power and Social Forces*, pp. 37–64.

47. Ben Ross Schneider, "The Material Bases of Technocracy: Investor Confidence and Neoliberalism in Latin America," paper presented at the CEDLA conference "Technocracy and the Politics of Expertise in Latin America," Amsterdam, September 1995.

48. Joel S. Migdal, "The State in Society," p. 16.

49. Cf. Luis Roniger, "*Caciquismo* and *Coronelismo:* Contextual Dimensions of Patron Brokerage in Mexico and Brazil," *Latin American Research Review,* vol. XXII, no. 2, 1987, pp. 71–99; Jorge Casteñeda, *Utopia Unarmed,* pp. 366–73. In Chile one has tried to avoid this phenomenon; see Brian Loveman, "Chilean NGOs: Forging a Role in the Transition to Democracy," in Charles A. Reilly, *New Paths to Democratic Development in Latin America,* pp. 134–7.

50. An exhaustive analysis of this phenomenon is offered by David Lehmann in *Democracy and Development in Latin America: Economics, Politics and Religion in the Post-War Period* (Philadelphia: Temple University Press, 1990).

51. Reilly cites the *Guide to Directories of NGOs,* recently published by the Inter-American Foundation, which mentions over 11,000 Latin American NGOs; my own experience leads me to believe this is a modest estimate; Charles A. Reilly, "Public Policy and Citizenship," in Charles A. Reilly, *New Paths to Democratic Development in Latin America,* p. 13.

52. This is based on extensive interviewing in August/September 1994 with top administrators of key central government institutions in eight Andean and Central American countries as part of an EEC mission to evaluate development cooperation policies with Latin America; see Menno Vellinga and Martine Vanackere, *Orientaciones para la Cooperación con América Latina en el Sector Rural* (Brussels: European Commission/DG-1, 1994).

53. The United Nations Economic Commission for Latin America and the Caribbean sketched the contours of this new model of development in *Changing Production Patterns with Social Equity: The Prime Task of Latin American and Caribbean Development in the 1990s* (Santiago: ECLAC, 1990).

54. Cf. Robert Wade, "State and Market Revisited: How Interventionist Should Third World Governments Be?" *The Economist,* April 4, 1992, p. 77. The World Bank's *World Development Report 1991* (Washington, D.C.: World Bank, 1991) underlines the responsibilities of the state in the areas of physical and social infrastructure, a rather radical change from earlier positions; see also the Inter-American Development Bank publications *Report on the Eighth General Increase in Resources of the Inter-American Development Bank,* pp. 57 ff., and *Elementos para la Modernization del Estado,* passim.

55. Robert Wade, "State and Market Revisited," p. 77.

56. "The Myth of the Powerless State," *The Economist,* October 7, 1995, pp. 13–4. Nico Colchester emphasizes the external constraints on authority, controls, and the power of the state in "State of the State," letter to the editor, *The Economist,* October 28, 1995, p. 6. For a similar view, see Gary Gereffi, "Contending Paradigms for Cross-Regional Comparison: Development Strategies and Commodity Chains in East Asia and Latin America," in Peter H. Smith, *Latin America in Comparative Perspective: New Approaches to Methods and Analysis* (Boulder: Westview Press, 1995), pp. 33–58, especially pp. 44–6; Hobsbawm emphasizes the in-

dispensable functions of the state in the redistribution of national income, functions that cannot be carried out by private agencies or through market mechanisms. E. J. Hobsbawm, "The Future of the State," *Development and Change*, vol. 27, 1996, pp. 267–78.

57. This includes, obviously, wide differences among individual countries: In 1994 the United States increased spending 33 percent while Sweden increased spending 68 percent. See "The Myth of the Powerless State," p. 14.

58. See Inter-American Development Bank, *Economic and Social Progress in Latin America 1993* (Washington D.C.: Inter-American Development Bank, 1993), p. 302.

59. Luiz Carlos Bresser Pereira, "Economic Reforms and Economic Growth"; also Jorge Casteñeda, *Utopia Unarmed*, p. 414.

60. See Peter B. Evans, Dietrich Rueschemeyer and Theda Skocpol, eds., *Bringing the State Back In* (New York: Cambridge University Press, 1985).

61. Richard Morse, "Claims of Political Tradition," p. 99.

62. Tensions created because of the acquired privileges of major political actors and the simultaneous imposition of stabilization programs and public sector reforms present additional complicating factors. See Eduardo A. Gamarra, "Market-Oriented Reforms and Democratization in Latin America: Challenges of the 1990s," in William C. Smith, Carlos Acuña, and Eduardo A. Gamarra, eds., *Latin American Political Economy in the Age of Reform*, pp. 1–16.

2

Historical Determinants of the Latin American State

Howard J. Wiarda

In 1985 a group of political sociologists and political economists published a book in which they attempted to "bring the state back in."[1] In Latin America, however, the state has always played a commanding, directing role, and one is left wondering why anyone would think the state had ever "gone away."[2] For clearly, while the state is obviously shaped and influenced by class, economic, and sociological variables, it also has an autonomy of its own—and particularly so in the bureaucratic-patrimonialist, corporatist, centralist, and authoritarian tradition of Latin America.[3]

The purpose of this chapter is to trace the origins of the Latin American state and to understand its historical determinants as well as its contemporary directions. We begin with an exploration of the beginnings of state-society relations in the Iberian Peninsula, then look at how the "Hapsburg model" of sociopolitical organization was carried to the New World; next we examine the collapse of this model in the Wars of Independence and the efforts to rebuild a new, "republican" state system in the nineteenth century and also look at the efforts to create corporatist and semicorporatist systems in Latin America beginning in the 1930s. Although more recent themes and developments are taken up by other authors, the analysis concludes with an assessment of both neoliberalism and neocorporatism in Latin America, the possible triumph of the one over the other or the continued overlap and fusion of the two.

Origins

To understand the role of the state[4] in Latin America, one needs to go back to its origins in Spain and Portugal. Few of us who began life as political scientists studying the contemporary era contemplated becoming also medieval historians, but that is what we must do to understand the kind of state and the system of state-society relations that Spain, and Portugal in a less well-articulated and forceful way, carried over to Latin America.[5]

The Iberian state and the dynamics of state-society relations in Iberia emerged long before there were nation-states called "Spain" or "Portugal." Instead, the peninsula was organized (when it was organized at all) on a more local or regional basis that included the kingdoms of Galícia, Navarre, Aragon, Castile, Leon, and Portugal (or Lusitania). The Iberian state system grew out of a confluence of factors that included the following:

1. the wild, unsettled, unruly, underpopulated character of Iberia during much of the medieval period, especially the heartland area known as "Old Castile," the north and center of the peninsula. The very unruliness of this vast, empty territory seemed to call forth the need for centralized, authoritarian government.[6]
2. the long (722–1492) Reconquest of the Peninsula from the Moors, which was one of the great, determining influences in Iberian history and made Iberian feudalism different from the French[7] (paradigm) case: more militaristic, less tolerant in a religious sense, again more authoritarian, and with the ownership of land and peasants tied to conquest and military service.
3. the number of groups and forces active during the Reconquest: several military orders (Alcantara, Hospitalers, Templars, etc.) who often carried the fight against the Moors and had an existence and history *prior to* the creation of any state organization; the Roman Catholic Church and various religious orders whose existence also preceded (both in time and in the church's hierarchy of loyalties) the state concept; various towns and regions that had some degree of self-governing autonomy; and the emerging state systems, as the Moors were driven further south, in such recently formed kingdoms as Aragon, Castile, León, and Portugal.[8]

With these opening comments, which clearly require greater details, examples, and fleshing out, we are now in a better position to understand the early concepts of the state and of state-society relations in Iberia. The initial Iberian states (plural) in León, Castile, and Aragon grew out of military and territorial conquest. They sought to govern over a vast, often unruly territory during a centuries-long struggle against the Moorish infidels, where the tide of battle ebbed and flowed (which helps explain the numerous castles and walled, enclave cities in Spain and Portugal).[9] As these early states began to emerge, they faced two struggles at the same time: one against the Moors and one against the autonomous corporate units (military orders, religious bodies, towns and municipalities, the fascinating economic corporation—among the most powerful of all, especially in later stages of the Reconquest—known as the *mesta*, or sheepholders' guild,[10] and eventually the medieval universities, which similarly had their own charters of independence and self-government, and represent the beginning of the Latin American concept of university autonomy).

The corporative ordering of society was closely bound up with the formative period as well as the successes of the early Spanish state.[11] The difficulty (one among many) of these emerging kingdoms or state systems was that many of the corporate units over which they sought to rule had a longer temporal existence than did the new states of Iberia; and, in the evolving Thomistic/Iberian hierarchy of law, some of them, such as the church and the religious orders had strong claims to having a legitimacy *above* that of the state. This is not the only reason for these phenomena, but one can see in these historical concepts why still today such institutions as the church and the military constitute virtual fourth or fifth "branches" of government and have seldom been fully subordinated to "mere" civilian authority.[12]

The nation-states of Spain and Portugal, among the first in Western Europe, were hammered out and forged between the twelfth and fifteenth centuries. They emerged in the midst of warfare, a constantly shifting frontier, and great social upheaval. One of the crucial arenas in the formation of these states involved the contest and tug-of-war between the emerging state systems and the autonomous, pre-existing, largely self-governing military orders, religious bodies, towns and municipalities, universities, and eventually other corporate units that made up "society." The emerging states of Aragon, Castile, León, and others, both to wage the war effort against the Moors more effectively and to enhance their own authority, sought to increase centralization and, with it, their own power—often at the expense of these corporate units—while the societal groups sought to preserve their autonomy. Like the war with the Moors, this contest also ebbed and flowed over a several centuries-long period, with first the emerging states gaining power and at other times society's corporate bodies gaining strength. This struggle between developing absolutism on the one hand and the *fueros* (rights) of society's corporate units on the other appears to be *the* crucial issue in the whole Spanish tradition.[13] The long-term trend, however, was toward enhanced power for the state and reduced power for the "*autonomías*."

The agencies of these corporate group rights and freedoms were the medieval *cortes* (parliaments) that emerged in Aragon, Castile, and León.

The *cortes* stood against the centralizing power of the monarchy and of royal absolution. Representation in the *cortes*—which also waxed and waned depending upon the need for assistance in struggle against the Moors and the power of royal authority but preceded the organization of parliaments in the north of Europe—was *both* by the traditional estates (noble, clerical, common) and by the corporate entities. In this way, both the class and the functional organization of society began at about the same time; frequently the two sets of categories overlapped. But the Spanish *cortes* never developed the independent law-making and tax-reviewing powers of the English parliament. Moreover, in the long struggle against royal absolution, the *cortes* steadily lost ground. By the time of Ferdinand and Isabella and later the Hapsburgs, the *cortes*—and with it, corporate group representation as well as the Spanish concepts of rights and freedoms—had all but been completely eliminated.[14]

Two interruptions in the narrative need to be made at this point. The first involves the question of causation. Was it economic factors, institutional factors, cultural factors, or military factors that shaped this struggle or were its ultimate causation? The question is akin to asking if it was the chicken or the egg that came first. The answer is: We do not and cannot know and, in the long run, the question doesn't matter very much. In this case, I am convinced, economic, sociological, institutional, military, and cultural factors were all involved in complex and overlapping ways; and it may be that one or a group of causative factors was important at certain times, while others were more important at others. Moreover, we know from anthropology, for example, that many social, economic, institutional, and even military factors may become so embedded in a culture that they take on a life of their own, becoming independent variables. That is probably what happened with such traits as bureaucratic-patrimonialism, corporatism, centralism, and authoritarianism as discussed here.[15]

The second digression in our historical narrative concerns some implications of this struggle between an emerging, self-aggrandizing state and the efforts of autonomous, corporate, societal units to retain their independence. The first implication is that the notion of "rights" in Iberia, and by extension in Latin America, tended historically to imply group or corporate rights (autonomy, self-government as a *group*) over the more individualistic notion of rights that eventually emerged in the Anglo-American, common law legal tradition.[16] The second, related implication is that in Iberia and Latin America historically "freedom" and "democracy" were largely defined in terms of the existence and protection of these corporate group rights, not in the individualistic and more process-oriented conceptions of Locke, Montesquieu, or Madison. A third, again related implication, is that "constitutionalism" in Iberia (less so in Latin America) was based on an "equilibrium" between the monarchy on the one hand and the independent regional kingdoms, social groupings, and corporate bodies on the other.[17] Constitutionalism was hence defined as a system of government where the rights of the autonomous units were protected in law and charter (constitution or organic laws) and a "just balance" existed between the state and society's component corporate bodies.[18]

But as Spain and Portugal began to near the end of the centuries-long struggle against the Moors and as the emerging nation-states (now consolidated into three: Aragon, Castile, and Portugal) gained greater power vis-à-vis the corporate units that made up society, this "just balance" was upset and all but entirely destroyed for centuries thereafter. This process reached its culmination in the reign of the "Catholic monarchs," Isabella (of Castile) and Ferdinand (of Aragon) and was consolidated under the subsequent Hapsburg monarchy. First, Aragon and Castile were united and further centralized by the marriage of wily Ferdinand (the model for Machiavelli's *Prince)* and the tough, shrewd Isabella—although their efforts to bring Portugal into the fold by dynastic arrangements ultimately failed. Second, *within* their kingdoms, especially Castile, the process of internal concentration of power continued, and the autonomous rights of the societal corporate units were stripped away. Initially, Isabella took away the separate, autonomous charters of the several military orders; then she eliminated the independence of the nobility by giving them glorious titles and luring them to her court; she also put the universities to work in the service of the crown justifying royal absolutism and a hierarchical, top-down state. The last, dying rebellion against this aggrandizing central authority was the *comunero* revolt of 1520, an effort by the previously autonomous towns and municipalities to hang onto the vestiges of their power but which was brutally put down by the *Spanish* (as distinct now from a regional) *army* (as distinct from the older, decentralized military orders).[19]

From this point on, at least until the nineteenth century, royal absolutism triumphed; the tradition of local or corporate-functional autonomies was snuffed out and nearly died. Eventually, it was revived in Spain but only weakly in Latin America (one of the area's problems, as we shall see)—in a republican form that was almost unrecognizable. We return to this theme later in the discussion. For Latin America, however, it is important to emphasize that it was the system of royal absolutism, what I have elsewhere termed the "Hapsburg model,"[20] that triumphed, with almost no sense of the earlier and opposed traditions of government by contract, just balance between central authority and society's component units, and constitutional government infused with group rights and liberties. I would summarize the Hapsburg model in the following terms:

1. Political. Centralized, authoritarian, top-down rule, with power arranged in a hierarchy of absolutions from king to viceroy to captain-general to local land owner.
2. Economic. A monopolistic mercantilist system based on exploitation and oriented toward milking the colonies dry for the sake of the mother countries.
3. Social. A rigid, two-class/caste (in the New World) system based on principles of patrimonialism and seigniorial authority.
4. Religious. A similarly (parallel to the state system) closed, monopolistic, top-down, absolutist, authoritarian body of beliefs and institutions that often served as an arm of royal authority.
5. Intellectual. A closed system of ideas and education similarly based on revealed, absolute truth, rote memorization, and the deductive method; in short, scholastic, pre-Enlightenment, pre-scientific revolution.

A close analysis of these five characteristics, which cover virtually all areas of existence, reveals that the institutions that Spain beginning in 1492 brought to the New World are the characteristics of a pre-1500, pre-modern, medieval, semi-feudal society. The institutions of Latin America are the institutions of the Counter-Reformation, of Spain's (and in a less rigid form Portugal's) efforts to restore and perpetuate the status quo ante, the institutions of pre-modern Europe. In this project Spain succeeded magnificently for over three hundred years but at enormous costs for future democratization. One can profitably speculate on the contrasts of this Hapsburgian model with the practices and institutions brought to the North American Dutch and British colonies over a century later, by which time in *these* mother countries the yoke and hold of medieval institutions had been substantially broken.[21]

In the New World

At the time of the Spanish conquest of the Americas beginning in 1492, royal absolution in Spain (and to only a somewhat lesser extent in Portugal) was in full flower. The processes of centralization of the Spanish kingdom and of royal aggrandizements of power had been occurring over centuries, reached their culmination in the reign of Ferdinand and Isabella, and were further consolidated and bureaucratized under the sixteenth-century Hapsburg monarchy of Charles V and Phillip II. But at the same time, the constituent elements of Spanish society, now subordinated to the power of the state, were the estates and a multitude of functional corporations that included the army, the church, merchants' guilds (*consulados*), artisans' guilds (*gremios*), towns and municipal organs, the *mesta* as well as cattlemen's guilds, and other corporate units. Each of these bodies had, historically, a separate juridical status and relation to the state (now largely eclipsed), expressed in *fueros*, *leyes organicas* (organic laws), *ordenanzas* (bylaws), or *reglamentos* (rules and regulations). Hence, while the state was increasingly centralized and absolutist, Iberian society remained essentially corporatist in the sense that it was the group or corporate body, sanctioned by and defined in law, rather than the individual, that constituted the fundamental building blocks. What was called the *estado estamental* was a conception of a "dual state" consisting of an increasingly absolutist monarchy and the corporate, anti-absolutist units of society represented through the *cortes*, with the two existing in a constantly dynamic tension.[22]

This same structure of an absolutist state coupled with the corporate organization of society—and the ongoing dynamic between the two—was carried to the New World. On the one hand, the Spanish (and Portuguese) colonial systems were based on the principles of absolute, top-down, royal authority centered in Madrid and Lisbon. On the other, colonial society was corporately organized with the most important colonial corporations being the church, the *cabildos* (local government), the *consulados* and *gremios* (guilds), the military, the *ayuntamiento*, the *haciendas* (large estates) and the *pueblos indios* (Indian villages). During the formative sixteenth century and through most of the seventeenth (the period of Hapsburg rule), the disintegrative, fissiparous tendencies in the colonies' social structure were held in check by the centralizing and legitimizing power of the Iberian patrimonial states, but later, as the state weakened, power began to return to society's more autonomous corporate units, which led eventually to independence.[23]

Colonial Latin America's political structure was, like that of the Iberian Peninsula, both statist and corporative. As in the Old World, society was organized by *groups* that constituted the basic units (family, parish, *gremio*, etc.) of political and administrative life. These groups derived legal personality from their privileges and responsibilities and often exercised—within a system of top-down royal authority—considerable autonomous control over both their own affairs and the individuals within their jurisdictions, frequently through a system of private courts and administrative agencies similarly hierarchically and corporately organized.[24] "The corporate principle," John Leddy Phelan has written, "was a basic principle of the whole system of government in the Indies, namely . . . that the individual's rights, privileges, and obligations were derivative from the particular estate and functional corporations to which that individual belongs . . . whose privileges and responsibilities were usually spelled out in specific charters."[25] And as Roland Ebel and James Henderson state, "Colonial Latin America's political structure was segmented by function and stratified by class, with those corporate groups which represented persons of higher estate having greater political power than those composed of persons of lower prestige."[26]

In the New World, however, there were significant differences from the corporate model of the Old World. First, the estates were less clearly defined; although there were large *haciendas* and eventually a native-born (*criollo*) aristocracy, there was no real nobility in the New World as in the Old. Second, in the New World the Spanish found a large indigenous population that did not fit neatly into the compartmentalized functional societal arrangements of the mother countries. In many cases the Spanish therefore created a new set of corporative arrangements (*ejidos, comunos*) for indigenous elements; but they also created a series of categories (*mestizo, castizo, morisco, chino, salta atras, gibaro, albarazado, cambujo, zambaigo,* etc.) to structure society in terms of castes as well as estates and corporations.[27] A third difference was that in the New World there was no *cortes* as there was in the Old (however, weakened) and therefore no self-government, no system by which estates, castes, and corporate bodies were directly represented or could make their voices heard in an organized fashion.

The power, authority, and legitimacy of the Spanish Crown, moreover, changed over time. As the Hapsburg monarchs declined in health, power, and legitimacy in the seventeenth century, their control over the colonies gradually eroded, allowing societal and corporate groups in the New World to achieve some greater autonomy. Moreover, royal authority was far away and travel and communications difficult; hence, while the colonies consistently exhibited formal obedience to the crown, in practice they were quite selective about the laws actually implemented. Then, in the eighteenth century, the new Bourbon monarchy, replacing the Hapsburgs, sought to recentralize imperial control and even abolished or put limits on the New World's corporate units such as the church and, in particular, the Jesuits. But these steps antagonized the colonies, which eventually determined to reestablish their autonomy by moving toward independence.[28]

The power structure of colonial Latin America was characterized by royal absolutism emanating from the mother countries on the one hand, as well as a continuous tension between absolutist and decentralized patterns of patrimonial authority on the other.[29] This tension manifested itself in a number of ways: in the dichotomy between the formal principle of a strict chain of authoritarian command versus the right of lower colonial officials to appeal directly to the crown over higher officials; in the right of colonial subjects to disregard royal authority when they thought it was inadequately informed concerning local conditions; and in the fluctuating power of the corporate bodies, which, as Ronald Newton writes, "in clothing themselves in legal charters, *fueros*, and customary privilege, achieved, especially under weak monarchies, a near parity of *de facto* power with the Crown."[30]

The Spanish colonial system, fluctuating between its absolutist and its decentralized tendencies, was, as Roland Ebel states, "a gigantic network of individual and corporate privilege depending for its ultimate sanction and operability on the legitimacy and authority of the monarch."[31] Thus, when the empire showed greater stresses and strains in the later eighteenth century and eventually cracked in the early nineteenth, so did the colonial power structure—both as an *empire* and within the existing viceregal and lower-level jurisdictions that became the geographic bases for the newly created states of Latin America. The network of clientage, patrimonialism, and interconnected corporate bodies that had provided a certain amount of social and political cement to the empire and to the vast, near-empty (in both a population and associational sense) territory of Latin America—and that had provided a considerable degree of legitimacy, direction, and coordination under a central authority—disintegrated into a collection of poorly organized, disarticulated, regional units presided over by local men-on-horseback or creole oligarchs. As Richard M. Morse concluded, "for a newly erected Spanish American political system to achieve stability and continuity it had to reproduce the structure, the logic, and the vague pragmatic safeguards against tyranny of the Spanish patrimonial state."[32]

Independence

By 1824 Spanish America had achieved its independence from the mother country and Brazil from Portugal. Our purpose, as in preceding sections of the chapter, is not to focus on the chronology of these and subsequent events but to provide an interpretive overview focused on the role of the state and its relations with Latin American society.

The withdrawal of the crown and of royal authority left a legitimacy vacuum in the colonies. The crown had not always been effective, but it had provided legitimacy, a centralizing focus, a gravitational pull for the distinct corporate, class, and caste interests that might otherwise spin off into separate orbits. In addition the crown, even in its weaker years, performed the role of a "moderative power."[33] That is, it moderated between contending societal forces and thus prevented either civil war or societal disintegration into separate sovereignties, either geographical or functional. But now, with independence, these useful integrative and moderating functions of the crown disappeared.

The results of the withdrawal of royal authority were disastrous throughout Latin America. The economies of many areas reverted to a more primitive form of subsistence. The societies based on class, caste, and corporate privilege were severely disrupted. Many of these groups lost their charters, special privileges, or place in society as a result of the independence struggle and the sociopolitical breakdowns that followed. Unity vanished as the continent broke up into smaller and smaller entities—"city states," to use Roland Ebel's term for the Central American republics.[34] There was no agreed-upon organizing principle; there was no one to "moderate" among the contending groups; and many areas slipped into anarchy. Into the legitimacy vacuum occasioned by the withdrawal of the crown came the independence armies, various regional men-on-horseback, and in some cases, such as Chile, the creole elite. But these patterns, which sound peaceful and regular, should not disguise the anarchy, disruption, and disintegration that occurred throughout the region.[35]

A few far-sighted independence leaders like Bolívar foresaw the disintegrative forces at work and sought to compensate for them. Bolívar tried to maintain the unity of the continent in a kind of pan-Latin American arrangement, but in this he failed. He flirted with the idea of a local or home-grown monarchy, but that idea also languished in the new republican climate. Recognizing the anarchic tendencies threatening to tear Latin America apart, coupled with the realization that the vast continent lacked the integrating webs of associability that De Tocqueville so admired in North America, Bolívar also considered the restoration of absolute central power (with himself as dictator); but that idea was not accepted by his contemporaries either.[36]

The Latin American "founding fathers" faced a terrible dilemma, and they were quite ingenious in finding a solution for it. On the one hand, the Enlightenment, Rousseauist ideas, the French Revolution, the (North) American Revolution, as well as independence sentiment and the desire for liberty in their own countries all dictated that the form of government they should follow would be republican. On the other, they realistically recognized the disintegrative, anarchic tendencies at work in their own societies; that Latin America lacked a sufficiently strong social, economic, and political base; that the area (to use the familiar refrain of modern authoritarians) "was not ready for democracy." So in the laws and constitutions of these new states, they arrived at an ingenious set of compromises. Strong power (not altogether different from that of the old, now ousted monarchy), combined with vast emergency powers, was concentrated in the executive branch, at the expense of the legislative and judicial branches. The franchise was severely restricted so that only literate and property holders (the creole elites or "nobility") could vote and hold office. Corporate privilege was restored: The army and the church were elevated to virtual fourth and fifth branches of government, with vast and special responsibilities. The executive or the army, succeeding the crown, now played the role of the "moderative power." Meanwhile, new controls were devised to keep the lower classes and castes in their place.[37]

The period between 1824 and the mid-1850s in most Latin American countries was disorganized, confused, often anarchic; but during the next period, 1850s–1880s, some order eventually emerged out of the prevailing chaos. The first banks were chartered. Population increased and began to fill the empty spaces; new lands were opened to cultivation. Foreign investment and foreign immigration both increased. An infrastructure (roads, port facilities, telephone and telegraph, railroads) began to be built. The economies of the area began to recover; society became more organized; the political systems began to stabilize.[38]

The better organization of "society" in Latin America, defined in terms of corporate bodies, associational life, and *"civilización"* (the opposite of *"falta de civilización,"* which had long plagued the area) was, during this period, accompanied by the corresponding growth of the state. The traditional four ministries (armed forces, treasury, foreign affairs, and public works) now expanded to include more state functions and hence more state ministries and agencies. The centrifigulism of the early decades of independence gave way to greater centralization.[39] New national armies replaced the rag-tag regional, caudillo-led armies of the past. Similarly, a national bureaucracy began to grow and to extend its sway over more areas of national life. Porfirio Díaz in Mexico is the paradigm example of the newer centralizing, development-oriented, "order-and-progress" (the positivists' message, then the dominant ideology in Latin America) leadership.[40]

The period of the 1850s to the 1890s is usually considered the period when the "pre-conditions for takeoff" (to use Rostow's aeronautical metaphor[41]) were established in Latin America; the "takeoff" occurred during the next period, 1890–1930, which is also frequently referred to as either the "twilight of the middle ages" or the "heyday of oligarchic rule." This was a period of unprecedented prosperity in Latin America; as late as the 1920s Argentina had a per capita income greater than that of the United States. It was also a period of social and political consolidation, actually under three patterns. One was stable, peaceful, oligarchic rule (Chile, Argentina, Brazil, Peru); another was order-and-progress dictatorship (Díaz, Gómez in Venezuela, Heureaux in the Dominican Republic). The third (sometimes combined with the first two) was U.S. Marine occupation in many of the smaller, weaker, less-institutionalized countries of Central America and the Caribbean but which accomplished many of the same tasks as the previous two patterns: social peace, political stability, centralization of military and bureaucratic functions, infrastructure development, and economic growth.[42]

By this point, almost a hundred years after the first stirrings of independence, Latin America was finally returning to the same level of development it had under colonial rule. Interestingly, this was a period when both a strong state *and* strong societal organizations were growing. Moreover, a genuinely Latin American political process, otherwise known as *criollo* politics, later baptized as the "Andersonian model,"[43] had begun to emerge. The economic, social, and political development of Latin America in the early decades of the twentieth century had given rise to new social and political forces that had either to be accommodated or repressed, co-opted or coerced. The Anderson model, based on a close examination of the processes involved, posited that a new social, economic, or corporate group could be accommodated to the political system provided two conditions were met: (1) the group had to demonstrate sufficient size or power capability to be taken seriously as a power contender; and (2) the group had to agree to moderate its demands and not resort to revolutionary methods that would destroy other groups in the system. Elections, a well-executed coup d'etat, or the use of carefully orchestrated violence that fell short of revolution were all "coinage" of the political system, a way of demonstrating a new group's power capability and that its demand to be admitted as a partner in the still-prevailing patrimonialist political system should be recognized. Under these rules and conditions, first the emerging business elites around the turn of the century and then the rising middle classes (rather, middle sectors) in the 1910s and 1920s (Argentina, Chile, Mexico) were admitted to "the system."

These examples and processes indicate that Latin America's prevailing corporatist, centralized, patrimonialist, and often authoritarian structures could be more accommodative to change than is ordinarily thought. They generally bent to change and sought to accommodate the new groups rather than being overwhelmed by them. They proved—within limits—to be flexible, even somewhat modernizing. Moreover, these changes took place within a political tradition that, while borrowing from other countries, was uniquely Hispanic, *criollo*, indigenous. That tradition owed a great deal to the colonial and Iberian past but was not entirely inimical to progress. However, with the market crash of 1929, the global depression that set in thereafter, and then the accompanying collapse of the Latin American political regimes (between 1930 and 1934, Latin America had no less than fourteen full-scale revolutions),[44] this system of traditional, co-optive, *criollo* politics came crashing down. In this sense the "middle ages," the feudal past in the sense of what we have termed the Hapsburg model, ended not in the 1820s with independence but only in the 1930s in ways that involved both the disintegration of the old system and the calling forth of a new system to replace it.

Manifest Corporatism

Up to this point we have been talking about corporatism in its traditional, historical, medieval, and what Ronald Newton called its "natural" sense.[45] That is the sense in which I offered some twenty years ago my still-controversial formulation of "the corporative model" of Iberian and Latin American development.[46] But in the 1930s a new model of corporatism and of state-society relations emerged that we will term "manifest corporatism." This form of corporatism owed something to the historical past, but it was also a product of new forces: the growth of a manifest ideology of corporatism, the desire or need for the state to get more directly involved in central planning, fascist influences, the emergence of state capitalism, and the need for authoritarian political controls to hold in check some of the new social forces, accompanying the desire for industrialization and economic growth.[47]

The dominant economic growth model in Latin America from the 1930s to the 1970s was import-substitution industrialization (ISI)—the substitution of industrial goods produced domestically for those previously imported. Other chapters in this volume will deal with this strategy in greater detail; suffice it to say here that state-led ISI in the economic sphere also called for the state to regulate or control more closely the social, political, and corporate groups that make up society. The earlier, pre-1930 period, we have seen, was one of the emergence of both strong states and a strong corporate or societal group life in Latin America, as well as a generally accommodative political process to incorporate the new groups; but now that trend was about to be reversed—once again. Although the process was often chaotic, varied greatly from country to country, and was at times interrupted by democratic interludes, the general trend after 1930 was toward a more statist or bureaucratic-authoritarian form of corporatism. In short, state capitalism and ISI in the national economic life required similarly statist and authoritarian controls in the social and political sphere.[48]

There were actually several influences shaping Latin American corporatism during this early period. One was simply the historical corporatist tradition as described above. A second was the Catholic *ideology* of Christian corporatism that had its roots in mid-nineteenth-century Catholic thought and found later expression in the papal encyclicals *Rerum Novarum* and *Quadregessimo Anno*.[49] A third was the bureaucratic-authoritarian version of corporatism, as found, for example, in Franco's Spain and Salazar's Portugal.[50] Other influences on Latin American corporatism came from integralism, fascism, and solidarism, though these latter carried less weight in Latin America than the first three. Most Latin American forms of corporatism in the 1930s and subsequently represented mixes, fusions, and sometimes alternations of historical or "natural" corporatism, manifest Catholic corporatism, and the bureaucratic-authoritarian or "statist" form.

Almost every regime that came to power in Latin America in the 1930s and subsequently showed some degree of corporatist influences. The more prominent examples include Vargas's Brazil, Perón's Argentina, Cárdenas's Mexico, Ibáñez's Chile, Trujillo's Dominican Republic, Stroessner's Paraguay, Arías's Panama, Velasco's Peru, Frei's Chile, Pinochet's Chile, and many others. Corporatism seemed to be ubiquitous: In a great variety of regimes that did not claim to be corporatist, corporatism seemed nevertheless to be present in the labor codes, the social welfare system, the structure of industrial relations, and other social and public policy programs.[51]

If corporatism was so ubiquitous, its usefulness as an explanatory factor is thereby somewhat diminished; several qualifications and distinctions hence need to be introduced. First, *nowhere* in Latin America was a complete, full-scale corporatist regime introduced comparable to Salazar's Portugal, with a corporately organized economy, full functional representation, a corporate chamber, and the complete corporate organization of society (even Salazar's Portugal, a model for many Latin American regimes, was never fully corporatist);[52] instead, Latin America was at most partially corporatist. Second and related, Latin American corporatism, because of (I am convinced) its setting in the *American* hemisphere rather than the European, continued to be influenced as much by liberal (U.S.) influences of representation, etc., as by corporatist ones. Third, the strong historical corporatism in Latin America and its medieval roots meant that Latin American corporatism included such groups as the church or the army and was never limited only, as in recent European corporatism, to such economic groups as farmers, business, and labor. Fourth, there were quite different forms of corporatism in Latin America, as the list of regimes in the preceding paragraph indicates, ranging from leftist (Cárdenas) to rightist (Pinochet), from Christian-Democratic (Frei) to secular, and from military (Trujillo, Velasco) to civilian (Arías). However, it should be noted that, if one considers the whole list, military and bureaucratic-authoritarian regimes seem to have a closer and stronger affinity for corporatism, especially in its statist or control-mechanisms forms, than do civilian, elected democratic regimes.[53]

A fifth consideration is the constantly changing nature of corporatism in Latin America. In *no* regime was corporatism or its precise form constant. Rather, corporatism changed over time in response to changes within regimes and to changing societal conditions and because of alternations in power from one government to another. Corporatism took an often open and manifest form in the 1930s when, as Manoilesco had proclaimed,[54] it seemed to be the wave of the future. After World War II and the defeat of the Axis powers, corporatism seemed to be discredited because of its association with those regimes; hence, many Latin American countries dropped their more manifest forms and the corporatist label, even while continuing often to practice a disguised form of corporatism. For example, Brazil's Vargas put in place in the 1930s a corporatist system of labor relations; and even though Vargas and his regime were later repudiated, the corporatist system of labor relations remained in effect until the constitutional and legislative changes of 1987—and may, de facto, still be partially in effect.[55]

Similarly, while many regimes of this period called themselves democratic and pluralist, they continued to practice the Andersonian model—essentially corporatist—of co-opting new groups into the system (now extended to organized labor and peasants) but under state control and direction. However, as some Latin American countries shed their long-time dictators in the late 1950s to early 1960s in favor of what turned out to be a short democratic interlude, they also shed much of their earlier corporatist infrastructure and control mechanisms or disguised them under "liberal" labels. However, as these democratic regimes again gave way in the 1960s and 1970s to a major wave of bureaucratic-authoritarian regimes, the corporatist structures and control mechanisms came back—often with a vengeance. In some analyses of this period,[56] corporatism and authoritarianism were viewed as likely permanent features of the Latin American political landscape.

Beginning in the late 1970s, however, a new wave, this time a democratic one, swept over Latin America. People became disillusioned with the corruption, brutality, and inefficiency of bureaucratic-authoritarianism; civil society began to revive after a decade and more of statism; pro-democracy sentiment spread; and the United States and the international community pushed and offered encouragement. By the mid-1990s all the countries of the area save Cuba were under varying forms (often mixed or halfway forms) of democratic rule, a dramatic reversal from two decades earlier when fourteen of the twenty republics were under authoritarian rule. With the authoritarians into oblivion often went the corporatist and bureaucratic-authoritarian interpretations of Latin American state-society relations that had been prominent in previous decades. The question remaining is whether such a consignment to the dustbins of history is premature, both of authoritarian and corporatist regimes and of the models used to interpret the area.

Toward the Future: Neoliberalism or Neocorporatism?

Latin America's transitions to democracy from the late 1970s began as purely *political* transitions aimed at holding elections, reestablishing the rule of law, restoring civil society, and respecting human rights. Initially, there was little thought given to the possibility of dismantling, reducing, or privatizing state bureaucratic institutions or of moving away from the statist ISI economic policy. Nevertheless, even at the beginning of this process some wondered if Latin America could have political liberalization without undergoing economic liberalization too.[57] For just as in the earlier period when statism in the economic sphere was associated with authoritarianism and corporatism in the political spheres, could political freedom now be carried forward without it being accompanied by a free economic marketplace?

While Latin America was still discussing the issue, events worldwide soon outpaced the policy debate. The collapse of the Soviet Union and Eastern Europe, the revelations of the many economic failures of both Marxist-Leninist and statist regimes, and the superior economic performance of capitalist economies in East Asia and worldwide over either Marxist or etatist ones pointed to the fact that there was now only one route to modernization: the liberal-democratic-free-market one. Moreover, to be competitive in the modern world, Latin America understood, in a context where there would be little United States or other foreign aid and where they could no longer use the Cold War to wring benefits out of the competing superpowers, they would have to modernize, rationalize, and make more efficient both their economies and their governmental systems. Most Latin American governments came to these conclusions by themselves; if they needed any prodding, the United States, the World Bank, and the International Monetary Fund were there to apply the pressure.[58]

The result, for a time, was a quite remarkable turnabout in thinking about the state. Led by Chile, Mexico, and Argentina, the by-now large, bloated, corrupt, inefficient, patronage-dominated Latin American state began to be reduced in size, decentralized, made more efficient, and privatized. The process was by no means peaceful, easy, or steady; in many countries there was at least as much sleight-of-hand for U.S. and IMF consumption (some public employees were fired with great publicity while others were quietly hired; state enterprises were "sold" to other state enterprises or simply consolidated into larger state enterprises so that the total number appeared to be reduced) as there was real public sector reform or privatization. But eventually in almost all countries the movement toward free markets took root; correspondingly, the economies of Latin America began to recover from the "lost decade" of the 1980s. Some economies even showed spectacular growth, comparable to the "tigers" of East Asia.[59]

Within the United States, the movement and pressure toward free markets had, as would be expected, been mainly a Republican approach from

1980 to 1992; my sense is that at first many Latin Americans "went along" only to please the Americans (*"para Inglés ver"*) and the IMF, and thus to qualify for sorely needed loans and loan guarantees. Only later, observing the spectacular economic growth of Chile and others, did this become a genuine and hemispheric-wide movement. The promise of free trade and greater access to U.S. markets a la NAFTA accelerated this process, as virtually every country in the hemisphere clamored to work out a free trade agreement with the United States. The Clinton administration, however, was split on the subject; some officials favored the free trade-privatization agenda while others favored a continuation of central planning, vast welfare programs, and a statist approach. This latter group provided encouragement to those, now in the minority, in Latin America who had never been convinced by the free-market approach and wished to continue with a *dirigiste* model. Hence, at the Hemisphere Summit in Miami in December 1994, we were treated to the new phenomenon of the traditionally statist Latin Americans being now more in favor of free trade and privatization than the historically private enterprise-oriented Americans.[60]

Within Latin America, meanwhile, the debate over corporatism and the proper ordering of state-society relations had been revived, but in new terms. Many Latin Americans have concluded that in order to have a more efficient economy and a more efficient and democratic government, they would have to dismantle the vast web of corporate controls, privilege, and entrenched interests that had built up over the preceding sixty years.[61] At this point corporatism no longer meant the ideology and system of functional representation popularized in the 1930s but now was used disparagingly to refer to entrenched, corrupt, privileged groups—labor unions, business groups, bureaucratic interests—who had penetrated the state over the previous decades, most often with official blessing; hived off whole sectors for themselves; had established vast sinecures of privilege and inefficiency; and, now most important, were holding back both democracy and greater government efficiency. Hence, the conclusion was this: For democracy and economic modernization to go forward, the entire corporative structure built up over decades and even centuries would have to be dismantled.[62]

We are now at the point of the current debates in Latin America. How much state is necessary? The Latin American state clearly needs to be streamlined for greater governmental and economic efficiency, but what about the dire social and equity issues that, presumably, demand a greater state role? A smaller, leaner state will reduce the opportunities for corruption and inefficiency, but what about all those patronage obligations that must be fulfilled if even democratic governments are to have a chance to survive and thrive? Dismantling corporatism may be rational for some economic and governmental reform purposes, but might it also result in the elimination of large parts of civil society and of some of Latin America's most important—and very fragile—webs of associability? By pushing too hard or too rapidly to dismantle corporatism, do not we in the United States run the risk of destabilizing the very countries that we would least want to see destabilized—e.g., Mexico? Throughout Latin America the historical forms and institutions of corporatism are being undermined, but they are by no means gone; meanwhile, the liberal-pluralist forms are growing but they are not well established or fully institutionalized yet.

Several currents will likely continue to operate at the same time. On one level there will be ongoing pressures to continue with neoliberal economic reforms; on others there will be pressures (now reinforced by the fallout from the Mexican peso crisis, which in some quarters is being interpreted as a repudiation of the neoliberal model) to maintain a large state role, to slow the pace of privatization, and to maintain the patrimonial systems. In some systems there will be sentiment in favor of dismantling the corporatist system; in others there will be pressures to keep corporatist privilege intact. In Mexico, for example, the official corporatist structure is undergoing change both from within and without; and meanwhile new associations are being formed that operate in a liberal-pluralist framework, not the corporatist one.[63]

My guess is that in all these areas, as on so many policy issues in the past, Latin America will end up with a mixed system—various blends, overlaps, and halfway houses. It seems likely that the Latin American state will continue to be reformed and perhaps somewhat reduced; but it also seems unlikely that a continent with such a long, strong historical tradition of statism and with such strong interests in preserving it—like France—will abandon that system quickly or easily. Similarly, with state-society relations: Latin America may be in the process of dismantling its older corporatist system and moving toward greater political liberalism and pluralism; but we should not be too surprised if, alongside these liberalizing changes, the region also moves toward new, updated forms of neocorporatism that also blend liberal with European-style neocorporatist forms.[64]

Conclusion

Historically, and today, the fate and future of the Latin American state are tied to its larger system of state-society relations. The relative weight and power of these two have fluctuated over time: often a strong state, rarely a strong society, and at times a kind of balance between the two. It is during these times of balance that Iberia, or by extension Latin America, have been thought to be governed "constitutionally" and "democratically." This combination of a strong state with autonomous corporate bodies is a form of democracy that has little to do with Locke, Jefferson, or Madison but has a great deal to do with Aquinas, Suárez, and the great Spanish neoscholastic tradition of the sixteenth century, updated in Rousseauist, positivist, corporatist, and now neocorporatist ways. Elsewhere I have called this system a "contract state";[65] one hopes, without holding out great optimism, that American policymakers understand the different conceptions of democracy involved and can frame appropriate policy responses accordingly.

We have also seen that both the Latin American state and the form of corporatism and state-society relations have varied over time. The region has gone from an absolutist or Hapsburgian state to a form (Rousseauist) of a republican state to a, currently, more liberal and pluralist state. Similarly with its omnipresent corporatism: we have seen traditional, historic, semi-feudal, or "natural corporatism"; manifest, albeit mixed, corporatism in the twentieth century; and the beginnings of modern neocorporatism. But the key has always been to achieve that "just balance" (Thomistic), that delicate equilibrium between state and society that enables Latin America to function more or less democratically. In the shifting quicksands of Latin American politics, where the state-society balance is a matter of constant nuance and virtually everyday renegotiation among the various actors, that equilibrium is always difficult to achieve, no less so today than in earlier times.

Notes

1. Peter B. Evans, Dietrich Rueschemeyer and Theda Skocpol, eds., *Bringing the State Back In* (New York: Cambridge University Press, 1985).

2. Howard Wiarda, *American Foreign Policy toward Latin America in the 1980s and 1990s: Issues and Controversies from Reagan to Bush* (New York: New York University Press, 1992). See especially chapter 8.

3. Claudio Veliz, *The Centralist Tradition in Latin America* (Princeton: Princeton University Press, 1980); Alfred Stepan, *The State and Society: Peru in Comparative Perspective* (Princeton: Princeton University Press, 1978).

4. The state is here defined, following Weber, as the continuous administrative, legal, bureaucratic, decision-making, and coercive system that governs the polity. It seeks to structure state-society relations and often seeks to influence the internal affairs of civil society as well.

5. Throughout the analysis we use "ideal types" to simplify and make clear the analysis, recognizing that numerous qualifications and country variations are also required.

6. E. Ramon Arango, *Spain: Democracy Regained* (Boulder: Westview Press, 1995).

7. On France, see Marc Bloch, *Feudal Society* (Chicago: University of Chicago Press, 1961). On the *Reconquest* as *the* defining feature of Spanish history, see Americo Castro, *The Structure of Spanish History* (Princeton: Princeton University Press, 1954).

8. James F. Powers, "The Origins and Development of Municipal Military Service in the Leonese and Castilian Reconquest, 800–1250," *Tradition*, XXVI (1970), pp. 91–111; Elena Lourie, "A Society Organized for War: Medieval Spain," *Past and Present*, 35 (December 1966), pp. 54–76; Jose Antonio Maravall, "The Origins of the Modern State," *Journal of World History*, 6 (1961), pp. 789–808; Evelyn S. Proctor, "The Towns of Leon and Castille as Suitors before the King's Court in the Thirteenth Century," *English Historical Review*, CCXC (January 1959), pp. 1–22; and especially Angus Mackay, *Spain in the Middle Ages: From Frontier to Empire, 1000–1500* (London: Macmillan, 1977); and Archibald R. Lewis, *The Development of Southern French and Catalan Society, 718–1050* (Austin: University of Texas Press, 1965). No one could read these works without being convinced of the power of the corporative tradition in Iberia and Latin America; see also Anton-Hermann Chroust, "The Corporate Idea and the Body Politic in the Middle Ages," *Review of Politics*, IX (October 1947), pp. 423–52; and Antony Black, *Guilds and Civil Society in European Political Thought from the Twelfth Century to the Present* (Ithaca, NY: Cornell University Press, 1984).

9. Claudio Sánchez-Albornoz, "The Frontier and Castilian Liberties," in Archibald R. Lewis and Thomas F. McGann, eds., *The New World Looks at Its History* (Austin: University of Texas Press, 1963), pp. 27–69.

10. Julius Klein, *The Mesta: A Study in Spanish Economic History, 1273–1836* (Port Washington, NY: Kennikat Press, 1964).

11. Ibid., n. 8; also Charles Julian Bishko, "The Iberian Background of Latin American History," *Hispanic American Historical Review*, XXXVI (February 1956), pp. 50–80; Alfonso Garcia Gallo, "Aportación al Estudio de los Fueros," *Anuario de Historia del Derecho Español*, 26 (1956), pp. 425–40. Corporatism is here defined as a sociopolitical system in which the group, sanctioned by and defined in law, constitutes the basic unit of social and political life, rather than the individual.

12. For an extended discussion, see Howard J. Wiarda and Harvey F. Kline, "Introduction," in Howard J. Wiarda and Harvey F. Kline, eds., *Latin American Politics and Development*, 4th ed. (Boulder: Westview Press, 1995).

13. Bernice Hamilton, *Political Thought in Sixteenth Century Spain* (Oxford: Clarendon Press, 1963); J. H. Parry, *The Spanish Theory of Empire in the Sixteenth Century* (Cambridge: Cambridge University Press, 1940).

14. Joseph F. O'Callaghan, "The Beginning of the Cortes of León-Castile," *American Historical Review*, LXXIV (June 1969), 1503–37; Lesley Byrd Simpson, "The Cortes of Castile," *Americas*, XII (January 1956), pp. 223–33.

15. For recent treatments of these issues, see Aaron Wildavsky and David Laitin, "Political Culture and Political Preferences," *American Political Science Review*, 82 (June 1988), pp. 589–96; Harry Eckstein, "A Culturalist Theory of Political Change," *American Political Science Review*, 82 (September 1988), pp. 789–804; Lucian Pye, *The Mandarin and the Cadre: China's Political Cultures* (Ann Arbor: University of Michigan Press, 1988); Ronald Inglehart, *Culture Shift in Advanced In-*

dustrial Society (Princeton: Princeton University Press, 1990); Howard J. Wiarda, "Political Culture and National Development," *Fletcher Forum,* 13 (Summer 1989), pp. 193–204.

16. Actually, both individual and corporate group rights were present in the early Iberian conception, but the group conception became paramount. See McKay, *Spain in the Middle Ages,* passim.

17. McKay is again the best source; also Gaines Post, *Studies in Medieval Legal Thought: Public Law and the State, 1100–1332* (Princeton: Princeton University Press, 1961).

18. The point is elaborated in Howard J. Wiarda, "Constitutionalism and Political Culture in Mexico: How Deep the Foundations?" in Daniel B. Franklin and Michael J. Baun, eds., *Political Culture and Constitutionalism: A Comparative Approach* (Armonk, NY: M. E. Sharpe, 1995), pp. 119–37.

19. John Lynch, *Spain under the Hapsburgs* (Oxford: Basil Blackwell, 1965).

20. Howard J. Wiarda, *Latin American Politics: A New World of Possibilities* (Belmont, CA: Wadsworth, 1994).

21. Louis Hartz, ed., *The Founding of New Societies* (New York: Harcourt, Brace and World, 1964). See especially chapter 5, Richard M. Morse, "The Heritage of Latin America," pp. 123–77.

22. L. N. McAlister, "Social Structure and Social Change in New Spain," *Hispanic American Historical Review,* LXIII (August 1963), pp. 349–70; Bishko, "The Iberian Background of Latin American History," passim.

23. McAlister, "Social Structure"; C. H. Haring, *The Spanish Empire in America* (New York: Harcourt, Brace and World, 1947); Charles Gibson, *Spain in America* (New York: Harper, 1966).

24. Ronald C. Newton, "On 'Functional Groups,' 'Fragmentation,' and 'Pluralism' in Spanish American Political Society," *Hispanic American Historical Review,* L (February 1970), pp. 1–29.

25. John Leddy Phellan, *The Kingdom of Quito in the Seventeenth Century: Bureaucratic Politics in the Spanish Empire* (Madison: University of Wisconsin Press, 1967). This book is a classic of historical analysis; its implications reach far beyond the Ecuadorian case study.

26. Roland H. Ebel and James Henderson, "Patterns of Continuity in Latin American Society: Political and Historical Perspectives," *Annals of the Southeast Conference on Latin American Studies* (March 1976), pp. 91–122.

27. Nicolas Leon, *Las Castas del Mexico Colonial* (Mexico, D.F.: 1924); Richard Kowetzke, "Estado y Sociedad en las Indias," *Estudios Americanos,* III (1951), pp. 33–58.

28. John Leddy Phelan, "Authority and Flexibility in the Spanish Imperial Bureaucracy," *Administrative Science Quarterly,* V (June 1960), pp. 42–65; L. N. McAlister, *Spain and Portugal in the New World* (Minneapolis: University of Minnesota Press, 1984).

29. Patrimonialism is a form of personal authority in which the ruler doles out benefits, privileges, and positions in return for loyalty and service. See Magali Sarfatti, *Spanish Bureaucratic Patrimonialism in America* (Berkeley: Institute of International Relations, University of California, 1966); Sidney Greenfield, "The

Patrimonial State and Patron-Client Relations in Iberia and Latin America" (Amherst: University of Massachusetts, Program in Latin American Studies, Occasional Papers Series No. 1, 1976); and Raymundo Faoro, *Os Donos do Pader: Formação do Patronato Político Brasileiro* (Rio de Janeiro: Ed. Globo, 1958).

30. Ronald C. Newton, "Natural Corporatism and the Passing of Populism in Spanish America," *Review of Politics*, XXXVI (January 1974), p. 46.

31. Ebel and Henderson, "Patterns of Continuity," passim.

32. Richard M. Morse, "The Heritage of Latin America," in Hartz, ed., *The Founding of New Societies*, pp. 123–77.

33. See Alfred Stepan, *The Military in Politics: Changing Patterns in Brazil* (Princeton: Princeton University Press, 1971).

34. Roland Ebel, "Governing the City State: Notes on the Politics of the Small Latin American Countries," *Journal of Interamerican Studies and World Affairs* (August 1972), pp. 325–46.

35. Tulio Halperin-Donghi, *The Aftermath of Revolution in Latin America* (New York: Harper, 1973); David Bushnell and Neill MacCaulay, *The Emergence of Latin America in the Nineteenth Century* (New York: Oxford University Press, 1994).

36. Glen Dealy, *The Public Man: An Interpretation of Latin American and Other Catholic Countries* (Amherst: University of Massachusetts Press, 1977).

37. Glen Dealy, "Prolegomena on the Spanish American Political Tradition," *Hispanic American Historical Review*, 48 (1968), pp. 37–58.

38. Roberto Cortes Conde, *The First Stages of Modernization in Latin America* (New York: Harper & Row, 1974); Richard Graham, *Britain and the Onset of Modernization in Brazil* (Cambridge: Cambridge University Press, 1968).

39. Veliz, *The Centralist Tradition in Latin America*.

40. Harry Hoetink, *The Dominican People, 1850–1900: Notes for a Historical Sociology* (Baltimore: Johns Hopkins University Press, 1982).

41. W. W. Rostow, *The Stages of Economic Growth* (Cambridge: Cambridge University Press, 1960).

42. Bruce Calder, *The Impact of Intervention: The Dominican Republic during the U.S. Occupation of 1916–1924* (Austin: University of Texas Press, 1984).

43. Charles W. Anderson, *Politics and Economic Change in Latin America: The Governing of Restless Nations* (New York: D. Van Nostrand, 1967).

44. Howard J. Wiarda, *Critical Elections and Critical Coups: State, Society, and the Military in the Processes of Latin American Development* (Athens, OH: Center for International Studies, Ohio University, 1979).

45. Newton, "Natural Corporatism."

46. Howard J. Wiarda, "Toward a Framework for the Study of Political Change in the Iberic-Latin Tradition: The Corporative Model," *World Politics*, 25 (January 1973), pp. 206–35; also, Howard J. Wiarda, *Corporatism and National Development in Latin America* (Boulder: Westview Press, 1981).

47. Andrew Shonfield, *Modern Capitalism* (Oxford: Oxford University Press, 1965); Philippe C. Schmitter and Gerhard Lehmbruch, eds., *Trends toward Corporatist Intermediation* (Beverly Hills: Sage Publications, 1979).

48. Guillermo O'Donnell, *Modernization and Bureaucratic Authoritarianism* (Berkeley: Institute of International Studies, University of California, 1973); but

also David Collier, ed., *The New Authoritarianism in Latin America* (Princeton, NJ: Princeton University Press, 1979).

49. Howard J. Wiarda, "Corporatist Theory and Ideology: A Latin American Development Paradigm," *Journal of Church and State*, XX (Winter 1978), pp. 29–56.

50. Howard J. Wiarda, *Corporatism and Development: The Portuguese Experience* (Amherst: University of Massachusetts Press, 1977).

51. Additional details are in Howard J. Wiarda, "Corporatism and Development in the Iberic-Latin World: Persistent Strains and New Variations," *The Review of Politics*, 36 (January 1974), pp. 3–33.

52. Wiarda, *Corporatism and Development*.

53. James Malloy, ed., *Corporatism and Authoritarianism in Latin America* (Pittsburgh: University of Pittsburgh Press, 1977).

54. Mihail Manoilesco, *Le Siecle du Corporatisme* (Paris: Félix Alcan, 1934).

55. Kenneth P. Erickson, *The Brazilian Corporative State and Working Class Politics* (Berkeley: University of California Press, 1977).

56. Philippe Schmitter, "Still the Century of Corporatism?" *The Review of Politics*, 36 (January 1974), 85–131; Malloy, *Authoritarianism and Corporatism*; Wiarda, *Corporatism and National Development*.

57. Michael Novak, *The Spirit of Democratic Capitalism* (New York: Simon and Schuster, 1982); and Peter L. Berger, *The Capitalist Revolution* (New York: Basic Books, 1986).

58. Abraham F. Lowenthal and Gregory F. Treverton, eds., *Latin America in a New World* (Boulder: Westview, 1994); Howard J. Wiarda, *Latin American Politics: A New World of Possibilities* (Belmont, CA: Wadsworth, 1994).

59. Among the best sources are the United Nations Economic Commission for Latin America and the Caribbean, *CEPAL News*, especially the January issues reporting on the economic performance for the previous year; and Inter-American Development Bank, *Annual Report* (Washington, DC: IADB, yearly).

60. Based on author interviews and participant observation. See also, Mark Falcoff, "The Miami Summit: Perils and Possibilities," *Latin American Outlook* (Washington, D.C.: American Enterprise Institute, December 1994).

61. Jorge Bustamante, *La República Corporativa* (Buenos Aires: EMECE Editores, 1989).

62. See the author's review of the Bustamante book, "Dismantling Corporatism: The Problem of Modernization in Latin America," *World Affairs*, 156 (Spring 1994), pp. 199–203.

63. Neil Harvey, ed., *Mexico: Dilemmas of Transition* (London: British Academy Press, 1993).

64. The model for a mixed liberal and neocorporatist formula may well be Spain; see Howard J. Wiarda, *Politics in Iberia: The Political Systems of Spain and Portugal* (New York: HarperCollins, 1992).

65. Wiarda, *American Foreign Policy toward Latin America*, especially chapter 8.

3

The Rise and Fall of the Developmental State in Latin America

Peter H. Smith

The role of the state in Latin America has generated controversy, confusion, and occasional dismay. Pluralist and radical theory both tended to interpret the state as an essentially residual phenomenon, either as the result of competition among societal interest groups or as a "pact of domination" among predatory elites. In response to this dismissiveness, social scientists in the 1980s made a concerted effort to "bring the state back in."[1] Around this same time, however, international advisers and policy analysts were proposing to banish the state from the economic sphere, ardently insisting that governmental intervention had contributed to poverty and backwardness throughout the region. By the 1990s the terms of debate began shifting again, as leaders and pundits came to the realization that fledging democratic regimes in Latin America needed powerful institutional capacity in order to address the challenges of inequality, governability, and development of human resources. Strong states are not inherently bad, according to this view; it depends on how they are used.

This chapter analyzes the rise and demise of the "developmental state" in Latin America from the 1930s through the 1980s. Through a broad reassessment of the economic role of the Latin American state, I intend to show not only that the state has always been active in economic matters, as its critics would agree, but also that it has often been effective. Latin America's developmental problems have arisen not so much from the state or state intervention per se but mostly from other causes. Principal among them have been the region's disadvantageous location in the world economy as well as internal contradictions within the long-run economic strategies. By implication, I suggest that the answer to Latin

America's modern-day problems lies not in the dismantling of the state but in a redefinition of its role within a plausible strategy for long-term economic growth.[2]

Concepts and Clarifications

Let us begin with definition. Following the Weberian tradition, I regard the state as a set of institutions claiming control over territory and people through a monopoly of legalized force. In Laurence Whitehead's minimalist formulation, the state displays three interrelated characteristics: territoriality, administration, and command over resources.[3] And as Evelyne Huber has observed, the state performs a variety of functions—administrative, legal, coercive, and extractive. "In its most basic sense," Huber continues, "state strength is the capacity of the state to preserve itself and the territory and people over which it claims control. This means that a strong state is capable of ensuring security from external attacks and from internal challenges to its monopoly of organized force."[4]

It is essential to distinguish between the state and the regime. Essentially, the character of the regime—democratic, authoritarian, or subtypes thereof—defines rules for access to political power and decision-making processes. The quality of the state concerns institutional capacity to maintain authority and achieve policy goals. One has to do with inclusiveness, the other with effectiveness. Of course there seems to be a pattern of association between regimes and states, as leaders of democratic and authoritarian regimes tend to develop and apply state strength in different ways and issue areas. (Normatively, too, one might wish for democratic regimes to have strong states at their disposal and bureaucratic regimes to have weak states, but that is still another issue.) Theoretically, these are distinct concerns: Democratic or authoritarian regimes could coexist with almost any kind of state.[5]

Beginning in the 1930s, state organization underwent considerable development in Latin America. In Whitehead's estimation:

> Enormous strides had been taken toward the consolidation of "modern states" throughout Latin America. . . . Between 1930 and the early 1980s nearly all of Latin America underwent a remarkable process of state organization; the ambitions, resources, and capabilities of nearly all the region's public authorities were incommensurably greater than they had been a half century before.[6]

Bureaucracies gained strength, lines of authority sharpened, commitment to performance improved. Put simply, states were able to accomplish much more in the 1980s than a half century before.

During this period as well, Latin American leaders (democratic and authoritarian alike) attempted to construct what has come to be known as the "developmental state." As described in the Asia/Pacific region, the developmental state not only establishes the rules and regulations for economic activity; it also establishes priorities and preferences for the structure and content of economic development. According to Chalmers Johnson, it has several key characteristics.

A developmental elite creates political stability over the long term, maintains sufficient equality in distribution to prevent class or sectoral exploitation (land reform is critical), sets national goals and standards that are internationally oriented and based on nonideological external referents, creates (or at least recognizes) a bureaucratic elite capable of administering the system, and insulates its bureaucrats from direct political influence so that they can function technocratically. It does not monopolize economic management or decision making, permit the development of political pluralism that might challenge its goals, or waste valuable resources by suppressing noncritical sectors (it discriminates against them through disincentives and then ignores them).

Policy choices by the development state must be "market-conforming" in order to work, and they must be based on economic and not political agendas. Moreover, Johnson suggests, the developmental state is "normally authoritarian."[7]

Despite its utility and popularity, the idea of the "developmental state" has one central difficulty: the conflation of structure and function. Properly speaking, the "structure" of a state has to do with its institutional characteristics—its internal coherence, organizational structure, and relative autonomy—while its "function" has to do with promoting economic growth on an outward-oriented model, providing clear incentives and guidelines for a cooperating private sector. This distinction is fundamental, and it will pose a basic concern of this chapter.

Historical Patterns of State Activism

States in Latin America have a long history of intervention in economic matters. Soon after Columbus arrived in the Americas in 1492, the Spanish crown applied the prescriptions of then-predominant "mercantilist" theory.[8] According to this approach, the goal of economic activity was to enhance the power and prestige of the nation and the state. The point bears emphasis: The purpose of economics was to strengthen the state—in this instance, the Spanish crown—both in its control over domestic society and, especially, in its relationship to other sovereign states. The accumulation of power was to be measured through the possession of precious bullion—that is, gold or silver. Mercantilist policymakers thus sought to run a favorable balance of trade, with exports exceeding imports, because this would increase the store of coinage or bullion. (It was this emphasis on trade that would give the doctrine its name.) Mercantilist theory entailed two central premises: first, a de-emphasis on the individual pursuit of prosperity; and second, a presumption that the state should take an active role in the regulation of commerce and finance.

Following this logic, Spain attempted to establish a monopoly over wealth discovered in the New World. The first target was mining, first gold then silver, to increase the royal supply of bullion. The second was to maintain complete control over commerce, thus assuring a favorable balance of trade for the metropolis (and a negative balance for the colonies). As a result, Spanish authorities gave low priority to economic development within the colonies. They paid little attention to agriculture, for example, and they actively discouraged manufacturing, which could reduce the market for Spanish goods in the Americas. A central pillar for the colonial economy, especially on the Spanish American mainland, was labor provided by culturally diverse indigenous peoples whom the conquerors called "Indians." Natives supplied labor through a variety of legal mechanisms—as conquered vassals, slaves, indebted peons, and, ultimately, wards of the crown under systems known as *encomienda* and *repartimiento*. It was their work that extracted precious metals from the mines. It was their tribute that filled the coffers of the crown and its appointed emissaries. And it was the decline in the Indian population, as a result of conquest and, especially, disease, that would lead to the weakening of the mercantilist economy.

Brutal as it was, mercantilism enjoyed substantial success. Spain acquired considerable wealth from the New World. It maintained effective control of its far-flung holdings for nearly 300 years, and in so doing, it created a powerful and capable bureaucracy.[9] Ironically enough, it was the success of the mercantilist enterprise—especially the extraction of bullion from the Americas—that contributed to the ultimate debilitation of the Spanish economy in the seventeenth and eighteenth centuries. The mercantilist formulation contained the seeds of its own destruction; to achieve its goal (and its demise), however, it required the construction of a strong and efficacious state.

Eventually Spain proved unable to maintain its hold, and almost all of Spanish America (except Cuba and Puerto Rico) attained independence by the mid-1820s.[10] In the ensuing years, most of Latin America reduced its links with the world economy. Creole landowners converted their holdings into autonomous, self-sufficient entities rather than producing goods for domestic or foreign markets. Mining came to a standstill, partly as a result of the general physical destruction caused during the Wars of Independence. Manufacturing was modest, done mostly by artisans in small establishments. Politics became a crude power struggle among rival caudillos, swashbuckling leaders of paramilitary bands that assaulted the national treasury for private gain. In some countries rival camps described themselves as "liberals" or "conservatives," though the ideological difference between them was often obscure. The state began to wither away.

The Industrial Revolution in Europe precipitated the next major transformation in the political economy of Latin America. By the mid-nineteenth century the process of industrialization in England and elsewhere was producing strong demand for agricultural commodities and raw materials. In response to this new opportunity, Latin American leaders turned toward economic "liberalism," an emphasis on the exportation of raw materials in exchange for the importation of manufactured products from abroad. Instead of attempting to close the region to outside influence, as in the case of mercantilism, liberalism would seek to exploit the "comparative advantage" of Latin America's resource endowments through intensive interaction with the industrializing centers of the world economy. At least rhetorically, the emphasis would be on freedom of trade and laissez-faire.

This did not mean a minor role for the state. On the contrary, the liberal state in Latin America took decisive steps to facilitate and sustain the region's new insertion into the evolving world economy. Especially in former centers of the Spanish empire, the state set out to destroy neofeudal remnants of colonial society—the structures of patronage and privilege that threatened to inhibit the development of capitalism. One key achievement of the liberal state was to reduce the economic power of the Catholic Church, particularly its hold over land, a step that opened up financial markets and made possible the emergence of a new, profit-oriented agricultural elite.[11] In Mexico and other countries the granting of individual land titles within traditional Indian communities had a dual effect: One was to make high-quality land available for purchase and incorporation into commercial haciendas; another was to create a landless laboring class available for employment as peons.[12] In addition, the liberal state actively courted foreign investment, especially for the development of infrastructure, and particularly railroads. In Argentina the government actually guaranteed a minimal profit margin to a British railroad concession; in Mexico the government eventually purchased a majority share in railways, not so much for the purpose of creating a state enterprise as to rescue the indebted companies.[13]

The nineteenth-century liberal state assumed considerable responsibility for the labor force. Wherever workers were scarce, elites sought to import them from abroad. In the 1880s Argentina and Brazil began aggressive campaigns to encourage immigration from Europe; Chile received a smaller but substantial flow of workers. Wherever workers were abundant, particularly in countries with large indigenous populations, the liberal state undertook to discipline the work force. In Guatemala, for example, the government supervised and enforced the seasonal migration of workers from traditional villages to coffee plantations; in El Salvador, it monitored labor relations between displaced peasants who had come to be employed by capitalist landlords. On banana plantations and in other settings, the nineteenth-century state consistently opposed labor organization, broke strikes, and championed the interests of the capitalist class.

In short, the liberal state played an active role in the promotion of Latin America's export economies. But the ultimate goal of this activism contrasted sharply with mercantilism. Instead of seeking to enhance of the power of the state, liberalism sought to facilitate the performance of the economy. Turning mercantilist logic on end, the liberal state placed its efforts and resources at the service of the economy—and of dominant economic forces in society. Partly for this reason, the liberal state was inconsistent in performance. There existed no clear prescription for state roles. Its very activity posed a contradiction: According to liberal ideology, the state should have only a minimal role in matters economic. Almost by definition, there could be no long-term developmental "plan," and, not surprisingly, the nature and extent of governmental involvement in economic matters varied from country to country.[14] Policymakers tended to follow market signals and, more decisively, to carry out the wishes of economic elites rather than to pursue an overall design.

With regard to politics, the central challenge for the state was maintaining stability and social control. In Argentina and Chile, for example, landowners and other economic elites took direct control of the government. They built strong, exclusive regimes, usually with military support, forms of "oligarchic democracy" that proclaimed legitimacy through adherence to constitutions superficially resembling U.S. and European models. An alternative political model involved the imposition of dictatorial strongmen, often military officers, to assert law and order-again, for the ultimate benefit of the landed elite. Porfirio Díaz of Mexico, who took power in 1876, is perhaps the most conspicuous example, but the pattern also appeared in Venezuela, Peru, and much of Central America. In contrast to oligarchic democracy, where elites exercised direct political power, here it was the indirect application of elite rule through dictators who did not themselves come from the upper ranks of society. Thus emerged a paradox: As applied in nineteenth-century Latin America, economic liberalism offered a justification for political authoritarianism.

Despite internal contradictions, liberal economic policies achieved their fundamental goals. The major Latin American countries underwent startling transitions from the 1880s onward. Argentina, with its vast and fertile pampas, became a leading exporter of agricultural and pastoral goods—wool, wheat, and beef. Chile resuscitated the production of copper, an industry that had fallen into decay after the independence years. Cuba produced coffee as well as sugar and tobacco. Mexico came to export a variety of raw material goods, from henequen to sugar to industrial minerals, particularly copper and zinc. As development progressed, investment flowed into Latin America from the industrial nations, particularly England. And in return, Latin Americans purchased European textiles, machines, luxury items, and other finished products in steadily growing quantities. In practice, liberal policy thus led to the promotion of export-import development.

Consolidation of the export-import model of growth prompted fundamental changes in the region's social structure. First in sequence, if not in importance, was the modernization of the upper-class elite. Landowners and property owners were no longer content to run subsistence operations on their haciendas; instead, they sought commercial opportunities and the maximization of profits. Second was the appearance and growth of middle social strata. Occupationally, these consisted of professionals, merchants, shopkeepers, and small businessmen who profited from the export-import economy but who did not hold upper-rank positions of ownership or leadership. Third was the emergence of a working class. Near the turn of the century, laborers began to organize themselves, first in mutual-aid societies and later in unions. Their role in vital sectors of the export-import economies—especially in transportation (railways and docks)—gave them critical leverage. And their contact with comrades and movements outside Latin America (such as the International Workers of the World, or "wobblies") offered examples and prescriptions for activism.[15] Partly as a consequence, the years between 1914 and 1927 saw a remarkable surge of labor mobilization.

Eventually, these social trends would lead to the unraveling of liberal states. Especially in the larger and more developed countries, the entrance of middle- and working-class sectors into the political arena meant an inexorable shift from elitist regimes to mass politics. Sometimes these new groups were accommodated, often they were repressed—but they could not be ignored. As the citizenry became more sophisticated and complex, so would public policy. From the 1930s onward, politics in major nations of the region would never be the same.

Industrial Developmentalism

The Great Depression initially had catastrophic effects on the export-import economies of Latin America. International demand for coffee, sugar, metals, and meat was sharply reduced—and Latin American leaders could find no alternative outlet for their products. Both the unit price and the quantity of Latin American exports declined, with the result that their total value dropped significantly from 1925–1929 to 1930–1934. Economic crisis exerted great pressure on the political systems of Latin American countries, many of which suffered military coups (or attempted coups). Within a year or so after the October 1929 stock market crash army officers had sought or taken power in Brazil, Chile, Peru, Guatemala, El Salvador, and Honduras. (This occurred in Argentina as well, but for somewhat different reasons).[16] It would be an exaggeration to say that the economic effects of the Depression alone caused these political outcomes, but they cast into doubt the viability of the export-import model of growth, helped discredit ruling political elites, and made the citizenry more prepared to accept military regimes.

Given the global economic situation, Latin American rulers could pursue two major options. One was to forge even closer commercial linkages to the industrialized nations in order to secure a steady share of the market, whatever its size and dislocations. Argentina adopted this approach. Under the Roca-Runciman Pact of 1933, Britain promised to uphold its import quotas for Argentine beef (and to allow for state participation in the meat-packing business) in return for firm commitments on the peso-pound exchange rate and on preferential tariffs for British-made goods. Controversial from the moment it was signed, the Roca-Runciman treaty represented the consummate effort by a Latin American nation to resurrect the benefits of the liberal *economía agroimportadora*.

An alternative tack, not necessarily inconsistent with the first, was to embark on a program of industrialization—what I here call industrial developmentalism. Pursuit of this option took time. In the 1920s and 1930s industrialization was generally seen as a supplement to agricultural development not as a replacement for it. To some extent this early turn toward industry had a "defensive" quality, as a fortuitous and not entirely desirable response to a downturn in external conditions. For many policymakers it was a second-best option, and they consistently stressed their belief in the compatibility of industry and agriculture. Indeed, there was considerable skepticism about the feasibility of long-term industrial development. Policymakers approvingly cited the Ricardian distinction between "artificial" and "natural" industries, based on national factor endowments, and firmly withheld support for artificial (largely manufacturing) activities throughout most of the 1930s. In Brazil, government loans to artificial industries were prohibited as late as 1937, and Banco do Brasil did not begin making significant loans to manufacturers until 1941. In Mexico, too, Nacional Financiera was established in 1934 but did not extend serious support to industry until the early 1940s. Much the same applied to Chile's famous Corporación de Fomento (CORFO).[17]

Gradually, however, industrialization acquired a clear sense of purpose. Even in Argentina, paragon of export-import liberalism, policymakers began promoting domestic investment. None other than Luís Duhau, the minister of agriculture, described the rationale in late 1933:

> The historic stage of our prodigious growth under the direct stimulus of the European economy has finished. . . . After writing off the external stimulus, due to the confused and disturbing state of the world economy and policy, the country should look into itself, with its own resources, for the relief of its present difficulties. The plan proposes to stimulate efficiently industrial output using two different means: the construction of reproductive public works and by adjusting imports to the country's real capacity to pay.

To dispel any possible ambiguity, Federico Pinedo, the minister of the treasury, made clear that tariff protection was intended to promote domestic industry:

> The execution of a vast program of public works will result in an immediate increase in the demand for a great quantity and variety of goods which Argentina produces, or could produce. And here we reach a point which must be noted: the preventive control of imports will enable us to avoid such a demand stimulating imports, so that it will be used to promote domestic economic activities.[18]

Public investment plus protective tariffs would provide incentives for industrial development.

In other words, the most plausible form of industrial development was not simply to copy the paths traced by nineteenth-century Europe. Instead, Latin America's economies started producing manufactured goods that they had formerly imported from Europe and the United States— hence the name for this approach: "import-substitution industrialization," also known as ISI.

As political leaders promoted this strategy, they began to forge near approximations of the classic "developmental state." They sought long-term political stability, often resorting to authoritarian methods of control; even in cases of electoral democracy, economic decision making followed a highly autocratic style.[19] Policies focused on means of achieving and assuring economic growth, and the state assumed an openly *dirigiste* role. Ministries and bureaucracies attempted to set goals and policies without regard for social pressure; not always successful in this regard, the technocrats in charge nonetheless prized the idea of insulation from political influence. At times they also espoused redistributive policies, if not necessarily land reform. One of the distinctive characteristics of developmental states in twentieth-century Latin America, in contrast with the Asia/Pacific region, is that they usually promoted inward-looking industrialization rather than export-led growth, but in other respects they bore close resemblance to the prototype.

Ideological and theoretical support for industrial developmentalism would not emerge until the 1940s, and it would come from two principal sources. One was nationalism, the long-held desire for autonomy and self-determination. As intellectuals and policymakers surveyed the results of the nineteenth-century liberal experiment, many concluded that the nations of Latin America could achieve true political independence only on the basis of economic independence. For them this meant industrialization.

A second inspiration came from an initially unlikely source: a technocratic body of the United Nations known as the Economic Commission on Latin America (ECLA).[20] Created in the late 1940s and led by the remarkably able Argentine economist Raúl Prebisch, ECLA began publishing throughout the 1950s a series of technical reports demonstrating that, over time, commercial relationships worked to the systematic disadvantage of primary-producing countries. Because the price of manufactured goods increased faster than the price of agricultural and mineral commodities, the developing countries of Latin America obtained less and less real value for their export products. Though ECLA refrained from explicit policy recommendations, there were three logical solutions to this dilemma: One was to establish international commodity agreements; a second, for the larger countries, was to undertake industrialization; a third was to pursue economic integration among countries of the region and thus expand consumer markets.[21]

One of the goals of industrial developmentalism, often supported by the military, was to strengthen economic independence. The idea was that by building its own industry, Latin America would become less dependent on Europe and the United States for manufactured goods. The Latin American economies would become more integrated and self-sufficient, in other words, and consequently less vulnerable to the kind of shocks brought on by a worldwide depression.

A second goal was job creation. Concentrated almost entirely in cities, the Latin American proletariat was growing in size but still struggling to organize and sustain union movements. In contrast to the previous generation, however, it was now beginning to exert power as a social force. In some countries, such as Chile, union movements were relatively free of arbitrary government involvement. Elsewhere, as in Mexico and Brazil, politicians recognized labor as a potential political resource and took a direct hand in stimulating (and controlling) labor organizations. Whether perceived as ally or threat, the urban working class was seeking secure employment, and Latin American leaders saw industrialization as one way to respond.

From the late 1930s to the 1960s, at least in major countries, ISI policies met with relative success. The Depression and World War II afforded tacit protection and explicit opportunity for infant industries at home. States would play major roles in taking advantage of this situation. Governments restricted foreign competition through tariffs and quotas, encouraged local investment through credits and loans, stimulated domestic demand through public-sector expenditures, and, perhaps most important, took direct part in the process through the formation of state-owned companies. As a result, larger countries of the region—Argentina, Brazil, and Mexico—developed significant industrial plants.

Table 3.1 displays rates of economic growth from 1951 to 1980. Output expanded fairly steadily from the early 1950s through the mid-1970s, as regional growth hovered in the 5–6 percent range for much of the period (the annual average was 5.1 percent in the 1950s, 5.4 percent in the 1960s, and 6.7 percent in the early 1970s). On a per capita basis, too, regional output expanded by 2.4 percent per annum during the 1960s, compared with 2.1 percent in the 1950s, and climbed to 3.8 percent in the period 1970–1974. Prime movers behind this performance were Brazil and Mexico, each with strong gains in the manufacturing sector. Indeed, both these countries would receive international acclaim for economic "miracles"—Mexico during the 1950s and 1960s, Brazil for its spectacular performance in the period 1968–1973. (With its smaller domestic market and greater reliance on international trade, Argentina fell victim to a "stop-go" pattern of economic cycles, but it too had sustained periods of growth.) At least until the mid-1970s, ISI appeared to work.

The social consequences of ISI were complex. One was the formation of an entrepreneurial capitalist class or, in other words, an industrial bourgeoisie. In Chile, members of this group came principally from the families of the landed elite. In Mexico and Argentina, they came from more modest social origins and therefore presented a potential challenge to the hegemony of the traditional ruling classes. But the basic point remains: Industrialization, even of the ISI type, created a new power group in Latin American society. Its role would be much debated as the century continued.

The political expression of industrial developmentalism took two distinct forms. One was extension of a kind of "co-optative democracy," through which industrialists and workers gained (usually limited) access to power through electoral or other competition. An example was Chile, where political parties were reorganized to represent the interests of new groups and strata in society, especially labor and business. A more common response involved the creation of multi-class "populist" alliances. The emergence of an industrial elite and the invigoration of the labor movement made possible a new, pro-industrial alliance merging the interests of

Table 3.1   Rates of Growth in Gross Domestic Product, 1951–1980 (in percent)

Year	Latin America	Argentina	Brazil	Mexico
1951	5.8	3.9	6.6	7.0
1952	3.4	–5.1	8.4	3.4
1953	4.7	5.2	2.8	4.4
1954	6.0	3.8	9.1	6.2
1955	6.3	6.3	6.9	8.2
1956	4.2	2.5	4.0	5.4
1957	6.2	4.9	7.7	7.3
1958	5.0	5.8	8.6	4.6
1959	3.0	–6.0	6.0	4.9
1960	6.3	7.5	8.4	6.7
1961	6.0	6.7	9.8	4.6
1962	4.3	–1.4	5.6	4.6
1963	3.0	–2.4	1.3	7.6
1964	7.0	9.3	3.0	10.9
1965	4.3	8.4	0.3	6.4
1966	4.3	0.8	3.8	6.8
1967	4.8	2.8	5.5	6.0
1968	6.6	4.2	10.3	7.7
1969	6.9	8.2	9.6	6.3
1970	6.8	5.1	9.3	6.6
1971	5.9	3.8	11.3	4.0
1972	6.6	2.0	12.0	8.4
1973	8.4	3.3	14.0	8.2
1974	5.9	5.7	8.3	6.0
1975	2.8	–0.5	5.0	5.5
1976	6.0	–0.3	10.2	4.2
1977	4.8	6.6	4.9	3.3
1978	4.4	–3.3	4.9	8.2
1979	6.4	7.1	6.8	9.2
1980	5.9	2.0	9.2	8.2

Source: James W. Wilkie, Carlos Alberto Contreras, and Christof Anders Weber, eds., *Statistical Abstract of Latin America,* 30 (Los Angeles: UCLA Latin American Center, 1993), Part 2, Table 3423. Reprinted by permission.

entrepreneurs and workers—in some cases, directly challenging the long-standing predominance of agricultural and landed interests. Each of these alliances was created by a national leader who exploited and relied upon the power of the state. Thus did Getílio Vargas build a multi-class, urban-based populist coalition in Brazil in the late 1930s; so would Juan Perón in Argentina in the 1940s.

Most populist regimes shared four central characteristics. First, they tended to be authoritarian: They usually represented coalitions of one set of interests against some other set (such as landed interests) that were by definition prevented from participation, and this involved some degree of both exclusion and repression. Second, as time would show, they represented interests of classes—workers and industrialists—that were bound to conflict. Third, the maintenance of such regimes therefore depended in large part on the personal influence of individual leaders (such as the charismatic Perón or the manipulative Vargas). Fourth, the reconciliation of differing interests led to the frequent use of unifying rhetoric and symbols—particularly, and most conveniently, nationalism. The internal contradictions within populist coalitions also meant that, with or without magnetic rhetoric or leadership, they would be hard to sustain under conditions of economic adversity.

Partly in an effort to smooth over differences with such coalitions, states in Latin American countries—especially in countries undergoing ISI—began to serve as a source of employment and patronage. This would ameliorate class differences, soften lines of conflict, and secure adherence to the system and regime.[22] What this tactic created was a dual structure within the state: one for meritocratic advancement and policy-making, the other for patronage. Needless to say, these two tendencies were at odds with each other, and their coexistence would lead to incoherence and inefficiency. As James Malloy observed in the case of Brazil in the late 1970s:

> The concept of a meritocratic elite civil service was consistently undermined by the expanding reality of a politically controlled patronage-based civil service. This fact contributed to the paradox evident especially after 1945 that, while the state apparatus grew in size and formal power, its capacity to act effectively in a number of important policy areas actually declined. The power of the state receded in part because its administrative apparatus was colonized and parcelled among a complex array of political and labor leaders.[23]

One major consequence was, of course, to dilute both the will and the capacity of Brazil's would-be "developmental state."

Ultimately, the economic trajectories of Argentina, Mexico, and (to a lesser extent) Brazil illustrate the weaknesses of ISI development. Typically, import-substitution industrialization produces a spurt of growth in the short run but encounters limits in the medium and longer term: National markets, especially in countries with modest populations, fall subject to saturation; production processes continue to require substantial imports of capital goods; higher production costs are passed on to consumers in protected markets; near-monopoly discourages investment in technology. Once established under state protectionism and sheltered by tariff walls, highly subsidized and inefficient local firms are unable to compete in the international market. Moreover, the concentration of resources on industrial development tends to weaken the agricultural sector. Eventually, policymakers in major Latin American countries would turn away from industrial developmentalism in search of yet new strategies.

The International Environment

Both the design and the outcome of Latin America's development strategies were greatly affected by the international environment. This was conspicuously true during the Depression of the 1930s, which promoted the first push toward ISI, and during World War II, when Latin America produced commodities for the Allied cause. Both these experiences hastened the process of state organization.[24] But beyond such direct economic impacts, international forces also exerted attitudinal and ideological influence over Latin America's perception of the range and content of plausible choice. This point becomes apparent through examination of the 1960s and the 1980s.

It was in response to the Cuban Revolution that newly elected President John F. Kennedy launched the Alliance for Progress, a bold new initiative to promote economic growth, social development, and political democracy (and thus deter potential communist inroads). At a historic meeting in August 1961 representatives from the United States and Latin America (minus Cuba) gathered to put Kennedy's sweeping vision into practice. They advocated redistributive policies, including land reform; they called for external assistance, a total of $20 billion over the course of the decade; moreover, they laid down a requirement for participating countries to draw up comprehensive plans for national development. These plans were to be submitted for approval or amendment by an inter-American board of experts ("the nine wise men," as they promptly came to be known).

Sponsored as it was by the United States, the Alliance for Progress conferred an international seal of approval upon state activism in economic affairs. Latin American governments were encouraged to plan, guide, and shape their patterns of development. They were to embark on programs of reform, pursue technocratic standards, and insulate bureaucracies from undue domestic influence (if not from the nine wise men or from Washington). In effect, the Alliance for Progress amounted to an endorsement of the developmental state.

How things would change during the debt crisis of the 1980s. Confronted by a windfall of "petro-dollars" in the wake of OPEC-induced price hikes on oil, bankers in the mid-1970s turned to Latin America—especially the so-called upper tier (Argentina, Brazil, Venezuela, and Mexico). Moneylenders were quite comfortable in dealing with public agencies and state enterprises, believing that repayment would be guaranteed by governments; countries may not be able to pay, according to a well-known dictum, but neither they nor their debts disappear. Meanwhile borrowers were encouraged by modest interest rates (at some junctures real interest rates were actually negative). Under these circumstances, Latin America's total foreign debt swelled from $28.6 billion in 1970 to $242 billion just ten years later.

As global inflation began accelerating, U.S. Federal Reserve chairman Paul Volcker responded with a substantial increase in interest rates. In the meantime, the value as well as the volume of traditional Latin American exports—from coffee to nonferrous metals to petroleum—was sharply plummeting. As the cost of debt service was rising, in other words, Latin America's capacity to pay was declining. In 1984 debt service amounted to 46 percent of the region's total earnings from exports.

By the early 1980s both lenders and borrowers were overextended. In August 1982 Mexico declared its inability to meet obligations on external debt, and other countries later followed suit. During the first stage of the decade-long crisis, from 1982 to 1985, bankers and debtors attempted to "muddle through" what they saw as problems of "liquidity." Their decisions assured successful rescue of the banks. Negotiators proudly proclaimed that their goal was to avoid financial panic, which could have harmful consequences for the entire international community, but in practice this entailed protection of private banks, some of which were seriously overexposed. A central premise of all negotiations was the continuation of interest payments. And as a result, the banks managed to survive: As Pedro-Pablo Kuczynski has observed, no major bank failed during the 1980s because of its Latin American loans.[25]

A second stage in response to Latin America's debt crisis began in 1985, when U.S. treasury secretary James A. Baker III stressed the importance of economic growth for indebted countries—acknowledging in effect that countries faced crises of solvency, not just liquidity. Recognizing the dearth of commercial lending, Baker called for an injection of $20 billion in developing countries that were willing to undertake market reforms. In March 1989 Baker's successor, Nicholas F. Brady, announced a plan to offer a broad portfolio of debt reduction and restructuring alternatives along with U.S. government support to countries undertaking market-based economic policies. Long anathema to the banks and to the Reagan administration, debt relief was thus legitimized on the basis that it could provide efficiency gains for both the debtors and the banks.

For Latin America, of course, the 1980s became the "lost decade." Economic and social progress was negligible at best, negative at worst. Renegotiations and restructurings led to reliance upon continuous lending (and borrowing), which forced the region's external debt up from U.S.$242 billion in 1980 to U.S.$431 billion by 1990. Meeting their contractual obligations, Latin American countries transferred a net amount of more than U.S.$200 billion to advanced industrial countries. Economic growth came to a virtual halt. As shown in Table 3.2, the regional growth rate was negative in 1982, 1983, and 1989; negligible in 1981 and 1988; and never more than 4 percent. On a per capita basis, output declined by 8.3 percent for the decade as a whole.[26] Unemployment swelled and wages plummeted. For Mexico, whose conduct set a model of good behavior for other debtor countries, real wages declined by nearly 50 percent during the course of the decade.

As it sought to plumb the causes of this crisis, the international financial community eventually arrived at the conclusion that Latin America required fundamental economic reform. A principal source of the region's difficulty was held to be structural distortions resulting from import-substituting industrialization. Of course, the debt crisis itself was largely due to factors outside of (and outside the control of) Latin America. Notwithstanding this self-evident truth, economists and policymakers in major international institutions—from the U.S. Treasury to the World Bank and the International Monetary Fund—issued a clarion call for economic restructuring in Latin America.

What came to be known as the "Washington consensus" entailed three sets of prescriptions.[27] First, Latin American governments should support the private sector; second, they should liberalize policies on trade; third, and perhaps most important, they should reduce the economic role of state. They should exercise fiscal discipline (as commonly preached, but rarely practiced, by Washington itself), and they should concentrate their resources not on social subsidies but on health, education, and infrastructural investment. They should deregulate their national economies, letting market forces operate without political or bureaucratic constraints. In effect, the Washington consensus called for dismantlement of the developmental state in Latin America.

This neoliberal vision contained at least one major paradox. A centerpiece of the entire program was reducing the role of the state; but at the same time, implementation of these policies could be accomplished only by a powerful state. Economic reform was bound to encounter resistance from entrenched groups—sheltered entrepreneurs, unionized workers, public-sector employees. Imposition of broad, equitable, and effective tax codes, another of the Washington proposals, would generate opposition from almost everyone. It would take a strong and autonomous state to

Table 3.2   Rates of Growth in Gross Domestic Product, 1981–1990 (in percent)

Year	Latin America	Argentina	Brazil	Mexico
1981	0.1	−7.0	−4.4	8.8
1982	−1.3	−5.8	0.6	−0.6
1983	−2.9	2.6	−3.3	−4.2
1984	3.7	2.4	5.3	3.6
1985	3.4	−4.4	8.0	2.6
1986	3.8	6.0	7.4	−3.8
1987	3.1	2.1	3.5	1.8
1988	0.9	−2.8	−0.3	1.4
1989	1.3	−4.4	3.3	3.1
1990	−.11	−.55	−4.7	3.9

Source: James W. Wilkie, Carlos Alberto Contreras, and Christof Anders Weber, eds., *Statistical Abstract of Latin America,* 30 (Los Angeles: UCLA Latin American Center, 1993), Part 2, Table 3423, part ii. Reprinted by permission.

overcome such pressures.[28] Proponents of the consensus often tried to resolve this paradox by advocating small but efficient government, but this formulation did not clearly address fundamental questions about the role and extent of state participation in economic affairs.

Ultimately, Latin America's developmental state collapsed under the weight of the debt crisis. Rightly or wrongly, the dismal economic performance of the 1980s totally discredited the policies of import-substituting industrialization. Either from desperation or conviction, Latin American leaders sought to implement much of the Washington consensus.[29] And to the extent that excessive state intervention was held to be responsible for structural deformities, the notion of dirigisme fell into widespread disfavor. Ultimately, the crisis of the 1980s resulted in delegitimation of the developmental state.

Concluding Reflections

Over the course of history, the state has performed an activist role in the economic development of Latin America. Such a pattern is by no means unique to the region. Even in allegedly laissez-faire capitalist societies, such as the late nineteenth-century United States, the state has performed vital economic functions. Indeed, the whole concept of a laissez-faire state exists only as theoretical construct not as empirical reality, and it is tautological even then: The state would adopt a minimalist posture toward economic matters on the basis of a political decision, rather than in deference to some abstract higher truth. A state that chooses to refrain from economic activism is nonetheless making a choice.

Nor does the economic role of the Latin American state in itself provide a convincing explanation for the persistence of poverty, underdevelopment, or backwardness throughout the region. It must be noted, first, that there have been periods of substantial growth and transformation throughout Latin American history. Within its own terms, the mercantilist strategy of the colonial period achieved a considerable measure of success for Spain; so did the liberal approach of the nineteenth century and the import-substitution model of the twentieth century for Latin America. Second, the inherent limitations within these strategies derived not from the performance of the state. The central difficulty came not from incapacity within the state—ignorance, corruption, inefficiency—or from the extent of state participation in the economy.

Whatever the reason, repeated cycles of innovation and experimentation have not left Latin America with the developmental capabilities that have recently become so evident in postwar Asia. Why has Latin America not been able to emulate the experience of Japan or of the "four tigers"—Singapore, South Korea, Taiwan, and Hong Kong? Let us immediately dispense with "national character" explanations and with simple-minded culturalist arguments about the "Confucian ethic" and the "Hispanic legacy." They are circular (Asians act like Asians because they are Asian, Mexicans act like Mexicans because they are Mexican). They are ahistorical (because they cannot account for change over time). They are atheoretical (because they cite culture as a cause but do not explain the cause of the culture itself). They tend to discourage social inquiry rather than encourage it. And they are for the most part superficial and deterministic.

Nor is it a matter of bureaucratic competence. As in Japan, the colonial Spanish-American bureaucracy recruited its membership from the most capable and well-trained segments of society. Likewise, the liberal state in Argentina and elsewhere staffed its ranks with skilled and highly educated elements. Industrial developmentalism drew its inspiration from the work of such celebrated international economists as Raúl Prebisch and the "Chicago boys," who, as their nickname suggests, received advanced training at a prestigious U.S. university and who served the Pinochet regime in Chile. To be sure, Latin American public bureaucracies may not possess the intellectual depth of their Asian counterparts— that is, they probably have not had equivalent levels of training and skill at lower and middle ranks—and this would no doubt have an impact on policy implementation. In and of itself, however, governmental capacity cannot account for the discrepancies in regional economic performance.

The question persists: Why has Latin America been unable to sustain the kind of "developmental state" that has been so essential to Asian success? This query raises two separate but related issues. One has to do with the structure of the Latin American state; another has to do with its economic performance.

Several governmental episodes in Latin America bear close resemblance to the developmental state. For better or worse, the mercantilist state of the colonial period more or less met the definitional criteria (revealingly enough, Chalmers Johnson from time to time describes the developmental state in Asia as "neomercantilist"[30]). Some of the liberal states in Latin America, particularly under Porfirio Díaz in Mexico (1876–1910) and perhaps the Generation of 1880 in Argentina (1880–1930), shared key features of the developmental model. But it was the post-1930s state in Latin America that came closest to the developmental prototype. Brazil under military rule (especially the 1964–1974 period) and Chile under Augusto Pinochet (1973–1988) would be plausible candidates for inclusion in this general category; so might Mexico during the heyday of the Partido Revolucionario Institucional (PRI).[31]

Yet even these resemblances are partial, imperfect, and infrequent. The fact is that Latin America was rarely, if ever, able to construct a full-fledged developmental state.[32] Why not?

The first obstacle was the political necessity for populist regimes to serve clientelistic purposes. In order to keep coalitions together, leaders relied on the state to provide patronage—jobs, favors, subsidies—to crucial client groups. Key among these were the urban middle sectors and the unionized working classes. The coexistence of meritocratic bureaucracy with institutionalized favoritism gave rise to unyielding contradictions within the Latin American state and fatally comprised its functional efficiency.

Second was the relative weakness of the capitalist class in Latin America. The developmental state in Asia has typically relied on a collaboration with a vital and vigorous private sector. The prototypical case entails massive industrial conglomerates: *zaibatsu* or *keiretsu* in Japan, *chaebol* in Korea. These private firms have provided capital, accepted risk, and reaped rewards from economic change. There has been nothing comparable in Latin America. Suggestively enough, episodes that bear some resemblance to the developmental state—Argentina under the landed oligarchy, Brazil under the generals—have occurred in times and places where the private sector has been relatively strong. For the most part, however, the private-public partnership characteristic of the developmental state has not flourished for a simple reason: One of the key partners has been missing.

Third was the low degree of state autonomy. Theoretically and empirically, the developmental state enjoys a large degree of autonomy: it can define goals on the basis of economic rather than political criteria, it can impose its decisions on unwilling segments of the private sector and society, and it can implement policy over sustained periods of time. Stability and continuity enable the developmental state to persist in "plan-rational" behavior in the medium to long term.

Since the 1820s, if not before, Latin American states have had only modest degrees of autonomy, at least by Asian standards. They have been subject to constant internal and external pressures, and their decisions have been susceptible to veto by power groups at home (such as the landed oligarchy or organized labor) or abroad (such as the United States). Dominant interests have often sought to exploit the state, especially during the liberal phase, rather than build up its autonomy. There have been instances of harmony between the public and private sectors—when, in its crudest form, the state has functioned as an "executive secretariat" for domestic or foreign capital—but these have been transitory episodes that have relied on enormous amounts of authoritarian repression. With the possible exception of postrevolutionary Mexico, even the populist authoritarian states that often initiated ISI policies proved unable to insulate themselves from political and societal pressures.

These structural imperfections (or characteristics, in more neutral language) help explain the economic performance of Latin America's putative developmental states, but only to an extent. An additional consideration stems from the internal logic of the development strategies themselves. In Latin America none of the major alternatives—mercantilism, liberalism, or industrial developmentalism—could provide a long-term path toward self-sustaining economic growth with social equity. Within its historical context, each strategy enjoyed a good deal of ideological support, and each had political backing. But each one also contained internal contradictions that proved ultimately fatal. And it is revealing, here, that these successive experiments took place within evershortening time frames: Mercantilism lasted for centuries, liberalism thrived for perhaps half a century, and import-substitution industrialization endured only for a matter of decades. Time has been growing short in Latin America.

A final factor concerns the international environment. Japan and the four tigers flourished most dramatically during the period of the (now defunct) Cold War. This brought considerable benefits in terms of both aid and trade. Latin America, on the other hand, entered the world economy at a much earlier stage, and in the postwar period it never counted as a "front-line state" in the struggle against international communism.[33] It was always a backyard of the United States, physically and figuratively; the Alliance for Progress was nothing like the Marshall Plan. And the debt crisis of the 1980s, though not entirely of Latin America's making, had a devastating impact on countries and peoples of the region. In other words, Latin America always had to confront harsh realities deriving from its marginal importance to the global economy and from the continuing expression of U.S. hegemony throughout the hemisphere. In such a context as this, the developmental state had little prospect for continuing success.

Notes

1. Peter Evans, Dieter Reuschemeyer, and Theda Skocpol, eds., *Bringing the State Back In* (Cambridge: Cambridge University Press, 1985).

2. Portions of this chapter are adapted from Peter H. Smith, "The State and Development in Historical Perspective," in Alfred Stepan, ed., *The Americas: New Interpretive Essays* (New York: Oxford University Press, 1992), pp. 30–56.

3. Laurence Whitehead, "State Organization in Latin America since 1930," in Leslie Bethell, ed., *The Cambridge History of Latin America*, Vol. VI (New York: Cambridge University Press, 1994), pp. 3–95. See also Oscar Oszlak, "The Historical Formation of the State in Latin America," *Latin American Research Review* 16, no. 2 (1981): 3–32.

4. Evelyne Huber, "Assessments of State Strength," in Peter H. Smith, ed., *Latin America in Comparative Perspective: New Approaches to Methods and Analysis* (Boulder: Westview Press, 1995), pp. 163–93, with quotes from pp. 165–6.

5. For this reason, analyses of bivariate associations between political regime and policy effectiveness may overlook a crucial intervening variable—the strength and capacity of the state. See Karen L. Remmer, "Democracy and Economic Crisis: The Latin American Experience," *World Politics* 42, no. 3 (April 1990): 315–35.

6. Whitehead, "State Organization," pp. 11–12.

7. Chalmers Johnson, "Political Institutions and Economic Performance: The Government-Business Relationship in Japan, South Korea, and Taiwan," in Frederic C. Deyo, ed., *The Political Economy of the New Asian Industrialism* (Ithaca: Cornell University Press, 1987), pp. 136–64, with quotes from pp. 142–5. See also Chalmers Johnson, *MITI and the Japanese Miracle: The Growth of Industrial Policy, 1925–1975* (Stanford: Stanford University Press, 1982), especially chapter 1 on "The Japanese 'Miracle.'"

8. Here I focus largely on the Spanish empire in America. The Portuguese crown placed less emphasis on New World holdings for at least three reasons: Portugal had more extensive interests in the Far East, there was no indigenous civilization comparable to the Aztecs or the Incas, and Brazil did not offer much silver or gold. And because the Portuguese monarchy fled to Rio de Janeiro in 1808, the Brazilian path to independence would be unlike that of Spanish America.

9. Strong in the sixteenth century, the colonial bureaucracy declined in quality and influence during the seventeenth century and recuperated during the eighteenth century.

10. For a majestic treatise on the evolution of creole patriotism, see D. A. Brading, *The First America: The Spanish Monarchy, Creole Patriots, and the Liberal State, 1492–1867* (Cambridge: Cambridge University Press, 1991).

11. Arnold Bauer, "Rural Spanish America, 1870–1930," in Leslie Bethell, ed., *Cambridge History of Latin America,* IV (Cambridge: Cambridge University Press, 1986), p. 177.

12. See Charles A. Hale, *Mexican Liberalism in the Age of Mora, 1821–1853* (New Haven: Yale University Press, 1968); Charles A. Hale, *The Transformation of Mexican Liberalism in Late Nineteenth-Century Mexico* (Princeton: Princeton University Press, 1989); and Brading, *First America,* chapter 29.

13. Steven Topik, "The Economic Role of the State in Liberal Regimes: Brazil and Mexico Compared, 1888–1910," in Joseph L. Love and Nils Jacobsen, eds., *Guiding the Invisible Hand: Economic Liberalism and the State in Latin American History* (New York: Praeger, 1988), p. 136.

14. Topik, "Economic Role of the State," pp. 117–44.

15. See Charles Bergquist, *Labor in Latin America: Comparative Essays on Chile, Argentina, Venezuela, and Colombia* (Stanford: Stanford University Press, 1986).

16. Peter H. Smith, "The Failure of Democracy in Argentina, 1916–1930," in Juan Linz and Alfred Stepan, eds., *The Breakdown of Democratic Regimes* (Baltimore: Johns Hopkins University Press, 1978), Part III, pp. 3–27.

17. Joseph L. Love, "Structural Change and Conceptual Response in Latin America and Romania, 1860–1950," in Love and Jacobsen, eds., *Guiding,* pp. 1–33, especially pp. 23–5.

18. As quoted in Carlos F. Díaz-Alejandro, *Essays on the Economic History of the Argentine Republic* (New Haven: Yale University Press, 1970), pp. 104–5.

19. See Peter H. Smith, "Crisis and Democracy in Latin America," *World Politics* 43, no. 4 (July 1991): 608–34.

20. As former European colonies in the Caribbean acquired independence, the organization later changed its name to the Economic Commission for Latin America and the Caribbean (ECLAC).

21. Joseph L. Love, "Raúl Prebisch and the Origins of the Doctrine of Unequal Exchange," *Latin American Research Review* 15, no. 3 (1980): 45–72. During the 1950s ECLA also published reports warning that ISI could work only in countries with large-scale domestic markets.

22. According to one cross-national study, over 60 percent of people in the "professional or technical" category were employed in the public sector in 1980; cited in Whitehead, "State Organization," p. 35.

23. James M. Malloy, *The Politics of Social Security in Brazil* (Pittsburgh: University of Pittsburgh Press, 1979), p. 78.

24. Whitehead, "State Organization," p. 13.

25. Pedro-Pablo Kuczynski, *Latin American Debt* (Baltimore: Johns Hopkins University Press/Twentieth Century Fund, 1988), p. 86. The statistics in the previous paragraphs also come from this volume.

26. United Nations, Economic Commission for Latin American and the Caribbean, *Changing Production Patterns with Social Equity* (Santiago: ECLAC, 1990), p. 20.

27. The classic (and controversial) formulation of this consensus appears in John Williamson, "What Washington Means by Policy Reform," in John Williamson, ed., *Latin American Economic Adjustment: How Much Has Happened?* (Washington: Institute for International Economics, 1990), pp. 7–20.

28. See Stephan Haggard and Steven B. Webb, eds., *Voting for Reform: Democracy, Political Liberalization, and Economic Adjustment* (New York: Oxford University Press/World Bank, 1994); and Stephan Haggard, "The Reform of the State in Latin America" (unpublished paper, 1995).

29. See Dani Rodrik, "The Rush to Free Trade in the Developing World: Why So Late? Why Now? Will It Last?" in Haggard and Webb, eds., *Voting for Reform,* pp. 61–88; and Sebastian Edwards, *Crisis and Reform in Latin America: From Despair to Hope* (New York: Oxford University Press/World Bank, 1995), especially chapter 3.

30. Johnson, MITI, p. 17.

31. A socialist "command economy" does not qualify as a developmental state.

32. This applies not only to Latin America; as Evelyne Huber observes, "strictly developmental states are a rare breed." "Assessments," p. 168.

33. See Peter Evans, "Class, State, and Dependence in East Asia: Lessons for Latin Americanists," in Deyo, ed., *Political Economy;* and Laurence Whitehead, "Tigers in Latin America?" *Annals of the American Academy of Political and Social Sciences* 505 (September 1989): 142–51.

4

Neoliberalism, Democratization, and the Rise of Technocrats

Patricio Silva

Since the early 1980s many Latin American countries have been undergoing political and economic transition simultaneously. As authoritarian regimes have relinquished power to democratically elected governments, a large majority of Latin American economies have abandoned the traditional pattern of state-led industrialization and adopted neoliberal free-market policies. In recent years these double transitions have been the source of fertile debate among political scientists and economists about the nature and the outcome of economic adjustments programs and the specific political circumstances in which they have been implemented.[1]

These studies unanimously emphasize the strategic role played by technocrats[2] in the formulation and application of economic and financial policies of the new democracies. Because the analysis has focused mainly on economic adjustment programs, however, most scholars have implicitly tended to make too narrow a link between these policies and the increasing importance of technocrats in defining state economic and financial policies. As a result, the long-term dimension of technocratic ascendancy in Latin America, manifested in the 1960s and 1970s under democratic as well as authoritarian regimes, is less well understood. Furthermore, little attention has been devoted to the long-term political consequences of technocratic ascendancy *beyond* the application of structural adjustment programs, particularly to its impact on the very nature of the new democracies.

Since the restoration of democratic rule, technocrats have acquired great public presence and a much higher degree of credibility and legitimacy among the political elite and the general population.[3] This, cannot be explained solely because of their central role in the implementation of recent stabilization programs or because they are now operating in a legitimate democratic environment, however. In this chapter I consider the importance of two other factors in explaining the new pivotal position of technocrats: the impact of collective memories of previous democratic and authoritarian periods and the fundamental changes in Latin American political culture, notably the growing appreciation of liberal democracy, that have occurred over the last decade, particularly in left-wing sectors. I argue that the current technocratization of the decision-making process is not a temporary phenomenon associated with the political and economic requirements of democratic transition and the application of structural adjustment programs but has become, rather, an integral feature of many Latin American democracies.

I focus on the case of Chile, where technocrats have had a central role in the decision-making process for two decades. This case also allows us to "delink" the narrow connections between structural adjustment, democratization, and technocratization because in Chile technocratic ascendancy has survived neoliberal economic reforms and even political regimes. Although technocracy mainly characterized the period 1975–1982, the technocratization of the decision-making process survived the era of Augusto Pinochet, becoming a permanent feature of the Chilean political reality.

Political Regime and Technocracy

The technocratic phenomenon in Latin America has yet to be systematically studied from a regional perspective. Instead, there have been numerous country studies that use dissimilar theoretical frameworks and in which the technocratic phenomenon is not always given a central focus. In general, little attention has been devoted to the role of specific regime type in the generation and strengthening of technocratic groups. Even in the case of Mexico, where the discussion of technocracy is by far the most well developed in the region, this question has been systematically ignored because the authoritarian nature of the political regime has constituted for many decades an unchanging variable.[4] But regime type is critical for the examination of technocracy in the context of transitions from authoritarian to democratic rule.

Although neoliberal economic reforms implemented since the early 1980s have clearly strengthened the position of technocrats in the decision-making process, it is instructive to view the technocratic phenomenon in much broader historical perspective. The presence of technocrats in governmental circles in Latin America is a relatively old phenomenon. In addition, authoritarian regimes have historically shown a marked inclination to rely on the support of technocrats for the running of state affairs. For instance, as early as the 1890s, Mexican dictator Porfirio Díaz incorporated in his government a group of intellectuals and professional men known as the *Científicos*, who aspired to introduce "scientific" state administration.[5] In the 1920s and 1930s several authoritarian regimes emerged that were also characterized by an alliance between military men and civil technocrats. This was the case during the first government of Colonel Carlos Ibáñez del Campo (1927–1931) in Chile, in which young technocratic-minded *ingenieros* were appointed to top positions within state institutions in order to implement profound economic and administrative reforms.[6]

The "selective affinity" between technocracy and authoritarian regimes became even more apparent during the 1960s and 1970s when a series of bureaucratic-authoritarian regimes were established in the Southern Cone. In his seminal work on this new type of political regime, O'Donnell identified the civilian technocracy as one of the military's principal allies in the "procoup" coalition and as key figures in the execution of the military regime's economic policies. Both actors shared a rejection of party politics and a belief in technical and "apolitical" solutions for the country's problems. Under military regimes in Argentina, Chile, and Uruguay, a selected group of economists and financial experts acquired unprecedented discretional powers in the formulation and implementation of radical financial and economic reforms.[7] In the case of Chile, a group of young technocrats, the so-called "Chicago boys," emerged as the primary designers and executors of the neoliberal economic policies of the Pinochet regime. They eventually became key ideologues of the regime as they attempted to explain the coexistence of economic liberalism and political authoritarianism.[8]

In Chile, O'Donnell's model was not well received among intellectuals who opposed the military regime. The main criticism concerned O'Donnell's thesis that one of the basic objectives of bureaucratic-authoritarian regimes was to "deepen" the industrialization process. In contrast, the Chilean military government opted to "deindustrialize" by deliberately allowing less expensive and better quality imports to compete with domestically produced goods and by instituting an export-oriented economic strategy based mainly on primary products.[9] In addition, the model was criticized because the Chilean military regime had evolved from an impersonal bureaucratic government of the armed forces into an autocracy.[10] O'Donnell's model was finally rejected completely, relegating the technocracy issue to the sidelines. Although O'Donnell's theory illuminated the relation between technocracy and political regime, his work focused exclusively on authoritarian regimes. How technocracy operates in democratic regimes is still relatively unexplored.

In the 1950s and 1960s, technocrats played a key role in the processes of industrialization and regional integration in many countries under democratic rule.[11] In Chile, for instance, the Eduardo Frei government (1964–1970) relied heavily on the assistance of hundreds of young *cuadros técnicos* in the formulation and execution of his developmental programs, including profound agrarian reform.[12] Nevertheless, the increasing technocratization of decision making was officially ignored because of its negative, elitist implications. In a climate of strong ideological polarization, the official discourse adopted a populist character, stressing the notion of "popular participation" as the government made efforts to integrate new actors, such as the urban poor and the peasantry, into the political scene. In comparison with earlier democracies, what we see is not so much a greater presence of technocrats at the highest levels of policymaking but their greater visibility and acceptance.

During the 1980s, the end of military regimes and the restoration of democratic rule produced a marked shift in the academic debate surrounding the dynamics of democratic transition and consolidation. Scholars who had been concerned exclusively with the political dimension of the transitions reoriented their research toward the study of constitutional and institutional issues, party and electoral politics, civil-military relations, and human rights-related issues.[13] The link between technocracy and military regimes suggested by O'Donnell may have strengthened the idea that the two were intrinsically related. From this assumption, it would implicitly follow that a move toward democracy would lead to a diminishing, if not the disappearance, of the importance of technocrats. In any case, the democratic wave during the 1980s produced a shift in scholars' interest toward the processes of democratic transition, in which the technocratic aspect was largely ignored.

Economic Adjustment and the Strengthening of Technocracy

Mexico's dramatic announcement in August 1982 that it was unable to meet its international financial commitments to repay its foreign debt marked the initiation of a profound shift in the development strategies followed in the entire region. Following the outset of the debt crisis, the traditional pattern of import-substitution industrialization was strongly criticized by domestic and international financiers, who demanded the adoption of market-oriented reforms and austerity measures. Initially, many Latin American countries decided to apply nonorthodox stabilization programs (e.g., the Austral Plan in Argentina, the Cruzado Plan in Brazil, and the Inti Plan in Peru) in an attempt to diminish the social costs of austerity policies. By the late 1980s, however, it had became clear that these and other stabilization programs had failed to bring about the expected economic recovery. As Green indicates, "once 'easy' heterodox solutions had been discredited, neo-liberalism spread rapidly across the region; these were the years when the long-term structural adjustment of Latin America's economy gathered pace. Trade liberalization, government cutbacks, privatization and deregulation have since then become the norm in almost every country."[14]

The adoption of orthodox adjustment programs has almost always been accompanied by the appointment of technocratic-oriented neoliberal economists in strategic governmental positions (ministries of economic affairs and finance, central banks, planning agencies, etc.) responsible for the formulation and application of these new economic guidelines. The extreme visibility given to the economic teams is a means for governments to send the right signals to both the domestic and international business communities.[15] Moreover, Latin American technocrats generally embrace neoliberal economic thinking, which since the early 1980 began to achieve almost uncontested hegemony. As Stallings points out:

> Technocrats who had long argued for more open economies and a bigger role for the private sectors suddenly found increased backing from the outside. They could count on political support from the United States and other advanced industrial countries, intellectual reinforcement from the IMF and World Bank, and empirical evidence of successful performance from countries that had followed an open-economy model.[16]

These technocrats have played a strategic role in conducting negotiations with industrialized countries as a means to reschedule existing debts and to obtain new credits and financial aid. As Kaufman indicates:

> these technocrats are more than simply the principal architects of economic policy: they [are] the intellectual brokers between their governments and international capital, and symbols of the government's determination to rationalize its rule primarily in terms of economic objectives. . . . Cooperation with international business, a fuller integration into the world economy, and a strictly secular willingness to adopt the prevailing tenets of international economic orthodoxy, all [form] a . . . set of intellectual parameters within which the technocrats could then "pragmatically" pursue the requirements of stabilization and expansion.[17]

In this manner, local neoliberal technocrats have become the national counterparts of foreign financial experts from lending institutions who assess the performance of the Latin American economies and their adjustment programs. Communication between the foreign financial experts and the local technocrats has clearly been facilitated by their common social and academic backgrounds. Centeno points out that they:

not only share the same economic perspectives, but perhaps most impor-
tantly, speak the same language, both literally and metaphorically. . . . The
technocrats do not necessarily have to represent one ideological niche or
the other, they simply share a familiarity with a certain language and rationale. . . . The graduate degrees from U.S. universities . . . enable these persons to present arguments that their fellow alumni at the World Bank . . .
understand and consider legitimate.[18]

Their common backgrounds, however, are not always a guarantee for
a solid alliance. In certain cases strengthening the position of technocrats
increased conflict. As Kahler indicates, the heterodox experiments in
Latin America during the 1980s that did not follow the guidelines of international financial institutions (IFIs) "were, by and large, designed by
economists with North American training and professional connections. . . . In middle-income developing countries, interlocutors may
share common training and discourse with IFI staff, but their ideological
preferences and bureaucratic positions may make them adversaries
rather than allies."[19]

Although international political and economic factors have played a
decisive role in legitimating and consolidating the position of technocrats
within the political elite, technocratic ascendancy is certainly not exclusively the result of *external* influences.

As the Chilean case shows, the rise of technocrats and the adoption of
severe neoliberal economic stabilization policies in the mid-1970s was
primarily a product of domestic political and ideological struggles resulting in a distinctive balance of power. The origins of Chilean neoliberals can be found in the late 1950s and 1960s debate between structuralists
and monetarists over the causes of the country's developmental problems. Monetarists criticized the dominant structuralist policies that favored large state intervention in the economy, citing state intervention as
one of the main sources of fiscal deficit, inflation, and low productivity.[20]
By the late 1960s, Chilean neoliberals had proposed the liberalization of
financial markets, the encouragement of private initiative, the reduction
of state bureaucracy, the sale of public enterprises, the opening of the
economy to international competition, and the end of government discretion in economic decisions.[21] It was evident, however, that the political climate at that time was not favorable to their radical neoliberal
recipes, which had almost no chance of obtaining the required political
support.[22] Following the military coup of September 1973, however, political conditions changed in favor of the adoption of market-oriented
policies. As would happen in the rest of the region a decade later, the
adoption of an orthodox neoliberal economic program in Chile came after
previous moderate, heterodox economic reforms had failed.[23]

It is important to stress that both the authoritarian regime and the Patricio Aylwin and Frei governments have consciously attempted to insulate the economic teams from direct social pressures. As a result, since the mid-1970s technocrats have achieved a significant degree of relative autonomy vis-à-vis entrepreneurs, unions, political parties, and the like. During the military regime, the insulation of the economic team was motivated by Pinochet's aim to reduce the direct interference of right-wing *políticos*, entrepreneurial groups, and civilians in general in order to minimize politicization among the armed forces. Thus, the Chicago boys' emphasis on the application of a "neutral" economic model based not on political but on "technical and rational" grounds was in tune with his own objectives. The idea of applying a uniform economic policy to all the economic sectors without exception also fit well with Pinochet's desire to fashion himself a "supra-actor."[24]

Following the restoration of democracy in 1990, the government continued the strong technocratic orientation. As did the Chicago boys earlier, a new group of technocrats, the so-called "CIEPLAN monks," emerged as the most powerful strategic group inside the government.[25] By appointing a team of very prestigious economists, Aylwin sought to reduce fears among right-wing political sectors and entrepreneurs that old populistic policies would be adopted or that an economic crisis would ensue. Because the military left power during a period of strong economic growth, one of the main challenges for the new government was to prove itself capable of maintaining or even improving the economy. In this respect, the insulation of the economic team was also meant to contain the explosion of social and economic demands expected to be made by marginal groups—which ultimately did not occur. Last but not least, the Aylwin government was well aware that the maintenance of financial and economic stability was indispensable for democratic consolidation.

Collective Memories

That technocratic decision making in Latin America has taken on permanent features over the last decade cannot be explained solely in terms of the forces that have *favored* it—international financial institutions, entrepreneurial circles, right-wing political parties, and the like. In my opinion, an even more important factor for the consolidation of technocratic politics has been the dramatic weakening and—in some countries—a virtual disappearance of the forces that traditionally have *resisted* it—left-wing parties, unions leaders, and other progressive groups. This also helps to explain the reason that since the restoration of democratic rule, most countries have adopted or maintained neoliberal economic policies.

One must remember that the existence of technocratic economic teams and the application of neoliberal economic policies constituted main features of the former military regimes. Thus it is remarkable that following democratic restoration, electoral formulas that openly or implicitly supported neoliberal policies (for example, Alberto Fujimori's in Peru and Carlos Menem's in Argentina during his reelection) have become successful.[26] This certainly has to do with the global hegemony achieved by neoliberal ideology, the pressure from international financial organizations, the perceived lack of economic alternatives, and the increasing apoliticism among the Latin American population. However, I think the more profound reason that large segments of civil society are beginning to accept the new technocratic and neoliberal reality lies in quite traumatic events of the recent political past.

The military dictatorships inaugurated in the 1970s dealt a deadly blow to the politics of populism in many countries in Latin America, based on clientelistic relations between the state and civil society. What has not been sufficiently stressed until now is that populism also suffered a decisive psychological defeat as many people, rightly or wrongly, internalized the view that populism had been one of the main causes for the economic and political crisis that had precipitated the breakdown of democracy. This is partly why almost no social sector was inclined to support the adoption of populistic policies after the departure of the military. The Chilean case is very illustrative in this respect.

At the root of Chile's political stability and economic health are—along with the economic policies it pursued so successfully—psychological and emotional factors that have shaped a distinctive set of political attitudes and behavior among the country's key actors. It can be said that Chilean society, as a whole, is still traumatized by its recent political history.[27] For right-wing sectors, the memories of social conflict—strikes, street violence, shortages of food and consumer goods—and the real or imagined communist threat from the Unidad Popular (UP) government had a deep psychological impact. Their conspicuous uncritical and passionate support for the military government cannot be understood without taking into account the political effects of this trauma. For those who supported Salvador Allende, the unforgettable memories of that Tuesday—11 September 1973—still produce intense sadness and bitterness. All previous certainties about the "irreversibility" of the socialist process were mercilessly destroyed in an instant. In addition, the physical mistreatment and torture, uncertainty about work, political oppression, and, for many, the hard experience of exile deeply shocked the Chilean left.[28]

These psychological factors have also influenced the attitudes and behavior of the major political actors during the democratic transition. The almost obsessive search for agreements and consensus between the democratic authorities and the opposition—which indeed has been crucial for the success of the democratization process—reveals the existence of deep-seated apprehensions on both sides. Since 1990 the strong willingness of both government and opposition to reach comprehensive agreements and compromises on several economic, political, and social issues had been accompanied by their mutual efforts to depoliticize issues that could provoke conflict.[29] As Tulchin and Varas correctly assess:

> After seventeen years of military dictatorship, Chilean political leaders all across the political spectrum began to put an end to a long tradition of bitter confrontations, and slowly to value more and more democratic stability through compromise. An important modernization of political life occurred under the authoritarian regime. It consisted of a more pragmatic, nonideological approach to political issues and a consensual commitment to the maintenance of democratic rules of the game. The trauma of the military coup and its long and bloody aftermath were powerful incentives for all political sectors not to recreate the same conditions that produced the breakdown of democracy.[30]

This "more pragmatic, nonideological approach" has strengthened the readiness of political actors and the population to support technocratic forms of decision making. In my view, since the restoration of democratic rule, the technocratic teams working on sensitive economic issues have been functioning as "moderating mediators" between competing social and political forces that deeply mistrust each other. The technocratic teams within the Aylwin and Frei governments have, in fact, provided some minimum guarantees to all parties involved in the proper administration of state institutions and the economy. In doing so, technocrats have played an important role in the deactivation of potential ideological clashes between government and opposition, thus helping to facilitate political stability.

It is true that Chile, in contrast to other countries in the region, inaugurated democratic rule under quite auspicious circumstances. For many years, the country's economy had steadily grown. In addition, Chile had previously had a long experience with democracy—a significant advantage over countries that must shape a democratic order for the first time.[31] Chilean politicians and citizens felt comfortable and familiar with the reestablishment of democratic procedures, which they experienced as a "re-encounter" with their national roots. However, as Valenzuela notes:

> Such cases of *reconsolidation* of democracy are . . . hampered by returning images of the crisis that led to their breakdown, which opponents of the democratic process will usually attempt to emphasize. Successful *redemocratizations* therefore require a deliberate effort on the part of the democratiz-

ing elites to avoid resurrecting symbols, images, conducts, and political programs associated with the conflicts leading to prior breakdown.[32]

As mentioned, one of the major apprehensions was whether the Aylwin government would be able to maintain the economic and financial stability inherited from the military government. The attitude that unions would take toward the government and the business sector—now that they were free to strike and to demand improvements in their salaries and working conditions—was a particular source of insecurity. The government, however, was resolute in its goal to be successful in the management of the economy. The *Concertación* (Consensus) coalition wanted to destroy the myth that an authoritarian government is better than a democratic one in achieving economic growth and development. If the Aylwin government could provide even higher levels of growth, this would not only legitimize democratic rule but also weaken civilian support for authoritarian solutions. The frenetic work of Finance Minister Alejandro Foxley to guarantee the continuation of economic prosperity becomes comprehensible only if one takes into consideration the weight of the collective memories of the past. As Oppenheim writes:

> Chileans remembered well the turbulent and chaotic days that had preceded that fall of Salvador Allende, along with the violence that ensued. The country had suffered a collective trauma. As a result, Chileans were extremely sensitive to situations that they thought might recreate previous crises. For example, many Chileans associated inflation and economic dislocation with the Allende government; consequently, the Aylwin government made the day-to-day management and stability of the economy a major priority.[33]

The Aylwin government began a new practice of regular consultations with opposition parties, entrepreneurial organizations, and unions in order to obtain a broad political and social basis for the implementation of economic policy. This practice, which has been continued by Frei, has clearly helped to reduce the traditional high levels of distrust in Chilean politics. This *"política de acuerdos,"* as it has been called, made possible tax increases to finance social programs, an increase in the minimum wage, and legislation to benefit labor. The relatively good relations among government, opposition groups, and entrepreneurs has undeniably to do with the fact that the *Concertación* government continued to apply the neoliberal policies of the military regime.[34] Indeed, the Aylwin and Frei governments have accepted important economic postulates introduced by the Chicago boys, including the subsidiary role of the state in economic activities; the reevaluation of the role played by foreign capital and the local private sector in achieving economic development; the adoption of market mechanisms and efficiency criteria as main instruments for the allocation of fiscal financial resources; and the need to keep public finances healthy and to achieve macroeconomic stability. Right-wing parties and entrepreneurial circles were, in general, satisfied by the economic path followed by the new authorities. Furthermore, they were reluctant to adopt a more oppositional stance, which could lead to a strengthening of the more radical sectors within the *Concertación* and, in turn, to a partial or complete abandonment of neoliberal economic policies.

The *Concertación* government realized that political stability would not be achieved by simply guaranteeing macroeconomic and financial equilibrium. Attention had to be given also to improving the living conditions of the millions of Chileans who had been excluded from the benefits of economic growth. Combating poverty had to be done very cautiously, however, because any government initiative could be interpreted in right-wing circles as a disguised attempt to pursue populist or even socialist objectives. The *Concertación* governments have consciously depoliticized such social issues. In contrast to the precoup period, social inequalities today are not approached in ideological terms but rather from the perspective of modernization. The consensus is that a country like Chile, which is experiencing an accelerating process of modernization and is quickly reaching satisfactory standards of development, simply cannot afford to have large segments of its population in extreme poverty, which is seen not only as ethically deplorable but also as technically unacceptable in a modern nation. Thus, in technocratic terms, social justice is presented as the efficient elimination of poverty. In this way, the principle of social justice has been integrated with the goals of economic efficiency and political stability.

Changes in Political Culture

The remarkable absence of active criticism of or resistance to the technocratization of decision making is, in my view, intimately related to the impact of the breakdown of democracy and the authoritarian experience on contemporary Latin American political culture, particularly the left. The process of deradicalization experienced by many left-wing groups during the 1980s and early 1990s has led to the disappearance of one of their most traditional demands, which in the past impeded the unconstrained expansion of technocratic practices: to expand popular participation in the decision making process. In this section I discuss the main factors leading to this change, which, in the end, produced an increasing acceptance of many neoliberal principles and, as a result, facilitated the rise of neoliberal technocracy. In the Chilean case, changes in the political culture of large sections of the left eventually led to the adoption of a technocratic-oriented vision of the administration of the state and economy and the way to deal with civil society. In other words, not only did the resistance to technocratic decision making vanish over time, but important sectors of the opposition against Pinochet began to adopt similar technocratic orientations.[35]

In order to understand this drastic change in political attitudes among the Chilean left, one must consider the process of ideological renovation that took place during the Pinochet regime. Following the military coup, a wide-ranging debate was initiated both within and among the left-wing parties and movements regarding the causes for the collapse of the socialist experiment. With the passing of time, a process of demythologizing of the Unidad Popular experience occurred in which the Allende government's own errors and deficiencies were underlined. An increasing number of political leaders under Allende began to talk about the *fracaso* (failure) of the UP experiment, stressing the coalition's own responsibility in the debacle.[36]

These leaders were particularly critical of Allende's economic policies, which were identified as a key factor in causing the economic crisis in 1972–73 (expressed in hyperinflation, serious food and consumer goods shortages, and a huge fiscal deficit). A second major self-criticism focused on the inability of the Unidad Popular coalition to maintain the support of the middle classes and to forge a political alliance with the Christian Democrats. In retrospect, a majority of the left accepted the fact that in order to implement radical social and economic reforms, the UP government needed a clear majority of the population behind it—and it did not have it. This was an implicit acceptance of the idea of majority rule, a central element of liberal democracy.

The brutality of the military coup and the innumerable atrocities perpetrated by the military government deeply marked the psyche of left-wing parties and their followers. The dictatorial and authoritarian nature of the Pinochet regime caused many Chileans, at home and abroad, to adopt a firm anti-authoritarian stance. Eventually this led to a veritable reformulation of attitudes about liberty, democracy, dictatorship, pluralism, and ideological tolerance.

The most important changes involved thinking about economic issues. During the first years of the military government, there was an near-general agreement among the left that the neoliberal economic strategy adopted by the military was not viable and could not last long. People predicted a rapid collapse of the economy and, with this, the end of the military government. By the late 1970s, however, it had become clear that the new economic system had become consolidated and that Chile had broken radically with the old system of state interventionism in the economy.

Many left-wing economists had already recognized the viability of the economic strategy followed by the military regime: The rate of inflation and fiscal deficit were severely reduced while the economy, in general, and exports, in particular, experienced continuous growth.[37] Although many correctly stressed the enormous social costs of these economic achievements, they also realized that economic growth and the maintenance of financial equilibrium constituted a precondition for improving the living standards of marginal segments of the population.

The former Minister of Economic Affairs, Carlos Ominami, an influential member of the Chilean Socialist Party, identified Chile's economic challenges for the future in a way that shows a clear continuity with the neoliberal policies of the former regime:

> Chile will face three challenges in the next decade. First, macro-economic stability must be maintained. Second, Chile must keep a solid competitive position in the demanding international markets. The consolidation of our export development requires a qualitative jump in the organization and magnitude of our presence abroad. Third, we must take advantage of the transition to democracy to attain greater social harmony, both in the country as a whole and within enterprises. The first point refers to the elimination of poverty and exclusion; the second poses the need to modernize labor relations, recognizing that the country has an enormous gap that the democratic system will help to close.[38]

In other words, the lessons of the economic failure of the UP period, combined with the relative economic success of the neoliberals, finally convinced many socialists that change in economic policies would not benefit anyone.

Not only left-wing sectors but perhaps the entire nation has assimilated the discourse of modernity and efficacy introduced by the Chicago boys. Not rhetoric but real socioeconomic and financial achievements have become the measures to evaluate the quality of government performance. Presidents Aylwin and Frei have continuously stressed the need to be more efficient and to modernize society in all aspects. Chilean socialists realize that the population will measure their viability as a political force and their performances in the Aylwin government by looking at the level of inflation, unemployment, growth of exports, increase of foreign investments, stability of the markets, and the general growth of the economy. After many decades of overideologized discourse, everyone in Chile has become extremely wary of demagogy and populistic rhetoric.

Toward "Techno-Schumpeterian" Democracies?

What are the implications of the adoption of the neoliberal paradigm and the subsequent technocratization of decision making for the very

nature of the new democratic regimes in the region? At the beginning of
the democratization process in Latin America, Cammack suggested that
the new democracies could adapt a Schumpeterian pattern, in which
political participation would be limited in the interest of rapid industrial development. He stressed the existence of a parallel with Western
Europe following the Second World War in the conscious decision by
the political class to limit citizen participation in political affairs and the
imposition of elitist control over the government decision-making
process during the phase of postwar reconstruction.[39] At the time, Cammack's idea for the "Schumpeterization" of Latin American democracies was not well received by political analysts, who found it difficult to
digest. Moreover, during the 1980s the democratic governments in
Brazil, Argentina, and Uruguay (upon which Cammack's analysis was
based) showed no apparent signs of adopting "European-style" democratic features. In addition, the Pinochet regime was firmly in power at
that time, and the possibilities for restoring democratic rule seemed
very remote.

Although Cammack's hypothesis did not pan out earlier, I think that
since the restoration of democracy in Chile, the country's political system
has indeed acquired distinct Schumpeterian features. During the last few
years, the concept of democracy has lost much of its Rousseauist connotations, with its participatory and egalitarian aspirations toward the decision-making process. The Schumpeterian view—one in which democracy is merely a *method* for arriving at political decisions and in which
citizens reserve the right to decide by whom they will be governed,
through elections in which various elites compete for the electorate's
vote—is beginning to be tacitly accepted in practice.

Today, the Chilean right, center, and left seem to have definitively
abandoned the use of populist political styles. Since democratic restoration, the search for consensus has been realized in the upper echelons of
the political class, while political debate at the lower levels has been systematically avoided. Furthermore, both parliament and government have
been identified as the sole legitimate sources of power in the political decision-making process. Today, traditional methods of civil pressure and
protest (such as property seizures, unauthorized street protests, politically motivated strikes, etc.), are generally considered illegitimate acts.
The democratic governments have also felt the need to demonstrate their
authority and ability to act decisively in containing the social and economic demands of the popular sectors and to show their ability to rule to
right-wing sectors and the armed forces.

In contrast with other countries in the region, the relative strength of
the political party system in Chile has permitted the political class to

maintain a firm control on the political process. In addition, the technocratization of the Chilean political class and the support for it from important sectors of society have reached beyond that of other Latin American countries.

The new democratic authorities have clearly adopted meritocratic criteria in recruiting top officials who have generally obtained advanced academic credentials abroad.[40] However, it must be stated that although one can observe some elements of continuity in the predominance of those possessing expertise under the military regime and under the new democratic governments, there are also important differences. In Chile, the struggle between the dictatorship and advocates of democracy led to the creation of two distinct technocratic strata: the pro-government technocrats who fought from their "trenches" in ministries and the antigovernment technocrats who fought from private research institutes controlled by the opposition.[41] The struggle, and their identification with it, greatly reinforced democratic awareness among the opposition technocrats (now in government), given that the dictatorship-democracy conflict was central (although not always explicitly so) to the arguments and debates with the Chicago boys.

The efficient management of the economy and the achievement of sustainable economic development have become key objectives for the *Concertación* governments, which, in itself, reinforces the economists' and financial experts' position in the inner corridors of power. The change of regime has also made it necessary to adopt new democratic styles of "doing politics" and reforming the judiciary inherited from the dictatorship. This has meant that sectors drawn from the traditional intelligentsia, such as lawyers and political scientists, have increased their political importance vis-à-vis the technocracy. The members of the economic team, for example, rarely participate in matters that are currently of central importance, such as human rights questions and relations between the government and the armed forces.

Nevertheless, technocrats *have* become a key actor in the new Chilean political landscape. This can also be said about other countries in the region, although in many cases the importance of this phenomenon is still not much known at the local level. In Chile, negative collective memories about the populist past, profound changes in the political culture of major left-wing sectors, together with the recent neoliberal transformations have allowed the almost unchallenged ascendancy of technocrats. One can expect that as long as neoliberal economic policies remain hegemonic in Latin America, technocrats will continue to assert their huge influence in the administration of the state affairs.

Notes

1. See Joan M. Nelson et al., *Fragile Coalitions: The Politics of Economic Adjustment* (New Brunswick: Transaction Books, 1989); John Williamson, ed., *Latin American Adjustment: How Much Has Happened?* (Washington, D.C.: Institute for International Economics, 1990); Stephan Haggard and Robert R. Kaufman, eds., *The Politics of Economic Adjustment* (Princeton: Princeton University Press, 1992); Stephan Haggard and Robert R. Kaufman, eds., *The Political Economy of Democratic Transitions* (Princeton: Princeton University Press, 1995); Stephan Haggard and Steven B. Webb, eds., *Voting for Reform: Democracy, Political Liberalization and Economic Adjustment* (New York: Oxford University Press, 1994); and Sebastián Edwards, *Crisis and Reform in Latin America: From Despair to Hope* (New York: Oxford University Press, 1995).

2. Technocrats are "individuals with a high level of specialized academic training which serves as a principal criterion on the basis of which they are selected to occupy key decisionmaking or advisory roles in large, complex organizations—both public and private." David Collier, "Glossary," in David Collier, ed., *The New Authoritarianism in Latin America* (Princeton: Princeton University Press, 1979), p. 403.

3. This is reflected, among other things, by the great popularity of the leaders of technocratic-oriented economic teams, such as the Ministers of Finance Alejandro Foxley in Chile, Fernando Henrique Cardoso in Brazil, and Domingo Cavallo in Argentina.

4. Although Merilee Grindle has explicitly recognized the importance of regime type for the "technocratization" of a bureaucratic system, she failed to integrate this factor in her analysis. See Merilee Grindle, "Power, Expertise, and the 'Técnico': Suggestions from a Mexican Case Study," *Journal of Politics*, 39 (May 1977), p. 402.

5. See Miguel Jorrín and John D. Martz, *Latin American Political Thought and Ideology* (Chapel Hill: The University of North Carolina Press, 1970), pp. 132–8; and Leopoldo Zea, *El Pensamiento Latinoamericano* (Mexico, D.F.: Editorial Ariel Seix Barral, 1976 [1965]), pp. 399–406.

6. See Adolfo Ibáñez Santa María, "Los Ingenieros, el Estado y la Política en Chile: Del Ministerio de Fomento a la Corporación de Fomento, 1927–1939," *Historia*, 18 (1983), pp. 45–102; and Patricio Silva, "State, Public Technocracy and Politics in Chile, 1927–1941," *Bulletin of Latin American Research*, 13, 3 (1994), pp. 281–97.

7. See David Collier, ed., *The New Authoritarism in Latin America*, passim.

8. See Pilar Vergara, *Auge y Caída del Neoliberalismo en Chile* (Santiago: FLACSO, 1985); and Juan Gabriel Valdés, *Pinochet's Economists: The Chicago School in Chile* (New York: Cambridge University Press, 1995).

9. See Robert N. Gwynne, "The Deindustrialization of Chile, 1974–1984," *Bulletin of Latin American Research*, 5, 1 (1986), pp. 1–23.

10. See Lois Hecht Oppenheim, *Politics in Chile: Democracy, Authoritarianism, and the Search for Development* (Boulder: Westview Press, 1993), pp. 118–20.

11. See Gary W. Wynia, *Politics and Planners: Economic Development Policy in Central America* (Madison: The University of Wisconsin Press, 1972).

12. See Sergio Molina, *El Proceso de Cambio en Chile: La Experiencia 1965–1970* (Santiago: Editorial Universitaria, 1972).

13. See Guillermo O'Donnell, Phillipe Schmitter, and Laurence Whitehead, eds., *Transitions from Authoritarian Rule* (Baltimore: The Johns Hopkins University Press, 1986); James Malloy and Mitchell Seligson, eds., *Authoritarians and Democrats: Regime Transition in Latin America* (Pittsburgh: University of Pittsburgh Press, 1987); and Scott Mainwaring, Guillermo O'Donnell, and J. Samuel Valenzuela, eds., *Issues in Democratic Consolidation: The New South American Democracies in Comparative Perspective* (Southbend, IN: University of Notre Dame Press, 1992).

14. See Duncan Green, *Silent Revolution: The Rise of Market Economics in Latin America* (London: Cassell and Latin American Bureau, 1995), p. 69.

15. See Ben Ross Schneider, "The Material Bases of Technocracy: Investor Confidence and Neoliberalism in Latin America," in Miguel A. Centeno and Patricio Silva, eds., *The Politics of Expertise in Latin America* (London: MacMillan, 1997).

16. Barbara Stallings, "International Influence on Economic Policy: Debt, Stabilization, and Structural Reform," in Stephan Haggard and Robert R. Kaufman, eds., *The Politics of Economic Adjustment* (Princeton: Princeton University Press, 1992), p. 84.

17. Robert R. Kaufman, "Industrial Change and Authoritarian Rule in Latin America: A Concrete Review of the Bureaucratic-Authoritarian Model," in David Collier, ed., *The New Authoritarianism in Latin America*, pp. 189–90.

18. Miguel A. Centeno, "The New Leviathan: The Dynamics and Limits of Technocracy," *Theory and Society*, 22 (1993), pp. 325–6. This is what Gouldner has called the "culture of critical discourse" that defines and unites the technical intelligentsia and creates an exclusionary "speech community." This technical discourse not only creates a special solidarity among the technocrats by the sharing of a language, but it also unifies those who use it and establishes distance between themselves and those who do not. See Alvin Gouldner, *The Future of Intellectuals and the Rise of the New Class* (London: MacMillan, 1979), p. 30.

19. Miles Kahler, "External Influence, Conditionality, and the Politics of Adjustment," in Stephan Haggard and Robert R. Kaufman, eds., *The Politics of Economic Adjustment*, p. 130.

20. See Cristóbal Kay, *Latin American Theories of Development and Underdevelopment* (London: Routledge, 1989).

21. See Juan Gabriel Valdés, *Pinochet's Economists*, passim.

22. Phil O'Brien, "The New Leviathan: The Chicago Boys and the Chilean Regime 1973–1980," *IDS Bulletin*, 13, 1 (1981), pp. 38–50.

23. See Pilar Vergara, *Auge y Caída del Neoliberalismo en Chile*, passim.

24. See Genaro Arriagada, *Pinochet: The Politics of Power* (Boston: Unwin Hyman, 1988).

25. See Patricio Silva, "Technocrats and Politics in Chile: From the Chicago Boys to the CIEPLAN Monks," *Journal of Latin American Studies*, 23, 2 (1991), pp. 385–410.

26. See Rosario Espinal, "Development, Neoliberalism and Electoral Politics in Latin America," *Development and Change*, 23, 4 (1992), pp. 27–48.

27. See Pamela Constable and Arturo Valenzuela, *A Nation of Enemies: Chile under Pinochet* (New York: W.W. Norton, 1991).

28. Patricia Politzer, *Fear in Chile: Lives under Pinochet* (New York: Pantheon, 1989 [1985]).

29. This has been particularly the case in the parliament. So, for instance, the socialist Senator Ricardo Núñez, vice president of the congress, has observed "the notable decline of the political dimension of the legislative activities." He further pointed out that "many senators are convinced that the parliament's activities are completely divorced from politics . . . intending to give it a technico-neutral connotation." *El Mercurio*, February 1, 1996, p. 10.

30. Joseph S. Tulchin and Augusto Varas, "Introduction" in Joseph S. Tulchin and Augusto Varas, eds., *From Dictatorship to Democracy: Rebuilding Political Consensus in Chile* (Boulder: Lynne Rienner, 1991) p. 4.

31. Laurence Whitehead, "International Aspects of Democratization," in Guillermo O'Donnell, Philippe Schmitter, and Laurence Whitehead, eds., *Transitions from Authoritarian Rule*, pp. 23–4.

32. J. Samuel Valenzuela, "Democratic Consolidation in Post-Transitional Settings: Notion, Process, and Facilitating Conditions," in Scott Mainwaring, Guillermo O'Donnell and Arturo Valenzuela, eds., *Issues in Democratic Consolidation*, p. 79.

33. Lois Hecht Oppenheim, *Politics in Chile*, p. 207.

34. James Petras and Fernando Ignacio Leiva, *Democracy and Poverty in Chile: The Limits to Electoral Politics* (Boulder: Westview Press, 1994).

35. See Patricio Silva, "Technocrats and Politics in Chile," pp. 385–410; and Jeffrey M. Puryear, *Thinking Politics: Intellectuals and Democracy in Chile, 1973–1988* (Baltimore: Johns Hopkins University Press, 1994).

36. See Manuel Antonio Garretón, *Reconstruir la Política: Transición y Consolidación Democrática en Chile* (Santiago: Editorial Andante, 1987), pp. 252 ff.

37. See Paul W. Drake and Iván Jaksić, eds., *The Struggle for Democracy in Chile* (Lincoln: University of Nebraska Press, 1995).

38. Carlos Ominami, "Promoting Economic Growth and Stability," in Joseph S. Tulchin and August Varas, eds., *From Dictatorship to Democracy*, pp. 21–2.

39. Paul Cammack, "Democratisation: A Review of the Issues," *Bulletin of Latin American Research*, 4, 2 (1985), p. 45.

40. See Patricio Silva, "Technocrats and Politics in Chile," passim.

41. See Jeffrey M. Puryear, *Thinking Politics*, passim.

5

The State in Retreat in the Economy

William Glade

Reversing a historical trend that, on the world scene, began with Otto von Bismarck if not earlier,[1] the state in Latin America has appeared to be in full retreat since Chile introduced pioneering structural adjustment policies in the mid-1970s and economic restructuring spread to other countries during the 1980s. In the process, large areas of policy territory have been evacuated—even in countries where one might have anticipated greater resistance to this shift than actually occurred. The dismantling of complex and ultimately incoherent structures of subsidies, the abandonment of nontariff trade barriers and lowering of tariffs, and the reform or abolition of a variety of regulatory schemes that had been cobbled together during decades of political and economic improvisation amounted to a sea change in policy that has aptly been called a "silent revolution," the comparative silence of which has been all the more remarkable because of the adjustment costs that so many bore during the implementation of stabilization and restructuring programs.[2] It seems unlikely that this acquiescence has come about for intellectual reasons: namely, through a widespread recognition that the social costs of structural adjustment, hard though they may be to bear, are less than the social costs of not restructuring.

Of special interest in this process of change has been the programs of privatization that, though less sweeping in their impact on allocational decisions than the alterations in trade, exchange rate, monetary, and fiscal policies that have been made during structural adjustment, are emblematic of the larger set of social, political, and economic transformations that restructuring promotes.[3] Perhaps because privatization deals so explicitly with the jurisdictional boundaries of the state, the very paladin of the new national projects that evolved over most of this century, these policies have functioned, at least at the outset, as a lightening rod for all the discontents and anxieties that were generated by the shift in policy models. Leaving aside the many interests that had a fairly direct stake in the old interventionary mechanisms, whence came all kinds of rent-generating privileges, the transfer of ownership of assets that were often especially prominent sometimes galvanized a formidable assortment of groups into active opposition—the most conspicuous instances being, perhaps, in Venezuela and Brazil. In the former, the opponents of policy reform actually succeeded, with the downfall of Carlos Andrés Pérez, in reversing the new policy direction, while in the latter, the bureaucratic and political foot-dragging that occurred in the two administrations that preceded that of Fernando Henrique Cardoso revealed a notable disinclination to follow through on the realignment of the public and private sectors.

In Argentina, too, the forces of resistance remained strong throughout the Alfonsín period, when the Radical government was clearly sympathetic to the old modalities of economic nationalism. Despite the success of the Carlos Menem government in effecting the sale of huge parastatal assets, it is clear that many politically conscious people outside government remain unconvinced of the validity of this transfer. In Peru, the issue helped defeat one leading candidate for the presidency (Mario Vargas Llosa) in the post-Alan García clean-up period, although the winner, the canny Alberto Fujimori, turned out to be, by stealth, a privatizer and restructurer after all. Costa Rica, it is clear, still harbors many in positions of political influence who have strong reservations about privatization and the rest of the reform package. Even in Mexico, where, after a certain amount of initial sham, privatization was carried out with breathtaking speed, the *inquietudes* that hovered about the privatization issue generated no small part of the popular support for the left opposition in the election that brought Carlos Salinas into office to consolidate policy directions pioneered under the Miguel de la Madrid presidency. What would happen were the petroleum monopoly and the main part of the electric power industry to be put on the auction block remains to be seen, but it is reasonable to suppose that at the least their privatization would occur amid much contention.

This and the concomitant revision of controls over such processes as foreign direct investment and technology transfer appeared to many in the intellectual and policy establishment, very much like a case of Essau selling his birthright for a mess of pottage—if not outright institutional parricide. Yet, whereas a decade or so ago there was much discussion about the feasibility and even desirability of privatization, today it is a fait accompli on a far grander scale than one might reasonably have anticipated when the first conferences were held to look into this policy option.[4] Largely discarded, too, are many of the suppositions that informed so much policy discussion in the 1960s and 1970s, most notably the *de-*

pendencia-inspired reading of the possibilities of international economic relations, with respect to both trade and investment flows, and the habit of assigning comprehensive social and economic responsibilities to the state as the spearhead of national development efforts. Indeed, along with privatization, the opening of national economies to much more extensive interaction with an increasingly globalized system constitutes a profound paradigmatic shift in both policy construction and the analysis that underlies policy. What the enthronement of the market meant for adaptations in the policy conversation was compellingly indicated, for Mexico, when some, especially among the Partido de la Revolución Democrática (PRD) and its sympathizers, went so far as to speak of a return to the *Porfiriato*.[5]

Several interesting questions are suggested by this striking turnaround in policy, a shift that, of course, reaches far beyond the margins of the Western Hemisphere and was nowhere more dramatically presented than in systemic implosion that occurred in Central and Eastern Europe in 1989 and, shortly thereafter, in the former Soviet Union. First and foremost is how to account for the sweeping reorientation of policy. What explanation is most plausible, particularly given the extraordinary geographical incidence of the phenomenon? The improbability of there having been a mass conversion along the Damascene road forces a search for structural factors that would account for the geographical and systemic prevalence of this policy alteration, particularly since in only one instance of many—the initial unfolding in Chile—did a concurrent application of force appear to give it a somewhat imposed character.

Secondly, what light does the withdrawal of the state from its customary policy margins shed on the lengthy literature on the secular growth of the public sector, for which development so many helpful, if inconclusive, explanations have been proffered? And what does the transformation of state policy tell us about the theory of public sector failure—and about the baleful macroeconomic populism that for so long characterized the workings of the policy machinery in most of Latin America?

At the same time, an examination of the course of policy since the silent revolution tells us much about certain achievements of state-managed development that may be underappreciated amid today's general reaction against the policies of the past, while the current policy agenda, in its way, evinces a maturation of economic structure that calls for new, if more nuanced, forms of state involvement, not simply beating a retreat from economic responsibility.

Too often, perhaps, for a full understanding of the situation that prevails today, the thought structure of neoclassical economics has inhabited contemporary analysts as a regulative idea, as Kant might have put it. But by failing to bring to the examination of contemporary trends a highly developed historical sense, the intellectual authority of this approach as well as its perspicacity has been lessened—however much this perspective has contributed to elucidating the assorted public sector as well as market failures that have bedeviled recent Latin American economic history. Yet in combination with explanatory paths opened up by neoinstitutional and neostructural economics, the analytical power of the conventional approach to development can be substantially enhanced by giving us more peripheral vision, as it were, and providing a richer contextualization of the subject.

Sources of Policy Transformation

The proximate source of the change in prevailing policy was in virtually every instance a compelling one: namely, economic breakdown. Not everywhere were the circumstances of the breakdown the same, but a common triggering element seems to have been the simple inability to continue doing what had been customary. The previous policy model had come to the end of the road—been exhausted, to use a customary Latin American expression.

For Chile the breakdown had its origins in the abrupt dislocations of production processes that were occasioned by the government's abruptly nationalizing not only the commanding heights of the economy (the copper mines and major industries), in the Fabian style, but a great deal else as well. Indeed, while the agitated political climate that prevailed just prior to and during the Salvador Allende regime probably made such a sweeping seizure inevitable, politically and ideologically speaking, what was taken into the state sector very likely exceeded in short order what the Unidad Popular coalition had proposed at the time of the election, though it is possible that the real intentions were all along closer to the outcome than to the initially stated electoral position. Be this as it may, the result of this kind of economic adventurism was, after a short growth spurt thanks to the Keynesian effects of stepped-up public spending, an acute case of organizational indigestion. The administration of production (and public administration) fell apart, no doubt in some measure because of internecine political and bureaucratic struggles among the allies in the coalition government; investment plummeted; inflation soared; and the balance of payments situation rapidly worsened. Viewed in this light, the liberalization programs introduced under Augusto Pinochet were necessarily rehabilitative in intent, not unlike the introduction of the New Economic Policy in 1921 to repair the damage of war communism in the fledgling Soviet Union.

For the countries where policy switching came a decade later, the precipitating cause was the onset of the debt crisis, which threw into bold relief 'the received policies' lost viability. Wittingly or unwittingly, the interventionist growth policies to which most countries had become so attached had eventuated in a stronger support for consumption than for investment, in a failure to promote exports (except in Colombia and Brazil), in the discouragement of foreign investment, in fiscal and monetary indiscipline, and in a stop-and-go rhythm of growth that tended to produce repeated balance-of-payments problems, as has been explained so clearly in Dornbusch and Edwards' *The Macroeconomics of Populism in Latin America.*[6] Though for most countries the end of the ancien régime in policies came less dramatically than it did in Chile, the impossibility of continuing to rely on a stream of external borrowing forced a departure from the model that had guided growth for so many years but that gradually foreclosed the main options to foreign borrowing for tapping the external resources needed to support growth.[7] Access to grants from aid-promoting agencies was curtailed as donor countries and institutions redirected their efforts to poorer parts of the world. Foreign investment was generally inhibited by tighter regulations and in some countries further deterred by the "fade out" policy of the Andean Group. Discriminatory policies had, meanwhile, hampered investment in export industries of the traditional varieties to the detriment of foreign exchange earnings. Under these circumstances, even the possibilities for debt-led growth turned out to be limited when the magnitude of the problem became clear to all concerned, most especially the banks that had participated with so little restraint in the run-up of the debt.

Restarting growth thus required every country to embrace policies quite distinct from those that had dominated the picture theretofore.[8] Fortunately for those who would sort out the dependent and independent variables in this process, so dramatic has been the substitution of new national projects for the old that a wealth of literature, much of it in a political economy vein, is now available to help make sense of what has occurred.[9] Particularly useful are some of the country studies of restructuring.[10] To be sure, a range of interpretations is offered in these analyses, but most seem to converge on the state, its composition and its behavior, as a key factor in producing these changes once external conditions no longer permitted a resumption and continuation of the previous policy model.[11] To be sure, external conditions do not appear paramount in the policy switch that occurred in Chile, a case dominated by the internal factors that produced economic contraction, but there, too, the complexion of the state and the ramifications of its behavior were the forces that propelled the search for new policy solutions. In short, the thesis of the provocative and immensely useful book brought out a decade ago by Evans, Rueschemeyer, and Skocpol—*Bringing the State Back In*—seems amply confirmed by the centrality of the state in the diagnostic and therapeutic work of recent times, though in truth, for Latin American research at least, the state had hardly ever been left out as a major dimensioning factor in social analysis.[12]

In retrospect, the denouement of the 1980s appears to have been built into the modus operandi of Latin American economic systems from very nearly their inception. The fairly straightforward policy rationale for intervention put forward by the Comisión Económica para América Latina (CEPAL) in its early years gradually gave way to a certain loss of coherence in policy design as interventionary measures proliferated and, on more than a few occasions, worked at cross purposes with one another. The state moved, for example, from a relatively measured and targeted protectionism at the outset to a more promiscuous allocation of its favors, sheltering, within its capacious policy field, a very wide range of private firms from external competition at a time when internal markets were often not competitively structured, so that there was neither an internal nor external impetus to increased efficiency. Export industries were in fact frequently penalized by policies, and discrimination against the agricultural sector was also a fairly common practice. The veritable menagerie of parastatal enterprises that came to compose the state's portfolio of direct investments[13] was, more frequently than not, especially burdensome for the state in terms of capital budgets because a fair number of the state's holdings were in capital-intensive lines. Meanwhile the soft-budget constraint that was common to parastatal companies in most of the countries meant that operating deficits had to be covered by the public sector as well—and this by a fiscal system that had undergone only limited reform and improvement during the 1960s when a strengthening of public finance was one of the declared policy objectives promoted by the Alliance for Progress. Although the deficits of the state-owned companies were both overt and covert (the latter, however, being sometimes wholly or partially concealed by cross-subsidization), national economies were also weighed down by what were in effect disguised deficits in the private sector: i.e., the operating deficits that would have appeared had not protectionism and regulation permitted prices to be administered with varying degrees of monopoly power in captive domestic markets. In short, maladroit policy was pandemic, though the consequences were manifested differently in the balance sheets of the firms of the public and private sectors.

With the advantages of hindsight, it is possible to see with reasonable clarity what was going on during the approximately half-century of state expansion. What began, generally in the 1930s and early 1940s, as an attempt to employ public policy to cope with externally induced economic disruptions brought on by depression and war,[14] gradually took on a more defined profile as industrialization came to be the centerpiece of national policy, and "national development," particularly as conceived by CEPAL, became the watchword of the policy community. With urbanization gradually accelerating and the economic and social structure growing more complex, while developments both internal and external undermined the old power system, the state's evolving role can be seen as guided by two types of considerations. On the one hand, it was deliberately employed by elite consensus to rescue national economies from the disruptive external forces and to serve in a catalytic role to promote newer forms of production.[15] But side by side with this proactive role, if we may call it that, the state was also reacting to the increasing systemic complexity of the day by responding to ever more varied pressures from new interest groups or constituencies. Foreign investors, who could spot the opportunities for rent generation this system entailed, were only too happy to join in the game—sometimes alone, sometimes in partnership with local private interests, sometimes in partnership with the state and its enterprises.[16]

The siren song of the state in this era of policy-induced development was sung by a fairly numerous chorus invoking all the usual economic and political arguments as justification for their agenda, though in many respects the institution expected to be omnicompetent suffered a considerable number of shortcomings that tended to blunt its efficacy as a vehicle of policy implementation. The very weakness of the state and the political system through which it operated made the apparatus of public power vulnerable to the ambitions of the varied social forces, which were only partly captured, conceptually speaking, by the fruitful notion of macroeconomic populism. From an early date, a number of studies of national development processes began to reveal the symbiotic relationship that was evolving between contemporary public policy mechanisms on the one hand and the evolving constellation of economic interests on the other.[17]

Weak political parties, compliant legislatures, subordinated judiciaries, and chief executives who had to cast about for constituencies purchasable with government blandishments (i.e., rent-seeking opportunities) were complemented by self-aggrandizing bureaucracies that, as one of the more strategically placed factions of the "middle sector"—to invoke John Johnson's famous, if much debated, term—used the public sector's expansion to expand their employment base and enhance the perks of office.[18] Given the general weakness of the mechanisms of administrative surveillance and control in the executive branch, alongside the limitations of legislative and judicial oversight, the kinds of behavior described by Niskanen, Downs, Rourke, and many other students of modern bureaucracy, to say nothing of Buchanan and other public choice theorists, were put on display as if to confirm the social science literature that was spawned by the process of development.[19] Indeed, the contributors to La Palombara's classic volume of thirty years ago were nothing if not accurate in tracing the contours of power and patterns of decision-making in societies in which bureaucratic politics tended to occupy center stage.[20] For that matter, from a purely scholarly point of view, it is reassuring how well captured were the dynamics of this system in the huge volume of social science literature that poured forth during the past thirty-five years or so.

In retrospect it would seem that the process of state expansion rested on a self-feeding dynamic in which the interaction of bureaucrats (together with political leaders) and the rent-seeking constituencies their favors cultivated exemplified a kind of Say's Law of public-sector products, a perverse political economy in which the supply (of policy-engineered income streams) generated its own demand (in terms of the constituencies these income streams nurtured). The notion of bureaucratic authoritarianism applies to a subset of the type of process involved, and variants of corporatism apply to a somewhat larger (and overlapping) subset, but the pattern of dynamics that was generic went beyond both. The overarching type of system appears to have been something resembling Michal Kalecki's concept of intermediate regime in which, for circumstantial or structural reasons, a Bonapartist-style regime could exercise public-sector leadership, providing bureaucratic and political guidance at a time when the dislocating impacts of depression and war during the 1930s and 1940s and increasing urbanization and market-based industrial development combined to erode the power base of the regimes that had prevailed during the heyday of classic export-led growth in Latin America. Assisting in this structurally induced process of state expansion were the capacity of technocratic leadership to draw on policy blueprints fabricated by the Economic Commission for Latin America (ECLA), World Bank country missions, and other external sources; their ability to tap major external sources of funding and technical assistance; and, in general, their role in managing key relations of resource exchange with the rest of the world. Indeed, orchestration of these key external inputs, especially during the 1950s and 1960s, seems, along with the allocation of parastatal output, to have been part of the strategies for political survival.[21]

As much ink has been spilled in the controversy over the relative autonomy of the state, there is no need to recapitulate the churrigueresque features of that discussion, much of which had to do with intramural delineations in Marxism as reflected, for instance, in the famous Miliband/Poulantzas exchange. It is sufficient to remark that dirigisme or etatisme, with varying degrees of state autonomy and state capacity, responded to conditions that were widespread in the developing world, which suggests a structural rather than cultural basis[22] in the kinds of social formations that emerged from the interplay of national economies and societies with the world market of capitalism.[23]

What began, in one sense, as a crowding-in process wherein government investment was welcomed as a catalyst for the private sector ended with a great deal of crowding out as the bloated public sector with its ever burgeoning financial requirements became an increasing drag on the economy.[24] Given the pattern of political economy that was consolidated during the 1930s–1960s interval, the very success of developmentalism, the guiding doctrine of the era, fostered an increasingly complex economic and social structure and multiplied the interest groups that had to be placated while reinforcing the capacity of these groups to make demands on the state. The result was that the fiscal crisis of the state, which O'Connor foresaw for advanced industrial societies, came home to roost with a vengeance in Latin America when the debt-led strategies of growth of the 1970s, which had been used to finance a reprieve for the system of state-guided growth, reached their unavoidable end in 1982.[25]

The demise of the institutional order that brought an increasing number of supernumeraries onto the payroll of an expanding state responded not only to the internal structural contradictions outlined above. External structural factors were involved as well, most notably in the increasing globalization of the economic structures that today organize the world economy: the spread of transnational production, marketing, research and development, and finance systems; the growing cultural openness of consumer preferences; and the implications for the growing relative importance of cross-border economic transactions in economies characterized by rising per capita incomes and increasing complexity in the structure of production. In the emerging world system with the constraints it poses for national policy choices, acquired comparative advantages have come to count for more than those based on natural resource endowments, and both scope and scale economies have rested increasingly on the environment in which firms operate (though internal economies of scale and scope remain crucial, as is indicated in the spread of multinational firms).

Thanks to these developments and to the capacity of the more than 37,000 multinational enterprises that, with their more than 170,000 affiliates and myriad other business relations (such as licensing and contracting agreements, strategic business alliances, and the like), organize so much of international exchange, significant portions of cross-boundary factor and product flows are nowadays intra-industry and, in many instances, even intrafirm in nature.[26] Mastery of the political ropes in a given location may still be a necessary condition of profitability (whereas it came close to being a sufficient condition in the protected national economies of the past), but international competitive standing and, hence, managerial prowess in a technical sense have become the decisive determinants of economic viability in a global economy in which national barriers have necessarily been dissolving.

Exploring the Organizational Moraine

What has been left behind as the boundaries of the state have receded during restructuring yields insights that are relevant to the likely future course of policy in Latin America. Inspection of this institutional detritus reveals that during the decades since the 1930s much of the expansion of the state took place along what might be described as the extensive margin rather than along the intensive margin. This is understandable in the light of the political economy of state expansion. The tendency to stake out new territory subject to intervention through adding to the administrative undertakings of the state and through taking on business activities as collectively financed and managed functions responded in no small measure to the task of adding or consolidating constituencies. All the while the process bypassed the more intensive development of state capacity that would have been less relevant to this objective, if indeed it would not have ended up antagonizing important constituencies. The advancing margin of state operations, then, created a kind of hollow frontier, for behind the frontier of intervention there was absent the kind of in-filling that would have been necessary to strengthen the essential power of the state but that might have rendered more difficult the conciliating and placating of the groups that had gained resources behind the mantel of public policy.

In the nature of the case, the triggering circumstances for restructuring in most of Latin America made plain the essential weakness of fiscal systems—despite the ostensible efforts to rectify their shortcomings that were made in the 1960s under external prodding. Thus, these earlier efforts notwithstanding, fiscal reform has generally been part of the conditionality requirements of latter-day stabilization and structural adjustment assistance from the World Bank and the International Monetary Fund (IMF). In this overhaul, both the design of the tax system and its administration are being changed, and new auditing and managerial control systems are being devised to regulate more effectively the flows of public expenditures. Reregulation in public finance has become, in effect, the point of departure for establishing sound macroeconomic management.

It is also patent that past promotional efforts in the field of money and banking, where much was accomplished in building up a workable financial infrastructure, were seldom backed up by the installation of equally significant new regulatory programs to ensure the integrity of capital markets and the safety of such financial intermediaries as banks and insurance companies—with the result that the capacity to withstand adverse shifts in the international flow of resources, to which all national systems are increasingly exposed, has been diminished. For their part, the security exchanges that are being counted on to function as allocative switchboards in the new market-based systems have been unusually volatile and vulnerable to speculation. Although Chile has made great headway in increasing the transparency of its capital markets, it is less clear how much has been done to promote similar conditions elsewhere. Problems in U.S. investment banking, the precarious state of the huge Japanese banks, and the recent collapse of Barings serve as a reminder that in this field the regulator's work is never done.

Not every Latin American banking system reached the depths of mismanagement that transpired in Venezuela, but in Mexico, Argentina, and Brazil, to go no farther, the stability of banking institutions has posed a decided threat to national economic well being in recent times—and this despite the instructive negative example provided by Chile more than a decade ago when its reprivatized and overextended banks collapsed and had to be salvaged by state intervention. Few problems, in fact, are so urgent as the modernization of bank supervision and the regulation of financial conglomerates to ensure the smooth functioning of these pivotal institutions and broaden access to credit. For that matter, the prevailing tendency in Latin American banking to follow continental practice in allowing close relationships between the major banks and the economic groups or conglomerates—the *kereitsu* or *chaebol* of the Americas—may ultimately require the state to revisit this policy area out of a concern with the possible antisocial effects of concentrations of economic power— though the opening of national economics provides some safeguards against the abuse of this power, and it could be argued that such national concentrations might play a countervailing role vis-à-vis foreign and multinational enterprises.

Closely related to the proper functioning of security exchanges and the cultivation of a more numerous investor class, not to mention the broadening of capital ownership through investing intermediaries, is the field of public utility regulation. Already a great many of the state's holdings in telecommunications, electric power generation and distribution, and similar basic services have been privatized in the hope of increasing their operating efficiency and raising the capital for tackling the pent-up demand that grew as a consequence of years of underinvestment and indifferent management. More are sure to follow along the privatization route. For the desired social results to be achieved, however, along with a much needed updating of technology in many cases, and for the shares and bonds issued by newly privatized companies to take on the character of guilt-edged or blue chip securities will in large measure depend on a fine calibration in the regulatory schemes that are being put together to provide public surveillance of these firms. Both the consuming public (including the industrial and commercial users) and the investing public (including household and institutional investors) have an interest in the installation of regulatory systems that will enable these offerings to maximize their potential role in the elaboration of capital markets by offering low-risk options for portfolio diversification.

Health and education systems have likewise grown in scale but with quantitative gains usually insufficient to meet the need and with a qualitative deterioration that has come to pervade much of the systems that have been established. In consequence, differences in access to opportunities for forming human capital (in both formal education and in-job training and experience) seem to have contributed increasingly to the maldistribution of wealth and income in most of the region. What is more, in spite of early efforts to introduce relatively advanced social legislation for the benefit of semiprivileged groups of workers, the refinement and adaptation of these programs to changing demographic and economic conditions fell behind, and many began to look almost parodistic. Thus it is that the worst (i.e., most unequal) income distribution among the high performing Asian economies has turned out to be better than the best (least unequal) income distribution among the major Latin American economies.

The list goes on. Ambitious programs of infrastructure construction, for example, have rarely been followed by commensurate provision for maintenance and repair. Regulation of technology transfer was rarely matched by systematic and effective support for local research-and-development programs, notwithstanding the prodigious productivity of modern technology. It is true that over the years more varied consumer products have figured in GDP, thanks to aggressive industrial policy, but with limited progress in upgrading product standards, imposing product liability requirements, and providing for consumer protection both to increase local welfare and to enhance the possibilities of penetrating more exacting foreign markets. Though here and there one finds notable exceptions in the achievement of product standards that are competitive in an international frame of reference, by and large this remains a field crying out for a realignment of responsibilities in the public and private sectors and for constructive collaboration between the two. One need hardly add, in view of the almost continuing discussion of recent years, that environmental degradation has come to be a frequent accompaniment to the growth of both agricultural and manufacturing production, offsetting private production gains by substantial social costs.

By the 1990s, in short, the social architecture of the region came to exhibit a great deal of what is called, in the real estate business, deferred maintenance: i.e., dilapidation. Consequently, the accumulated social deficit—in shelter, nutrition, urban and regional infrastructure, and so on—hangs like a huge liability over future increases in output. There is every likelihood that the troubled recent history of Chiapas prefigures issues that will confront the whole region in the years immediately ahead, although the panegyrists of the market who have lately dominated the reading of social and economic trends have tended to miss this aspect of the situation.

Many of the public sector failures that marred the record of the half century of state-managed growth stemmed from faulty program design and multiple inadequacies in implementation. But behind these, as today's rather more transparent environment reveals, lay a set of nested problems that ranged from the vagaries of bureaucratic politics and a certain opaqueness in policy formation and execution to the spread of informal markets for government-dispensed privilege and a pervasive lack of accountability. Asymmetries in access to information and in institutional problems, both rife in the organizational sprawl of the state, were combined with wide, even widening, disparities in the distribution of access to the political process—with all the complications this has entailed for tracking and formulating an elusive social demand. Not least among the problems has been the conspicuous frailty of anything resembling the ingredients that compose a civic culture and civil society. For these and other reasons, while public decisional processes have frequently proven no more adept than private decisional processes in reckoning social gains and social costs, we can, thanks to a covert privatization of the public sector, at least clarify how this has come about and what its consequences have been.

At the same time, the very speed with which privatization programs have been implemented in most countries reveals another side of the coin, an aspect of institutional evolution that is no less consequential in determining what lies ahead. For all the failings of the now-abandoned system, the fact is that it managed to achieve significant real gains in aggregate output and productivity over a protracted period.[27] Further, the ease with which substantial parastatal assets have been transferred to private ownership, such as the Mexican telephone company, the large Brazilian steel mills, and the huge Argentine state petroleum enterprise Yacimentos Petrolíferos Fiscales (YPF), implies the emergence of a perhaps hitherto unsuspected capability on the part of the national private sectors, as does the participation of Chilean and Brazilian firms in the privatization of the Argentine steel industry or the acquisition by Brazilian capital of the erstwhile parastatal airline in Ecuador. National capital markets and financial intermediaries have proven adept at facilitating such transfers, even when past maladroitness left much for the new owners to set right. A case in point is the rapid turnaround of the YPF, formerly one of the worst-managed petroleum enterprises in the Americas. Sooner than one would have thought possible, its heavy operating losses were converted into profits, and it was even able to embark on a program of foreign expansion as its financial status moved from the ludicrous to the lucrative. The massive rehabilitation effort involved attests both to a high level of managerial and technical competence and to the availability of a wide variety of specialized service firms for feeding expertise into the production of goods: consulting engineers, accountants and financial advisors, geologists, geophysicists, management and marketing specialists, and so on down a rather lengthy list of specialized forms of human capital. One has only to compare the yellow pages of the telephone directory in any good-sized Latin American city with its predecessor of, say, thirty years ago to see how much ground has been gained in developing the organizational capital of a modern industrial economy.

By the same token, the capacity of the system of higher education in Latin America is today vastly superior to what was found there when ECLA began its labors. Research institutes, centers for advanced technical and professional training, and such have, for all their shortcomings, utterly transformed the domestic development of skills and knowledge. Thanks to the enormous accumulation of organizational capital and to the in-job learning experiences offered by an increasingly diversified, technically dense, and versatile production complex, the human resources of the area are far richer than they have ever been before. Increasingly, in other words, we are coming to appreciate the understandings of the original institutionalists, the old-fashioned structuralists, and, indeed, many of the early development scholars of other persuasions of the critical importance of institution building and how innovation in institutions or organizational structures promotes not only agricultural improvement (the field on which much of the institution-building literature was centered) but also the evolution of the service sector, of industry, of public administration, and even of society as a whole.[28]

When the Latin American countries first launched their respective national development projects, some of them before there was available either significant expert experience in development design and implementation or a field of development studies as such, no blueprints were readily at hand to assist in the new social endeavor. And in the earliest instances, there were few sources of financial or technical assistance from the outside.[29] The state, consequently, found itself very much in the position of that early venture capitalist, Isabella, for there were at the time scant alternatives for providing initiative, assuming risks, and mobilizing resources beyond what was already devoted to the incipient market-in-duced industrialization that had been underway for some decades.

Mistakes were made in abundance in moving through what was initially uncharted territory, but taking an ample view of all the achievements as well as the deficiencies, one would have to conclude that the state did essentially fulfill the catalytic role it first took on when it set about spurring industrial development and that its investments in building an industrial economy, as a kind of public good, were at the end of the day outlays that produced a significant positive return. That the process of in-filling behind the hollow frontier now remains as a kind of "old business" on national agendas indicates that the state's resources, relieved of the burden of operating deficit-ridden parastatals and overblown bureaucracies, will be available to be redeployed in a more focused fashion to build administrative capacity in critical areas, drawing on the superior competencies of the younger technocrats who have come out of the evolutionary changes of the past thirty years or so. With these new resources at hand, we may reasonably expect Latin American governments to seize the opportunity both to learn from the ongoing efforts of the industrially advanced countries to fine-tune their more matured regulatory systems and to produce imaginative homegrown innovations for coping with the continuing problems of institutional adjustment. To be sure, there is nothing foreordained about such an optimistic scenario. Yet if one considers the burst of institutional creativity that ensued from the structural changes of fifty to sixty years ago, there is certainly some basis for assessing the probabilities as favorable in the current round of institutional renewal.

Notes

1. Alexander Gerschenkron in *Economic Backwardness in Historical Perspective* (New York: Praeger, 1965) suggests an even earlier emergence of state-led development efforts.

2. Inter-American Development Bank, *Economic and Social Progress in Latin America, 1991* (Baltimore: Johns Hopkins University Press, 1992), pp. 29–38, uses the term and succinctly describes the principal features of the policy changes so characterized.

3. For several detailed reviews of policy changes in this period, see Bela Balassa et al., *Toward Renewed Economic Growth in Latin America* (Washington, D.C.: Institute for International Economics, 1986); William Glade, ed., *Privatization of Public Enterprises in Latin America* (San Francisco: ICS Press, 1991); John Williamson, ed., *Latin American Adjustment: How Much Has Happened?* (Washington, D.C.: Institute of International Economics, 1990); and Felipe Larrain and Marcelo Selowsky, eds., *The Public Sector and the Latin American Crisis* (San Francisco: ICS Press, 1991).

4. See, for instance, the concerns and doubts expressed by a number of the contributors to William P. Glade, ed., *State Shrinking: A Comparative Inquiry into Privatization* (Austin: Institute of Latin American Studies, University of Texas, 1986). See especially chapters 2 and 3.

5. The sensitivity of reopening the economy to foreign investment, as well as domestic investment, on a less restricted basis is succinctly explained in Paul E. Sigmund, *Multinationals in Latin America: The Politics of Nationalization* (Madison: University of Wisconsin Press, 1980). Sigmund's book, written just at the high tide of nationalism, depicts parallel developments in other countries as well.

6. Rudiger Dornbusch and Sebastian Edwards, eds., *The Macroeconomics of Populism in Latin America* (Chicago: University of Chicago Press, 1991).

7. The single major country to escape the debt crisis, Colombia was a notable exception in several respects. It had not overborrowed; it had not developed such a pervasive parastatal sector; its interventionism was, arguably, more moderate; and it had not repressed the agricultural sector to the degree that was common elsewhere. Moreover, Colombia began in the 1960s to promote export diversification and expansion.

8. By now the literature describing and assessing these changes has become abundant. Some works deal with the whole set of complementary policy modifications put forward in the new agenda: e.g., Bela Balassa et al., *Toward Renewed Economic Growth in Latin America;* John Williamson, ed., *Latin American Adjustment;* and Lance Taylor, ed., *The Rocky Road to Reform: Adjustment, Income Distribution, and Growth in the Developing World* (Cambridge, MA: MIT Press, 1993). Others examine more specific facets of reform policy or reform in particular countries: e.g., Hernan Buchi Buc, *La Transformación Económica del Chile* (Santiago: Universidad Nacional Andres Bello, 1992); *"El Ladrillo": Bases de la Política Económica del Gobierno Militar Chileno* (Santiago: Centro Estudios Públicos, 1992); see especially the prologue by Sergio de Castro; Domingo Cavallo, *Volver a Crecer: Un Desafio y un Compromiso para todos los Argentinos: Bienestar sin Inflación* (Buenos Aires: Sudamericana/Planeta, 1984); Moisés Naim and Ramon Piñango, *El Caso Venezuela: Una Ilusión de Armonia* (Caracas: Ediciones IESA, 1988); Moises Naim, *Paper Tigers and Minotaurs: The Politics of Venezuela's Economic Reforms* (Washington, D.C.: Carnegie Endowment for International Peace, 1993); William Glade, *Privatization of Public Enterprises;* William Glade, ed., *Bigger Economies, Smaller Governments: The Role of Privatization in Latin America* (Boulder: Westview Press, 1995); Werner Baer and Melissa Birch, eds., *Privatization in Latin America: New Roles for the Public and Private Sectors* (Westport, CT: Praeger, 1994); Manuel Sanchez and Rossana Corona, eds., *Privatization in Latin America* (Baltimore: Johns Hopkins University Press, 1994); Ahmed Galal, Leroy Jones, Pankaj Tandon, and Ingo Vogelsang, *Welfare Consequences of Selling Public Enterprises* (New York: Oxford University Press, 1994); Rolf Luders and Dominique Hachette, *Privatization in Chile: An Economic Appraisal* (San Francisco: ICS Press, 1993).

9. Joan M. Nelson, ed., *Economic Crisis and Policy Choice: The Politics of Adjustment in the Third World* (Princeton: Princeton University Press, 1990); Joan M. Nelson, ed., *A Precarious Balance: Democracy and Economic Reforms in Latin America* (San Francisco: ICS Press, 1994); John Williamson, ed., *The Political Economy of Pol-*

icy Reform (Washington, D.C.: Institute of International Economics, 1994); Anne O. Krueger, *Political Economy of Policy Reform in Developing Countries* (Cambridge, MA: MIT Press, 1993); Stephan Haggard and Robert Kaufman, eds., *The Politics of Economic Adjustment: International Constraints, Distributive Conflicts, and the State* (Princeton: Princeton University Press, 1992); Merilee S. Grindle and John W. Thomas, *Public Choices and Policy Change: The Political Economy of Reform in Developing Countries* (Baltimore: Johns Hopkins University Press, 1991).

   10. Felipe de la Balze, *Remaking the Argentine Economy* (New York: Council on Foreign Relations Press, 1995); Nora Lustig, *Mexico: The Remaking of an Economy* (Washington: Brookings Institution, 1992); Pedro Aspe, *Economic Transformation the Mexican Way* (Cambridge, MA: MIT Press, 1993); Maria Lorena Cook, Kevin Middlebrook, and Juan Molinar Horcasitas, eds., *The Politics of Economic Restructuring: State-Society Relations and Regime Change in Mexico* (La Jolla: Center for U.S.-Mexican Studies, University of California, San Diego, 1994); Dwight S. Brothers and Adele E. Wick, eds., *Mexico's Search for a New Development Strategy* (Boulder: Westview Press, 1990); Peter M. Garber, ed., *The Mexico-U.S. Free Trade Agreement* (Cambridge, MA: MIT Press, 1993.

   11. See, for example, the reading of events in several countries by contributors to Felipe Larrain and Marcelo Selowsky, eds., *The Public Sector and the Latin American Crisis;* see also Fundación de Investigaciones Económicas Latinoamericanas, *El Fracaso del Estatismo: Una Propuesta para la Reforma del Sector Público Argentino* (Buenos Aires: Editorial Sudamericana/Planeta, 1987); and Fundación de Investigaciones Económicas Latino Americanas, *Los Costos del Estado Regulador* (Buenos Aires: Ediciones Manantial, 1989); Moises Naim and Ramon Piñango, *El Caso Venezuelano: Una Ilusión de Armonia,* passim.

   12. Peter B. Evans, Dietrich Rueschemeyer, and Theda Skocpol, eds., *Bringing the State Back In* (Cambridge: Cambridge University Press, 1985). That the state has long been recognized in Latin American development studies as a critical variable is illustrated by the uniquely, even startlingly, candid picture of the state painted by a team of foreign specialists in the World Bank's Economic and Technical Mission to Cuba, *Report on Cuba* (Washington D.C.: World Bank, 1951).

   13. The odd assortment of enterprises operated by the Peruvian state, for example, ranged from basic public utilities to mining and petroleum to airlines and shipping to banks to plantations to a great variety of industrial firms (cement, iron and steel, textiles, papermaking, plywood, chemicals and fertilizers, food processing) and even included trading companies, fishing fleets, hotels, restaurants, and a pornographic motion picture theater. See Armando Gallegos, Amparo Lozano, and Jhony Pacheco, *Mapa Económico Financiero de la Actividad Empresarial del Estado Peruano* (Lima: Escuela Superior de Administración Nacional, 1985). An equivalent dispersion of public sector resources was present in Mexico where, according to a tally made by the Office for Public Sector Studies of the Institute of Latin American Studies of the University of Texas, the number of state-owned and mixed enterprises reached almost 1,500 by the end of the José Lopez Portillo administration.

   14. In some instances, interventionism antedated the years of the Great Depression and World War II: e.g., that born of the revolutionary agenda in Mexico

after 1917 and the early twentieth-century efforts by Brazil to prop up the coffee market. As I endeavored to show in William Glade, *The Latin American Economies: A Study of their Institutional Evolution* (New York: American Book Company, 1969), the interventionism that became so pronounced from the 1930s onwards had a good many antecedents in prior decades, to say nothing of the policy bias of the whole colonial period. See also Rosemary Thorp, ed., *Latin America in the 1930s: The Role of the Periphery in World Crisis* (New York: St. Martin's Press, 1984).

15. The main official rationale, elaborated from the original CEPAL doctrine, is well presented in "Public Enterprises: Their Present Significance and their Potential in Development," *Economic Bulletin for Latin America*, vol. XVI, no. 1, 1971, pp. 1–70. But the case for direct intervention went beyond this; see, for example, Alexander Eckstein, "Individualism and the Role of the State in Economic Growth," *Economic Development and Cultural Change*, vol. 6, 1958, pp. 81–7; L. Mark, "The Favored Status of the State Entrepreneur in Economic Development Programs," *Economic Development and Cultural Change*, vol. 7, no. 2, 1959, pp. 422–30; and Alexander Gerschenkron, *Economic Backwardness in Historical Perspective*, chapter 1. This is not to mention, of course, the appeal of confiscation for reasons developed by Martin Bronfenbrenner in his famous article on that subject, "The Appeal of Confiscation in Economic Development," *Economic Development and Cultural Change*, April 1995, pp. 201–18. Harry Johnson's own essay in Harry G. Johnson, ed., *Economic Nationalism in Old and New States* (Chicago: University of Chicago Press, 1967) is much to the point here.

16. Peter Evans in *Dependent Development: the Alliance of Multinational, State, and Local Capital in Brazil* (Princeton: Princeton University Press, 1979) examines some of these relations in Brazil. A point of friction, however, was that the multinational corporation, with very different and internationally defined opportunity costs from the local partners, whether private or public, was often less beholden to Latin American policymakers than were local investors—particularly when so many attractive investment opportunities beckoned from Europe and, in time, Asia.

17. Representative of the earliest works of this genre are George Wythe, *Industry in Latin America* (New York: Columbia University Press, 1946), and Sanford Mosk, *Industrial Revolution in Mexico* (Berkeley: University of California Press, 1950). Close on the heels of these came Frank Brandenburg, *The Development of Latin American Private Enterprise* (Washington, D.C.: National Planning Association, 1964); Albert Lauterbach, *Enterprise in Latin America: Business Attitudes in a Developing Economy* (Ithaca, NY: Cornell University Press, 1966); Alcira Leiserson, *Notes on the Process of Industrialization in Argentina, Chile, and Peru* (Berkeley: Institute of International Studies, University of California, 1966); Seymour M. Lipset and Aldo Solari, eds., *Elites in Latin America* (New York: Oxford University Press, 1967); and Nathaniel Leff, *Economic Policy-Making and Development in Brazil, 1947–1964* (New York: Wiley, 1968). During the 1960s, ECLA sponsored and published a series of country studies of entrepreneurship, an example of which is Aaron Lipman, *El Empresario Industrial en America Latina: Colombia* (Santiago: CEPAL, 1963). Slightly later came Henry Kirsch, *Industrial Development in a Traditional Society: The Conflict of Entrepreneurship and Modernization in Chile*

(Gainesville: University Presses of Florida, 1977); Frits Wils, *Industrialization, Industrialists, and the Nation-State in Peru* (Berkeley: Institute of International Studies, University of California, 1979); Fred Jongkind, *Venezuelan Industrialization: Dependent or Autonomous* (Amsterdam: Centro de Estudios y Documentación Latinoamericanos [CEDLA], 1981); and Jorge Hidrobo, *Power and Industrialization in Ecuador* (Boulder: Westview Press, 1992). The Mexican economy is especially well covered. See, for example, Flavia Derossi, *The Mexican Entrepreneur* (Paris: Organization for Economic Development and Cooperation, 1971); Dale Story, *The State and Public Policy in Mexico* (Austin: University of Texas Press, 1986); and Roderic Ai Camp, *Entrepreneurs and Politics in Twentieth-Century Mexico* (New York: Oxford University Press, 1989). Among other insightful studies of industrial policy in the same country are Merle Kling, *A Mexican Interest Group in Action* (Englewood Cliffs, NJ: Prentice Hall, 1961); Timothy King, *Mexico: Industrialization and Trade Policies since 1940* (Oxford: Oxford University Press, 1970); Robert Shafer, *Mexican Business Organizations* (Syracuse: Syracuse University Press, 1973); John F. H. Purcell and Susan K. Purcell, "Mexican Business and Public Policy," in James Malloy, ed., *Authoritarianism and Corporatism in Latin America* (Pittsburgh: University of Pittsburgh Press, 1977); René Villareal, "The Policy of Import Substituting Industrialization, 1929–1975," in José Luis Reyna and Richard Weinart, eds., *Authoritarianism in Mexico* (Philadelphia.: Institute for the Study of Human Issues, 1977); Menno Vellinga, *Economic Development and the Dynamics of Class: Industrialization, Power and Control in Monterrey, Mexico* (Assen: Van Gorcum, 1979); Carlos Arriola, *Las Organizaciones Empresariales y el Estado* (Mexico, D.F.: Fondo de Cultura Económica, 1981); and Stephen H. Haber, *Industry and Underdevelopment: The Industrialization of Mexico, 1890–1940* (Stanford: Stanford University Press, 1989). Later examples of studies that illuminate the conditions of policymaking in Latin America are Richard D. Mallon and Juan V. Sourrouille, *Economic Policymaking in a Conflict Society: The Argentine Case* (Cambridge, MA: Harvard University Press, 1975); Jean Carriere, ed., *Industrialization and the State in Latin America* (Amsterdam: CEDLA, 1979); Albert Berry, *Essays on Industrialization in Colombia* (Tempe, AZ: Center for Latin American Studies, Arizona State University, 1983); E. Basualdo and Daniel Azpiazu, *Cara y Contracara de los Grupos Económicos: Estado y Promoción Industrial en la Argentina* (Buenos Aires: Cantaro Editores, 1989); Paul H. Lewis, *The Crisis of Argentine Capitalism* (Chapel Hill: University of North Carolina Press, 1990); Pierre Ostiguy, *Los Capitanes de la Industria: Grandes Empresarios, Política y Economía en la Argentina de los Años 80* (Buenos Aires: Legasa, 1990); Moisés Naim, *Las Empresas Venezolanas: Su Gerencia* (Caracas: Ediciones IESA, 1989); Ben Ross Schneider, *Politics Within the State: Elite Bureaucrats and Industrial Policy in Authoritarian Brazil* (Pittsburgh: University of Pittsburgh Press, 1991); and Stephan Haggard, Chung Lee, and Sylvia Maxfield, eds., *The Politics of Finance in Developing Countries* (Ithaca, NY: Cornell University Press, 1993).

18. John J. Johnson in his classic *Political Change in Latin America* (Stanford: Stanford University Press, 1958) anticipates in an interesting way the argument advanced much later by Benedict Anderson in *Imagined Communities: Reflections on the Origins and Spread of Nationalism* (London: Verso, 1991). Harry Johnson's

essay on economic nationalism, cited in note 15, complements the picture and fleshes out the political dynamics of state expansion, as does an important recent World Bank study, *Bureaucrats in Business: The Economics and Politics of Government Ownership* (New York: Oxford University Press, 1995).

19. William A. Niskanen, Jr., *Bureaucracy and Representative Government* (Chicago: Aldine, 1971); Anthony Downs, *Inside Bureaucracy* (Boston: Little, Brown and Co., 1967); Francis Rourke, *Bureaucracy, Politics, and Public Policy* (Boston: Little, Brown and Co., 1969); James Buchanan, Robert D. Tollison, and Gordon Tullock, eds., *Toward A Theory of the Rent-Seeking Society* (College Station, TX: Texas A&M University Press, 1980).

20. Joseph La Palombara in *Bureaucracy and Political Development* (Princeton: Princeton University Press, 1963) captures much of the process at work in developing countries in general, providing a larger backdrop for the interpretation offered by Albert O. Hirschman in "The Political Economy of Import-Substituting Industrialization in Latin America," *Quarterly Journal of Economics*, vol. 82, no. 1, 1968, 2–32. The country studies that illustrate the process and its results are numerous, those focusing on Peru exemplifying the literature particularly well. In addition to the works mentioned in note 17, see also Pedro Pablo Kuczynski, *Peruvian Democracy under Economic Stress: An Account of the Belaunde Administration, 1963–1968* (Princeton: Princeton University Press, 1977); Richard C. Webb, *Government Policy and the Distribution of Income in Peru, 1963–1973* (Cambridge, MA: Harvard University Press, 1977); and E. V. K. FitzGerald, *The Political Economy of Peru, 1956–78: Economic Development and the Restructuring of Capital* (Cambridge: Cambridge University Press, 1979). A particularly insightful study of Brazil is Ben Ross Schneider, *Politics Within the State.* For another look in another setting at the topic covered by Richard Webb, see Pedro Aspe Armella and Paul Sigmund, eds., *The Political Economy of Income Distribution in Mexico* (New York: Holmes & Meier, 1984).

21. Michal Kalecki, *The Last Phase in the Transformation of Capitalism* (New York: Monthly Review Press, 1972). Barry Ames in *Political Survival: Politicians and Public Policy in Latin America* (Berkeley: University of California Press, 1987) shows how political leaders have used public expenditures as key policy instruments but for fine-tuning the polity rather than for macroeconomic management.

22. This is not to deny the relevance of the cultural approach, which has been put forward so compellingly by Howard Wiarda and Glen Dealy, among others, but it is to suggest that the determining factors inhered in the structure of the world economic system.

23. Two volumes trace the rise of a state-managed development process in a variety of regions: Hugh G. J. Aitkin, ed., *The State and Economic Growth* (New York: Social Science Research Council, 1959), and Gustav Ranis, ed., *Government and Economic Development* (New Haven, CT: Yale University Press, 1971).

24. Still helpful in understanding this process are Rudolf Goldscheid, "A Sociological Approach to the Problem of Public Finance," reprinted in Richard Musgrave and Alan T. Peacock, eds., *Classics in the Theory of Public Finance* (New York: St. Martin's Press, 1994), and the concept of fiscal sociology Joseph Schumpeter put forward in "The Crisis of the Tax State," another classic that was reprinted in *International Economic Papers*, no. 4, 1954.

25. James O'Connor, *The Fiscal Crisis of the State* (New York: St. Martin's Press, 1973. This would need emendation to apply to the case of newly industrialized and less developed countries, but this would merely involve amplifying his concept of social capital to include a broader set of the institutional accoutrements of industrial capitalism.

26. Of particular help in discerning the institutional geography of the globalized economy are recent volumes of the annual *World Investment Report* produced by the Economic and Social Development Department of the United Nations.

27. See Angus Maddison et al., *The Political Economy of Poverty, Equity, and Growth: Brazil and Mexico* (New York: Oxford University Press, 1992), which indicates that the two largest economies of the region, both of which were afflicted with an ample assortment of public sector and market failures, were, from 1929 to the early 1980s, among the fastest growing economies of the world, with quite respectable gains in total factor productivity.

28. The allusion here is not only to the work of John R. Commons, Douglass North, and others who have written in a kindred vein but also to a large and diverse body of insightful literature that comes out of both development experience and economic theorizing: e.g., Vincent Ostrom, David Feeny, and Hartmut Picht, eds., *Rethinking Institutional Analysis and Development: Issues, Alternatives, and Choices* (San Francisco: ICS Press, 1988); Jerald Hage and Kurt Finsterbusch, *Organizational Change as a Development Strategy: Models and Tactics for Improving Third World Organizations* (Boulder: Lynne Rienner, 1987); Arturo Israel, *Institutional Development: Incentives to Performance* (Baltimore: Johns Hopkins University Press, 1987). On the theoretical side, see, for example, John E. Tomer, *Organizational Capital: The Path to Higher Productivity and Well Being* (New York: Praeger, 1987), and Yuichi Shionoya and Mark Perlman, eds., *Innovation in Technology, Industries, and Institutions: Studies in Schumpeterian Perspectives* (Ann Arbor: University of Michigan Press, 1994).

29. U.S. assistance to the Mexicans for setting up the Altos Hornos steel mill, the Brazilians for establishing the Volta Redonda steel project, or the Peruvians for getting a fishing industry underway did not come until the war years.

6

Argentina: The Politics of Economic Liberalization

Pablo Gerchunoff and Juan Carlos Torre

The process of economic change taking place in Argentina in recent years is part of a more general regional trend. Since the mid-1980s a surge of structural reforms have radically transformed the economic institutions established after World War II. Structural reforms came about as a result of two parallel developments. The first was the learning process spurred by the acute economic emergency that came in the wake of the foreign debt crisis. Repeated failures to correct macroeconomic imbalances through short-term adjustment policies increased pressures for more comprehensive solutions. At the same time, a powerful consensus began to build around the neoliberal discourse that dominated economic thinking within international financial institutions and within government circles in creditor nations. According to this view, the macroeconomic imbalances experienced by Latin American countries were caused by their dysfunctional inward-looking and state-led patterns of development. The 1985 Baker Plan summarized this diagnosis and advocated the rationalization and reduction of the economic role of the state and closer integration into the world economy.[1]

These policy developments—the search for more radical solutions on the part of Latin American policymakers and the structural adjustment programs recommended by multilateral credit organizations—converged at a single point: the demand and supply of financial lending. The conditions attached to International Monetary Fund (IMF) and World Bank loans—that structural reforms be put in place—became, then, a vehicle through which neoliberal economic policies made their way onto Latin American government agendas. One after another, Latin American countries began to implement far-reaching reform packages, the final goal of which was to reverse the historical role of the state as the engine of economic development as well as to alter the traditional balance between domestic and international markets.

Although the current direction of economic change in most of Latin America is similar, the extent and rhythm of implementation of reforms has been predictably different. Each country has shifted course under particular economic and political circumstances. This chapter describes and explains the reform of Argentine economic institutions, emphasizing the ways in which it was influenced by the context of policy choices. The approach leaves aside the normative perspective, which, claiming the principle of the universal rationality of structural reforms, tends to focus on the analysis of whether a given strategy fits or doesn't fit a prescriptive model. Instead of considering the process in terms of the transition to the market economy, the focus will be upon the concrete dynamics of the economic transformation, with the aim of distinguishing the distinctive traits of Argentina's emerging economic order.

A useful point of departure for understanding the peculiarities of the Argentine economic transformation is Albert Hirschman's distinction between chosen and pressing problems.[2] Chosen problems are those decision makers select to tackle based on their own preferences; pressing problems are forced upon policymakers through pressure from actors outside government or because of an impending emergency. Using this distinction, two contrasting contexts for reform policies can be identified.[3] In the first, government leaders face an economic situation that, despite recurrent signs of imbalance, is still considered manageable. Under such circumstances, they decide to act preventively, putting forward policy changes aimed at correcting the macroeconomic imbalances. It can be said that these policy changes have the characteristic of a chosen problem because decision makers retain the capacity to define the scope and pace of the implementation. In the second, government leaders are confronted with a pressing problem that forcefully invades their agendas. A hyperinflationary crisis that threatens to bring about social chaos or institutional instability by dramatically undermining the state's capacity to extract resources and provide services would be an example. In the face of an emergency, the conviction that it is necessary to act on all fronts surfaces quickly and schematically, paving the way for launching real policy reforms. In this context, debates about the scope and pace of the reform process become irrelevant, and reform measures have a more reactive than proactive character, being inextricably linked to government efforts to regain control over a potential economic crisis.

These contrasting contexts of policy choice have clear implications for the political dynamics of the decision-making process and the nature of the reform initiatives. In a noncrisis context, reform policies are one of a number of alternative options; their chances will depend greatly upon the political ability of decision makers to organize bureaucratic resources and mobilize societal support. In a crisis context, the persuasive force of circumstances opens by itself the political space for reformist policymaking. The nature of the reform policies, when pushed through under strong pressure, will be characterized by a significant amount of improvisation and little evaluation of costs and benefits. Contrary to what tends to be the case when policymakers have more room for maneuvering, reform initiatives will be considerably simpler in technical and administrative terms and will bear the imprint of the urgencies that dominate the context of policy choice.

When reforms are chosen as part of a preventive strategy, the decision-making process may be more demanding politically but, in principle, the quality of the reform design is higher. Quite the opposite occurs when reforms are launched in the face of a crisis, where there is always a tendency to underestimate the complexity of adjustment. These contrasts became apparent in the process of Argentina's economic transformation because, as we shall see, it was carried out in different contexts of policy reform.

Launching the Structural Reforms

Although Argentina took similar initiatives in previous years, the process of economic transformation began in earnest at the end of 1989 when the Carlos Menem administration launched a combination of extremely radical stabilization policies and structural reforms.[4] To account for this dramatic shift toward pro-market strategies, two sets of factors are relevant.

The first is the hyperinflationary surge that derailed the Argentine economy in the May–August 1989 period and that literally led to the collapse of public finances. The crisis dramatically ended a series of failed stabilizing efforts made during the second half of the 1980s. At the beginning of 1989, a deteriorated fiscal situation, growing government indebtedness at increasingly unfavorable terms, and low international reserves were compounded by the uncertainty about who would win the forthcoming presidential election. As a result, there was a generalized tendency to convert australes to dollars, the value of which rose twenty-five-fold against the australe in only six months. The inflation rate, which averaged 14 percent a month in 1988, topped 200 percent in July 1989.

The fiscal and financial collapse resulted in the government's inability to ensure the functioning of the state's apparatus or even to guarantee law and order. This dark scenario forced President Raúl Alfonsín to resign from office five months ahead of schedule, precipitating the inauguration of Menem, who had been elected in May. Faced with a crisis that could potentially mean political annihilation, the new Peronist president, surprising followers and adversaries alike, jettisoned his populist electoral program and adopted neoliberal policies in an attempt to secure the support of the major foreign and domestic economic agents who controlled the market and determined the sustainability of the government.

The second set of factors affecting the shift to a pro-market strategy was a classic problem of credibility. Menem was now trying to resolve an economic crisis by adopting as his own the very policies that he and his political movement had traditionally repudiated. Indeed, a major determinant in the onset of hyperinflation was the uncertainty that infected financial markets when preelection polls anticipated the imminent victory of a Peronist presidential candidate. This evoked the traumatic memory of the most recent experience of Peronism in government between 1973 and 1976. Menem's political credentials and his electoral message only augmented the fears. When Menem announced policy promises diametrically opposed to the ones that had been instrumental in his victory, a problem of credibility naturally arose.

Upon his inauguration, Menem confronted two challenges that pushed him to act promptly and audaciously: the macroeconomic fiscal crisis and the political problem of credibility. Understandably enough, the collapse of public finances called for quick action and compelled the president to use all the means at his disposal. But the need to dispel deep doubts had the same effect because it forced Menem to go further than he would have in the absence of a credibility gap.[5] In fact, Menem's first decisions were crafted so as to provide clear signals of his present commitments and future intentions for the purpose of gaining the elusive confidence of the business community. Shortly before taking office, Menem disclosed to the press that his future finance minister would be a top executive of the Argentine transnational holding company Bunge & Born. He was rewarded with a positive reaction in the financial markets. Although the Bunge & Born executive was soon to be replaced, the commitment underlying his nomination was preserved. Except for a brief period, Menem excluded Peronists from the management of economic policy, the handling of which he entrusted to figures appointed with the consent of the business community. In economic matters, the Peronists ended up being the guests of their own government.

Simultaneous with the launching of stabilization measures, structural reforms began to take shape with the congressional approval of two key pieces of legislation: the Economic Emergency Law and the State Reform Law. The first dealt a serious blow to the heart of Argentine post-war capitalism by suspending for 180 days—which would later be extended indefinitely—industrial and export promotion subsidies and the preferential purchase regime for local manufacturers. It also authorized personnel dismissals in the public sector and canceled some special salary systems for state employees. The State Reform Law marked the beginning of the end of another traditional pillar of Argentine development by providing the legal framework to privatize a large number of state enterprises and services including the telephone, airline, railroad, shipping, and highway companies; the public television and radio stations; and several petrochemical firms. Through the enactment of these laws, within a peremptory term and with no amendments, the congress delegated to the executive branch the power to legislate the details of the new policies by decree. Besides granting these institutional powers, the congress further expanded executive privilege by passing a law that increased from five to nine the number of Supreme Court justices. After the nomination and appointment of justices sympathetic to his administration, Menem managed to block any potential veto by the Supreme Court in the interests of those affected by his policy initiatives. Soon he accumulated all the institutional means necessary to concentrate decision-making power in the executive and set the stage for sweeping economic reforms.

The daunting problems that Menem faced at the beginning of his term can account for the scope and timing of his policy choices. However, in order to understand why he was able to carry out his policies, it is necessary to consider additional factors: the effects of the acute economic emergency on public tolerance for hardship, the discrediting of the prevailing economic institutions, and Menem's political capital as a leader.

Considering these factors in order, it should be pointed out that the threat of social chaos and institutional breakdown triggered by hyperinflation not only led Menem to make a bold U-turn toward radical economic reforms, it also increased public tolerance for policies that had been strongly resisted during the previous government. The thirteen general strikes launched against the adjustment efforts of the Alfonsín administration are proof of the extent of this opposition. To place Menem's political advantage in context, we should recall one of the classical dilemmas of implementing reform policies—their costs are felt immediately and tend to be concentrated while their benefits surface only after some delay and are more diffuse in nature.

Consequently, one can expect a reformist government to face the resistance of those who consider themselves negatively affected well before it is able to mobilize the support of the prospective beneficiaries of the reforms. Because in a democratic system political leaders depend on the backing of public opinion and on the results of forthcoming elections, this asymmetrical relationship between winners and losers constitutes a serious obstacle to reform policies.

However, the evaluation of costs and benefits of structural changes may be altered by certain circumstances. Among them are those in which reform programs are implemented as an integral part of a stabilization

package aimed at overcoming a grave economic emergency. After suffering the devastating effects of hyperinflation, even the prospect of economic stability will produce a feeling of relief that overrides the distributional consequences of reform policies. In other words, the cost of
economic changes and the social reactions to them are not always closely
correlated. Rather, they are mediated by evaluations of the maintenance
of the status quo. Consequently, as in Argentina in 1989, reformist governments may count on the acquiescence of losers who perceive that reforming the status quo, despite the sacrifices and the financial hardship it
imposes on them, is the best available alternative to stop further deterioration of their economic position.[6]

Second, it should be underscored that the historical performance of the
economic institutions to be reformed in Argentina had been highly unsatisfactory. In contrast to Brazil, for instance, Argentina's inward-ori-
ented and state-led pattern of development was not associated in the
public mind with a long trend of economic growth. The last fifteen years
had been particularly marked by wide economic fluctuations, the deterioration in the provision of public utilities, and a diffused sense of economic decline. These experiences were fertile soil for the emergence and
acceptance of a popular vision, borrowed from the preachings of the neoliberal ideologues, who attributed the macroeconomic disequilibrium to
the pathology of a statist and protectionist economic system. In such a
context, the advocates of old policies and practices could not mount a
credible and coordinated defense and were forced to retreat. The general
discrediting of the prevailing economic order gave Menem great leeway
to initiate his reform policies with little opposition.

A third factor played the final key role: Menem's capacity to abandon
the traditional postures of the Peronist ideology and to embrace new policies and forge new alliances without losing the support of his followers.
To account for this, we must turn our attention to what originally generated the distrust and reservations of the private sector: Menem's political
credentials.

Menem gained a position of preeminence in the 1988 primary election
of the Peronist presidential candidate, and he won it by appealing to a
plebeian and messianic populism, with deep roots within the Peronist
movement. Thus, with Menem's victory, for the first time since Perón's
death in 1974, Peronism was unified around a leadership accepted by all
the internal factions of the movement. Consequently, when he took office,
Menem brought with him the political capital necessary to legitimize his
policy options. Had they been carried out by a political leader without
Menem's credentials, his innovations in policies and alliances would not
have been equally well received. In the critical hours of 1989 we saw an
old political paradox come true: Leaders from the left can readily adopt

right-wing policies without unleashing the disapproval of the left and vice versa.[7] Menem's successful turnabout proved that a president from a populist tradition could launch a nonpopulist economic strategy and come through with flying colors.

Nevertheless, as a consequence of the government's policies, there were major strains among rank-and-file Peronists, but dissidents lacked compelling political alternatives. Some unions and party members pressed for confrontational strategies, but most were unwilling to take a course of action that could jeopardize their access to the political and economic resources of state patronage. Menem exploited this opportunity and, skillfully applying the politics of stick and carrot, managed to keep his followers in line. Only a handful of deputies dared to challenge official policies in congress, and the majority of trade union leaders chose to collaborate or to adopt a wait-and-see attitude. As a result, Menem was able to build an unprecedented and powerful government coalition that combined the institutional power of the Peronist electoral majority with the backing of the major economic groups.

In brief, the sociopolitical landscape we have just outlined—the effects of hyperinflation upon public tolerance for hardship, the general discredit in which existing economic institutions were held, and Menem's leadership in the Peronist movement—opened a window of opportunity for policy changes that would otherwise have been politically unfeasible.

The First Wave of Structural Reforms

In what follows we focus on the first wave of structural reforms implemented during the initial phase of the Menem administration between 1989 and 1990.[8] In a situation less characterized by pressing fiscal problems, stabilization and reform policies can conceivably be addressed as sequential tasks, with stabilization as the first step. However, in the Argentina where Menem came to power in mid-1989, the macroeconomic context was quite different, and this had important consequences. When economic emergency forces governments to implement stabilization and reform initiatives together as part of a single policy package, the reforms tend to be made with a view toward achieving stabilization. This means that they are aimed primarily at reducing fiscal deficits and inflation rather than at increasing the global productivity and competitiveness of the economy.

Privatization Policy

The rush to privatize was so great that within a year, by October 1990, almost all the targeted public enterprises had been transferred to the private sector. The list of assets to be privatized in the first phase included the telephone and airline companies, which Menem made paradigmatic of his new economic course. These public utilities monopolies received special priority for both economic and political reasons.[9] First, those companies had been on Alfonsín's privatization agenda. The Radical president had tried without success—because of Peronist opposition in congress—to sell 40 percent of each to private operators. For a president eager to make clear that his new pro-market convictions were to be taken seriously, the failed attempts of his predecessor constituted in practice an unavoidable point of departure. Furthermore, the sharp deterioration in services provided by the state-owned companies and their tainted public image made the privatization policy a popular initiative. Finally, considering the government's financial urgencies, the privatization of the public utilities monopolies was expected to produce significant liquid funds with which to reduce substantially foreign debt obligations.

The literature on the privatization of public enterprises abounds in arguments in favor of the state's retaining considerable stock holdings, of restructuring prior to sale, and of transparent and competitive bids.[10] Menem's government took heed of none of these recommendations. When the time came to make the decisions, the intentions of the authorities were made evident in the privatization methodology. They wanted to sell state assets as quickly as possible and to leave no doubt about their firm commitment to radically change the role of the state.

The context of the privatization process was disadvantageous to the government: Its imperative need to collect funds quickly and gain credibility gave the potential buyers great leverage. The government had to create a set of protective regulations and guarantees to facilitate access by the new private owners to market reserves and to quasi-rents. As a result, the state-owned companies were sold under warranty that all the benefits of monopoly would be maintained. The sale of the state-owned companies under different terms, that is, in a competitive environment, would have brought considerably lower prices for the assets, which was not acceptable given the government's fiscal urgencies.

Thus, privatization policies led to a change in property relations but not in the relationship between the firm and the market. The newly privatized firms operate within a framework in which rules of market competition are as alien as they were under the previous policy of protected industrialization. The survival of this old pattern was not counterbalanced by the creation of effective regulatory frameworks. The haste with which the privatization policies were adopted and the long-standing weaknesses of the Argentine state worked against the creation of regulatory agencies capable of controlling the market power of the new private companies or of promoting policies for stimulating competition.

Trade Liberalization

Trade reform is another clear example of the subordination of reform policies to the demands of the stabilization policy. Upon taking office, the new economic authorities made their goals public: to cut import tariffs to 20 percent and to eliminate most nontariff barriers (quotas, licenses, and import bans). To achieve these goals, they set a four-year deadline. Curiously enough, seen from the perspective of the present, the administration's approach to economic issues indicates that it wanted to bring about a relatively gradual opening of the economy to foreign competition. Yet this step-by-step approach to trade reform could not be sustained. By the end of 1990, all quantitative barriers on imports had been virtually lifted. As for tariffs, the terms set for their reduction were shortened. In October 1989 the average tariff was 26 percent; by the end of 1990 it was 17 percent. In March 1991 a new scheme was introduced for lowering tariffs on a gradual basis, with no tariffs on raw materials, 11 percent on industrial inputs, and 22 percent on manufactured goods. As a result, the average tariff dropped to 10 percent.[11]

Macroeconomic avatars accelerated the rhythm of the changes. But the responses by interest groups calling for trade reform were not always the same. In practice the tariff policy could contribute to economic stability in two ways: as a mechanism for disciplining domestic price makers and as a backup for achieving a balanced budget through import duties. This explains why throughout this agitated first phase there were several changes in policy. As they were moving towards trade liberalization and under pressure to meet their fiscal goals, they often resorted to increased nominal tariffs or to temporary import surcharges. Thus, between October 1989 and March 1991, the maximum and minimum tariffs were altered no less than eleven times. By the first quarter of 1991, the conflict over the tariff policy that dominated these marches and countermarches inclined toward a more open trade regime. The exigencies of the anti-inflationary struggle, along with the government's explicit willingness to demonstrate to local and international financial sectors the vigor of its new tenets, canceled any possibility of implementing a piecemeal strategy. As in the case of privatizations, changes in this policy area were fast and deep and had impacts far beyond short-term negative effects on public sector revenues. Even more important, they involved a high real cost in terms of productive resources: In the absence of complementary policies, they forced many business to close, generating high and long-lasting unemployment.

The Tax Reform

From the moment Menem took office, the need to balance public accounts and, consequently, to bolster tax revenues became a pressing issue. To do so, the economic authorities resorted to the same instruments that had often been used by the former administration: taxes that could provide prompt yields and were easy to control, such as taxes on agricultural exports and financial transactions. These instruments were useful to finance the posthyperinflation emergency for a very limited time and allowed the administration to gain time to prepare its tax reform bill.[12]

The new tax system was based on three major changes. The first was the concentration of the tax structure on a few taxes: the value-added tax and the income tax. For both, the tax base was expanded, tax rates were increased, and withholding mechanisms were broadened, which allowed better control. In addition, these taxes were supplemented with a fuel tax and customs duties. The tax reform effort initially rested upon the value-added tax, which was easier to collect; only later did the income tax become increasingly important.

The second major change was introduced by the Economic Emergency Law. As indicated, this law reduced partially or totally industrial and regional promotion subsidies, which, in general, contained important tax exemptions. This contributed to the increase of tax receipts and constituted a further signal of the new economic orientation: subsidies for investment promotion that undermined the tax base had to disappear.

The third change was institutional. A new criminal tax law was passed to ensure payment of taxes by the citizenry. Under the new law, the punishment for tax evasion was made harsher, and the tax collection agency was strengthened and entrusted with the collection of all taxes—including social security contributions. It should be underscored that this reform took a zigzag course dominated by fiscal urgencies. The priority was collecting taxes to finance a bankrupt state; long-term implications of the reform received only marginal attention. Neither the distributional consequences of the new tax structure nor the incentives for saving and investment it creased were central concerns of the government.

Evaluative Comments

In sum, structural reforms made their way into the Menem administration's agenda through a discourse advocating a new economic order centered on the market and foreign trade. However, the implementation of reforms was little influenced by this discourse, which was more than anything else part of the official strategy to gain credibility. In fact, the reform policies were just one of the instruments the government used to deal with the economic emergency. Under such circumstances, the government could not afford to make more meditated and technically complex decisions that might have improved the quality of the reforms.

The nature of the first reforms also reflected the weak credibility of Menem's government. His sudden conversion to economic liberalization raised doubts. Consequently, both foreign creditors and local economic groups began to exert pressure on the government in order to take advantage of Menem's political ability to neutralize the resistance of Peronism. The reform process could then be accelerated and eventually made irreversible. Thus, the idea that reforms had to be implemented no matter how began to take root, allowing Menem to gain reputation and the advocates of pro-market reforms to foreclose any potential attempt to turn back the clock.[13] Finally, the simultaneous character of reforms allowed the government to devise a strategy for negotiations in different areas with the most important economic groups. Thus, the big enterprises that were negatively affected by one reform—opening the economy— were compensated by another—the privatization policy. Consequently, how the reforms were packaged also played a role in the consolidation of Menem's newly gained economic support.

The Difficult Road to Economic Stabilization

Menem's political and ideological conversion was not enough to deactivate the state of alert among the business community. Prior experiences of failed attempts at economic stabilization made for deep-seated skepticism.

The First Failed Attempts at Stabilization

During the first eighteen months of Menem's term, a succession of three finance ministers struggled to control inflation through emergency taxes, adjustments in the exchange rate, and income policies negotiated with the private sector.[14] At the beginning, the monthly inflation rate was temporarily reduced from 200 percent to 6 percent. But between December 1989 and March 1990 speculation against the exchange rate triggered a new outbreak of hyperinflation that was followed by new emergency taxes, suspension of payments to suppliers, and deep cuts in public service expenditure. Faced with a desperate situation, the government forced the conversion of current-time deposits in the banking system to long-term dollar-denominated public bonds.

Although it dealt a severe blow to public confidence in the local banking system, this decision enabled economic authorities to initiate in

March 1990 a restrictive monetary policy that put an end to hyperinflation that very month. This was made possible because of the previous implementation of a floating exchange regime and because of the strict reduction of government payments to the level of fiscal revenues. Moreover, in order to reassure and attract investors, the restrictions on the movement of foreign and domestic capital were eliminated, and the remission of royalties abroad was made easier. Nevertheless, the results were again discouraging: The inflation rate remained high, 25 percent a month, and the economy went into recession, with investment dropping 10 percent.

The credibility the Menem administration acquired among domestic and international economic agents began to deteriorate as the stabilization attempts continued to fail. Monetary restriction led to excess demand for money, which in turn led to a large overvaluation of the domestic currency. When fiscal payments could no longer be postponed and the fiscal deficit climbed again, a new round of speculation against the exchange rate was inevitable. The third hyperinflation episode was less severe than the second, but its ultimate impact would be greater. In February 1991 Domingo Cavallo was appointed finance minister.

To that point, the failure of stabilization attempts overshadowed the performance of the economic reform that were heralded as the definitive solution to Argentina's chronic economic crisis. But their potential positive effects were not appreciated by the public, who were constantly subjected to increasingly radical measures in the context of a stagnant economy punctuated by recurrent inflationary episodes. Menem's honeymoon period began to fade. His government's popularity was at its lowest point in the first quarter of 1991.

Economic failure was compounded by growing rumors of corruption at high levels. In fact, the critical turning point in the difficult road to economic stabilization came only with the introduction of the so-called "Convertibility Plan" engineered by Cavallo in March 1991.

The Convertibility Plan

It is true that some of the measures taken earlier were instrumental to the Convertibility Plan, particularly the policy of accumulation of international reserves implemented in 1990. However, it would be a mistake to view the previous stabilization attempts as part of the same scheme. From the beginning, the Convertibility Plan stood out for its ambitious goals and radical instruments. Given that its objective was not only to reduce inflation but also to establish a new currency and exchange rate regime, it cannot be considered an ordinary stabilization program.

Rather, it should be viewed as a structural reform, like the privatization policies, trade reform, and deregulation.

The Convertibility Plan provided for a fully convertible currency pegged to the dollar and prohibited any currency emissions not backed by hard currency reserves in the Central Bank. The plan, established by congressional statute, eliminated government discretion over the monetary and exchange rate policy. The effect was similar to placing Argentina on a gold standard and limiting the Central Bank's role to that of a currency board. There are only a few cases of currency boards and convertibility regimes in the world: Gibraltar, Bermuda, Hong Kong, Estonia, and Lithuania. All resulted from exceptional situations, a state of emergency, or a combination of both. In some, such as the financial havens, this monetary and exchange rate policy was chosen because of its simplicity and expediency: However unsophisticated, it facilitates negotiations and, at the same time, does not clash with other goals. In other cases, convertibility was adopted as a last resort. Hong Kong's economic success is threatened by its imminent annexation to China, which has forced the government to peg the local currency to the issuing bank of an economically healthy country. In Estonia and Lithuania the situation is similar. The new national states created after the dissolution of the Soviet Union are still fragile and, consequently, so is confidence in their currencies.

In Argentina, the state's reputation and the credibility of its currency were severely tarnished by long-standing economic instability and, in particular, by the 1989 and 1990 hyperinflation episodes. Against such a backdrop, the logic behind the convertibility option rested on a strategy of "self-binding." Like Ulysses, who commanded that he be tied to the mast so that he could not steer toward the treacherous songs of the Sirens, the government gave up the use of key economic instruments to make more credible its commitment to fiscal and monetary discipline.[15]

The fixed exchange rate managed to stabilize the volatile expectations of the financial markets. On April 1, annual interest rates fell from 44 percent to 22 percent, while the value of the dollar remained stable. Inflation began to drop gradually but steadily. The first favorable results of this program, together with a standby credit granted by the IMF and the beginning of foreign debt rescheduling under the Brady Plan, increased confidence. Reversing initial pessimistic forecasts, the government won the mid-term elections in the third quarter of 1991 with 40.3 percent of the votes cast. The Radical Party, its main opposition, obtained 30.5 percent of the votes. The electorate chose to ignore blatant signs of corruption in official circles and voted for the new promises to achieve stability. The success in the battle against inflation and the electoral victory allowed Menem to regain control of the economic and political process.[16]

The Inflow of Foreign Capital

After three years of sustained decline in economic activity, the Menem administration might have expected a moderate reactivation of the economy. Unlike other anti-inflationary packages that encourage a contraction of aggregate demand, the Convertibility Plan combined orthodox and heterodox instruments with a view to expanding the economy. In fact, the promise to reach fiscal balance in the short term, the sine die pegging of the local currency to the U.S. dollar, and some informal pressures by economic authorities on powerful businessmen caused inflation to drop sharply. Within a very short time, the economic landscape changed completely. Companies stopped preventive price increases and bank deposits began to grow, allowing banks to start lending money again. Because of the virtual elimination of the inflationary tax, the purchasing power of the urban population rose. A reactivated economy went hand in hand with stability.

Yet it was not just a moderate reactivation. Its success in achieving stability allowed the Menem administration to take advantage of a favorable shift in international markets: As a result of a sharp fall in interest rates caused by recession in the developed economies, capital began to flow abroad in search of more attractive opportunities in the so-called "emerging markets."[17] At this point, Argentina was not only implementing the structural reforms recommended by the World Bank and the IMF, it also offered prospects of monetary and exchange rate stability. Moreover, the influx of foreign capital was accompanied by a vast inflow of Argentine funds returning from abroad, where they had been sent during the 1980s. These circumstances gave an extraordinary boost to the financing of aggregate demand.

However, they had a twofold negative counterpart. On the one hand, the rapid reactivation of the economy produced a relative price structure that deteriorated foreign competitiveness, which stimulated imports and discouraged exports. As a result, the trade deficit widened, introducing an element of uncertainty in the highly indebted Argentine economy. On the other hand, the wave of optimism accompanying the first results of the Convertibility Plan increased consumption among large sectors of the population, further intensifying the economy's chronic inability to save. In the long run, the noncompetitive price structure and the low level of savings raised doubts about the sustainability of the program.

But in the short run, the inflow of foreign funds could not have been more timely. Without it, the consequences of the trade imbalances and of the decline in the savings rate would have been even more serious. The fixed exchange rate could not have been maintained, inflation would have decreased at a slower pace, and the growth rate would have been lower. In fact, it was capital inflow that altered the course of the Argentine economy. The painful adjustment associated with the implementation of structural reforms was superseded by an expansionary process that would last almost four years.

The Happy Combination of Structural Adjustment and Economic Expansion

The new and now more nuanced economic landscape had two dimensions. First, between 1991 and 1994 GDP grew at a rate of 7.7 percent per year. The increase in GDP was boosted by consumption, which grew 40 percent, and by investment in machinery and equipment, which, having stopped dead during the fiscal crisis, grew significantly in response to the stabilized currency, resurgence of credit, and liberalization of trade. Notwithstanding the greater demand, inflationary results were excellent. The growth rate of consumer retail prices dropped from 171.7 percent in 1991 to 24.9 percent in 1992, 10.6 percent in 1993, and 3.9 percent in 1994. The boom in demand helped, in turn, to balance the fiscal deficit. In fact, a fiscal surplus was achieved in 1992 and 1993, largely because the reformed tax system centered on high excise taxes.[18]

The second dimension of the auspicious macroeconomic evolution relates to the hard conditions imposed by the new economic rules. Income distribution, which had worsened during the inflationary and recessive 1988–1990 period, did not improve in the 1991–1994 period. This is quite noteworthy if we take into account that the Argentine economy has always reduced inequalities during periods of prosperity and enhanced them during recessions.[19] In the new distributional pattern, the richest 10 percent segment of the population was the only one that conspicuously increased its share. Moreover, even though it took place in a context of decreasing inflation, the evolution of relative prices had an uneven impact on the population. The low-income strata benefited from stable food prices but were harmed by unemployment. Important segments of the middle class, for whom subsidized services were central, had to bear the increased costs of private services—especially health and education—and privatized public utilities. Wages and employment were also affected unevenly in different sectors. For activities connected closely with international trade, domestic economic expansion had an almost nonexistent impact. By contrast, opening the economy and fixing the exchange rate resulted in the simultaneous decline in wages and employment in the domestic sectors: Between 1991 and 1994 real wages dropped 17.2 percent and employment shrunk. Finally, although reactivation offered further business opportunities for self-employed workers, small entrepreneurs, and professionals, the improvement in tax management and control meant that these individuals had to start paying taxes that they had been evading.[20]

All in all, the balance of the asymmetrical effects of the economic program implemented between 1991 and 1994 was favorable to the government. The economy began to revolve around a positive feedback process: Foreign financing improved almost all the economic performance indicators and facilitated the implementation of reforms, which, in turn, galvanized confidence and stimulated the influx of fresh cash. Equally important was what happened at the symbolic level: The Menem administration effectively recast the framework of the economic debate. The main tenets of the Convertibility Plan—fiscal discipline and structural reforms—became a consensual standard against which all other programs of the major Argentine political contenders are measured.

The New Context of Economic Reforms

The Convertibility Plan and the improvement of economic indicators altered the context for policy choices within which structural reforms unfolded. The gravity of the problems that ravaged the first phase of the Menem administration—the fiscal crisis and the lack of credibility—lessened significantly yet temporarily. It can be said that the government was no longer operating in a context dominated by pressing problems. Its capacity to choose policies and to influence their content and the timing of their implementation increased. Greater fiscal resources and room for maneuvering provided a firmer foundation for the government to enhance the efficiency and political sustainability of the reform process. In turn, the macroeconomic logic established by the Convertibility Plan gave a new boost to structural reforms. By relinquishing monetary instruments to gain credibility, the government moved the center of gravity of economic policy.

Given the institutional arrangements that forbade the issue of new money to finance the public sector or devaluation, the management of macroeconomic imbalances would necessarily have to rely on instruments different from those applied in the past. Insufficient savings and relative price distortions—the two major problems that accompanied the Convertibility Plan for a long time—had to be tackled with commercial and fiscal policies and with structural reforms aimed at encouraging savings, productivity, and price flexibility. The economic authorities did use these policy instruments (in particular, structural reforms), which became a basic tool to accommodate the functioning of real economy to a fixed monetary rule.

The implementation of the second phase of economic reorganization was facilitated by the team of well-trained professional economists that

Cavallo brought with him to the ministry of finance. In its new position, the economic team improved the administrative and technical capacities of the government, thus reducing the permeability of the decision-making structure to pressures from nongovernmental actors.

Indeed, the general orientation of the changes under way would continue to be defined by the government's dependence on the interests and preferences of the big business groups and foreign creditors. However, these influences would no longer have direct access to the decision-making process. They were now mediated by the economic team, who sought to channel and redefine them according to the logic of economic rationality and to the political needs of Menem's administration. In spite of the fact that they agreed on the general course of the reform process, the economic team and the representatives of the business community would not always agree on the sequencing of reforms, the instruments for their implementation, or the distribution of reform costs.

Moderating Reform Costs

The change in the context of policy choice can be seen first with regard to structural adjustment costs. In fact, the policy directed toward expanding domestic demand associated with the Convertibility Plan mitigated the distributive costs of the reform process. In the literature on reform policies, the problem of compensation occupies a prominent place.[21]

From an economic viewpoint, compensation schemes, designed to alleviate the "social costs" of adjustment, used to be regarded as measures that put the consistency of reform programs at risk. Still, their presence or absence often makes all the difference in the political feasibility of structural changes. A major question for any government undertaking structural adjustments in a democratic setting is—according to John Waterbury—to calculate how a process will affect the various members of its ruling coalition. In Waterbury's view, the key to coalition management is to avoid alienating too many groups at once.[22] Thus, even when compensation schemes conflict with economic efficiency in a narrow sense, they may allow governments to ride out opposition and to buy support for the reform efforts.

Stability and the boom following the introduction of the Convertibility Plan sidelined the threat of a return to recession and put mechanisms in place to buffer the distributional consequences of the reform process. We have deliberately used the term "mechanisms" instead of "policies" to stress that we are referring to the indirect effects of macroeconomic decisions rather than to the direct effects of compensatory policies. Achieving the latter was conspicuously absent from the government agenda.[23] Still, stability and the policy of stimulating internal demand associated with the Convertibility Plan had an extra impact that contributed to moderating the structural reform costs.

The proportion of households below the poverty line in metropolitan Buenos Aires, which had peaked at 38 percent by the end of 1989, decreased to 14 percent in 1993. This reveals that in spite of the worsened income distribution, the benefits of the economic boom had reached the lowest levels of the social structure. The unemployment generated by privatizations, the opening of the economy, and to a lesser extent the reorganization of the public sector was more than compensated, in aggregate terms, by the impact of economic expansion on employment. Thus, the percentage of employed people grew from 35.7 percent in 1990 to 37.4 percent in 1993.[24] Finally, the economic reactivation attenuated business closings, which typically accompany trade liberalization policies.

Furthermore, the economic boom facilitated the implementation of a set of policies that had so far lacked financing and credibility. Greater fiscal affluence allowed the government to increase public expenditure, which had been severely restricted prior to the Convertibility Plan and to the massive inflow of capital. In particular, public expenditure increased considerably in the area of social policy, reaching a fifteen-year high in 1994.

Redesigning Reforms

After the inauguration of the Convertibility Plan, the government managed not only to mitigate adjustment costs but also to improve the design of structural reforms. The privatizations are a case in point. Although in the first stage of the privatization, the primacy of fiscal goals led to results that were almost incompatible with the creation of a competitive economy, in the second phase the privatizations were implemented in a more relaxed fiscal environment and focused more on improving productivity and efficiency. Furthermore, more competitive bidding processes improved the privatization procedures.

The privatization of the production, transportation, and distribution of electric energy and gas illustrates the new trend. In contrast to previous experiences, in these cases the sale of state assets was carried out by establishing regulatory frameworks aimed at promoting competitiveness and public utility rates that would not aggravate relative price distortions. Within a few years, these privatizations exhibited results in terms of service and costs that were in sharp contrast to the privatizations of the phone and airline companies. In addition, the second wave of privatizations was carried out in a more peaceful setting because the government's promises to distribute some of the new companies' shares among workers were fulfilled. Moreover, unions were given assistance so that they could participate in the purchase of state assets.[25]

With more room to maneuver, the government was able to improve the design of the reforms. No longer under pressure to overemphasize their pro-market credentials and with the advantage of an increasingly positive fiscal situation, the authorities sought to strengthen sustainability on the external side by means of specific policies aimed at reducing the trade deficit and meeting the demands of industrial entrepreneurs. Unilateral decisions made in the first years, for example in the opening of the economy, were partially reversed, and some moderate protective measures were taken in order to curb the avalanche of imports and prevent massive bankruptcies in the industrial sector. On the export side, the fiscal stimuli that had been suspended in 1991 were reintroduced and taxes affecting competitiveness were reduced. Moreover, certain measures in support of the industrial sector were reintroduced after having been canceled by the 1989 Economic Emergency Law, in particular, the automobile industry initiative, which brought back the old industrialist aspiration to modernize economic sectors under temporary protection.

The free trade zone established under Mercado Comun del Sur (Southern Common Market, or MERCOSUR) is another example of how the government revised its maximalist policies. Having inherited regional economic integration from the Alfonsín administration, Menem initially decided to deepen it and quicken its pace in order to—as in the case of the privatizations—ensure a rupture with the past. Highly ambitious goals were set, and the government mandated that all deadlines be met at any cost, even if haste affected the quality of the process. However, following the Convertibility Plan, the government began to show concern for rationalizing the process of economic integration, resorting to special regimes on certain products, safeguard clauses, quotas, and continued negotiations with the MERCOSUR member countries.

Redesigning reforms involved not only introducing some limits to the scope of economic liberalization but also deepening it in some areas. This was the case with the deregulation measures taken to promote competitiveness in the goods and services sectors sheltered from international trade, just as the opening to foreign trade had promoted competitiveness. Several measures were introduced by the end of 1991, which included the lifting of limiting regulations on retail trade operations, the practice of liberal professions, and the supply of insurance services; the dissolution of price-regulating bodies in some agriculture and livestock markets; and the creating of more flexible working conditions in ports and the promotion of competitiveness in the transport of cargo and passengers.

Negotiating Reforms

The policies launched by the Menem administration were not limited to macroeconomic management or to the redesign of structural reforms. The authorities also had to respond to interests groups who, as the climate of economic emergency abated, became increasingly demanding and outspoken and were in a better position to exert pressure. In fact, the profile of this second phase of the stabilization and structural adjustment program was also influenced by the changes in the political dynamics of the decision-making process. The implementation of reforms became politically arduous: The government was now, more often than not, compelled to negotiate with representatives of its own party in congress as well as with special interest groups.[26] The favorable economic situation removed the costs of structural adjustment from the forefront and facilitated better articulation of sectoral and political interests. Now the process of structural adjustment required more careful political management in order to maintain the government's coalition. By resorting to better packaging and sequencing of policy reform, Menem tried to alter the interest groups' strategy and avoid the risk of open confrontations.

The social security system reform process is a case in point.[27] The aim of the official project was to replace the old and bankrupt public pay-as-you-go scheme by a compulsory private fully capitalized system that would also provide for a minimum universal income. The reform blueprints were inspired by the Chilean experience. The project abandoned the principles of intergenerational solidarity and instead proposed an individual saving accounts system, administered by state-authorized pension funds among which workers could choose freely. As a byproduct, pension funds would serve to strengthen the long-run capital markets.

The shortcomings of the government initiative were basically two: first, the low priority given to equity considerations, which were reduced to a rather low universal minimum income; and second, the fiscal implications of the transition. Moving from a pay-as-you-go scheme to a fully capitalized system implies that today's workers, who will be accumulating financial assets for their accounts, will no longer be paying for today's pensioners. Consequently, pensioners become a fiscal liability, which causes problems for the management of public finances.

Parliamentary deliberations lasted almost two years and entailed various important changes in the official project. Legislators first favored workers who had retired under the previous system by acknowledging their past contributions. Then, the minimum universal income was increased. Later, the retirement age for women was reduced from 65 to 60 years. Finally—and this was the main change—the social security system ultimately approved by congress included both the old public pay-as-you-go scheme and the new private capitalized system and allowed workers to choose between them.

The law passed by congress improved the solvency of public finance in the long run, although to a lesser degree than the executive's initial project. In our opinion, there are two reasons that account for the authorities' departure from their original objectives. First, the current fiscal bonanza created room for negotiating that had been unthinkable before the success of the Convertibility Plan. Second, having already been made public, the reform had to be upheld; failure to do so would have brought about a loss of confidence, and, probably, lower external financing. The need to display a successful and uninterrupted process of structural reforms had become essential to preserve the political credibility of Menem's government.

A vital element of the reform was the parallel privatization of the state oil giant Yacimientos Petrolíferos Fiscales (YPF), the highest-priced state asset sold. The privatization of YPF had begun in previous years with the partial sale of oil and gas fields, refineries, and transport fleets and a deep restructuring of the company as part of the structural reform of the hydrocarbons market. In 1993, the year of the social security reform, this process was completed with the sale of a major portion of its stock package on the New York market. In contrast to other privatizations, in which proceeds were used to finance public expenditure, most of the resources obtained were used to cancel state debts with pensioners in an attempt to neutralize their opposition to the social security reform. YPF shares were also distributed among some provincial governments that had long been creditors of the central administration, with the aim of securing the support of their deputies in congress.

A second example of the new political context of reforms is the relationship between government and unions. By 1989, the prevailing attitudes among union leaders towards the new economic course led, in practice, to a labor truce. Thus, the launching of the structural adjustment policies was followed by a series of isolated and short-lived conflicts. Soon labor mobilization was undermined by job uncertainty as well as by decrees that limited strike activities in public services and banned wage hikes not accompanied by productivity. The consequences of the economic crisis and institutional restrictions were compounded by the impact of the official strategy, which combined governmental inflexibility in the face of union opposition with the distribution of incentives and lateral payments to the more acquiescent labor sectors. For their part, union leaders chose to withdraw their attention from labor disputes and focused their meagre bargaining power on defending their organizations and the corporatist guarantees upon which they depended.

Only in December 1992, when the government announced its intention to put forward labor reform to introduce changes in collective bargaining, the union structure, and the control of welfare funds administrated by the unions, did labor leaders abandon their forced passivity and launch a general strike. Menem's response was to open negotiations that ultimately resulted in the phase-down of labor reform plans and in concessions such as the bailing out of union welfare funds' debts. The government renewed its attempts in 1993 and 1994 but, once again, with little success. Although union leaders showed themselves willing to agree to more flexible working conditions, they continued to hinder reforms that threatened their organizational positions, with the support of Peronist representatives in congress.[28]

Thus, when taking a global look at the reform process, we see the survival of certain institutions that contradict the neoliberal bent of government policies. Among them are pro-union corporatist guarantees such as, notably, the monopoly of representation and union preferential privileges in the supply of health services.[29] This illustrates how the government had to time its reform agenda to spread the burdens of adjustment in order to avoid harming key members of the political coalition.

Our last example of the self-imposed limits of the reform policy refers to the relationship between the executive and the Peronist Party machine, whose backbone has been the control of provincial administrations.[30] Since the outset of the Convertibility Plan, the improvement in fiscal accounts and the greater availability of financing gave respite to governors and in many cases allowed them to use their traditional clientelistic instruments more extensively. In this context, the national authorities entered into a series of agreements with the provincial administrations to establish a distribution of shared revenues different from the one stipulated by current legislation: basically the so-called *Pacto Fiscal* (Fiscal Pact), which was signed in 1992 and renewed in 1993.

In view of the increased tax revenues, the Fiscal Pact guaranteed a minimum amount—quite high in historical terms—of the shared revenues in exchange for a reduction in the percentages corresponding to the provinces, in order to correct imbalances in the social security system. The central administration also provided for a tax reduction on condition that the provinces did the same, especially for those taxes affecting the competitiveness of the export sector. The aim, only partially achieved, was to secure the support of provincial governments for the priorities on Menem's reform agenda. But this exercise entailed important concessions on the part of the Menem administration: The provincial social security systems—which are key tools for their provinces' clientelistic policies—were not subject to the type of reform the national social security system underwent; public enterprises remained under local authority control, channeling liquid funds to the provincial coffers; provincial state banks were not privatized, retaining their role as financial agents for the local authorities; and finally, public payroll continued to grow and was not affected by any rationalizing strategy.

Yet, the increased amount of public funds was not sufficient to avoid recurrent financial crises in the provinces, which triggered frequent and sometimes violent public employees' protests in 1993 and 1994. These protests, however, were successfully controlled by means of the timely financial assistance of the central authorities. In fact, reform policies in the provinces were never a pressing issue despite the fact that they were always mentioned in the agreements reached between central and provincial governments. Thanks to the suspensive effect that the economic boom had upon regional structural adjustment, the national authorities managed to obtain the necessary legislative support to move forward on the reform process without clashing with the Peronist Party structures.

To recapitulate, let us say that the favorable post-1991 economic conditions and the political use that Menem's government made of them were crucial to the success of the second phase of the stabilization and structural adjustment efforts. It was not surprising, then, that in the congressional elections of October 1993 Peronist candidates obtained 42.3 percent of the votes—2 percent more than two years before—against 30 percent for the Radical Party, a new victory that gave it nine additional seats in congress. The electoral performance in the province of Buenos Aires, where the vast majority of the blue-collar population lives, was particularly remarkable: Peronists won 48 percent of the votes cast. The electoral results sparked the government's confidence and galvanized Menem into mounting the political operation for his reelection. However, another reading of the same results reveals the existence of widespread discontent with the project of political hegemony and economic liberalization. The reasons were many, and not all of them would translate into electoral behavior. What we see is a rejection of Menem's political style, which combines a patrimonialist use of public resources with the discretionary manipulation of constitutional rules.[31] This political criticism often coexisted with the acceptance of the general orientation of the process of economic change. The discontent was also fueled by a sense of socioeconomic malaise caused by the double-edged effects of economic policies. Stability and growth between 1991 and 1994 yielded extensive benefits vis-à-vis previous years, but they also forced all the different social sectors to adapt to harsh new economic rules.

The Current Crisis and Its Challenges

The strategy that allowed the Menem administration to wade across the turbulent waters of economic adjustment for almost four years depended largely on the flow of foreign funds and on the steady expansion of domestic demand. These two factors made the program potentially fragile, which became apparent in 1994 when the Argentine economy felt the impact of the rise in U.S. interest rates and, especially, the Mexican peso devaluation. The macroeconomic weaknesses inherent in the policy thus emerged in the fiscal and external sectors.

In 1994 the government began to pay the costs of the strategy inaugurated with the Convertibility Plan. Relying on growing fiscal revenues, the authorities embarked on a reform program that in some cases involved sacrificing public resources. As we noted, that is what happened with the social security reform and with the reduction of taxes aimed at correcting relative prices. However, we have also seen that the growth in public expenditure in 1991 and 1994 made politically feasible the structural changes advocated by the executive and reluctantly accepted by some official party members. During the second semester of 1994, when reactivation began to ebb and, as a result, tax collection declined, the combination of the above-mentioned factors upset the balance of public accounts and raised doubts in the financial markets about the program's sustainability.

In the external sector, the setback suffered by the official policy was even greater. In early 1994 the increase in international interest rates raised the cost of financing the Argentine economy and caused the value of public bonds to drop. At the end of the year, these unfavorable circumstances were compounded by the Mexican devaluation, which radically changed the situation. To foreign investors, the Argentine adjustment and reform program closely matched Mexico's. When the Mexican peso was devalued in December 1994, word spread that Argentina might follow suit. This provoked a massive outflow of local assets, a sharp rise in country risk as calculated by foreign investors, and, consequently, a major recessive, fiscal crisis unique in Latin America.[32]

It was against this ominous backdrop that Menem was reelected, after the 1994 constitutional reform allowed him to run for a second term. Once again, the fear of the return to the economic instability of 1989–90 was an advantage to the government. Believing that any departure from official policies could bring the return of hyperinflation, the people gave Menem 50 percent of the vote, ensuring his victory in the May 1995 election. By then, however, the macroeconomic magic conjured up during the first years of the Convertibility Plan had vanished.

The Controversy over Economic Policies

The sudden change of fortune reinstated the debate over Menem's economic policy choices that had taken place during the previous years. Although the official decision to take advantage of the international credit markets' favorable conditions to bolster domestic demand was welcomed by the local business community, critical voices advocating alternative policies were heard in some financial and technical circles. Some recommended fostering austerity and increasing fiscal savings, others put forward proposals for freezing the money supply or for regulating capital movements. In both cases, the aim was to attain sustainable, though initially lower, growth.

The 1995 crisis seemed to vindicate these positions. However, when the government had to make choices, political rationality prevailed over any other consideration. The policy alternatives to Menem's program would not only have sacrificed the politically attractive goal of reactivating the economy in a democratic setting, they would also have limited the room for maneuvering necessary to reduce the costs of the reform process and to sustain the ruling coalition. In the face of the crisis, the simple mechanisms of the Convertibility Plan, which had till then promoted economic expansion, began to have the opposite effect. The lack of liquidity provoked by capital flight led to an increase in interest rates and, initially, a significant drop in consumption and investment. Collective pessimism brought on by the altered prospects deepened this trend. As a result, 1995 came to a close with a 4.4 percent drop in GDP, a sharp increase in the unemployment rate (which topped 18 percent), greater bank insolvency, and a growing fiscal imbalance generated by the fact that recession had caused a decline in tax collection, which is extremely dependent on the level of aggregate demand.[33]

This turning point brought to the fore two public policy issues that the previous climate of euphoria had removed from the government's agenda. The first was the question of the macroeconomic management of the convertibility regime in hard times. The second was the political sustainability of the reform process once the economy had entered a recessive phase and the costs of adjustment were becoming clearly visible.

Economic Management in Hard Times

In terms of macroeconomic management, the authorities were confronted with the classic dilemmas of gold-standard monetary regimes. First, there was fragility in the financial system: Faced with a crisis of confidence and with withdrawal of funds from banks after the Mexican peso devaluation, the Central Bank had less power to prevent the collapse of the banking system. Second, there were obstacles to adjusting relative prices to the new and stricter conditions imposed by foreign financing through deflation. Finally, instruments for the implementation of anticyclical policies that would deflect the risks of a prolonged recession were lacking.

The first problem was solved during 1995. With its few monetary tools and the crucial financial assistance from international organizations—which did not want the Mexican crisis to spread to the rest of Latin America—the Central Bank managed to contain the run on banks and start a deep restructuring of the banking system. Within a year, deposits in the financial system were higher than the total before the outset of the Mexican crisis, at no significant cost to the depositors or to public finances.[34]

The second problem—the adjustment of relative prices when devaluation is not available[35]—was handled with success. During 1995 and 1996 the recessive pressures on the capital and labor markets caused a drop in prices and forced many unions to accept changes in their collective bargaining agreements, which entailed a de facto deregulation of labor relations and a reduction of labor costs. In addition, many medium- and high-income employees, particularly public servants, suffered substantial wage reductions.

It should be noted that it was not necessary to resort to a deep and generalized deflation.[36] A set of internal and external factors contributed to the partial correction of relative price distortions that accompanied the Convertibility Plan from the beginning. First were productivity rises between 1991 and 1994 and the improved competitiveness resulting from supply side policies of tax reduction; second, and more important in quantitative terms, the international prices of Argentine goods sold abroad increased between 1994 and 1996 and exports to Brazil, which in 1995 was already buying 30 percent of Argentine exports, expanded further.

Yet the success in dealing with the relative prices problem is not definitive because these factors, especially the rise in the price of export goods, may change in the course of time. Besides, the other factors are not significant enough to lead to large investments in export activities. Nevertheless, this was not the main issue in 1995–96. Rather, it was the difficulty in coming out of recession and its consequences for tax collection and bank solvency. In spite of the fact that the financial crisis was overcome, the supply of credit recovered, and the problem of competitiveness no longer at center stage, recession deepened and extended over time because of the generalized pessimism that followed almost four years of expansion and optimism. Growing unemployment and a lower nominal income discouraged demand, and, given the resistance in financial circles, the government was unable to expand public expenditure. Thus reactivation of the economy was left to the spontaneous dynamics of the market, with the danger that recession might last even longer.

The new climate of economic emergency evoked the memory of the hyperinflation years, when Menem first came to power. As then, the executive demanded wide-reaching decision-making powers and implemented a succession of public expenditure cuts and tax increases. The still-pending privatizations were designed with haste and focused primarily on meeting fiscal goals. The new social security system—the result of many rounds of negotiation in better times—was in turn reformed with great dispatch by congress in order to limit the entitlements of public sector employees, making them dependent on the availability of financial resources.

Now the issues that had been put aside between 1991 and 1994 were back at the top of the reform agenda. The pressure for the integral deregulation of the labor market increased. The crisis-ridden provincial governments, affected by the financial crisis and declining tax revenues, in some cases to the point of being unable to pay salaries and pensions, had no alternative but to implement the reforms they had previously avoided. Backed by multilateral credit organizations and the national government, the provinces began to privatize many public companies and state banks while, at the same time, they transferred their social security systems to the central administration. The frequent changes the authorities were obliged to make during the crisis exposed the precarious nature of the novel economic institutions.

The Political Sustainability of the Reform Process

It can be argued that the need to sustain the ruling coalition constrained economic options. As a consequence, the stabilization and structural adjustment program moved forward on a tightrope: Austerity was sacrificed for the sake of reform; private consumption increased, and no anticyclical policies were attempted; public expenditure also expanded. Furthermore, the reforms of this second phase demanded substantial tax reductions. In sum, the government acted as if the inflow of foreign capital would be prolonged indefinitely, thereby making the economic program extremely vulnerable to external shocks. This became indisputably apparent with the 1995 crisis.

In light of our analysis, it is difficult to see the viability of a reform program similar to the one implemented since 1991 but carried out under conditions of greater austerity and lower growth. The Peronist legislators who voted for the reforms and the union leaders who endorsed them did not fully agree with Menem's project of economic liberalization, which looks rather like a "revolution from above." If they reluctantly backed Menem's program, it was because economic decisions made way for exceptional years of prosperity that mitigated adjustment costs and opened spaces for negotiating. Within the government coalition, it was the big business groups that exerted pressure in favor of structural reforms, but it was the Peronist leadership that implemented them and ultimately gave them their distinctive features.

At present, the circumstances that allowed Menem's government to postpone or avoid making difficult choices have changed. The growth rates of recent years will be hard to replicate in the near future, the negative distributional effects of structural reforms are quite conspicuous, and the advocates of economic liberalization are pressing with renewed vigor to accelerate the reform process with no regard to political considerations. It is not surprising to see how the tensions underlying the government coalition are now surfacing: Conflicts between the executive and congress proliferate, and there are recurrent clashes between the political wing of the administration and the economic team. It is not surprising either that an atmosphere of uneasiness pervades, for opposite reasons, both union circles and the business community.

In sum, the current economic and political challenges facing Menem are more serious than those he confronted during his first mandate. Since history is still in the making, it seems difficult to anticipate a denouement. Lacking the perspective that comes with the passage of time, any assessment of the present is necessarily conjectural. At first glance, the problems in the process of structural adjustment recall others that Argentina experienced in the past and was unable to solve. Its recent history features numerous occasions on which the country seemed to be on the brink of taking a new direction in its development only to lose, shortly after, the necessary momentum to sustain course. Indeed, at the beginning of the 1960s, efforts were made to further import-substitution industrialization. However, while Brazil would follow this course in a sustained fashion, making developmentalism the core of a vigorous modernization process, Argentina soon ground to halt. In the mid-1970s, the search was renewed, now in the opposite direction of economic liberalization. But while, at the same time, Chile dismantled the institutions of its state-led and protectionist economy and found a new development path. Argentina, after also paying high social costs, came to a dead end. Argentina stands out in Latin America for its ability to frustrate the various expectations it has sparked throughout its history as a nation.

However, there is an argument against historical parallelisms. Societies do not always confront and resolve dilemmas by resorting to their stock of ready-made options. This general argument applies particularly to Argentina, where historical patterns were deeply affected by the large-scale transformations that occurred at the level of both economic organization and social expectations. As to the first level, a new political economy has emerged that combines trends of the last twenty years with more recent developments. Let us consider briefly two of its most important features: the processes of transnationalization and economic concentration and the high unemployment rate.

The privatization of public utilities, the new opening of the economy, and the extension of MERCOSUR strengthened big national conglomerates and promoted the arrival of many transnational companies.[37] Today, these firms are leading the rapid modernization of Argentina's productive structure by heavily investing in equipment and machinery and by changing organizational patterns. They have fluent access to credit from international financial markets and are, therefore, prepared to pursue long-term strategies. This contrasts sharply with Argentine capitalism in the past, which was extremely dependent on state subsidies. The prominence acquired by the dynamic sector of large enterprises and the accelerated integration of the economy into supranational production and trading networks constitute changes that, together with financial deregulation, are setting new and more restrictive parameters for the choice of alternative economic policies.

The other feature of the new political economy is the high unemployment rate. The labor market situation has changed so drastically that it may be impossible to reverse it in the near future.[38] From the late 1930s until the 1980s, Argentina's unemployment rate was normally below 4 percent. During the 1980s, in spite of stagnation, the rate only rose to 6 percent. This was not because of the implementation of explicitly pro-job policies but to a closed economy with fiscal deficit, which produced growing inflation as well as some employment. Thus, the two-digit unemployment rate in the 1990s represents a radical departure from past trends. Such a high level of structural unemployment challenges the efficacy of traditional survival strategies and, consequently, severely affects social cohesion.[39] Furthermore, it has a dramatic political impact. As Tulio Halperín Donghi recently remarked,[40] the defense of job opportunities had been for years a key component of the implicit consensus that brought together union leaders and some important business groups because it also represented the defense of an economic structure on which both of them depended. Today, the existence of so many structurally unemployed seems to be marking the end of that consensus and, therefore, the weakening of political obstacles to the ongoing economic transformation.

Finally, when looking into the future, we should take into account not only the constraints of the new political economy but also the changes in social expectations. In this respect, let us recall the existence of critical junctures that periodically redefine the perceptions and preferences of political and social actors and whose effects are deep and lasting. To go through the experience of hyperinflation is clearly one of them. It is our view that the traumatic events Argentina experienced in 1989 and 1990 are bound to continue to influence the search for solutions to the crisis that currently dominates the vast economic, social, and political reorganization of Argentina.

Notes

The authors wish to thank Bernardo Kosacoff, Roberto Bouzas, Adolfo Canitrot, Franco Castiglioni, Eduardo Feldman, and Vicente Palermo for their comments.

1. We have dealt with structural reforms in Latin America in Pablo Gerchunoff and Juan Carlos Torre, "What Role for the State in Latin America?" in Simon Teitel, ed., *Towards a New Development Strategy for Latin America: Pathways from Hirschman's Thought* (Washington, D.C.: Inter-American Development Bank, 1992).

2. See Albert Hirschman, *Essays in Trespassing: Economics to Politics and Beyond* (Cambridge: Cambridge University Press, 1981), p. 146.

3. The concept of policy reform context has been formulated in further detail in Merilee S. Grindle and John Tomas, *Policy Choices and Policy Change: The Political Economy of Reform in Developing Countries* (Baltimore: The Johns Hopkins University Press, 1991), chapter 2.

4. In this section we have utilized the work of Juan Carlos Torre and Vicente Palermo, "A la Sombra de la Hiperinflación: La Política de las Reformas Estructurales en la Argentina." Manuscript, 1996.

5. See Dani Rodrik, "Promises, Promises: Credible Policy Reform via Signalling," *Economic Journal*, no. 99, 1995, pp. 756–72.

6. Here we follow Laszlo Brust's argument in "Why on Earth Would Eastern Europeans Support Capitalism? Democracy, Capitalism and Public Opinion." Manuscript, 1994.

7. Atul Kohli has pointed out that when government leaders are judged by their followers, what they claim to represent tends to be more important in the short run than the substance of the policies they advocate. Thus, in 1980–81, India's Prime Minister Indira Gandhi, taking advantage of her popular image as a leftist leader and of past nationalistic and antipoverty policies, was able to launch trade liberalization measures at little political cost. See Atul Kohli, "The Politics of Economic Liberalization in India," in *World Development*, vol. 17, no. 3, 1989, pp. 305–28.

8. For an analysis of this first phase, see Roberto Bouzas "Más allá de la Estabilización y la Reforma? Un Ensayo sobre la Economía Argentina a Comienzos de los 90," *Desarrollo Económico*, no. 129, 1993, pp. 3–27.

9. On privatization policy, see Pablo Gerchunoff and Guillermo Canovas, *Las Privatizaciones en Argentina: Impactos Micro y Macroeconómicos* (Santiago: Comisión Económica para América Latina [CEPAL], Proyecto Reformas de Política Pública, Documento No. 21, 1994.)

10. See Leroy P. Jones, Pankaj Tandon, and Ingo Vogelsang, *Selling Public Enterprises* (Cambridge, MA: The MIT Press, 1990).

11. On trade liberalization, see Bernardo Kosacoff, *La Industria Argentina: Un Proceso de Reestructuración Desarticulada* (Buenos Aires: CEPAL, Centro Editor de América Latina, 1993).

12. For an analysis of the Argentine tax reform, see Ricardo Carciofi, *Reformas Tributarias en América Latina* (Santiago: CEPAL, 1995).

13. Thus, Rudiger Dornbush claimed that "however crude, the school which holds that, as far as privatizations are concerned, it is more important to do it quickly than well, is right. Thus . . . in Latin America, governments should be less concerned about doing it right than about actually doing it." *Structural Adjustment in Latin America* (Washington, D.C.: The Woodrow Wilson Center, The Latin American Program, Working Paper 191, 1990).

14. The first attempts at stabilization are analyzed by Adolfo Canitrot in "Crisis and Transformation of the Argentine State (1978–1992)" in William C. Smith, Carlos H. Acuña, and Eduardo A. Gamarra, eds., *Democracy, Markets, and Structural Reform in Latin America* (Boulder: Lynne Rienner, 1993), pp. 75–102. For an excellent account of the economic and political aspects of the Alfonsín administration and of the initial phase of Menem's government, see Adolfo Canitrot and Silvia Sigal, "Economic Reform, Democracy, and the Crisis of the State in Argentina," in Joan Nelson, ed., *A Precarious Balance: Democracy and Economic Reforms in Latin America* (Berkeley: Institute for Contemporary Studies, University of California, 1994), pp. 95–142.

15. The concept of self-binding was elaborated by Jon Elster in *Ulysses and the Sirens: Studies in Rationality and Irrationality* (Cambridge: Cambridge University Press, 1978) and was used in relation to the Convertibility Plan by Vicente Palermo in his doctoral thesis, "¡Siganme! La Política de las Reformas Estructurales: El Caso Argentino, 1989–1993" (Madrid: Universidad Complutense, 1995).

16. Another reason for strengthening the government was the resolution of the conflict with the military, which had compromised the last part of Alfonsín's administration. Once in the presidency, Menem issued a partial pardon of military men convicted of human rights violations and of participating in military revolts. The ex-members of the military juntas were excluded. The measure fell short of putting an end to tensions because the high military authorities began to exclude those mid-rank officers who were hostile to the military hierarchy. They reacted in December of 1990 with a new uprising that was violently crushed by loyal forces. In January of 1991 Menem issued a second pardon of ex-members of the military juntas. Although this measure was strongly opposed by public opinion, it brought about a durable peace. See Carlos Acuña and Catalina Smulovitz, "Militares en la Transición Argentina: Del Gobierno a la Subordinación Constitucional," in Carlos Acuña, ed., *La Nueva Matriz Política Argentina* (Buenos Aires: Nueva Visión, 1995), pp. 153–202.

17. A preliminary examination of the impact of the inflow of foreign capital can be found in M. Damill, J. M. Fanelli, R. Frenketl, and G. Rozenwurcel, "Crecimiento Económico en America Latina: Experiencias Recientes y Perspectivas," *Desarrollo Económico*, no. 130, 1993, pp. 237–63.

18. Inter-American Development Bank, *Economic and Social Programs in Latin America: 1995 Report* (Baltimate: Johns Hopkins University Press, 1995), pp. 23–9.

19. See Luis Beccaria, "Estancamiento y Distribución del Ingreso," in Alberto Minujin, ed., *Desigualdad y Exclusión: Desafíos para la Política Social en la Argentina de Fin de Siglo* (Buenos Aires: UNICEF-Losada, 1993).

20. Inter-American Development Bank, *Economic and Social Programs*, pp. 23–9.

146   *Pablo Gerchunoff and Juan Carlos Torre*

21. Joan Nelson, "Poverty, Equity and the Politics of Adjustment" in Stephen Haggard and Robert Kaufman, eds., *The Politics of Economic Adjustment* (Princeton: Princeton University Press, 1992); Carol Graham, *Safety Nets, Politics and the Poor* (Washington, D.C.: The Brooking Institution, 1994), chapter 1.

22. John Waterbury, "The Political Management of Economic Adjustment and Reform" in Joan Nelson, ed., *Fragile Coalitions: The Politics of Economic Adjustment* (New Brunswick, NJ: Transaction Books, 1989), p. 39.

23. Workers losing their jobs received compensatory payments, but no complementary policies were adopted. For an analysis of the negative consequences of the lack of complementary policies for the privatization of a state steelworks, see Luis Beccaria and Aida Quintar, "Reconversión Productiva y Mercado de Trabajo: Reflexiones a Partir de la Experiencia de Somisa," in *Desarrollo Económico*, no. 139, 1995, pp. 401–17.

24. For statistics on poverty and employment, see Torre and Palermo, "A la Sombra de la Hiperinflación," passim.

25. Victoria Murillo's excellent paper on the changes in the trade unions in the past years includes numerous examples of their new activities. The Electricity Workers' Union bought 40 percent of the stocks in nine energy generators in the Argentine Northwest, 33 percent of the stocks in four energy generators in the Argentine South, and 20 percent of the stocks of the Sorrento energy generator in Rosario. It also obtained the concession for the state monopoly of coal exploitation, and participated in partnerships that bought 90 percent of the stocks of three energy generators in Santa Fé and Paraná. The Railroad Workers Union has started the administration of a number of cooperative workshops for the maintenance of trains in Santa Fé and participated in the privatization of one of the railroad lines. For its part, by 1993 the Oil Workers Union had organized 215 maintenance firms that gathered 7,194 laid-off workers and was organizing another 39 firms with 63 workers to be dismissed. Moreover, it bought part of the YPF fleet and shares of an oil equipment firm. These unions and many others have participated in partnerships with banks and have created with them pension funds after the social security reform. "Union Responses to Economic Reform in Argentina: Organizational Autonomy and the Marketization of Corporatism," paper presented at the 1994 annual meeting of the American Political Science Association, New York, September 1–4, 1994.

26. Vicente Palermo presents a thorough analysis of the change from a unilateral decision-making pattern to a more negotiated one in "Reformas Estructurales y Régimen Político," *Agora*, no. 3, 1995, pp. 95–113.

27. For an analysis of the social security reform, see Alberto Petrecolla, "El Sistema de Jubilaciones y Pensiones: Un Esquema de Análisis" (Buenos Aires: Instituto Torcuato Di Tella, 1996, mimeo); and Oscar Cetrángolo, *El Nuevo Sistema Previsional ¿Una Reforma Definitiva?* (Buenos Aires: Centro de Ciencias Económicas [CECE], Serie Notas No. 2, October 1994).

28. See Sebastián Etchemendy, "¿Límites al Decisionismo? El Poder Ejecutivo y la Formulación de la Legislación Laboral, 1983–1994," in Ricardo Sidicaro and Jorge Mayer, eds., *Política y Sociedad en los Años del Menemismo* (Buenos Aires: Universidad de Buenos Aires, Facultad de Ciencias Sociales, 1995), pp. 127–53.

29. The outcome of the negotiations for the deregulation of the unions' welfare funds' system did not change the situation substantially. The government proposed establishing a compulsory national health insurance system, providing for a free choice between the different agencies, union and nonunion, that supplied health services. Union leaders managed to limit the workers' free choice to the health suppliers of the union welfare funds system, which is bound to promote greater concentration in favor of the larger union organizations.

30. A detailed study of the financial relations between the national and the provincial governments during the Convertibility Plan can be found in Oscar Cetrángolo, *El Conflicto en Torno a las Relaciones Financieras entre la Nación y las Provincias. Segunda Parte: Desde la Ley 23548 hasta la Actualidad* (Buenos Aires: CECE, Serie Estudios No. 10, February 1996).

31. On constitutional practices under Menem, see Delia Ferreira Rubio and Mateo Goretti, "Gobernar la Emergencia: Uso y Abuso de los Decretos de Necesidad y Urgencia (1989–1993)," *Agora,* no. 3, 1995, pp. 75–94; and Ana María Mustapic, "Tribulaciones del Congreso en la Nueva Democracia Argentina. El Veto Presidencial bajo Alfonsín y Menem," *Agora,* no. 3, 1995, pp. 61–74.

32. For a study of the impact of the Mexican crisis on the Argentine economy, see Roberto Bouzas, *The Mexican Peso Crisis and Argentina's Convertibility Plan: Monetary Virtue or Monetary Impotence?* (Buenos Aires: Facultad Latinoamericana de Ciencias Sociales and Comisión Nacional de Investigación, Ciencia, Educación, y Tecnologia [FLACSO-CONICET], 1996, mimeo).

33. These developments are analyzed in Torre and Palerma, "A la Sombra de la Hiperinflación," passim.

34. For an excellent analysis of the financial crisis, see José Luis Machinea, "Causes, Consequences and Lessons: The Argentine Financial Crisis in 1995" (Buenos Aires: Instituto Torcuato di Tella, 1996, mimeo).

35. In Argentina and elsewhere in Latin America there have been many stabilization programs based on a fixed exchange rate. In general, they were used only temporarily. The Argentine peculiarity lies in the fact that the fixed exchange rate was established by law with the purpose of solving a problem of credibility. The success of the stabilization efforts led to public confidence in the economic program being dependent on the maintenance of the fixed exchange rate. There is a general belief that any change in this respect may drastically revert public expectations.

36. See Pablo Gerchunoff and José Luis Machinea, "Un Ensayo sobre la Política Económica después de la Estabilización," in Pablo Bustos, ed., *Más Allá de la Estabilidad: Argentina en la Epoca de la Globalización y la Regionalización* (Buenos Aires: Fundación Friedrich Ebert, 1995); José María Fanelli, Osvaldo Kacef, and José Luis Machinea, "Precios Relativos y Competitividad Industrial" (Buenos Aires: Unión Industrial Argentina, Documento de Trabajo No. 19, 1994).

37. The transnationalization process, the differences between national and multinational corporations, and the consequences of the new specialization pattern in the Argentine economy have been dealt with in greater detail in D. Chudnovsky, A. López, and F. Porta, "Más Allá del Flujo de Caja: El Boom de la Inversión Extranjera Directa en Argentina," *Desarrollo Económico,* no. 137, 1995, pp. 35–62.

38. The most optimistic hypothesis holds that only if employment grew at the same rate as in the 1991–92 boom period, which is quite difficult, would the unemployment rate be lower than 7 percent in the year 2011. On the causes of unemployment, see Pablo Gerchunoff and Osvaldo Kacef, "Macroeconomía y Mercado de Trabajo durante el Plan de Convertibilidad" (Buenos Aires: Instituto Torcuato di Tella, 1995, mimeo).

39. The magnitude of poverty and its spread to the middle classes in the 1980s has meant that Argentina's social structure has become more like that in other countries in Latin America. For details, see Silvia Sigal, "Argentine 1992–1995: Une Societé en Mutation," *Problèmes d'Amerique Latine*, no. 21, April 1996.

40. Tulio Halperín Donghi, *La Larga Agonía de la Argentina Peronista* (Buenos Aires: Ariel, 1994), p. 88.

7

The State in Retreat in the Administrative Field

Lawrence Graham

The redefinition of the role of the state throughout Latin American over the last decade cannot be separated from the process of economic and political transition that has swept across the hemisphere. The side of the equation that is probably best understood falls within the purview of economics, where the return to markets as the primary regulating force has led to a retreat of the state from intervention in the economy throughout the region. Globally, state shrinking is a consequence of neoliberal structural adjustment policies, which require major changes in the structure of the economy, the state, and society. To date, the most visible aspects of adjustment have been the use of monetary policy to end inflation and the opening of Latin American economies, previously dominated by state-owned enterprises and statist strategies for economic growth, to private sector firms. What has been much more difficult to achieve is structural change in the apparatus of the state itself.

As a consequence, it is easier to sketch out the parameters of the retreat of the state from the economy due to the primacy of a single dominant economic model emphasizing market solutions to the problems of economic growth than to identify commonalities in the strategies pursued in reform of the state *(reforma del estado)*. This is because restructuring the state touches on questions of political power and established relationships among organized groups inside and outside government. Thus, while there is a uniformity in the market-friendly strategies being advocated, there is no such uniformity in how the issue of state reform is being approached because the political transitions underway and the debates over how to consolidate more open forms of governance are derived essentially from internal changes in the relationship between state and society and the interplay between traditional and new political forces in each country.

The administrative systems in Latin American countries have evolved in conjunction with political and social institutions to produce twenty very different nation states. Although the point of departure in the building of states throughout Latin America historically derives from a common set of conditions and political outcomes—independence in the early nineteenth century from Spain and Portugal—at the end of the twentieth century what is striking is how varied the political and administrative behavior of individual states in the region has become.

Chile has advanced furthest in state reform. But administrative changes in Chile are the consequence of a particular set of political choices made during the authoritarian rule of Augusto Pinochet prior to the return to democracy in 1990. Elsewhere in Latin America, state reform is embedded in the politics of redemocratization and internal debates over how more open forms of governance are to be institutionalized. The countries in which the issue of state reform has been engaged most clearly are Mexico and Brazil. Because state reform issues have only begun to be seriously debated in Brazil since 1995, however, Mexico offers much clearer insights into how the direction of the political transition away from authoritarian practices toward more participatory forms shapes the debate over state reform. Indeed, state reform issues have been a part of the policy agendas of Mexican presidents since the administration of José López Portillo (1976–1982).

Because Mexican attempts at state reform span a twenty-year period, it is more useful to draw on a single theoretically relevant case to illustrate how changes in national politics have shaped the debate over state reform than to attempt to address these variations in national experiences only superficially across Latin America as a whole. My objective is to illustrate four points. First, it is imperative to understand how the process of state reform is being guided by internal political conditions. The economic and political transition in Mexico, which can no longer be controlled by the president, for example, bears no relationship to Peru's under Alberto Fujimori. Second, it is essential to see how variations in national politics have been the guiding force in shaping very different national administrative systems. Third, this particular combination of externally induced economic change and internally directed political and administrative change is leading to a retreat of the state from active involvement in social policy. Virtually every Latin American government that has grappled with the issue of how to reduce costs has found it necessary to cut back on social services that a decade ago were assumed to be a right. Fourth, as governments abandon the objective of building state autonomy by designing public administration systems with greater capacity to implement economic and social policy and as they look to economic and social forces outside government to guide socioeconomic development, they have increasingly restricted access to political power to the privileged; at the same time, decisions are made by an increasingly limited set of policymakers who use the rhetoric of majoritarian politics to promote the interests of a small group of actors, those who would use the resources of state power to their own advantage.

In Mexico the tension between sweeping internal political and economic changes and external conditionalities identified with structural adjustment policies is the greatest in the region. What makes this topic so complex and so fascinating is the juxtaposition of external pressures on the economy (the promotion of the primacy of markets and above all world markets) and internal pressures for political change as new groups entering politics have mobilized to redefine the concept of national community. The actions of Carlos Salinas de Gortari and Ernesto Zedillo in Mexico, of Fujimori in Peru, Carlos Saúl Menem in Argentina, and Fernando Henrique Cardoso in Brazil are producing very different sets of national outcomes from which it is increasingly difficult to generalize without abandoning a Latin American point of reference.

The Mexican Case

The economic and political crisis facing Mexico today has generated widely divergent interpretations of the transformations taking place in state and society, but most of the analysis has focused on developments outside government: indigenous revolt in Chiapas, the growing strength of the Partido Acción Nacional (PAN) in the north (especially in Monterrey and Nuevo León) and the center (in León and Guanajuato), the rapid decline in the value of the peso and the need for a U.S. bailout to keep economic reforms going, and social protest over the rise in prices and the return of inflation. Yet, within the regime—in the corridors of central governmental organizations where key policy decisions are made—equally significant changes that warrant greater attention are taking place. In bureaucratic terms, the issue has become how to reform the state in order to consolidate the changes achieved in the economy and, in so doing, how to separate party (that is, the Partido Revolucionario Institucional, or PRI) from government.

At the core of the Mexican state is a highly centralized regime in the process of redefinition and movement away from the corrupt practices and ineffective programs that are the legacy of more than fifty years of PRI-dominated rule. Although analysts of these developments have identified the emergence of a new technocratic elite and call attention to a new and improved PRI in the making, below the political and administrative elites who consolidated their control over Mexican government during the Salinas *sexenio* remains a clientelistic bureaucracy. Jobs and promotions are awarded according to political and personalistic criteria, and there is a notable turnover in personnel with every change in political leadership. Effective reform is usually equated with the victory of opposition parties at the state and local levels and their instigation of new concepts of governance centered around performance criteria.[1] For party reformists, regime transformation has become embodied in the movement for a "New Federalism," in which state and local governments have set their sights on obtaining meaningful and real autonomy.

Defenders of the existing order and scholars who stress the reforms that have accompanied the economic and political openings inaugurated by Miguel de la Madrid (1982–88) and consolidated by Salinas (1989–94) also see a new regime in the making, but in very different terms. They call attention to an ever more clear demarcation between government by a technocratic elite (drawn from Mexico's new professional and business class) and a political process and party system dominated by the PRI at the national level, although increasingly under attack from below at the state and local levels. Support for these arguments stem from analysis of economic policies linked to market reforms and privatization. Here the emphasis falls on the consequences: considerable success in creating a more open and competitive economy but severe economic dislocations that can be measured in terms of job compression and increased costs for goods and services. PRI supporters argue that poverty alleviation strategies, in the form of programs undertaken by SEDESOL (Secretaría de Desarrollo Social), have accompanied structural adjustments in the economy and continue to contribute a great deal toward compensating those groups most affected by the dislocations engendered by economic reforms.[2] But critics, as Victoria Rodríguez and Jon Shefner elaborate in their chapters, have made equally great claims that activities of SEDESOL and Solidarity (Solidaridad) are linked to grass-roots strategies designed to benefit the PRI and sustain popular support for the party at the ballot box.

The People Who Dominate the
Institutions of Government in Mexico

In the midst of the public debates over the direction the Mexican transition is taking and of competition between government and the opposition to control the process, economic reform continues. Despite differences over the direction and content of the political opening, both sides generally concur that continued progress in economic reform is contingent on extensive changes in the state's administrative apparatus. Although calls for administrative reform are not new to Mexico, what is different about current discussions is the extent to which economic reform has now become linked to administrative reform. As a consequence, there is a new consensus emerging between the Mexican business community and the central government that civil service reform, emphasizing nonpartisan, merit-oriented criteria in recruitment and promotion, is in their best interest. This consensus is evident when one compares the programs of PAN in the states and major cities where PAN party members now hold office with those of the Zedillo administration in the federal bureaucracy.

This convergence between reformers in both camps must be juxtaposed against the increasing turbulence and uncertainty in politics as the pace of change accelerates in Mexican society. There is a simple reason this is the case. For all the problems and difficulties inherent in the present situation, Mexico continues to have a relatively strong state, and public officials in strategic sectors have considerable capacity to design and to implement the economic and social policies to which the government is committed. Groups in the center and on the right politically do not wish to see this resource squandered. The Mexican experience in state building stands in marked contrast with that of most other developing countries; in Latin America, only Chile can match the Mexican record. This new convergence among Mexican elites in business and government on the need for strong state capacity transcends partisan differences and must be factored in as an important part of the political equation: Despite all the signs of upheaval in Mexican society, this is not a regime bordering on collapse. Both sets of policymakers generally agree that smaller, more professional administrative apparatuses capable of implementing a broad range of social and economic policies are essential, at whatever level of government they are operating.

In the eyes of Mexican reformers a technocratic revolution is underway. Although set back by unexpected political assassinations, popular protest and revolts, and continued instances of police corruption, federal officials have not lessened in the least their push to consolidate a new regime based on the instrumentalities of a strong state. Those identified with "the New PRI" (the new alliance between professionals and party officials committed to greater transparency in politics) differ little, for example, from PAN government officials in the city of Monterrey or the state of Nuevo León. Furthermore, as Miguel Angel Centeno argues, when one examines elite interaction, separation between party (the PRI) and government has already occurred.[3]

Against the desiderata of these reformers must be juxtaposed more than half a century of partisan political practices. Reformers, operating at the apex of the political and economic systems, have the capacity to shape policy and control the reform agenda and wish to expand that capacity. But their success in determining macroeconomic policy does not translate into their ability to implement economic and social policy at the grass-roots level. For all the talk of reform, corruption and influence peddling abound at the state and local levels. At the middle and lower levels of government and society, party and government remain inseparable. Thus, one of the major challenges of the Zedillo *sexenio* is to move this debate over state reform out of the offices of the privileged (*los que mandan*) and into mass-based state and party organizations without derailing the prevailing presidentialist regime. As Centeno makes clear in his analysis of the technocratic revolution in Mexico, the past strength of the PRI—state alliance was its ability to sustain a political settlement in which the civilian bureaucracy retained the upper hand over politicians and the military within the framework of a single dominant party organization that could deliver mass support.[4]

As pressures increase for adjustments in social policy to ameliorate the further dislocations likely to occur as economic liberalization advances, the old formula of bureaucratic expertise at the top and political party patronage within the organs of the state can no longer work. In the older political world controlled by the PRI, public employment at the middle and lower levels was linked to job creation and enhancement for individuals who lacked employment opportunities elsewhere in the economy. This style of political clientelism is no longer compatible with either the demands for greater efficiency and effectiveness in government as economic reforms advance or with the opening of politics in ways that make government officials subject to public scrutiny and accountable for their actions.

One should not minimize earlier attempts to reduce central government personnel during the de la Madrid and Salinas administrations. Although there is fluctuation in year-to-year employment, public employment figures do show a decline over the ten-year period from 1983 to 1993, from a high of 1,432,968 in 1984 to a low of 818,775 in 1992. But one should also note that reductions have been made at the margins of the state and largely within the category often referred to as "parallel administration" (state-owned enterprises now subject to privatization, independent commissions, and a variety of autonomous government authorities). The current challenge is how to achieve the drastic downsizing of the state carried out in Chile under Pinochet at the very point when PRI dominance of the Mexican state is weakening and opposition politics is building. The current economic model, applied earlier in Chile and in vogue in Mexico today, cannot advance without a major reduction in government expenditures on public-sector salaries and programs.

The Institutional Framework
within which Reform Must Occur

At a time when so much attention is being focused on government crisis in Mexico, it is important to keep in mind the institutional setting that shapes Mexican politics because the constants—spin-offs from the settlement reached in Mexican politics in the 1930s—remain. They are integral parts of the framework that has provided stability and continuity in Mexican government and the basis for economic growth and progress during the 1950s and 1960s. Furthermore, although a new elite settlement seems to be in the making, if one accepts Centeno's arguments, these constants will remain a vital part of any new accord on the rules that will guide a political system in which party competition becomes the norm.

First, this is a highly centralized state in which power and policy initiatives are concentrated in the presidency. The rationalization of administrative structures that dates back to the administration of López Portillo began a process of tightening internal controls in such a way as to ensure that the president would have power to control public finances and personnel. This process has continued despite three major crises: in 1982 with the devaluation of the peso and economic restructuring; in 1988 with the rise of strong opposition movements on the right and the left that threatened PRI dominance for the first time; and in 1994 with political assassinations of key PRI officials identified with the reformist wing of the PRI and with a new economic crisis stemming from the precipitous fall of the peso at the end of the year. Yet despite press reports that would lead one to believe the system is bordering on collapse, economic and political reforms have continued, and Zedillo, like his predecessors, has accelerated efforts to consolidate a new basis of power. While many political analysts center their attention on changes within the PRI and on its relations with other parties, especially PAN, others have directed their attention to economic and social policy.

At the end of the Salinas *sexenio*, technocrats concluded that if the pace of economic restructuring was to be accelerated, there would have to be fundamental changes in government institutions. Over the past two decades a number of significant, albeit partial, reforms have been achieved. Ostensibly to increase rationalization, efficiency, and effectiveness, they have been designed to give power to the office of the Presidencia de la República to implement policies of immediate interest to the president. By 1995 an extremely powerful set of governmental organizations in the domain of economic policy had been put in place: the Presidency, the Ministry of Finance (Hacienda de Crédito Público), the Ministry of Commerce and Industrial Development (Comercio y Fomento Industrial), the Comptroller General (Contraloría), and the Central Bank (Banco de México). The current strategy is to expand this base, now that it has been coordinated and consolidated, to embrace other key public organizations essential to the control and regulation of the public agenda. These embrace economic areas directly linked to the NAFTA accord and outside the original set of key economic organizations (for example, Customs and PEMEX), as well as social and security affairs (SEDESOL and Gobernación).

Second, the Mexican state is federalist. Although standard textbook characterizations of Mexican politics always begin with statements to the effect that Mexican federalism has little substance, from a policy perspective the instruments of governance follow federalist precepts with a clearcut demarcation among federal, state, and local authorities. This gives to the Mexican state an internal complexity that is rarely appreciated by those who focus their attention on politics and society. The growth of the state apparatus since the 1940s has, as a consequence, engendered considerable institutional pluralism.

To trace the circuitous route that any policy must follow in moving from central governmental offices to the states and into the municipalities, intergovernmental relations must be a central concern. Although the institutional setting certainly is different from that of the United States, the same intricate mixture of federal, state, and local offices, officials, commissions, and authorities obtains. Not only are there multiple centers of power, some with greater or lesser degrees of importance, but there is also an extraordinarily complicated set of relationships among federal, state, and local officials.[5] Hence, although decision making is centralized, the president's authority is far from absolute. This can be seen most clearly by contrasting the instruments for macroeconomic policy management with those designed to deal with questions of social policy, control of the police, or corruption.

Third, because many of the instruments of governance follow European models more closely than those identified with the United States, partial reforms engineered within the state apparatus have produced staffing arrangements that divide government employees de facto into three groups that cut across internal organizational divisions: the administrative elite (secretaries/ministers, undersecretaries, charges d'affaires/*oficiales mayores,* and directors-general; occupants of middle-level positions (directors, subdirectors, department heads, and liaison personnel); and lower-level personnel (unionized workers and rank-and-file employees). One of the least understood mechanisms of governance in Mexico concerns public personnel management; yet, it is crucial in conceptualizing the relation between merit and ascription in personnel policies. At the apex are senior civil servants comprising an administrative elite or executive class who rotate among a select set of central (or federal) government organizations, some of which fall within the "direct" administration category while others belong to separately constituted public entities with greater or lesser amounts of autonomy. This is the administrative elite whom Centeno characterizes as technocrats allied with political leaders. His conclusions are that this group controls the policy agenda in such a way as to keep both PRI party officials and the military at a distance while they decide on key issues in economic and social policy.[6] According to the Finance Ministry, these people numbered 1,247 at the end of Salinas's term.[7]

Distinct from those who set the policy agenda is an administrative class of technicians (*personal de mando medio superior y de enlace*) adept at specific professional tasks. In the earlier literature on the Mexican state, these individuals were identified as the *técnicos* and were considered an important subset of actors, distinct from the *políticos*—the PRI political party leaders who dominated the regime and secured the linkages between the organs of government and the mass organizations that made the PRI and the state inseparable.[8] Among them, engineers, lawyers, economists, accountants, and other professionals predominate. Since the 1980s most political analysts have found the dichotomizing of Mexican officialdom into *técnicos* and *políticos* less and less meaningful, as roles between professionals and politicians have blurred. Few professionals rose to influence within the state without an active PRI affiliation, and fewer politicians could move into the inner corridors of power without extensive professional experience within state organizations involved in development programs and projects. Furthermore, as the political and administrative systems became more complex, specialization of roles occurred. Still, while Centeno emphasizes the waning affiliations with party among the administrative elite, rare are the instances of top officials (in both these categories) who have not spent time in IEPES (Instituto de Estudios Políticos, Económicos, y Sociales), PRI's research and policy institute.

Centeno records how bureaucratic roles have converged at the top and analyzes in detail the formation of this new bureaucratic elite: the technocrats. But here it is important to draw attention to the fact that *técnicos* also continue to exist as a distinct category of public employee and perform essential roles in the policy process. It is largely they who implement policy at the federal, state, and local levels. Their ranks are larger than those comprising the administrative elite, although they too constitute only a small percent (13) of total public employment.[9]

The third category is the much larger one of public functionaries (*personal operativo*) in a multitude of nonprofessional or nontechnical jobs for whom educational background is much less important than ability to respond to the mandates of administrative superiors. At this level patronage politics is alive and well, and it is here that administrative reform initiatives will have to be concentrated. Without the support of lower-level personnel—whatever the initiative and however innovative it may be—specific projects and programs become bogged down in a hopeless series of bureaucratic details and delays. The administrative reform issues of the day are thus not grandiose schemes but very practical and substantive concerns: customs administration, budget execution, accounting reforms, and the like. Employees in this category total 311,695, and it is here that party service, clientelism, and public employment overlap to the greatest extent.[10] Complementing these employees in the public sector but not reported in public pay records are medical personnel, contract personnel (*personal eventual*), consultants, teachers, and lower-level military personnel. The public payroll figures reported by the Dirección de Integración y Control in the Ministerio de Hacienda y Crédito Público indicate that these employees numbered 461,443 in 1994.[11]

The Relative Power of Civil Servants and Political Leaders

In a setting where tremendous political, social, and economic changes are underway, it is increasingly difficult to balance centrifugal and centripetal forces. The analysis of opposition politics, which ranges from the assessment of PAN state and local governments in the northern states to competition in the south between PRI and Partido de la Revolución Democrática (PRD) to indigenous revolt in Chiapas,[12] shows that major adjustments are underway in Mexican politics and records significant change in state and local governments as party competition has raised new demands for government to perform with greater effectiveness and efficiency. What this case material suggests is a twofold process: acceptance of increased state and local autonomy in regions where disaffection with PRI rule is the greatest and demands for political reform dominate the public agenda, coupled with a tightening of PRI control over the central governmental apparatus under the leadership of the reformist wing of the party. The task is thus no longer one of distinguishing traditional politicians accustomed to old-style clientelism and manipulation of the vote from younger, better educated technocrats. Instead, it has become one of identifying the political preferences of those occupying the centers of power, when their public discourse is couched in technical and apolitical terms. This is especially the case with the rhetoric used by the new PRI*istas* to secure external support from multilateral institutions for administrative reforms tied to economic liberalization. At their level, it is very difficult to separate politics and administration and, by extension, to determine when PRI identification is essential for appointments in the federal bureaucracy as opposed to professional appointments independent of party affiliation.

In such a context, keeping in mind that Mexican concepts of federalism follow much more closely the Spanish rather than U.S. model, regional autonomy in selected areas does not preclude an accommodation between the PRI and the PAN (in the same way that Catalán autonomy in Spain has laid to rest one of the most divisive issues in Spanish politics):

acceptance of PAN dominance in certain key states in the periphery (such as Nuevo León) in exchange for PRI dominance of the federal government. If the perspective provided by analysis of opposition politics is broadened to include the growing disaffection between PRI party officials and working-class individuals, in which older corporatist party divisions (such as the Confederación de Trabajadores de México, or CTM) are on the wane, the new territorially oriented PRI that is emerging is much closer to PAN in programs and practices. For these new leaders, commitment to the economic agenda of market liberalization and continued structural reforms precludes their willingness to let Mexican governance revert to the weak state characteristic of Mexico in the last century.

The impact of NAFTA and of sustained support for it among Mexican elites, despite the economic hardship if has engendered for major segments of the Mexican population, argue for sustained movement in the direction of a state that is less politicized at the middle and upper levels than conventional wisdom would suggest. Thus, when the revolt in Chiapas and the PRI's loss of Nuevo León and its capital Monterrey are viewed from an administrative context, it is not so clear that the Mexican transition is to be linked to democratization. These components call attention to the fact that while the movement away from old-style authoritarianism is irreversible, it is not at all certain that greater transparency in economic decision making will automatically generate greater transparency in government decision making and hence lead to democratic consolidation. Quasi-federalist experiments characteristic of Mexican governance since the late 1970s may well become the foundation for a quasi-democratic regime in the 1990s, with a strong state in the center identified with a new PRI, with greater respect for electoral majorities and greater political competition but without necessarily bringing an end to PRI dominance of national politics.

Conclusion

When the strength of opposition politics and its commitment to reform of the state are compared with that of the official organs of the state, it is certain that the Mexican transition will be a lengthy one, as was the case in Brazil. Given the resources both sides have at their disposal and the fact that neither can be excluded from power without resorting to unacceptable repression, what is to be expected is a new settlement in which business elites are accommodated more fully within the state without rupturing fundamentally the institutional framework developed for Mexican governance over the past fifty years. Skeptics of such an interpretation, among the various scenarios constructed to interpret the Mexican transition, should keep in mind that virtually no one in Mexico wishes to see recreated the conditions present at the beginning of the century or the mass upheaval that followed.[13]

In this particular setting, decentralization and regionalization have become highly politicized. What goes on within the administrative system is and will remain a function of changing political relationships in state and society at large as the PRI control of politics comes to an end and opposition groups gain a larger voice. Aside from the reducing the state's role in regulating the economy and making adjustments to accommodate economic policies to control inflation, manage the debt, and stimulate economic growth, administrative change will not so much be a case of the state in retreat. Rather, it will be the result of the competition for power and influence among different political actors and groups who dominate the internal administrative system and the external political system.

By extension, it is the larger political arena and the political forces active in national politics in each of the Latin American republics that will determine the outcomes in the administrative arena. In the Portuguese transition, once the restructuring necessary for economic reasons was accomplished, the state simply had to relinquish power to the new interest groups that had entered the political arena. This is what is likely to occur also in Latin America. Already, the state is being superseded by the force of events in Mexico; this is certainly also the case in Brazil and in many other countries. What happened in Peru under Fujimori—the dismantling of the state except for the reconcentration and recentralization of power in the presidency—is unlikely to occur elsewhere in Latin America. Much more likely will be variations on the Mexican theme: the domination of the state by the forces of society as competing groups vie for power and new accommodations are worked out in state and society. The driving forces will be the economy and the struggle to consolidate a new distribution of power. These forces will determine what changes take place within individual administrative systems. What is emerging, then, is not so much a retreat of the state in the administrative field as a movement toward a weak state dominated by social interests and groups undermining its capacity to implement broad development-related goals. What is underway is not just privatization in the economy but privatization of social policy in which social security systems, educational establishments, health systems, and other social institutions are no longer the exclusive domain of the state but arenas where social and political groups compete to determine policy content and design.

Notes

This chapter is a revised and updated version of a paper presented on May 26, 1995, to the Second Oxford-Texas Colloquium on Mexico and Latin America at the Latin American Centre, St. Antony's College, Oxford, England.

1. Victoria E. Rodríguez and Peter M. Ward, "Disentangling the PRI from the Government of Mexico," *Mexican Studies/Estudios Mexicanos*, vol. 10, no. 1 (Winter 1994), 163–86; Victoria E. Rodríguez and Peter M. Ward, "The New PRI: Recasting Its Identity," in Rob Aitken, Nikki Craske, Gareth A. Jones, and David E. Stansfield, eds., *Dismantling the Mexican State* (New York: MacMillan, 1995); Victoria E. Rodríguez and Peter M. Ward, *Opposition Government in Mexico* (Albuquerque: University of New Mexico Press, 1995); and Enrique Cabrero Mendoza, "The State of Guanajuato: An Innovative Model," and Mauricio Merino, "The Go-Between Government: Obstacles and Opportunities to Good Local Government in Mexico," in Robert H. Wilson and Reid Cramer, eds., *International Workshop on Good Local Government: First Annual Proceedings* (Austin: Lyndon B. Johnson School of Public Affairs, The University of Texas at Austin, 1995), 65–78.

2. By far, the most important new book to appear in this extensive literature on the Mexican state is Miguel Angel Centeno, *Democracy within Reason: Technocratic Revolution in Mexico* (University Park: The Pennsylvania State University Press, 1994). Illustrative of the more specialized literature on various aspects of these reforms and changes in Mexican governance are Pascual García Alba Iduñarte, *Testimonios de Política Económica, 1982–1988* (México: Universidad Autónoma Metropolitana, 1993); Antonio Argüelles and José Antonio Gómez, *La Desconcentración en el Proceso de Modernización Económica de México: El Caso de SECOFI* (México: Miguel Ángel Porrúa Grupo Editorial, 1992); and Secretaría de Desarrollo Social, Programa Nacional de Solidaridad, *La Solidaridad en el Desarrollo Nacional: La Nueva Relación entre Sociedad y Gobierno* (Mexico, D.F.: SEDESOL, 1993).

3. See Centeno, *Democracy*, especially chapter 5, "The Technocratic Vanguard."

4. Ibid., pp. 47–51.

5. For a discussion of why the intergovernmental relations construct is especially appropriate for understanding the difficulties in policy implementation in Latin America in general and Mexico in particular, see Lawrence S. Graham, *The State and Policy Outcomes in Latin America* (New York: The Hoover Institution/Praeger, 1990).

6. Centeno, *Democracy*. Although tangential to the discussion here, a crucial aspect of the stability of the Mexican political system is civilian control of the military. For a discussion of civil-military relations in Mexico, see Roderic Ai Camp, *Generals in the Palacio: The Military in Modern Mexico* (New York: Oxford University Press, 1992). For an analysis of the Mexican case in comparative perspective, see Zoltan Barany and Lawrence S. Graham, "Political Transitions and the Military: Iberia and Eastern Europe" (unpublished manuscript).

7. Archives, Dirección de Integración y Control, Ministerio de Hacienda y Crédito Público, 1994.

8. The first scholar to discuss the role of *técnicos* and the differences between them and the *políticos* was Raymond Vernon in *The Dilemmas of Mexico's Development* (Cambridge: Harvard University Press, 1963).

9. Archives, Dirección de Integración y Control.

10. Ibid.

11. Ibid.

12. See Rodríguez and Ward, "Disentangling the PRI"; Rodríguez and Ward, "The New PRI"; and Rodríguez and Ward, *Opposition Government.*

13. Wayne A. Cornelius, Judith Gentleman, and Peter H. Smith, "Overview: The Dynamics of Political Change in Mexico," in Wayne A. Cornelius et al., eds., *Mexico's Alternative Political Futures* (La Jolla: Center for U.S.-Mexican Studies, University of California, San Diego, 1989).

8

Centralizing Politics Versus Decentralizing Policies in Mexico

Victoria E. Rodríguez

The host of decentralization programs and policies implemented in Mexico by successive presidential administrations since the early 1970s is the legacy of the crushing overcentralization of economic and political power in the country's capital city. Although in theory Mexico is a federation with three separate branches and three separate levels of government, in practice it is a highly centralized state. Particularly during this century— partly as a result of the social and political restructuring following the Mexican Revolution and partly as a result of the demands of regulated economic growth—the Mexican system has evolved into one of the most effectively centralized systems in Latin America.

As is amply documented in the literature, a strong centralist tradition has prevailed in Mexico since the pre-Hispanic period although federalism did indeed exist under Spanish rule and for a short period after Mexico obtained its independence. But after the restoration of the republic, the need to unify the country led to political and economic centralization, first realized during the dictatorship of Porfirio Díaz (1876–1911) and later intensified after the Revolution of 1910. As the country attempted to regain control of its resources, the bureaucratic apparatus expanded considerably, and economic activity and decision making were increasingly concentrated in the capital city. The state was becoming increasingly centralist with two incontrovertible characteristics: an extremely weak federal system, which is reflected in a lack of autonomy for local governments and in the strong domination by a single political party; and a massive concentration of economic power, population, and bureaucracy in the metropolitan area of Mexico City.

But my purpose in this chapter is not to discuss how and why Mexico became so overcentralized; rather, I propose to review the efforts to undo

such centralization by offering an assessment of the formal efforts to decentralize economic and political power during the last five presidential
administrations: Luis Echeverría (1970–76), José López Portillo (1976–82),
Miguel de la Madrid (1982–88), Carlos Salinas de Gortari (1988–94), and
Ernesto Zedillo (1994–2000). Because none of the efforts to undo centralization in the capital has been spontaneous, this chapter argues that all attempts to decentralize have been motivated by political factors.

Building upon the argument made by Lawrence Graham in the preceding chapter, this chapter seeks to demonstrate that, from the beginning, decentralization in Mexico has been the policy product of politically induced
change, thereby leading to a de facto retreat of the state. As the state re-
treated in the administrative field, however, it managed until recently to reinforce its central position in the political sphere. What we are witnessing
now, with concerted efforts at political opening and increasing victories of
the opposition at the state and local levels, is a nascent retreat of the state in
the political field. Decentralization, under the banner of New Federalism,
may very well serve as the full embodiment of the Mexican state in retreat.

Mexico's Decentralization Policies, 1970–1995

Although former Presidents Echeverría and López Portillo showcased
decentralization as an important policy issue, in no way can it be regarded a central concern of either of their respective terms in office. It was
not until the early 1980s, when Miguel de la Madrid assumed the presidency, that decentralization would become a key issue in the presidential
policy agenda. From the time de la Madrid embarked upon his presidential campaign in 1981, he grouped the nation's problems in seven large
categories, one of which was "decentralization of national life." Salinas
essentially followed the de la Madrid line, making decentralization one
of the basic issues around which his governmental plan was organized.
By the end of his *sexenio*, although subsumed under the umbrella of Solidaridad, it remained a key issue. Under Zedillo's New Federalism program, decentralization has climbed to the peak of the government's policy agenda. A review of the formal policy efforts to decentralize enacted
during the last five presidential administrations will show that although
their success may be questionable, the decentralization policy of the de la
Madrid administration, in particular, must be regarded as the most forceful effort of the past twenty-five years because it provided the turning
point for de facto decentralization to begin in earnest.

The Echeverría and López Portillo Administrations

At least partially, centralization in Mexico derived from the fact that since
the 1940s the state has been the most important contributor to the coun-

try's economic development. The boom that began in the 1940s and lasted for the next thirty years was evident in massive state investment in infrastructure, cheap credits, and countless subsidies, all of which made Mexico a regional leader in productive capacity. Even in the 1970s Mexico experienced a period of extraordinary growth, mainly based on oil revenues. But as the number of federal programs increased, so did the penetration of the federal government into the state and municipalities; more important, this growth accelerated the already rapid concentration of resources in the center.

The administration of Luis Echeverría dramatically sought to change the old development strategy of "stabilizing development" (*desarrollo estabilizador*) to one of "shared development" (*desarrollo compartido*). The objectives included correcting problems of income distribution and unemployment, raising the population's standard of living, reducing external dependency, controlling foreign investments, stimulating national industry, and increasing international trade,[1] all of which required more balanced regional development to be successful.

Throughout the Echeverría *sexenio* a large number of measures were designed to decentralize the industrial, agricultural, and administrative sectors and to move population away from the Valley of Mexico. One of the most important strategies to balance regional development was to decentralize the economic activities of the larger cities via the creation of the so-called *polos de desarrollo*. These "development poles" were designed to alleviate the growing problems of the larger metropolitan areas (unemployment and underemployment, pollution, scarcity of public services, and high cost of infrastructure), to create new employment opportunities that would raise the standard of living in the poorer areas, and to deflect the rural migrating population toward areas other than the huge urban agglomerations.

Thus the primary focus was to be on regional development, based on a series of programs aimed at alleviating rural and urban problems. The most important rural program was the Programa de Inversiones para el Desarrollo Rural (Program of Public Investments for Rural Development, or PIDER). Among the urban programs the most noteworthy were those designed for industrial decentralization, in particular the iron and steel complex Lázaro Cárdenas-Las Truchas and the twin-plant manufacturing program along the U.S.-Mexican border. The formulation of the regional development programs reflected a holistic vision that included both the agricultural-rural and the industrial-urban sectors.[2] However, this holistic vision slowly gave way, toward 1973, to one in which urban problems dominated and rural ones were neglected. More important, however ambitious and effective the various programs appeared to be on paper, strong regional vested interests were determined to impede their implementation.

Just prior to the end of the Echeverría *sexenio* the Ley General de Asentamientos Humanos (General Law on Human Settlements, or LGAH) was passed, partly as an outcome of the international conference on human settlements and of the marked interest of the administration in this matter. The general objective of the law was to coordinate the three levels of government in their regulation of human settlements throughout the country by carefully planning the development of population centers. The law emphasized the need for formulating plans of urban development at the national, state, and local levels.[3]

The new López Portillo administration took up Echeverría's concern with the problem of urban development coupled with industrial decentralization, and in 1978 a Plan Nacional de Desarrollo Urbano (National Plan for Urban Development, or PNDU) was promulgated.[4] Thereafter, state and municipal urban development plans were also formulated. The major policies through which the PNDU proposed to achieve its objectives included, among others:

> discouragement of growth in the Mexico City metropolitan area; promotion of the decentralization of industry, public services, and a range of private sector activities by orienting them toward areas that the PNDU declares to be priority zones; [and] encouragement of the development of cities with regional services and of medium-sized cities with a potential for economic and social progress.[5]

Thirteen priority zones were established throughout the country to implement the PNDU. The Ministry of Human Settlements and Public Works (Secretaría de Asentamientos Humanos y Obras Públicas, or SAHOP) was established as the institution responsible for overseeing the PNDU's implementation. At the same time, two important programs were designed to facilitate implementation. The Desconcentración de la Administración Pública Federal (Deconcentration of the Federal Public Administration) intended to reduce the number of federal personnel and offices in Mexico City. As the head of SAHOP commented: "32 percent of the public sector employees . . . 31 percent of its budget . . . and 45 percent of those covered by the Institute of Security and Social Services for State Workers (ISSSTE) are concentrated in the Mexico City metropolitan area. . . . There is one public employee for every 24 inhabitants and more than 20 percent of the population depends on the federal public administration."[6]

The Estímulos para la Desconcentración Territorial de las Actividades Industriales (Incentives for the Territorial Deconcentration of Industrial Activities) focused on industrial decentralization. Its main objectives involved reducing industrial concentration in Mexico City and regulating growth in the other two industrial centers of the country, Guadalajara and Monterrey, through fiscal, tariff, and credit incentives, all of which are essential elements for determining industrial location.

One of the most important urban-rural development programs of the López Portillo administration was COPLAMAR (Coordinación General del Plan Nacional de Zonas Deprimidas y Grupos Marginados, or National Plan for Depressed Areas and Marginalized Groups). Initially COPLAMAR competed with Echeverría's PIDER and duplicated many of its services, a common practice between successive administrations in Mexico.[7] Efforts to decentralize encountered similar types of bureaucratic difficulties as well, as of other decentralization programs were formulated with the respective governmental reorganization.[8] What all these programs meant in terms of actual policy implementation is difficult to assess definitively, but the evidence indicates overwhelmingly that the programs had very little real impact upon decentralization away from Mexico City.

The most comprehensive plan of the López Portillo administration was the Plan Global de Desarrollo, 1980–82 (Global Development Plan), whose chief architect, incidentally, was then Secretary of Programming and Budget Miguel de la Madrid.[9] Although the Global Development Plan dealt with virtually every phase of life in Mexico, it was aimed primarily at urbanization problems.[10] Unfortunately, the plan was barely off the printing press when Mexico was struck by the economic crisis that brought all programs and plans to a grinding halt. At that point it became virtually impossible to sustain any decentralization effort.

Taken together, the programs for regional development and industrial decentralization of the Echeverría and López Portillo administrations had almost no impact whatsoever on the development of states and municipalities—as industry still tended to locate in the Valley of Mexico. To a certain extent, the absence of control over the location of industry can be explained by the opposition of powerful industrial groups who, when pressured to relocate outside the Mexico City area, reacted by reducing investments significantly. Matters were complicated further by the economic crisis because the government could hardly afford to maintain an autonomous and detached position vis-à-vis the transnational industrial investments it badly needed. Overall, big industry did not sympathize with the government's regional development strategy and preferred to have the continuity of concentration that produced economies of scale.

Medium- and small-sized industry, which felt more heavily burdened by the growing costs of location in big cities (higher real estate and labor costs), took a somewhat different perspective from that of the larger corporations. Through CANACINTRA (Cámara Nacional de la Industria de Transformación, or National Chamber of Manufacturing Industry), smaller industries repeatedly pressured the government to decentralize the growing economic concentration in the metropolitan area of Mexico City and to promote industrial expansion in other areas. To a large extent the pressure from the smaller industries explains the decentralizing measures taken by the government because of its need to maintain the traditional support offered to the PRI by CANACINTRA. In addition, the government was trying to reassure medium-level and small entre- preneurs that it was seriously attempting to solve the problem of indus- trial concentration.

The evidence from the Echeverría and López Portillo administrations, however, conclusively shows that the spatial concentration of industry and population continued without interruption from 1970 to 1982 and that the problems of unemployment and income inequality became more severe for both urban and rural areas.[11] Overall, the effects were quite dif- ferent from the objectives proposed in the multitude of plans and pro- grams: Very little was actually accomplished. By the time López Portillo left office, the decentralization effort, like virtually everything else in his administration (and certainly himself personally) was badly tarnished. The public's general perception was that during the most recent two *sex- enios* more harm than good had been done.

The de la Madrid Administration

Given that Miguel de la Madrid was the author of López Portillo's Global Development Plan, when he became the PRI's presidential candidate, it seemed likely that decentralization would become a major issue in his governmental program. One of the highlights and innovations of his presidential campaign, which has become a standard for his successors, consisted of holding a series of public meetings throughout the country to discuss a variety of local and national issues. At these *consultas popu- lares* (or popular consultations, as they came to be known) demands for decentralization, particularly in the form of pleas for municipal auton- omy, came up repeatedly, and thus decentralization became a major and widely trumpeted plank in his campaign. In his inaugural address de la Madrid renewed his support for decentralization and indicated that, in order to pursue it, he proposed to transfer the health and education sec- tors to the states, to amend Article 115 of the constitution in order to strengthen municipal governments, and to strongly oppose any further growth in Mexico City.[12] His administration's first major statement on de- centralization appeared in the Plan Nacional de Desarrollo, 1983–1988 (National Development Plan, or PND).[13] In essence, de la Madrid pro- posed three broad lines of action in order to resolve the problems of cen- tralization: to strengthen federalism, promote regional development, and invigorate municipal life.[14] A series of formal plans and programs were designed to achieve each of these goals.

Decentralization of the Federal Public Administration

In June of 1984 de la Madrid issued a decree directing all federal agencies to develop a program to decentralize, deconcentrate, or relocate. These programs were formally embodied in the Programa de Descentralización de la Administración Pública Federal (Decentralization Program of the Federal Public Administration), implemented beginning January 1985.[15] In formulating their programs each agency was to consider development proposals from the states in order to decide how best to share with the state governments the responsibilities for implementing these programs. Thus the decentralization measures contemplated far more than a simple transfer of offices and personnel from Mexico City to the states, although the program also proposed to relocate a large group of central agencies outside the Federal District and to create field agencies to ease the burden of the center. The Ministry of Programming and Budget (SPP) took responsibility for the coordination of this program, particularly for overseeing the three specific ways it would be carried out: by transferring federally administered parastatal organizations to the state governments; by transferring to the state governments the responsibility for coordinating the execution of development plans; and by deconcentrating administrative functions. In essence, the program sought to support regional development by enlarging and improving regional infrastructures.

In early 1985 the federal government announced the transfer of various programs to the states.[16] In 1986, the first regional centers for decision making were established in Jalisco and Nuevo León, and twelve ministries, the Office of the Attorney General, and two important parastatals delegated a wide variety of functions to their representatives in those states.[17] The reorganization that resulted from the September 1985 earthquakes in Mexico City led to some acceleration and enlargement of many of these plans.[18] The relocation of federal employees, for example, was speeded up. The Comisión Nacional de Reconstrucción (National Reconstruction Commission) reported that in the few months following the tremors 70,000 federal public employees (15 percent of the total number of federal employees in Mexico City) would be relocated.[19] Nonetheless, the effect the earthquakes had upon the scale of decentralization was probably only slight. By the end of de la Madrid's administration 62,000 public employees had actually been relocated, which represented 67 percent of the goal proposed for 1988.[20] Although these accomplishments are by no means negligible, they are nevertheless secondary to the two most important and widely publicized decentralizing programs in the federal administration's plan: education and health.[21]

The main purpose of the program to decentralize education was to transfer responsibility for elementary education and teacher training to the states through a series of agreements between the federal and state governments that facilitated the transfer of material and financial resources and also provided the framework for the administration of federal and state educational services. But in addition to this quite valid administrative rationale, the decentralization of education also had a major political component. The government's main educational institution for teachers (the Escuela Normal Superior de México) had become heavily politicized, with a markedly leftist inclination; teachers who trained there, allegedly, were heavily indoctrinated against the government. From the government's perspective, this political activity was a greater cause for concern than the efficacy of the teachers' academic training. Decentralization away from Mexico City seemed to offer a solution because this would break up the primacy of the center as a locus for teachers training for public education. Not surprisingly, the program to decentralize education was not uniformly well received, in particular by the large and powerful teachers' union (the Sindicato Nacional de Trabajadores de la Educación, or SNTE). Fearing that decentralization would weaken its national structure, the SNTE strongly opposed the program, although in the end the union's national leaders did throw in their support.[22] By 1987, the transfer of responsibility for elementary and teachers' education to the thirty-one states was complete.

The most important step taken to facilitate decentralization in the health sector was the reorganization of the Ministry of Health (Secretaría de Salubridad y Asistencia, or SSA). The President decreed the Ley General de Salud (General Law of Health) in 1983 and in 1984 issued another decree by which all health services of this ministry would be provided by the states. The same decree stipulated that the services provided by the IMSS-COPLAMAR community participation program of the Instituto Mexicano del Seguro Social (Mexican Institute of Social Security, or IMSS) would also now fall under the states' responsibility.[23] In addition, the Ley Sobre el Sistema Nacional de Asistencia Social (Law on the National System of Social Assistance), put into effect in early 1986, transferred all the functions of social assistance from the SSA to the DIF (Desarrollo Integral de la Familia), a family social welfare agency.[24] Because the SSA no longer provided services of social assistance, its name was changed from Ministry of Health and Assistance to Ministry of Health. Reportedly the health decentralization program made some significant progress in its initial stages, but in the final analysis, it was not as successful as hoped.[25] Even though by 1988 the Ministry of Health had signed agreements with approximately half the states, an effective decentralization of these services was carried out by only fourteen states; in the others, IMSS-COPLAMAR continued operating under central directive.

Regional Development

In the administrative reorganization at the beginning of de la Madrid's presidency, a new Subsecretaría de Desarrollo Regional was created within the Ministry of Programming and Budget to oversee the country's regional development and to liaise with states and municipalities. The importance given to this *subsecretaría*, coupled with the transfer of various duties that formerly belonged to urban planning departments, showed that for the de la Madrid administration the urban concept was to be displaced by that of region.[26] Chapter 9 of the National Development Plan (PND) referred to the policy for regional development as "the general basis of the decentralization policy,"[27] to be accomplished primarily by redistributing powers and responsibilities among the three levels of government, relocating productive activities, and directing economic activities to medium-sized cities. The PND also included provisions for decentralization that were subsequently built into the daily operations of all ministries and federal agencies and devised an elaborate formal mechanism for the implementation of decentralization. The target of the regional development policy was to foster more comprehensive development in each of the states. The institutional framework created to do so was the Sistema Nacional de Planeación Democrática (National System of Democratic Planning, or SNPD), which was intended to make the planning system more democratic. The SNPD emphasized the importance of coordination among all levels of government and other organized social groups for planning the regional and national development programs.[28]

The primary mechanism for promoting regional development was the Convenio Unico de Desarrollo (Development Agreement, or CUD), signed yearly between the president and the governor of each state. The CUD (Covenio Unico de Concertación under López Portillo) provided the framework for a variety of programs through which the federal government could attend more effectively the states' needs.[29] Through the first CUDs, the state governments received federal allocations for the education and health sectors only, but gradually allocations grew to encompass all other federal programs for regional development. In addition to the rather complex bureaucratic structure of the CUDs, another equally complex set of agencies and programs was established under the Programas de Desarrollo Regional (Programs of Regional Development, or PDR), which were similar to PIDER and overall proved to be relatively successful.[30] The government also targeted specific areas of the country as priority development zones. Partly to assist each state in the formulation and evaluation of their CUDs, COPLADEs (Comité de Planeación para el Desarrollo Estatal) were created to help coordinate the investment priorities of the federal, state, and municipal governments as well as the private sector. The SPP, at the federal level, also used the COPLADEs to include state priorities in federal expenditure decisions. To this day, the COPLADEs have remained critical players in intergovernmental planning and the allocation of resources.

The primary importance of the CUDs lay in their being formal agreements designed for the transfer of federal resources to the states. From a decentralizing perspective, this was an important first step toward a more effective federalism. The CUDs were also important because through them the federal and state governments promised to strengthen municipal governments, for instance, by transferring directly to them resources that in the past the federal government had retained. Federal revenues were to be allocated *directly* to municipalities, bypassing the states (although, as will become apparent, this did not happen). From 1983 to 1988 the total federal investment in the CUDs amounted to 1.8 billion pesos.[31]

The urban policy of the de la Madrid administration focused primarily on promoting the growth of medium cities. This was no longer the responsibility of the Ministry of Human Settlements and Public Works (SAHOP), which had been recast as the Ministry of Urban Development and Ecology (Secretaría de Desarrollo Urbano y Ecología, or SEDUE). Perhaps the most important program designed to address urban problems was the Programa Nacional de Desarrollo Urbano y Vivienda (National Program of Urban Development and Housing) of 1984. In essence, this was a watered-down version of López Portillo's National Urban Development Plan (PNDU), which now had two main purposes: to change the national population patterns of growth and to regulate the growth of larger cities. From a political standpoint, there was little love lost between de la Madrid and the physical planners (who had held considerable influence under his predecessor) because they had allied themselves with the expansionist lobby of the cabinet, which de la Madrid had strongly opposed.[32] It is not surprising, therefore, that he formulated no spatial policy as such and that, instead, his prime concern was with the economic development plan and its implementation at a regional level. In this context he developed the SNPD and the CUDs, which because of their major implications for program implementation in the states ipso facto had spatial implications for regional development. De la Madrid's programs reflected a policy aimed at decreasing inequalities between rural and urban areas and at reducing migration to the United States.

The Municipal Reform

The municipal reform of 1983 was the cornerstone of de la Madrid's decentralization policy. In response to the generalized pressure to decentralize brought to bear during the *consultas populares* of his campaign, de la Madrid sent to the congress only five days after assuming the presidency an initiative to modify Article 115 of the constitution dealing with municipal governments. In this initiative, the Iniciativa de Ley de Reformas y Adiciones al Artículo 115 Constitucional, the president outlined the historical, ideological, and juridical justification for the transformation of *municipios,* emphasizing that "the centralization that in an earlier period allowed the country to accelerate its economic growth and social development has outlived its usefulness and become a serious limitation on the country's national project. . . . Centralization has seized from the *municipio* the ability and the resources needed for its development and, without question, the moment has come to stop this centralizing tendency."[33] Through this constitutional amendment, approved by the congress on February 3, 1983, and effective as of January 1, 1984, *municipios* were to become more autonomous. Indeed, the whole purpose was to give them the self-governance to which they were entitled under the constitution, but which they had never actually enjoyed. As the first major step toward decentralization, it was meant to strengthen the municipalities and, in so doing, to strengthen Mexican federalism by making local governments more independent of the state and federal governments.

The devolution of municipal autonomy was de la Madrid's key to decentralization. The president supported his argument for decentralization by emphasizing the deep historical roots of municipal organization in Mexico from the *calpulli* of the Aztecs to the present.[34] He also emphasized that the Constitution of 1917 granted municipalities economic and political autonomy in theory but not in practice. His address to the congress indicated that decentralization demanded a revision of the constitutional arrangement that divided rights and responsibilities among the federal, state, and municipal governments in order to obtain a better equilibrium among the three. He appeared firmly convinced that this redistribution would begin by devolving to the municipality the direct government of the community.[35] The president forcefully stated that the "changes in Article 115 are aimed at strengthening the municipality's finances, its political autonomy, and all those faculties that somehow have constantly been absorbed by the states and the federal government."[36]

De la Madrid's proposal for devolution also attempted to deal directly with the major problems associated with the uncontrolled growth of Mexico City and other urban areas, as well as with the disparities among various regions of the country. In changing Article 115, he pointed out, special attention was given to the social and economic differences among municipalities, their stages of development, and the contrasts among them.[37]

The initiative to reform Article 115 is divided in ten sections, seven specifically related to municipal structures, two that are common to states and municipalities, and one (without any modifications to the earlier text) related to the states.[38] Early evidence, however, suggested that the political and financial autonomy promised by the reform did not materialize during de la Madrid's administration. Moreover, the little autonomy that municipalities were able to achieve brought with it a series of responsibilities that municipal governments often could not handle, which inevitably meant that the central government retained supervisory powers and continued to play a critical financial role. In short, it was a policy designed to grant a measure of autonomy to local governments by transferring *some* power and resources but with the underlying proviso that the center would retain ultimate control. Certainly this central control was further reinforced during the Salinas presidency.

More than ten years have passed since de la Madrid's reform, and we are now in a position to evaluate its accomplishments. Even though most analysts tend to be rather pessimistic because they see a continued dependency of the municipality on the higher levels of government, my contention is that *some* decentralization has occurred. If nothing else, whatever discretion that already existed at the local level became official with the Municipal Reform of 1983; at the very least the reform acknowledged it and formalized it. Nonetheless, a critical point to be recognized is that this discretion in decision-making procedures has become much more evident at the *state* level, even if intended for municipalities. Both the overall fiscal policy and the Municipal Reform, albeit perhaps unintentionally, allowed the states to develop significant methods of control over their municipalities, particularly through the distribution of financial resources—an authority that remains in the states' hands. As will be discussed below, the state level of government will apparently continue to be the most likely beneficiary of decentralization under Zedillo's New Federalism.

The Salinas Administration

During the Salinas administration, Solidaridad was the watchword. The Programa Nacional de Solidaridad (National Solidarity Program, or PRONASOL) became the all-encompassing program under which the Salinas administration grouped most of its welfare and regional policies, including decentralization. Even though throughout his administration Salinas spoke much more in terms of solidarity than of decentralization specifically, the latter was an important element in his administrative program from the beginning. During his presidential campaign, too, Salinas emphasized repeatedly the urgency to decentralize, and indeed some of the largest and most important meetings of his campaign dealt with municipal life, federalism, and regional development. Like de la Madrid, he held numerous *consultas populares* on these subjects throughout the country.

But rather than presenting a specific decentralization policy of his own, Salinas pledged to continue the decentralization efforts of his predecessor through an invigoration of the municipal reform and other programs for administrative deconcentration, most notably in the education and health sectors. He also pledged, like de la Madrid, to center his efforts to decentralize around the issue of redistributing political and economic power, and he focused his discourse on the link between decentralization and democratization. Like his predecessor, also, he picked up the *descentralizar es democratizar* slogan and emphasized the democratic principles involved in decentralizing. Although a detailed evaluation of the decentralization accomplishments of the Salinas administration cannot be presented in this chapter, our concern is to review the main directives of his *sexenio*'s efforts to decentralize. By far, the most important of these was Solidarity.

The National Solidarity Program

PRONASOL was originally conceived as the program to combat poverty. It was designed for *los que poco o nada tienen* (those who have little or nothing at all) and soon became, as one public official put it to me, "Salinas's ticket." Indeed, Solidarity began operations on December 2, 1988—one day after Salinas assumed the presidency—and thus became the first formal act of his government. On December 6, 1988, the *Diario Oficial* published the decree that created the Comisión Nacional del Programa Nacional de Solidaridad as the organism for coordinating and overseeing all programs of poverty alleviation and regional development. Immediately, Solidarity's importance became visible to anyone visiting any part of the country; indeed, into the Zedillo administration, Solidarity slogans and the logo's small flag can still be seen everywhere.

The stated objectives of Solidarity were to improve the living conditions of marginalized groups, promote balanced regional development, and promote and strengthen the participation of social organizations and local authorities in the development efforts. The initial Solidarity initiatives were intended to benefit indigenous communities and the poorest peasant and urban groups and focused on nutrition, regularization of land titles and housing, legal aid, creation and improvement of educational facilities, health, community electrification, provision of potable water, agricultural infrastructure, and preservation of natural resources.[39] As the program developed, these were grouped into three principal "areas of action": solidarity for social welfare, solidarity for production, and solidarity for regional development.[40] In time, the PRONASOL umbrella covered a multitude of programs of a very diverse nature: social welfare, including education, health, urban and rural development services, and basic needs provision for "high risk" sectors of the population; infrastructural development; and general sustainable development for low-income groups, farm workers, and indigenous communities.

Although in its beginning stages the program was run directly from the president's office, Salinas soon moved to create a new ministry in which to house Solidarity. He reorganized his cabinet, consolidating the Ministry of Urban Development and Ecology and the Ministry of Programming and Budget (SEDUE and SPP) to form the Ministry of Social Development (Secretaría de Desarrollo Social, or SEDESOL) in 1992. Throughout the remainder of the *sexenio*, the new ministry's functions were carried out through three main divisions—Regional Development, Urban Development and Infrastructure, and Housing and Real Estate—in addition to its branch agencies and delegations in the states. Two of the most important branch agencies are Empresas de Solidaridad, which supports investments in productive projects, and the Instituto Nacional de Solidaridad, a training organization for potential leaders engaged in Solidarity activities.

In no time SEDESOL became the most visible ministry of the Salinas cabinet, not least because it appeared to be the ministry through which all major budgetary resources were channeled.[41] The President appointed Luis Donaldo Colosio (then president of the PRI) as head of the new ministry and Carlos Rojas Gutiérrez as head of the Solidarity program (which, naturally, was the principal office of the new ministry). Through SEDESOL and through both Colosio and Rojas—Colosio in particular—Salinas was able to maintain extremely close ties with the program's activities.

Essentially, PRONASOL emerged as a community participation program that worked in a rather simple way: Any organized group, be it a state or local government, a residents' group, or a local association, could approach local Solidarity officials to propose a public works project. Once a project was approved, Solidarity put up most of the financial resources required, while the group contributed the labor force and, whenever possible, local resources. As is well documented in the literature, the benefits of local projects of this sort are legion, and although not new to Mexico, they gained increased popularity during Salinas's administration as a direct link between government and the people and as an effective device to eliminate bureaucratic red tape and reduce government inefficiency. Indeed, just as de la Madrid had claimed to have designed his decentralization policy in response to popular demand, Salinas pledged during his own campaign to create a program that met popular demands to do away with government inefficiency and paternalism and to involve community actors more directly in decision-making processes that affected their daily lives. These promises were embodied in Solidaridad.

Although in itself the program was not really new to Mexico and was in many ways a direct descendant of PIDER, its novelty rested in taking advantage of the bureaucratic mechanisms already in place to implement a program that ambitiously hoped to address the gaps in social service provision and promote more balanced regional development. All funding decisions for Solidarity projects, for example, were incorporated into each state's Convenio de Desarrollo Social (Agreement of Social Development, or CDS, the successor to de la Madrid's CUD), thereby taking advantage of the COPLADE planning and development bureaucratic structure already set up in each state.[42] What distinguished Solidarity from other regional development and poverty alleviation programs was a set of principles and guidelines that clearly favored decentralization and community involvement. Solidarity demanded, for example, community participation in the selection and implementation of projects through the local Solidarity committees, shared responsibility for program implementation with state and municipal authorities, and shared costs among the three levels of government and beneficiaries.

Although the overall impact of Solidarity is difficult to measure because the range of its programs was so vast, federal financing for Solidarity grew from US$500 million in 1989 to US$2.2 billion in 1993. The thirty-plus programs covered a wide range of investments, often designed to complement regular sector investments. For example, the Escuela Digna program funded the rehabilitation and construction of educational facilities, and the Niños de Solidaridad gave small scholarships to individual students; neither of these expenditures were included in the normal education budget. The overall results of the program at the end of the *sexenio*, the administration claimed, amounted to a total of 523,000 projects completed throughout the country between 1989 and 1994.[43]

The number of beneficiaries and projects completed under the Solidarity umbrella are indeed impressive, even though in many respects the political aspects of the program overshadowed its social welfare accomplishments. But even if to a large extent Solidarity was engineered as a mechanism of political consolidation and as a natural outcome of the economic development policies of the administration,[44] what is important to underscore is its intention to target specific regions and municipalities in a major effort of poverty alleviation.

The most significant contribution of Solidarity to decentralization was twofold: On the one hand, it provided a vehicle for greater citizen participation in government decision making through the Solidarity committees and municipal Solidarity councils, especially for projects implemented at the local level; on the other, it promoted greater control over public investment decisions by states and municipalities as well as more adequate input in the planning and implementation of public works and social programs in their own communities. Altogether, Solidarity effectively decentralized by allocating federal funds *directly* to project committees and their municipal councils instead of going through the state governments as intermediaries. If the main decentralization shortcomings of the municipal reform consisted precisely in making allocations to local governments via their state governments, then Solidarity may have served as the vehicle for assisting municipalities in moving toward the autonomy they had been unable to achieve thus far.

Other Decentralization Efforts

A key, if largely unacknowledged, outcome of Salinas' political and financial "opening" and restructuring is genuine decentralization. At least in geographic and economic terms—and particularly in the aftermath of NAFTA—indications are that the lead is being taken by the modern manufacturing *maquila* industries (assembly plants) located along the U.S.-Mexican border. If the *maquila*-type industries continue to expand from the border to other provincial areas of Mexico—what Leslie Sklair calls "the march to the interior"[45]—then it will constitute an important vehicle for shifting the tendency away from centralization. The dramatic reorientation of the economy toward export manufacturing since Mexico's entry into GATT in 1986 and especially since the implementation of NAFTA has meant that manufacturing industries are now the most dynamic and important contributors to GDP, superseding petroleum. Within the manufacturing sector *maquilas* are at the leading edge of contemporary Mexican industrial development,[46] and this has reinforced those cities, mostly in the north and center of the country, that have included *maquila* plants in their urban development strategies.

In the education sector, Salinas proposed *la modernización del estado y de la educación*, with the principal objectives of increasing the involvement of the states in the planning process, furthering teachers' training, and restructuring the teachers' unions. All these objectives were fulfilled in the first three years of the Salinas administration. The reforms to Article 3 of the constitution, the new Ley General de Educación and, more important, the Acuerdo Nacional para la Modernización de la Educación Básica (signed in 1992 by the SEP, the SNTE, and the state gov-

ernments) provided the basic framework for furthering decentralization in the education sector initiated under de la Madrid. The principal
steps consisted of transferring to the state governments both responsibilities *and* resources for education and granting full autonomy for
spending them. Although significant achievements resulted from this
transfer, in the end there were also a series of negative outcomes, most
notably an increase in the conflicts between the teachers' union and the
state governments and complaints on the part of states and municipalities about the insufficiency of financial resources to carry out their
newly assigned functions.

In the health sector, the decentralization program initiated under de la
Madrid, which had transferred responsibility for the provision of health
services to fourteen states, did not advance much further. Indeed, even
though the decentralization of this sector was included in the Plan Nacional de Desarrollo, 1989–94 and in the Programa de Salud, 1990–94, no
steps were taken to implement it. If anything, with the creation of Solidarity and SEDESOL the federal government centralized even further all
resources for building, maintaining, and administering hospitals. The
IMSS-Solidaridad program, for instance, provided health services without any involvement of either the state or municipal governments.

The Zedillo Administration

For President Zedillo, decentralization has become more than a standard
rhetorical element in a campaign speech or a governmental program. It is
the key element in his project of *Nuevo Federalismo.* Under tremendous
pressure to take immediate action to remedy the abuses of overcentralization, Zedillo has been left with no alternative but to carry out a de
facto redistribution of political and economic power.

The implementation of New Federalism embraces several major areas
of reform of the state. It requires reform of the judiciary; reform of the fiscal system of revenue sharing; greater and more effective separation
among the three level of government (executive, legislative, judicial); a
reduction in the powers of the presidency itself (both constitutional and
metaconstitutional); institutional strengthening of state and municipal
governments; increased autonomy for the lower levels of government;
separation between party (PRI) and government; further advances in
electoral reform and implementation of reform at the state and local levels; and the development of new forms and opportunities for both representative and participatory democracy in the process of government.
Quite literally, it is a comprehensive, thorough *reforma del estado.* Although it is still early in the *sexenio,* on the basis of my reading of the official documentation to date and discussions with senior public officials

charged with implementing the program, it seems likely that there will be five broad areas of decentralization.

First, there will be some level of reform to raise the revenue-sharing allocations to the states, but this is likely to proceed only insofar as new and additional responsibilities are also transferred. During the Salinas administration, there were rising claims from several states to raise the proportion from 18.5 percent to over 30 percent, especially from states loyal to the Partido Acción Nacional (National Action Party) and other wealthier states of the north.[47] While institutional resistance from the Ministry of Economics and Finance, the economic crisis, and the continually growing size of the federal bureaucracy make the proposed level of change unrealistic, it seems likely that some across-the-board increase may occur and that certainly there will be a redistribution to accompany the transfer of new sectoral responsibilities to the states. Specifically, there will be improvements and extensions to the existing decentralization of public education and health, which has till now proven to be unsatisfactory and incomplete. In addition, many areas of agriculture, communications, and transportation will be decentralized. The bottom line is that states will receive more resources only insofar as they respond positively to these new responsibilities.

Second, there will be an expansion of the states' capacity to raise income locally through taxation and other mechanisms. This is unlikely to occur through property tax because the right to collect this tax was transferred to the municipalities with the Municipal Reform of 1983. Nor is it likely to come from the Value Added Tax (IVA) because this tax has been centrally collected since 1990 and is not likely to be transferred back to the states. Therefore, the opportunities for raising state incomes will likely derive from developing other areas of taxation (e.g., automobiles, licenses, payroll, etc.) and from the collection of fees for services.

Third, the lion's share of funds assigned for regional and social development through RAMO XXVI (formerly PRONASOL, now renamed Superación de la Pobreza) will be to a far greater extent allocated to the states and thus controlled by state governments. As of 1996, the resources of RAMO XXVI are being distributed among three funds: Fondo de Desarrollo Social Municipal (Fund for Municipal Social Development); Fondo de Prioridades Estatales (Fund for State Priorities); *and* Fondo para la Promoción del Empleo y la Educación (Fund for the Promotion of Employment and Education). Of these, the largest share (65 percent) will go to the Fund for Municipal Development; the Fund for Employment and Education will have 30 percent; and the discretionary Fund for State Priorities will have the remaining 5 percent.[48] By 1998, the latter two funds are to be phased out entirely, and therefore all resources will go into the Fund for Municipal Development. Currently, the resources of this fund are to be distributed among the states according to a formula based on poverty indicators.[49] The four states taking the largest share of the fund are Chiapas, Oaxaca, Veracruz, and Puebla (in that order). SEDESOL remains in charge of designing social policy at a national level and retains control of the budgetary resources of RAMO XXVI. Thus, the mechanisms for the distribution of resources from the federal government to the states appear to be transparent and equitable, given that they favor the poorer states; however, the precise mechanisms of decision making regarding the allocation of these resources from the states to the municipalities remain unclear, which may potentially sustain the patterns of discretion that have existed in the past and that have caused inequitable development among municipalities.

A fourth element in the decentralization scheme is to increase and strengthen the administrative capacity of municipalities. In the past, one of the principal arguments against decentralization has centered around municipal officials, who are perceived to be poorly trained, corrupt, and inexperienced in administration. The problem has been exacerbated by a lack of training programs, low funding, and Mexico's three-year nonrenewable terms in office, all of which produce a lack of continuity in policy design and implementation. Under New Federalism, the responsibility for raising this institutional capacity at the municipal level will increasingly fall to state governments; there is also more discussion of instituting re-election provisions.

And fifth, there will be clarification of the distribution of administrative functions among federal, state, and municipal levels. Although this seems imprecise, it follows the premises first incorporated in the municipal reform meant to eliminate (or at least reduce) bureaucratic duplication and overlap.

The weight and direction of decentralization appears, then, to be targeted much more to the states than to municipalities. Indeed, in the emerging Pacto Federal between states and the federation, the position accorded to municipalities is that they form part of the *régimen interior* of each state. Although one assumes (and hopes) that their autonomy will be respected, there is little doubt in my mind that the principal political beneficiaries of New Federalism will be state governments.

Conclusion

Although at an earlier stage centralization was critical in the process of economic development and political consolidation in Mexico, in time it became so excessive that its negative consequences could no longer be ignored. Over the last twenty-five years one presidential administration after another has attempted to tackle the problems of overconcentration, with relatively little success. The policy of President de la Madrid, largely encompassed in the Municipal Reform of 1983, represents the most forceful effort to undo the damages wrought by the overcentralization of power and resources. To the extent that some decentralization *has* occurred in Mexico, it has been a result of his initiative, further consolidated under some initiatives of Salinas's National Solidarity Program. Under Zedillo, we are hopeful that we will see a further consolidation of a de facto decentralization with his marked emphasis upon a New Federalism.

The challenge for the future rests upon the effective withdrawal of the state in different spheres (administrative, political) and at all levels (federal, state, municipal). Decentralization cannot be expected to be the responsibility of the federal government alone; it requires the help of state and local governments, all of which must recognize that decentralization, like any major reform, will alter the status quo and impinge upon vested interests. Although some of the decentralization efforts may have been well intentioned, major questions arise about their effective implementation. One issue is whether policies and programs have been designed to eliminate, reduce, or simply recast the dependency of the lower levels of government on the higher ones; another is that they require local political heavyweights, state governors, and other high-ranking public officials to relinquish some power in favor of lower levels of government. Thus far, this has not much happened; to the extent that the decentralization efforts of the last twenty-five years have produced any changes, they have been in the emergence of a new brand of federalism, with larger powers concentrated at the *state* level.

Thus, Mexico's decentralization policies are illustrative of the retreat of the state in the administrative field only to the extent that one is able to separate the administrative from the political. The increased demands for an effective federalism in Mexico—which will inevitably require a recasting of the powers of the state at the federal level in favor of lower levels of government—and the growing number of victories of the opposition at the state and local levels (approximately 30 percent of all Mexicans are now governed by the opposition) all point to an effective (if unwilling) retreat of the traditional, centralized Mexican state. Altogether, the consequences of this retreat of the state in Mexico are multifaceted: more effective and efficient governance; more open and democratic government institutions (e.g., state and federal congresses); a genuine distribution of powers across levels of government *and* branches of government; more transparent electoral processes; the birth of a new political culture characterized by increased participation of the electorate in the governing process; and perhaps, in the long run, increased confidence of the Mexican people in their governmental system. Seen in this light, the retreat of the state in Mexico may well lead to the consolidation of a democracy that is now only in incipient form.

Notes

1. See Judith A. Teichman, *Policymaking in Mexico: From Boom to Crisis* (Boston: Allen and Unwin, 1988).

2. The programs explicitly intended to support regional development and economic decentralization were divided into three general categories: those aimed at rural areas, those aimed at urban areas, and those aimed at both rural and urban areas. Among the rural programs, in addition to PIDER, was a National Plan for New Ejido Centers; the urban programs included two important presidential decrees for industrial decentralization issued on November 23, 1971, and July 20, 1972, in addition to the Lázaro Cárdenas and twin-plant programs; the urban-rural programs included a Program for the Border's Economic Development and the Coordinating Commissions for the Development of the Isthmus of Tehuantepec and the Peninsula of Baja California. For more information on the Echeverría administration's regional development policy, see Alberto Rébora, "El Ordenamiento Territorial y Urbano en México: Problemas y Perspectivas." *Comercio Exterior,* vol. 20, no. 10, 1978, pp. 320–60; Luis Unikel, "Políticas de Desarrollo Regional en México." *Demografía y Economía,* vol. XI, no. 2, 1976, pp. 240–2.

3. In 1976 a series of important reforms were made to the constitution with response to policies concerning human settlements and the participation of the *municipios* in this matter: Municipalities became empowered to propose laws and regulations concerning the problems of urban administration and human settlements; in addition, municipalities were to participate with the state and federal governments in planning and regulating all population centers. These constitutional reforms became the basis for the Law of Human Settlements, in which the *municipio* played a most important role. For a detailed account of the changes in the constitutional provisions dealing with municipalities, particularly of Article 115, see Diego Valadés Ríos, "El Desarrollo Municipal como Supuesto de la Democracia y el Federalismo Mexicano." *Estudios Municipales,* no. 3, 1985, pp. 63–71.

4. The main objectives of the PNDU were "to rationalize population distribution and the distribution of economic activities throughout Mexican territory; to promote an integrated and balanced urban development; to favor conditions allowing the population to satisfy its needs for urban land, housing, public services and urban infrastructure and facilities; and to improve and preserve the environment of such human settlements." See *Comercio Exterior,* vol. 24, no. 12, 1978, p. 494.

5. Ibid.

6. Pedro Ramírez Vázquez as quoted in the daily *El Universal,* September 22, 1978.

7. As Merilee Grindle concluded, "partisans of the two programs continually sniped at each other. According to followers of COPLAMAR, it had fallen heir to PIDER's original functions which PIDER was not able to carry out. Par-

tisans of PIDER questioned the integrated nature of COPLAMAR's activities and decried its lack of attention to productive activities. In both cases, these tensions inhibited cooperative activity." In addition, even if PIDER was the most comprehensive effort of the Echeverría administration for regional-urban areas, it was ineffective because occasionally it applied incompatible investment criteria. For instance, financial resources were often allocated to resolving problems that elicited serious social protest even if there were low expectations for results; preference was frequently given to irrigation areas where the highest yields were assured, or PIDER simply gave in to the World Bank's pressures to grant loans to seasonal zones. COPLAMAR hoped to correct some of those problems. Merilee Grindle, *Official Interpretations of Rural Underdevelopment: Mexico in the 1970s* (La Jolla.: Center for U.S.-Mexican Studies, University of California, San Diego, 1981).

8. Well over a dozen such programs were designed under elaborate names and with equally elaborate objectives. For a description of the content of these programs see *Comercio Exterior*, vol. 24, no. 12, 1978, pp. 496–9.

9. In a speech delivered at the unveiling of the Global Development Plan, de la Madrid stated that "efforts will be made to control the excessive growth of the largest cities, to strengthen the cities of intermediate size, and to give a boost to those on the coast and in the border zones. This scheme of spatial distribution seeks to achieve more balanced regional development, to reinforce the federal pact." De la Madrid's speech reflected the plan's concern with urbanization and in some statements, such as "to reinforce the federal pact," gives an early indication of his concern with decentralization. See *Comercio Exterior*, vol. 25, no. 11, 1979, p. 195.

10. The plan called for an annual increase of 20 percent in regional funds to be channeled through both PIDER and COPLAMAR as well as the Convenios Unicos de Coordinación (Coordination Agreements, or CUC, the predecessors of de la Madrid's Convenios Unicos de Desarrollo and Salinas's Convenios de Desarrollo Social) and an overall annual increase of 11 percent in the expenditures of all state enterprises. The revenues from petroleum exports would provide part of the funds. The plan also called for rationalizing purchases, eliminating corrupt practices, ending the excessive fragmentation of public works, integrating federalism with strong state planning, and increasing efficiency through program-budgeting mechanisms. See *Global Development Plan, 1980–82: Synopsis* (Mexico, D. F.: Secretaría de Programación y Presupuesto, 1980), pp. 28–9.

11. For example, between 1970 and 1975 alone the percentage of industrial establishments in the federal district and the state of Mexico increased from 32.2 percent to 34.9 percent, the economically active industrial population increased from 45.6 percent to 46.7 percent, and manufacturing production increased from 50.6 percent to 52.1 percent. The population of the metropolitan area of Mexico City increased at an estimated rate of 5.5 percent annually, which means that a population of 8.8 million in 1970 jumped to 11.5 million in 1975. Many other indicators also illustrate this point; for instance the twin-plant program, whose purpose was to support regional industrial development, stipulated that these plants could not be located in areas of high industrial concentration, yet over 50 percent

of the 107 twin plants registered in the program between 1972 and 1975 alone were located in or near the three largest metropolitan areas. Luis Unikel and R. de la Peña, "Consideraciones sobre la Concentración Económica en México," in *Asentamientos Humanos* I. (Mexico, D. F.: Secretaría de la Presidencia, 1976).

12. Miguel de la Madrid, "Protesta de Ley como Presidente Constitucional de los Estados Unidos Mexicanos, 1o de Diciembre de 1982," in *Testimonio Político* (Mexico, D. F.: Presidencia de la República, Dirección General de Comunicación Social, 1984), vol. I, pp. 30–1.

13. See Secretaría de Programación y Presupuesto, *Plan Nacional de Desarrollo, 1983–1988* (Mexico, D.F.: SPP, 1983). A more detailed discussion of his decentralization efforts can be found in the Secretaría de Programación y Presupuesto, *Plan Nacional de Desarrollo: Informe de Ejecución, 1983* (Mexico, D. F.: SPP, 1984) pp. 89–98.

14. Miguel de la Madrid, *Manual Sintesis de Pensamiento Político* (Mexico, D. F.: Partido Revolucionario Institucional, Coordinación General de Documentación y Análisis, 1992), p. 96.

15. The predecessor to this program was the Programa Nacional de Descentralización Administrativa (National Program for Administrative Decentralization), formulated after the Ley Orgánica de la Administración Pública Federal (the comprehensive legal code of the federal public administration) was reformed on December 29, 1982. The 1984 general decentralization program of the federal administration included the widely publicized Programa de Simplificación Administrativa (Program for Administrative Simplification), designed to eliminate, or at least reduce, bureaucratic red tape. The program also sought to provide the public with easier access to the services of federal agencies.

16. For example, the Comisión Nacional de Zonas Aridas (National Commission for Arid Zones) was relocated in Saltillo, Coahuila; the Centro Nacional de Investigaciones Agrarias (National Center for Agrarian Research) moved to Cuernavaca, Morelos; the Centro Regional de Investigaciones e Infraestructura Hidráulica (Regional Center for Hydraulic Research and Infrastructure) to the capital of Tlaxcala; the administrative offices of the Empresa Nuevo Vallarta to Puerto Vallarta, Jalisco; and the Centro Internacional de Adiestramiento de Aviación Civil (International Center for Civil Aviation Training) to Santa Lucía in the state of Mexico. These are only some of the programs designated for relocation. One of the more widely publicized and successfully relocated institutions was the Instituto Nacional de Estadística, Geografía e Informática (National Institute for Statistics, Geography and Information, INEGI) to Aguascalientes, where it remains today.

17. Secretaría de Programación y Presupuesto, *México: Desarrollo Regional y Descentralización de la Vida Nacional. Experiencias de Cambio Estructural, 1983–1988* (Mexico, D. F.: SPP, 1988), p. 32.

18. For varying perspectives on the government's responses to the earthquakes, see the special issue of *Revista Mexicana de Ciencias Políticas y Sociales* (January–March 1986) entitled "Desastre y Reconstrucción."

19. Comisión Nacional de Reconstrucción, *Comité de Descentralización* (Mexico, D.F.: CNR, 1986), p. 374.

20. Secretaría de Programación y Presupuesto, *Mexico: Desarrollo Regional,* p. 34.

21. The Ministry of Health also published a series of five volumes entitled *Cuadernos de Descentralización* (Mexico, D.F.: Ministerio de Salud, 1985), which discusses in detail the sector's decentralization policies and programs. See also Yolanda de los Reyes, "Descentralización de la Educación," in Blanca Torres, ed., *Descentralización y Democracia en México* (Mexico, D. F.: El Colegio de Mexico, 1986), pp. 126–45; Elena Jeanetti Dávila, "Descentralización de los Servicos de Salud," in Ibid., pp. 146–62; and Susan Street, "Los Distintos Proyectos para la Transformación del Aparato Burocrático de la SEP," *Perfiles Educativos UNAM,* no. 7, 1984, pp. 34–49.

22. Cf. Joe Foweraker, *Popular Mobilization in Mexico: The Teachers' Movement, 1977–1987* (New York: Cambridge University Press, 1994).

23. *Diario Oficial,* March 8, 1984, pp. 6–8.

24. *Diario Oficial,* January 9, 1986, pp. 33–9. The DIF embarked on a very successful decentralization program that also provided large political payoffs. At the beginning of de la Madrid's presidency only the national DIF and several state DIFs existed; there were none at the municipal level. By the end of his term in office 1,838 municipal DIFs had been created. For a detailed discussion of the DIF's decentralization, see Victoria E. Rodríguez, "The Politics of Decentralization in Mexico: Divergent Outcomes of Policy Implementation" (Ph.D. dissertation, Department of Political Science, University of California, Berkeley, 1989).

25. Miguel González Block, et al., "Health Services Decentralization in Mexico: Formulation, Implementation, and Results of Policy," *Health Policy and Planning,* vol. 4, no. 4, 1989, pp. 301–15.

26. Secretaría de Programación y Presupuesto, *México: Desarrollo Regional.*

27. Secretaría de Programación y Presupuesto, *Plan Nacional de Desarrollo,* p. 375.

28. See Secretaría de Programación y Presupuesto, *Sistema Nacional de Planeación Democrática: Principios y Organización* (Mexico, D.F.: SPP, 1982); Luis Aguilar Villanueva, "El Federalismo Mexicano: Funcionamiento y Tareas Pendiente" (Mexico, D. F.: El Colegio de Mexico, 1995), mimeo.

29. Within each CUD, five major programs were subsumed including PIDER, the Programas Estatales de Inversión (State Investment Programs, or PEI), the Programa de Atención a Zonas Marginadas (Program for Marginalized Areas, or PAZM), the *Programas Sectoriales Concertados* (Sectoral Programs, or PROSEC), and the Programas de Desarrollo Estatal (State Development Programs, or PRODES). The implementation of these CUD programs met with varying success.

30. The PDR was specifically charged with administering three different programs: the Programas de Infraestructura Básica de Apoyo (Programs of Basic Infrastructure, or PIBA) to provide services such as electricity, telephones, and roads; the Programas de Infraestructura para el Desarrollo (Programs of Development Infrastructure, or PID) to provide rural and urban communities with nutritional, medical, social security, housing, and educational services; and the Programas Productivos (Productive Programs) to develop self-sufficiency in rural areas through the provision of supplies and basic needs.

31. Secretaría de Programación y Presupuesto, *México: Desarrollo Regional,* p. 379.

32. Judith A. Teichman, *Policymaking in Mexico,* passim.

33. See Cámara de Diputados del Congreso de la Unión, LII Legislatura, *Proceso Legislativo de la Iniciativa Presidencial de Reformas y Adiciones al Artículo 115 de la Constitución Política de los Estados Unidos Mexicanos* (Mexico, D. F.: Colección Documentos, 1983), p. 8.

34. The *calpulli* was the Aztecs' system of social and political community administration and is the first instance of municipal government in Mexico. *Calpullis* were somewhat similar to modern municipalities in that they were responsible for a population in a specified territory, and there was a group of public officials charged with maintaining order. They were efficient and well-organized institutions that endured until the first part of the colonial period.

35. Cámara de Diputados, *Proceso Legislativo,* p. 8.

36. Ibid., p. 10.

37. Variations among regions were also considered in restoring municipal autonomy and making it a national rule: "In accordance with the constitutional principle regarding the internal regimes of the states, the regulation of municipal communities will be guided by the local laws and constitutions in order for these to contain the norms that will correspond to the specific geographic, ethnographic, demographic, and economic characteristics that are distinctive of each one of the states." Camara de Diputados, *Proceso Legislativo,* p. 12.

38. The key provisions are II, III, and IV. Section II grants municipalities autonomy in the management of their finances and enables them to design their own rules and laws of governance; Section III deals with the provision of public services and specifies which services must be provided by the municipality; Section IV, the most important, specifically grants municipal governments all revenues collected from property taxes and from the provision of public services. For many municiplities, these have become critical sources of revenue. See Victoria E. Rodríguez, *Decentralization in Mexico* (Boulder: Westview Press, 1997).

39. Consejo Consultivo del Programa Nacional de Solidaridad, *El Combate a la Pobreza: Lineamientos Programáticos* (Mexico, D.F.: El Nacional, 1990), pp. 15–6.

40. Secretaría de Solidaridad, *Solidaridad: Seis Años de Trabajo* (Mexico, D. F.: SEDESOL, 1994), pp. 10–11.

41. However, contrary to this perception, the evidence indicates that PRONASOL never reached even 20 percent of federal spending.

42. The CUD became CDS in 1992, but it retained the same mission to serve as the coordinating mechanism for planning intergovernmental programs and investment. The only visible difference is that CDS emphasizes the links between planning and social development and incorporates the funding for carrying out these policies through Ramo XXVI. The COPLADES have had no changes in their composition and functions since 1983.

43. SEDESOL, *Solidaridad,* p. 25.

44. See Denise Dresser, *Neopopulist Solutions to Neoliberal Problems: Mexico's National Solidarity Program* (La Jolla: Center for U.S.-Mexican Studies, University of California, San Diego, 1991); Wayne Cornelius, Ann l. Craig, and Jonathan Fox,

eds., *Transforming State-Society Relations: The National Solidarity Strategy* (La Jolla: Center for U.S.-Mexican Studies, University of California, San Diego, 1994).

45. Leslie Sklair, *Assembling for Development: The Maquila Industry for Mexico and the United States* (Boston: Unwin Hyman, 1989).

46. Patricia Wilson, *Exports and Local Development: Mexico's New* Maquiladoras (Austin: University of Texas Press, 1992); Nora Lustig, *Mexico: The Remaking of an Economy* (Washington, D. C.: The Brookings Institution, 1992).

47. Victoria E. Rodríguez, *Decentralization in Mexico,* passim.

48. See *Diario Oficial,* December 22, 1995.

49. See *Diario Oficial,* January 5, 1996.

9

The Redefinition of State Policies in the Social Arena: The Case of Mexico

Jon Shefner[1]

The onslaught of the Latin American debt crisis and the application of neoliberal policies often referred to as "structural adjustment" is by now a well-known story. The crisis has been traced to the mid-1960s European recession, which lasted into the 1970s and was accompanied by increasing oil prices and accumulation of OPEC funds in western banks. The banks, holding a large amount of lending capital and unable to lend it profitably within the depressed western economy, increased lending to Third World and socialist nations. These nations, suffering balance of payments deficits because of steadily rising import prices, borrowed at unprecedented levels. Then, as the effects of the recession of the late 1970s and early 1980s became felt, few of the indebted nations could service their debts without severe domestic policy changes, such as cutting social welfare budgets and governmental subsidies for food, oil, and transportation.

The impact of debt and debt service on the Third World in the 1980s was devastating. The period from 1980 to 1983 saw a zero to negative growth rate of per capita production and income throughout the Third World.[2] Total indebtedness of the Third World at the end of 1984 was calculated at U.S.$895 billion and rose to $1.4 trillion by 1992.[3] This increase was largely a result of the rising burden of interest rather than new loans and continued into the latter part of the decade. In 1988, the World Bank reported a $43 billion negative flow of payments from the Third World to the industrial nations. Living standards and investment in Latin America fell drastically. During this period, inflation soared at rates of increase ranging from 57.6 percent to 11,000 percent in various nations throughout the region.[4] The credit rating of most Latin American countries had dropped to an abysmally low level.

International lending agencies such as the International Monetary Fund (IMF) and, to a lesser extent, the World Bank, operating under the mandate of their most powerful member nations, disburse loans and advise creditor nations on the domestic economic policies upon which these loans are contingent. The IMF asserts that conditional policies

> achieve a better balance of payments equilibrium in the medium term and a more efficient use of scarce resources by introducing a number of incentives and measures to generate more domestic savings, more investment, and more exports. These are programs aimed . . . at a more rational combination of economic policies in order to achieve a better balance of payments equilibrium, and thus open the way for more vigorous and lasting growth.[5]

The conditions suggested by these international lending agencies and imposed by national governments have consistently taken the form of "shock treatments" or "austerity policies" (also called structural adjustment policies) intended to elicit economic stabilization. John Walton found that

> borrowers were expected to introduce domestic reforms, including some combination of devaluation, reduced public spending, elimination of subsidies for food and necessities such as cooking oil and gasoline, wage restraint despite inflation, increased interest rates, taxes related to demand restraint, elimination of state-owned enterprises, greater access for foreign investment, reduced protection for local industry, import curbs, export expansion, and, at bottom, the application of new foreign exchange to debt service.[6]

These policies have had deep and lasting consequences for economy and society in dozens of indebted countries.

Not the least of these consequences have been changes in the role of the state. The state in Latin America has been periodically defined as populist, corporatist, and bureaucratic-authoritarian.[7] What all three descriptions hold in common is the recognition that the state maintains some responsiveness to societal sectors. These sectors vary from popular urban groups, labor, *campesinos,* the military, and technocrats to state functionaries themselves. The most commonly, and most powerfully, represented sector, however, has been small national capitalist classes because of their link with international capital.[8]

If the neoliberal state, as we may call it in the most recent period, has changed in Latin America during the debt crisis, it has been to increase responsiveness of the government to the interests of national and international capital. Subsequently, other sectors have lost influence. This is clear in the wide-ranging damage done to peasants and to the urban

working and middle classes, who have borne the brunt of neoliberal restructuring. Employment has decreased, in part due to reduced state size
but also because of removal of protections for domestic industry. Real
wages have fallen because of the rising costs of living and salary freezes.
Subsistence and small-market agriculture have suffered as large agribusi-
nesses gained even greater entry into domestic production, having a further adverse effect on employment opportunities and wages.

The policies of the neoliberal state, then, have increased the pro-
nounced inequalities already existing in Latin American societies. Yet
even as the logic of the neoliberal state forces it away from social responsiveness, the damaging impacts of the program force the state to apply
some remediating antipoverty policies. In Bolivia, for example, the Emergency Social Fund was created with the objective of alleviating poverty
while maintaining economic reform. The fund, administered by local
governments and nongovernmental organizations, helped build schools
and low-income homes and created jobs for some of Bolivia's urban poor.

In Chile, despite a general decline in social spending amid repressive
governing, antipoverty efforts for the poorest Chileans actually increased
during the Pinochet years. Although the general economic changes eliminated social welfare access to many, government programs temporarily
employed a large number of Chilean workers during the height of the
economic crisis. Antipoverty measures also helped protect the health of
the poorest Chileans.

Peru also instituted a temporary public works program that employed
many urban poor, although it was used largely to bolster the public
image of President Alan García's government. Its link to the government
and the basic clientelist process of its administration discredited it in the
eyes of many Peruvians.[9]

The Latin American state, under pressure from the neoliberal regime,
has moved away from some of the day-to-day social welfare provision.
The dramatic nature of this change, however, has left large sectors of the
population in even worse economic straits than before. The antipoverty
programs responded to these needs in largely piecemeal fashion, often
following political requirements for system maintenance rather than successfully addressing social problems. As we turn to the neoliberal experience and antipoverty efforts in Mexico, we see more evidence that state
policy is focused mostly on maintaining stability and legitimacy in a context of reduced social welfare delivery.

The Social Costs of Structural Adjustment

In Mexico, neoliberal structural adjustment proponents identified state
intervention in the economy as the source of many ills: disruption of in-

ternational and national competition; stagnation of production; stunted technological development; increasing fiscal deficit and taxes; and above all, the lack of efficiency and rationality in production. In response, both Presidents Miguel de la Madrid and Carlos Salinas de Gortari advocated the opening of the economy to international investment by sharply reducing all controls, regulations, and protections.[10] This effort reduced state intervention in the economy to allow the market to determine its own course, using privatization of state-owned enterprises as one principal tool. The domestic market was opened to the entry of foreign capital and trade by the removal of protections and controls that previously favored domestic industry. This was expected to lead to competition that would end all market distortions resulting from earlier state intervention.

Before structural adjustment, the Mexican economic development model yielded an increasingly unequal distribution of wealth but nevertheless produced a general increase in the standard of living among the urban working and middle classes. Throughout the 1960s and 1970s, real minimum wages rose steadily while prices of basic foods decreased. Growth was tied to oil revenues between 1978 and 1981, but growth proved illusory, with the official recognition of the debt crisis.

As Mexican policymakers prioritized debt repayment, national well-being plummeted. The outcome of two presidential terms that emphasized neoliberal policies was negative economic growth and reduction in social spending, followed by low economic growth. Wages decreased, unemployment increased, and quality of life was significantly impaired. The real economic growth rate averaged 0.3 percent each year between 1982 and 1987, recovering in the 1989–1992 period with an annual average increase of 3.75 percent.[11]

Recent economic growth has again slowed, with a 0.8 percent growth in gross domestic product in 1993 and 3.5 percent in 1994. In 1995 GDP showed a negative percentage of 6.9 as a result of the 1994–95 currency crisis. Other economic measures indicate stagnation or reduction of growth as well. Comparing 1992 to 1970, agriculture, industry, and manufacturing all fell as a percentage of GDP. Only the service sector, a weak propellant for the rest of the economy, expanded its percentage of GDP. And external debt itself became more onerous, doubling from U.S.$57.4 billion in 1980 to U.S.$158.3 billion in 1995. Concomitantly, the almost U.S.$11 billion in annual debt service increased to almost $U.S.20 billion over that same period.[12]

Wage decreases in formal sector employment were significant, with a 45 percent drop in real wages from 1982 to 1986.[13] Even more drastic was the drop in the minimum salary, which by 1992 was effectively 38 percent of the 1975 minimum salary. This drop was partially a result of increased prices but also resulted from stabilization policies limiting wage increases. With the December 1994 devaluation of the peso, the Mexican Federation of Labor, a group affiliated with the Partido Revolucionario Institucional (PRI), estimated that the purchasing power of minimum salaries fell between 30 and 40 percent virtually overnight. In sum, the working class lost almost half its buying power during the Salinas *sexenio*, 1988–1994.[14] Employment in the formal sector also fell between 1982 and 1987, with a concurrent rise in informal employment and a stagnation in overall employment.[15] By 1993, 56 percent of the working population worked outside the formal economy.[16] Unemployment rose from 2.7 million in 1981 to 4.6 million in 1984 and reached 8 million in 1988.[17] Rising unemployment was largely based in the cities, where manufacturing and construction activities had contracted sharply. This trend has continued in the 1990s. According to government figures, 1993 manufacturing industry employment fell 15 percent from 1992, translating into the loss of over half a million jobs. A further 400,000 workers lost jobs in 1994, and the employment fallout from the devaluation continues to grow.[18]

From 1983 to 1988, a period of heavy economic adjustment, government social spending per capital fell 40.2 percent and included cuts in basic food subsidies. The 1984 subsidy expenditure was 43 percent below that of 1983 in the shift from general to targeted subsidies. Clear results from these cuts were evident as early as 1983, when a survey showed poor families consuming less food, especially animal products. By 1985, the price of a basic food basket as a percentage of the minimum wage had increased to 50 percent from 30 percent in 1982.[19] Other figures show a much more dramatic increase in the prices of basic food basket items, with estimates ranging from 1593 percent to 6200 percent between 1982 and 1988.[20] Other clear indicators of the government's retreat from social welfare provision include the following reductions in spending (as a percentage of total central government expenditure) between 1980 and 1992: in education, from 18 percent to 13.9 percent; in health, from 2.4 percent to 1.9 percent; and in housing, social services, and welfare, from 18.5 percent to 13 percent.[21] Although these are federal expenditures, recent reports make it clear that the states have failed to make up for the reductions, as they are increasingly beset by their own debt.[22]

State Dominance and Popular Demands

Wide social unrest followed de la Madrid's neoliberal restructuring. After winning the 1988 presidential elections in dubious circumstances, Carlos Salinas was forced to address quickly some of the painful consequences of economic restructuring in order to bring unrest under control.

How does the state maintain control over a burgeoning population of urban poor? A large body of work on Mexico, especially from the 1960s through the 1980s, put forth a model to explain how the state dominates popular organizations. Rooted in a wider analysis of Mexico's corporatist governing system, this model describes how the state maintains legitimacy and power and how dissent and demand-making are channeled into state-sanctioned organizations, which limit alternative organizing and constantly recreate state power while incorporating dissident groups and leaders.

In the state dominance model, the dominant political party, the PRI, which is identified with the state, embodies the hope of the urban poor to better their lives. Local needs are expressed via local leaders' ties to state and party functionaries. Although these ties often result in manipulation or exploitation of the community, they also offer limited protection, advancement, and political participation. In return for using his influence with state or party officials, the leader receives support from the community, and the government receives expressions of loyalty.

Contacts with government and party officials are made in a notably nonthreatening manner. Community groups usually shy away from protest, which is thought futile and even damaging to relations with state and party patrons. Conventional strategies include offering to pay for urban services, exerting indirect pressure by publicizing demands to the media, and reminding visiting officials of their long-felt needs. The limited and local focus of demands means that once gains are satisfied, popular organizations disintegrate rather than shift the focus of their organizing. The need for personal and party contacts may even preclude independent organizing, and access to PRI patronage often dissolves dissidence.[23] The pressure on leaders to become "entangled" in the state-sanctioned organizations is great: The personal rewards are substantial, and the space for maintaining autonomy is small.

As formerly independent leaders enter the party or the government, their constituencies lose a voice. Eckstein has shown that even popular mobilizations that organize independently from the state may fall into the trap of incorporation. Survivors of the 1985 earthquake in Mexico City, for example, organized outside of the PRI umbrella and enjoyed some success in their efforts to rebuild their devastated community. These groups, however, entered into an agreement that bound them to state negotiations. Having failed to incorporate the newly mobilized groups within traditional mass organizations, the state found a new mechanism that fulfilled some popular demands, while convincing groups "to work with and not against the state. . . . (The accord) cleverly brought groups 'into line' and put an end to popular protests."[24] An organizational structure was imposed that the independent leadership was not allowed to head, thus superseding the previous organizing and reincorporating these groups. Despite the success they enjoyed, the disaster victims ended up reintegrated within a party/government structure. Eckstein summarizes the state dominance model in her comment:

> organizations of the poor help legitimate the regime, extend the government's realm of administration, and reinforce existing social and economic inequities through overt and covert collective incorporation and through overt and covert individual cooptation of leaders into the official power structure. . . . Cooptation of leaders and incorporation of local groups has served to establish and reinforce the status quo.[25]

Agreeing in general on the intent and effect of state dominance, Cornelius tries to understand the perpetuation of this relation from the poor urban dweller's point of view: "Their unwillingness to confront the system reflects a rational adaptation to the rules of the political game, a low propensity for risk-taking, and an awareness of which kinds of political action are rewarded by the authorities and which kinds are likely to be ignored or violently repressed."[26] Cornelius emphasizes, however, that the perpetuation of state dominance depends on the degree of community need to be met and that it can be done only when the economy is experiencing continued growth. The "lost decade" of the 1980s debt crisis, however, severely limited the expansion of the Latin American economies. Consequently, the maneuvering room for these types of "populist" solutions disappeared.

Popular Insurgency and New Demands on the State

Recent research has shown that opportunities for popular organizations to come together independently of state-sanctioned channels is presenting a greater challenge to the state than previously assumed. It builds upon earlier studies that showed popular organizations having wider strategic prerogatives than the state dominance model suggested.[27] The literature positing different relationships between states and popular organizations is based on field work done since the late 1970s and suggests a wider structural shift affecting changes in power relationships between popular organizations and the state.[28] Although these studies do not show the total displacement of clientelist or corporatist relations, they stress new, independent popular organizing as the activity to be watched. They have inspired an alternative interpretation of the relationship between state and civil society, one that has become known as the popular insurgency model.

New organizational postures range from rejection of clientism to a willingness to redefine clientelism. The conscious rejection of clientelist relations is evident when new organizations are built, and the urban poor refuse to enter into relations with previous patrons. Even where traditional state-society relations remain in place, however, their character has changed. Shorn of some frills, the new clientelism operates through naked transactions of goods and services in exchange for electoral support.

Several authors argue that a new definition of citizenship rights is emerging. Paul Singer sees an effort to " develop a new consciousness, an attitude of unity for self-help among the population," where "the demands made assume the character of demands for rights and not for favours to be obtained by bargaining with the representatives of the state."[29] The new consciousness is accompanied by a critique of clientelism, as new community organizations view exploitation and perpetuation of inequalities as inevitable results of this relationship. A new electoral activism accompanies the critique, with independent community leaders suggesting that residents refuse vote-buying efforts and assess candidates' value based on other criteria.[30]

The new citizenship is also expressed in new organizational forms. Groups recognize their similarities in demands and background and challenge ongoing state attempts to segregate and channel popular opposition.[31] Coalitions organize around extra-local issues that relate to the more general social problem of unequal access to resources, as in the participation of *favela* organizations in the civil society challenge to the Brazilian military regime.[32] Some of the newly organized poor perceive their actions as part of a wider struggle, their local fights advancing more comprehensive social transformation.[33] Mobilization goals are expressed as part of an attempt to "bring about popular participation in the institutions which control these aspects of urban life."[34]

The new political participation is increasingly militant, as organizations self-consciously break the state's rules of political conduct. Instead of ties with important functionaries, the new preferred leadership characteristics include a demonstrated solidarity with workers and the poor, a willingness to pressure the state, and active community participation.[35] But they are often representatives of the popular church, who advocate political action to attain rights. Christian-base communities help create new organizational forms and make consciousness-raising an explicit goal. Human rights groups also have deliberately attempted to create organizations that move away from patronage relations.[36]

Although clientelism is declining slightly, researchers recognize that it continues to be a strong force in structuring state-society relations. Radical and conservative tendencies coexist within urban politics, the latter maintaining clientelism. The state continues to look for new ways to reimpose some variant of traditional relations.[37]

Most of the research cited by advocates of the popular insurgency model does not focus on Mexico. However, social movement dissent in the debt crisis years in Mexico has likewise been largely anticlientelistic and has followed similar patterns.[38] One less evident, but still important, difference is that the state dominance model, as it applies both to Mexico and elsewhere in Latin America, is rooted in an understanding of the political economy of dependent development. The popular insurgency model celebrates the newly discovered democratic popular process without sufficiently linking it to political and economic change. In addition, the optimism inherent to the popular insurgency model has yet to be borne out by wide-scale political change. We must be careful of such optimism when we remember the enthusiasm generated by revolutionary movements from the 1960s through the 1980s.

The state dominance literature indicates the myriad strategies the state has used to quiet dissent. Although new strategies by challengers are important to recognize, we must also understand the state's capacity to change policy and rhetoric to confront new challengers. In the situation of increasing social tensions and state withdrawal from key social policy areas, this capacity is being tested to the limit.

Challenges of the 1990s

The dynamics of political life in Mexico are almost spectacular. In the recent past, political assassinations, a guerilla uprising, and the devaluation of the peso have provided dramatic evidence that the one-party government does not have the solid control over Mexican society it used to. Recent electoral defeats in Jalisco, Guanajuato, and Baja California, following the narrowest presidential victory ever claimed by the PRI, offer further confirmation. However, it is too early yet to assume the phasing out of the PRI-dominated political system. Opposition challenges have been met by a state taking concerted action to maintain control over increased societal conflict. The critique of the antisocial bias of neoliberal policies and their antidemocratic implications was met by governmental policies that attempt to meet both material needs and demands for popular representation. The question arises whether these policies are best understood as state attempts to reimpose clientelist relations or whether they form part of a distinct change in state strategy. A secondary question is whether local political power can influence policy regardless of the intention of federal policymakers. If local political power holders dispute the directions of reform driven by central authorities, this will have a significant impact on the extent and form of future change in the Mexican political system.

The local applications of President Salinas's flagship project, the Programa Nacional de Solidaridad (PRONASOL), provide some empirical evidence for the debate. Solidaridad has been variously described as an attempt to alleviate poverty and to include all sectors of Mexican society in a national process of democratization, or as an effort to relegitimize Mexican centralist politics.[39] Its importance as a policy instrument is confirmed in the growth of both its funding and mandate throughout the Salinas administration.

During the Salinas years, PRONASOL widened in scope and intention. From its inception it was used to quiet dissidents and neutralize the opposition in potentially dissident communities. For example, the austerity policies of de la Madrid had been challenged by a loose coalition of groups in the Movimiento Urbano Popular (MUP).[40] The Salinas administration created locally managed community organizations, the Comites de Solidaridad, in direct response to the demands of urban protestors. They became a new organizational vehicle sharing "responsiblity" in bringing urban services to poor areas.

Nongovernmental organizations (NGOs) posed another challenge to traditional politics. Representing diverse constituencies and political goals, they have organized in ways that challenge state strategies of isolation, fragmentation, and cooptation of the political opposition. Governmental policy responses to the activities of the NGOs originate in the same ministry that housed Solidaridad.

Here I examine two cases in which PRONASOL attempted to address problems identified by local communities and nongovernmental organizations. The first is an example of organizing in popular *colonias* in the *municipio* of Tlaquepaque, located southwest of Guadalajara, Jalisco. I look at how Solidaridad policies operated within local communities and assess the program's claims of independence from the ruling party. The experience of the Comites de Solidaridad in Tlaquepaque also offers an opportunity to analyze their interaction with both entrenched political power groups and independent political organizations in poor *colonias.* In the second case the government responded to the challenge presented by the emerging NGO sector by creating a state council of nongovernmental organizations. It was one of the first attempts in Mexico to create a setting in which relations between the state and NGOs could be institutionalized.

The state dominance and popular insurgency models of state-society relations provide a context within which Solidaridad can be evaluated, although neither may provide sufficient explanatory power for entirely understanding debt-induced state change in the social sector.

The National Solidarity Program

PRONASOL was created immediately upon Carlos Salinas's assumption of the presidency in December 1988. Solidaridad's genesis is evident in

Salinas's doctoral dissertation on the faltering relation between government and rural communities. The intellectual roots of the program are found in his suggestion to launch "a concerted effort by the PRI-government apparatus to promote the emergence of a new generation of leaders at the community level who could serve as more effective interlocutors between citizens and the state."[41]

The institutional goals of Solidaridad evolved even in its relatively short history. Initially created to ameliorate some of the social costs of modernization, the activity was to be carried out by targeted populations of poor people working in local committees. The expressed intentions of Salinas and the directors of PRONASOL soon became much broader and more ambitious: The Solidaridad program was presented as the formula through which state-society relations were to be recreated and the activities of the state in the social sector restructured.[42]

Even in the beginning, the PRONASOL program was advertised as a comprehensive attempt to attack root causes of poverty. "It is fundamental to emphasize that PRONASOL does not look to be a palliative for extreme poverty in which wide sectors of the Mexican population find themselves immersed; it is trying to attack the structural causes of poverty."[43] The Solidaridad program became the device through which the state would make amends for its previous negligence in rectifying socioeconomic inequalities.

New goals included the creation of social justice through participation in Solidaridad programs. Government publications emphasized the role that clientelist politics played both in delaying the arrival of democracy and in the perpetuation of poverty. Economic modernization requires political modernization, so that Mexico can "move into the twenty-first century strengthened in its sovereignty; prospering in its economy; in peace, freedom, and democracy; and able to create new horizons for well-being and justice for all Mexicans" in a political environment that abandons the old "paternalist and clientelist schemes."[44]

The transition from "clientelism, hierarchy, paternalism, and political conditionality" was to be made by following basic principles of community respect and democratic participation. The next step, according to PRONASOL managers, would be the creation of a new democratic political culture. Working together in organized communities required such common goals as "promoting participation," "strengthening the ties of commitment between organization members," "developing solidarity attitudes," "assuming democratic practices in decision making," and "strengthening autonomy." Joint work to attain these goals would result in benefits beyond accomplishing finite public works projects. "These works are important because we gain the awakening of a sentiment of solidarity and responsibility about the problems we have analyzed and

an establishment of commitments and agreements with responsibility
and consensus."[45]

Thus the goals of the Solidaridad program evolved from addressing
poverty to the creation of a new political culture, inducing "a consciousness of social solidarity." The creation of the new culture was itself instrumental to another goal, the restructuring of state-society relations:

> In the Solidaridad program, the process of redesigning the state-society re-
> lation is clearly expressed: Through the Comites de Solidaridad, the impov-
> erished groups of our country have been able to open practical and agile
> new channels for communication and coordination in dealing with the gov-
> ernment, making decisions, and resolving problems democratically.[46]

The transition from local committees addressing infrastructural needs
to coalitions of the same committees seeking and winning greater representation is the most comprehensive step in the evolution of Solidaridad
goals. By joining together with other permanent *comites*, Solidaridad literature suggested, organized Mexicans can participate directly and have
a voice in issues of both community and national development. The coalitions advocated by the Ministry of Social Development (SEDESOL)
would create a platform for vocal representation that would remain
strong and viable long after the completion of the initial public works.[47]
The rhetoric surrounding the *comites* transformed them from instruments
of poverty alleviation to carriers of a new democratic culture and ultimately to an expression of alternative representation and participation of
organized civil society in a democratizing Mexican political system.

Not surprisingly, the disjuncture between this institutional view and
the real-life practices of Solidaridad has received ample political and academic analysis. The political aspects of the program tended to over-
shadow the accomplishments in the area of social welfare provision, as
Victoria Rodríguez explains in chapter 8. Domestic political complaints
include charges by municipal presidents that PRONASOL discriminated
against non-PRI-supporting *municipios*. In addition, they charged that
PRONASOL resources were used by local PRI organizations as patronage
during electoral campaigns. Both academic and political critics point to a
more general use of PRONASOL to strengthen electoral possibilities of
the PRI by devoting more attention to opposition areas in order to recapture their support.[48]

Many of these complaints have been echoed in recent academic analyses. Denise Dresser interprets PRONASOL as a centralized effort to create a new social base allowing the continuation of neoliberal policies.[49] In
her view, dissident social reformers were incorporated into PRONASOL
projects, thus forging state ties with noncorporate social groups. Solidari-

dad programs strengthened both the presidency and the PRI, if not its corporate sectors, and provided support for the Salinas doctrine of social liberalism and the redefinition of state responsibilities in the social sector.

Critics of PRONASOL argue that participants were forced to work through official government channels, had to petition within predetermined constraints, and had to avoid public criticism of the government. Active grass-roots participation was present only in the implementation phase of the projects, not in the making of strategic decisions. Despite these nondemocratic elements, however, PRONASOL policies may have aided Mexico's transition from clientelism to citizenship, passing through some intermediary, "semiclientelist" phases in the process. Because social movements have gained resources by participating in PRONASOL programs, the strengthening of independent organizing may be a longer-term consequence of the program.[50]

Another view is that the effects of Solidaridad activities differed in areas where there is a previous history of strong autonomous movements from those where the PRI maintains a strong corporate presence. Where independent movements were strong, their access to PRONASOL resources and organizational legitimation may have reinforced their ongoing empowerment.[51]

Comites de Solidaridad and Local Power

The impact of Solidaridad depended heavily on the nature and strength of pre-existing political power structures. The potential for entrenched power to gain control over Solidaridad resources and manipulate them to its benefit, however, may have been as important as the possibility of empowering independent organizations.

At the local level, the process of program organization began by small groups of residents petitioning for aid in local Solidaridad offices or by Solidaridad promoters who visited local communities to publicize the program's potential benefits. These initial steps were followed by a general assembly of the residents in which Solidaridad workers explained the organizing process. Subsequently, the community selected the leaders of the local *comite* and defined priorities. The *comite* members wrote the formal project proposal, collected the residents' contribution to the community's share of expenses, negotiated with contractors, and oversaw the work.

In communities where PRI neighborhood groups had already been organized, their group leaders would be the new *comite* leaders. Whether they were selected by imposition of higher authority, by open election, or because of their leadership role in the community, local PRI domination would be reinforced. This, however, did not preclude struggle for control among different sectors of the PRI.

The experience in the *municipio* of Tlaquepaque exemplifies the struggle between local political power and the centralized policies of Solidaridad. After having had its municipal government controlled by one of PRI's corporate organizations, the Confederación Revolucionaria de Obreros y Campesinos (CROC), for forty years, Tlaquepaque finally elected a PRI municipal president who was not pro-CROC in 1991. Internecine conflict ensued on several fronts as CROC tried to maintain its prerogatives. For example, it organized large demonstrations to force the president to staff important local positions with CROC supporters rather than with persons of his own choosing. The conflict continued throughout his term, and CROC soon found the Comites de Solidaridad, with their attendant resources, a useful weapon.

These resources were extensive. Over 44 million new pesos were spent in the *municipio* in eleven separate programs in 1994 alone.[52] The funds were mostly directed at infrastructure projects in poor *colonias* and meant a reasonably large windfall for competing political forces to use in winning support in those areas. The CROC leaders recognized this, as did the federal SEDESOL delegate who in August 1993 asked the CROC leaders to separate themselves from the leadership of local Comites de Solidaridad. SEDESOL's attempt to keep Solidaridad resources out of the hands of the CROC supporters followed the program's expressed intentions to work outside the structures of local power. The conflict soon focused on control of these resources between two PRI factions—the *municipio* and the CROC—with Solidaridad/SEDESOL acting as a "third force." SEDESOL's effort was unsuccessful, and CROC supporters took over most of the *comites,* leaving only a few loyal to the embattled *municipio* president.

A battle for control of the *comites* ensued, with the nomination (and affiliation) of the municipal coordinator of the *comites* as the central issue. Both parties denounced violations of the Solidaridad principles of unrestrained committee functioning, free elections, and decisions over public works, and both organized protests.[53] The CROC finally succeeded in controlling the coordination of the *comites,* although the anti-CROC forces were promised a federal audit to keep watch over resources. Subsequently, nonaligned *comites* established an independent office because they assumed that CROC control could only lead to corruption. Despite its earlier attempt to separate the CROC from the power available through Solidaridad resources, SEDESOL continued to work with the *comites* as constituted.

This willingness to operate through the old PRI-dominated neighborhood political power structures constituted a major weakness of the program. Often it was difficult to bypass these old leaders, who would become key actors in the operation of the Solidaridad program despite the rhetoric about new structures of representation. In that way, PRONASOL helped maintain local power with a new source of patronage resources.

The relationship between Solidaridad and independent popular opposition was exemplified by the interaction between the CROC-dominated *comites* and the Union of Independent Settlers (UCI) in Tlaquepaque. UCI is a popular organization that explicitly rejected clientelist relations. Since its creation it opposed local CROC leaders who fraudulently sold lots in an area where UCI members had settled. With the entry of the Solidaridad program in the zone in 1990, the UCI charged that many of the *comites* were headed up by the same corrupt local leaders. The announcement that water and electricity were soon to be acquired through Solidaridad was therefore met with skepticism because such promises had been made before and the timing of the announcements and program start date coincided with local elections. Fraudulent procedures in the calculation and collection of the costs for the services to be charged to individual households led to conflicts between the parties. The UCI eventually won and succeeded in exposing the separation between the professed goals of the Solidaridad program and its operation in Tlaquepaque. Their charges included manipulation of the open assemblies, where nonresidents were imported to support the CROC agenda; leadership imposed by high CROC officials; open partisan proselytizing; and fraudulent accounting practices. Despite their intention to keep Solidaridad at arms length, UCI also criticized the CROC for trying to block Solidaridad's relations with independent organizations.

The insertion of Solidaridad in poor communities forced it to take a political character. In popular neighborhoods lacking urban services, the provision of the most basic necessities took on political meaning. As a policy instrument designed to offer services, the difficulty was whether Solidaridad would follow the independent path it advocated or be routed through preexisting political channels. Despite the Solidaridad rhetoric of independence from PRI corporate power, the experiences in Tlaquepaque illustrate how local power structures corrupted the expressed goals of the program by channeling it through preexisting organizational structures. Far from creating an alternative opportunity for community representation, Solidaridad resources were co-opted and used in the effort to maintain local power.

In this way, the Solidaridad program's expressed intentions to create independent representation were foiled, and local political power remained in place. In an area held by one dominant group, Solidaridad resources may have been used to maintain their power. In an area in which groups were struggling for power, the resources became a prize that solidified local control of one faction over others. The greater the resources brought by Solidaridad, the greater the likelihood that already powerful groups would try to control them.

The increased independence of neighborhood organizations and movements is one part of the changing Mexican political landscape. In addition to an increased willingness to step out of patron-client relations and work in independent organizations, neighborhood groups and nongovernmental organizations are increasing their common work, forming coalitions around issues of human rights, social services, democratization, support for the Chiapas uprising, and public security concerns. In Jalisco, the government response to nongovernmental organizations working together has been a policy initiative aimed, in the government's words, at creating a stronger government-NGO relationship. Given the PRI government's history of co-opting and diverting popular organization, its entry into the nongovernmental organization world was met with some skepticism.

The State and NGOs: The Jalisco Experience

The growth in importance of nongovernmental organizations is recognized in both government and nongovernment sectors as dating from a watershed event, the 1985 earthquake in Mexico City. During and after the earthquake, civil society manifested a great capacity for spontaneous organization that later acquired an institutional character, and in some cases civic groups evolved into nongovernmental organizations, working to resolve social needs, sometimes more effectively than the government. By the 1988 elections, it was clear that nongovernmental organizations had entered a new phase, marked by the "accelerated development of organizations of civil society and the filling of spaces that the state, in retreat, has left open."[54]

With the maturing of nongovernmental organizations, they have taken on new activities, including promoting organized collective action, advising popular groups, making research and policy links with academic institutions, and actively proposing policy for both specific group constituencies and the wider Mexican society. Their growing importance is further characterized by increased links among organizations, the creation of new networks, and their greater size, heterogeneity, and increased regional and national scope.

Government recognition of the new NGO role was confirmed in concrete policymaking. SEDESOL created the Social Concensus Unit in 1994 to support nongovernmental organizations "through the creation of mechanisms that facilitate dialogue and systematic information sharing, with the goal of linking their [NGOs] actions with analagous or complementary organizations."[55]

Nongovernmental organizations in Jalisco began working together in the 1980s, but it was not until 1992 that they formed a formal alliance. The founding of the Mutual Support Network for Social Action (Red de Ayuda Mutua en Acción Social, or RAMAS) offered a vehicle for open dialogue, collective projects, and problem solving. With the change in tax laws and the continuing economic crisis, much of their common work centered around financial survival.

The government responded with proposals addressing the financial and legal problems of NGOs, intended to institutionalize strategies through which NGOs could work with SEDESOL as their government representative. It created the Fondo de Conversión Social (FCS), which in Jalisco provided funding for NGO projects on a competitive basis.

This development was celebrated by SEDESOL as clear evidence of the state's goodwill in moving toward more democratic state-society relations and of its willingness to cooperate, through PRONASOL, with the NGOs. The attempts to fit NGOs into one area or another of the broadly conceived PRONASOL program followed, including proposals to turn NGOs into Comites de Solidaridad. NGOs resisted their integration into the PRONASOL framework, charging that the program was aimed at short-term solutions and not directed to resolving "structural misery"; that there was no redistributive aspect; that it did not address the problems resulting from structural adjustment; and that it was driven by the intention to avoid potential political instability bred by poverty and the retreat by the state in other social sectors.[56]

Despite their skepticism of the government's role, several Jalisco NGOs cemented their relationship with SEDESOL in subsequent months and gained access to financing. Thereafter, the government created a state council for the NGOs. RAMAS's members were especially sensitive to the possibility that the council would duplicate their independent efforts and felt that the state council's intention of securing financing was a preemption of one of RAMAS's goals and an effort to supersede them. The dilemma became more pronounced when financing through SEDESOL came through first. SEDESOL's efforts to forge closer ties to NGOs was interpreted as part of the government's well-tested strategy of diversion and co-optation. The dilemma was temporarily resolved by the decision that as an organization RAMAS would not work with SEDESOL, but member groups were free to participate. Subsequently, several members applied for and won project financing, and three members joined as representatives of the state council. Tensions between the two organizations continued, however. For some, participation in both RAMAS and the state council was seen as a precarious balancing act between maintaining RAMAS's consistent opposition stance—its undisguised goal of aiding civil society to build Mexican democracy—and using the project money available through SEDESOL. For others, the benefits in growing closer to SEDESOL were decisive and created possibilities for establishing different relations with other government groups. In addition, through their presence on the council they would be able to influence the government away from corrupt financial practices.[57] In practice, the relationship between SEDESOL as a representative of government authority and the less powerful NGOs remained an uneasy one.

In general, RAMAS members believed that the intention of PRONASOL's strategy toward NGOs was co-optation. They relied on their political sophistication as long-term NGO leaders and members of the opposition and on the shared solidarity among their coworkers to resist government manipulation and exploit available resources where they could. As much as they believed in their own capabilities to escape cooptation, however, they doubted other organizations' abilities. RAMAS members were responding to the dual effect of Mexican neoliberal policies, which have forced the retreat of the state from some social arenas, opening opportunities for new political participation by NGOs and popular organizations alike. At the same time, the economic devastation wrought by these policies limited the resources of these organizations and their constituencies in ways that made them even more vulnerable to the offerings of state patronage. All this happened at a time when the volume of international funding of local NGOs in Latin America was in sharp decline.[58] As a result, less money became available to Mexican NGOs traditionally dependent on this support. The institutionalized access to resources, however limited, thus became even more valuable for them. It remains one of the most directly successful strategies of the Mexican corporate system. As Eckstein writes, bringing relevant groups into the resolution of political crises defuses a wider challenge to the state.[59] This state effort has been recreated in the SEDESOL strategy of working with NGOs, although it is as yet unclear how successful it will prove to be.

Solidaridad has retained its importance under Ernesto Zedillo, but its focus has slightly changed. Responsibility for the allocation and administration of a considerable share of the funds dedicated to social welfare and regional development was handed over to the state governments, and the implementation of projects was assigned to newly created institutions as part of Zedillo's decentralization program, detailed by Victoria Rodríguez in chapter 8. In November 1996 the federal government announced a new antipoverty program—to be coordinated by SEDESOL with the participation of the Ministries of Health and Education. It is aimed at four million poor families in ten states and will complement ongoing antipoverty programs—for which funding, however, was reduced by 4.6 percent in the 1997 budget.[60]

Conclusion

The antipoverty program in Mexico may be considered part of the wider dynamic of the redefinition of the Latin American state. The neoliberal state, despite moving away from delivery of social welfare, must still maintain stability and legitimacy. To this end, less economically powerful social sectors have to be appeased. Piecemeal remediation of poverty through national antipoverty programs has been a consistent tool used by the neoliberal state for this purpose.

The prevalence of these programs testifies to the neoliberal states' recognition that the redefinition of the state has left a large percentage of their populations in precarious situations. Both government and opposition groups have recognized Solidaridad efforts as responses to failing social and economic policies and to the growing political discontent in Mexico. It is no accident that the first Solidaridad programs, the formation of the neighborhood *comites*, were intended to ameliorate disaffection with corporate politics and neoliberal policies at the local level. The urban popular movement had effectively challenged local PRI power in a way that made politics as usual untenable. The "new representation" offered in the *comites* intended to create new access to resources outside preestablished avenues while maintaining PRI dominance.

Even if the Solidaridad intentions were taken at face value, however, the program's experience in Tlaquepaque illustrates its basic failure. Entrenched power defied the will of the presidency, evident in the fruitless attempts by SEDESOL to divorce CROC cronies from the local *comites*. As local power tried to capture federal resources to maintain its local prerogatives, centralized power attempted a strategy of limited change to maintain longer-term dominance. This internal struggle ultimately helped the opposition. The Partido Acción Nacional (PAN) won the Tlaquepaque municipal government election in 1995. The lesson is clear. If central state elites are to continue their dominance, they will have to find new ways to confront local power. Solidaridad propaganda notwithstanding, its policies have not been able to supplant the ongoing corrupt machinations of local power.

Eckstein argues that "without institutionalized access to authorities, groups may not be able to follow their collective interests."[61] Institutional access represents a successful integration process supported by government and party functionaries to satisfy local needs. In many cases, the large expenditures of the Solidaridad program have clearly done so.[62] When needs are fulfilled, however—whether for individuals, popular organizations, or NGOs—it also creates an investment that participants may be unwilling to divest. State policy has followed the changes in Mexican society in turning away from strongmen leaders to a wider, more organizationally represented leadership. This does not necessarily bankrupt the strategy of co-optation, but it changes its target. The government no longer tries to integrate the strongman leader and through him the local association; instead the attempt is to co-opt organizations and the constituency they represent. The apparent independence of organizations may be undercut by strategies that do not act as a direct control but still channel opposition into government-sanctioned forms and processes, while offering access, financial and human resources, and representation through a government institution. In case of success, the independent critique generated by neighborhood groups and social movements may be suppressed. An unresolved question is how long an increasingly challenged government commanding declining resources can make strategic resource decisions that keep sufficient support within the fold.

One of the challenges facing NGOs has been self-definition not only of their own identities but of the needs of the sectors whose interests they represent. One element in this struggle is the creation of an agenda for change. PRONASOL policies have tried to impose an agenda on local communities and wider organizations. Those NGOs willing to accept the government's definitions often prove to be focused on social assistance rather than on more politicized activities. Greater recognition, promotion, and aid is likely to follow this acceptance. Although this helps to create a new support constituency for the state, the more politicized groups will remain on the outside. This means politicized NGOs will face yet another frustrating experience in their interaction with the government, and it may strengthen their resolve to redouble their efforts to establish a more democratic system. This, in the changing political economy of Mexico, may be the final legacy of PRONASOL.

Notes

1. Funding for the research conducted in Guadalajara, Jalisco, was obtained from UC Mexus. I am grateful for the comments of Fred Block, Susie Gerard, Myrna Goodman, Victoria Johnson, Estee Neuwirth, and John Walton.

2. Peter Körner, Gero Maass, Thomas Siebold and Rainer Tetzlaff, *The IMF and the Debt Crisis* (London, Zed Books, 1986), p. 9.

3. United Nations, *World Economic Survey, 1993/1994* (New York: United Nations, 1995), p. 103.

4. Sue Branford and Bernardo Kucinski, *The Debt Squads: The U.S., the Bank, and Latin America* (London: Zed Press: 1988), p. 3.

5. Cited in Jacques de Larosiere, *Does the Fund Impose Austerity?* (Washington D.C.: International Monetary Fund, 1984), p. 4.

6. John Walton, "Debt, Protest, and the State in Latin America," in Susan Eckstein, ed., *Power and Popular Protest: Latin American Social Movements* (Berkeley: University of California Press, 1989) p. 307.

7. James Malloy, ed. *Authoritarianism and Corporatism in Latin America* (Pittsburgh: University of Pittsburgh Press, 1977).

8. Fernando Henrique Cardoso and Enzo Faletto, *Dependency and Development in Latin America* (Berkeley: University of California Press, 1979).

9. The examples of Bolivia, Chile, and Peru were drawn from Carol Graham, "Mexico's Solidarity Program in Comparative Context: Demand-Based Poverty Alleviation Programs in Latin America, Africa, and Eastern Europe," in Wayne A. Cornelius, Ann L. Craig, and Jonathan Fox, eds., *Transforming State-Society Relations in Mexico* (La Jolla: Center for U.S.-Mexican Studies, University of California, San Diego, 1994), pp. 309–27.

10. Hector García Bedoy, *Neoliberalismo en Mexico: Características, Limites, y Consecuencias* (Guadalajara: Centro de Reflexión Teológica, 1992), pp. 11–26.

11. Carlos Tello, "Combatting Poverty in Mexico," in Mercedes Gonzáles de la Rocha and Agustín Escobar Latapí, eds., *Social Responses to Mexico's Economic Crisis of the 1980s* (La Jolla: Center for U.S.-Mexican Studies, University of California, San Diego, 1991), pp. 57–65; Inter-American Development Bank, *Economic and Social Progress in Latin America, 1996* (Baltimore: Johns Hopkins University Press, 1996), p. 420.

12. See the World Bank's *World Development Report* (New York: Oxford University Press: 1994), pp. 200–20; and *World Debt Tables, 1993–1994* (Washington D.C.: World Bank, 1994), pp. 170–1; Inter-American Development Bank, *Economic and Social Progress in Latin America, 1996*, p. 420.

13. Diane E. Davis, "Social Movements in Mexico's Crisis," *Journal of International Affairs*, vol. 43, no. 2, 1990, pp. 343–67; Nora Lustig, "Economic Crisis, Adjustment, and Living Standards in Mexico, 1982–1985," *World Development*, vol. 18, 1990, pp. 1325–42.

14. David Velasco, "Macroindicadores de la Economía Neoliberal en México," in R. H. Mora, ed., *Indicadores de la Modernizacíon Mexicana* (Guadalajara: Centro de Reflexión Teológica, 1992), pp. 45–78; *Siglo 21*, December 27, 1994, p. 14.

15. Diane, E. Davis, "Social Movements in Mexico's Crisis," p. 348.

16. "Los Salarios de México Han Perdido 61% de su Valor," *Siglo 21*, Feb. 4, 1994, p. 21.

17. Nora Lustig, "Economic Crisis," p. 1334; Carlos Tello, "Combatting Poverty in Mexico," p. 59.

18. "El Poder del Salario Cae 40%," *Siglo 21*, Dec. 27, 1994, p. 19.

19. Nora Lustig, "Economic Crisis," pp. 1335–6.

20. Hector García Bedoy, *Neoliberalismo en México*, p. 44.

21. International Bank for Reconstruction and Development, *World Development Report* (New York: Oxford University Press, 1994).

22. Roberto Gonzalez Amador, "Asciende a 26 Mil Millones la Deuda de Estados y Municipios," *La Jornada*, July 14, 1995, p. 14.

23. Carlos Vélez-Ibañez, *Rituals of Marginality: Politics, Process, and Culture Change in Central Urban Mexico, 1969–1974* (Berkeley: University of California Press, 1983).

24. Susan Eckstein, "Poor People versus the State and Capital: Anatomy of a Successful Community Mobilization for Housing in Mexico City," *International Journal of Urban and Regional Research*, vol. 14, no 2, 1990, pp. 221–46.

25. Susan Eckstein, *The Poverty of Revolution: The State and the Urban Poor in Mexico* (Princeton: Princeton University Press, 1988), p. 101.

26. Wayne A. Cornelius, *Politics and the Migrant Poor in Mexico City* (Stanford: Stanford University Press: 1975).

27. See Alejandro Portes, "Rationality in the Slum: An Essay on Interpretive Sociology," *Comparative Studies in Society and History,* vol. 14, no. 3, 1972, pp. 268–86; Anthony Leeds and Elizabeth Leeds, "Accounting for Behavioral Differences: Three Political Systems and the Responses of Squatters in Brazil, Peru, and Chile," in John Walton and Louis Masotti, eds., *The City in Comparative Perspective* (New York: John Wiley & Sons, 1976), pp. 193–248; Janice Perlman, *The Myth of Marginality* (Berkeley: University of California Press, 1976).

28. See Robert Gay's publications in, "Neighborhood Associations and Political Change in Rio de Janeiro," *Latin American Research Review,* vol. 25, no. 1, 1990, pp. 102–18; and Robert Gay, *Popular Organization and Democracy in Rio de Janeiro* (Philadelphia: Temple University Press, 1994); Susan Stokes, "Politics and Latin America's Urban Poor: Reflections from a Lima Shanty Town," *Latin American Research Review,* vól. 26, 1991, pp. 75–101; Susan Stokes, *Cultures in Conflict: Social Movements and the State in Peru* (Berkeley: University of California Press, 1994); Paul Singer, "Neighborhood Movements in São Paulo," in Helen Safa, ed., *Towards a Political Economy of Urbanization in Third World Countries* (Delhi: Oxford University Press, 1982), p. 301.

29. Paul Singer, "Neigborhood Movements," p. 301.

30. Robert Gay, *Popular Organization and Democracy,* passim.

31. Juan Manuel Ramírez Saiz, *El Movimiento Urbano Popular en México* (Mexico D.F.: Siglo XXI, 1986); Juan Manuel Ramírez Saiz, "Urban Struggles and Their Political Consequences," in Joe Foweraker and Ann L. Craig, eds., *Popular Movements and Political Change in Mexico* (Boulder: Lynne Rienner, 1990), pp. 234–46.

32. Ruth Cardoso, "Popular Movements in the Context of the Consolidation of Democracy in Brazil," in Arturo Escobar and Sonia E. Alvarez, eds., *The Making of Social Movements in Latin America* (Boulder: Westview Press, 1992), pp. 291–302.

33. Susan Stokes, "Politics and Latin America's Urban Poor," passim.

34. Paul Singer, "Neighborhood Movements," p. 302.

35. Susan Stokes, "Politics and Latin America's Urban Poor," passim.

36. Daniel H. Levine and Scott Mainwaring, "Religion and Popular Protest in Latin America: Contrasting Experiences," in Susan Eckstein, ed., *Power and Popular Protest,* pp. 203–40.

37. Robert Gay, *Popular Organization and Democracy,* passim; Susan Stokes, "Politics and Latin America's Urban Poor," passim.

38. Jaime Tamayo, "Neoliberalism Encounters Neocardenismo," in Joe Foweraker and Ann Craig, eds., *Popular Movements and Political Change in Mexico,* pp. 121–57; Juan Manuel Ramírez Saiz, "El Movimiento Urbano Popular," passim; Vivienne Bennett, "The Evolution of Urban Popular Movements in Mexico between 1968 and 1988," in Alvaro Escobar and Sonia E. Alvarez, eds., *The Making of Social Movements in Latin America,* pp. 240–59; Paul Haber, "Political Change in Durango: The Role of National Solidarity," in Wayne A. Cornelius, Ann L. Craig, and Jonathan Fox, eds., *Transforming State-Society Relations in Mexico,* pp. 255–80;

Oscar F. Contreras and Vivienne Bennett, "National Solidarity in the Northern Borderlands: Social Participation and Community Leadership," in Wayne Cornelius, Ann L. Craig, and Jonathan Fox, eds., *Transforming State-Society Relations in Mexico*, pp. 281–305; Jorge Regelado Santillán, "El Movimiento Popular Independiente en Guadalajara," in Jaime Tamayo, ed., *Perspectivas de los Movimientos Sociales en la Región Centro-Occidente* (Mexico, D. F.: Editorial Linea, 1986), pp. 121–57; and Jorge Regelado Santillón, "Movimientos Urbanos en Guadalajara," *Sociedad/Estado*, vol. 1, 1988, pp. 17–29.

39. Nora Lustig, "Solidarity as a Strategy of Poverty Alleviation," in Wayne Cornelius, Ann L. Craig, and Jonathan Fox., eds., *Transforming State-Society Relations in Mexico*, pp. 79–96; Enrique González Tiburcio, "Social Reform in Mexico: Six Theses on the National Solidarity Program," in Ibid., pp. 63–78; Denise Dresser, "Bringing the Poor Back In: National Solidarity as a Strategy of Regime Legitimation," in Ibid., pp. 143–66; see also Victoria Rodríguez's chapter in this volume.

40. Juan Manuel Ramírez Saiz, *El Movimiento Urbano Popular*, passim.

41. Wayne Cornelius, Ann L. Craig, and Jonathan Fox, "Mexico's National Solidarity Program: An Overview," in Wayne Cornelius, Ann L. Craig, and Jonathan Fox., eds., *Transforming State-Society Relations in Mexico*, p. 6. For a more extensive outline of the program, see Victoria Rodríguez's chapter in this volume.

42. Victor Ballinas, "Se Realizaron más de 500,000 Obras Mediante PRONASOL: Rojas," *La Jornada*, September 20, 1994.

43. Presidencia de la República, *El Esfuerzo Nacional de Solidaridad* (Mexico, D. F.: Dirección General de Comunicación Social, 1992), p. 15.

44. Secretaría de Desarrollo Social (SEDESOL), *Organización Social: Lineamientos* (Mexico, D.F.: SEDESOL, 1993), pp. 5, 8; and SEDESOL, *Los Comités de Solidaridad: Organización Social* (Mexico, D.F., SEDESOL: 1993), passim.

45. SEDESOL, *Organización Social*, p. 48.

46. SEDESOL, *Los Comités de Solidaridad*, p. 32.

47. SEDESOL, *Organización Social*, passim.

48. Guillermo Correa, "Alcaldes no Priistas Dicen que se les Hace a un Lado del PRONASOL," *Proceso*, no. 776, September 16, 1991, pp. 20–1; Salvador Corro, "PRONASOL, el Instrumento de Rescate de Posiciones e Imagen Presidencial," *Proceso*, no. 782, October 28, 1991, pp. 12–3; Juan Molinar Horcasitas and Jeffrey Weldon, "Electoral Determinants and Consequences of National Solidarity," in Wayne Cornelius, Ann L. Craig, and Jonathan Fox, eds., *Transforming State-Society Relations in Mexico*, pp. 123–42; Peter Ward, "Social Welfare Policy and Political Opening in Mexico," in Ibid., pp. 47–62; Denise Dresser, "Bringing the Poor Back In," passim.

49. Denise Dresser, "Bringing the Poor Back In," p. 144.

50. Paul Haber, "Political Change in Durango," passim; Jonathan Fox, "Targetting the Poorest: The Role of the National Indigenous Institute in Mexico's Solidarity Program," in Wayne Cornelius, Ann L. Craig, and Jonathan Fox, eds., *Transforming State-Society Relations in Mexico*, pp. 255–80.

51. Oscar F. Contreras and Vivienne Bennett, "National Solidarity in the Northern Borderlands," passim.

52. Programa Nacional de Solidaridad (PRONASOL), *Programa Operativo Anual: Inversión Aprobada* (Guadalajara:Unidad de Desarrollo Regional PRONA-SOL, 1994), p. 2.

53. José Diaz Betancourt, "La CROC Propone un Plebiscito para Solucionar el Conflicto," *Siglo 21,* July 4, 1994, p. 3.

54. SEDESOL, *Participación de las Organizaciones No-Gubernamentales en el Estado de Jalisco* (Mexico, D. F.: Unidad de Concertación Social SEDESOL, 1994), p. 2. The amount spent by Solidaridad in Tlaquepaque reached over U.S.$11.5 million.

55. Ibid., p. 3.

56. Carlos Ortega Nava, "Nuevas Relaciones Estado-Sociedad, Propuesta para la Modernidad: Continuidad ó Transición," in SEDESOL, *Memoria del Primer Encuentro: Acción Transformada* (Guadalajara: SEDESOL, 1994), pp. 5–12.

57. Author interviews with RAMAS and SEDESOL representatives, Guadalajara, 1994.

58. Mariano Valderrama, *Perú y América Latina en el Nuevo Panorama de la Cooperación Internacional* (Lima: Centro Peruano de Estudios Sociales, 1995), pp. 27–58.

59. Susan Eckstein, "Poor People versus the State and Capital," passim.

60. See "Se Inicia un Nuevo Programa de Desarrollo Social, *La Jornada,* November 27, 1996.

61. Susan Eckstein, "Poor People versus the State and Capital," passim.

62. John Bailey and Jennifer Boone, "National Solidarity: A Summary of Program Elements," in Wayne Cornelius, Ann L. Craig, and Jonathan Fox., eds., *Transforming State-Society Relations in Mexico,* pp. 329–38; The official SEDESOL estimates for five years of Solidaridad accomplishments include the delivery of 2.3 million land titles; paving of 41 million square meters in 7,344 *colonias;* access to water provided to 15.4 million people; 20 million provided access to electricity; 13.5 million provided access to sewer systems; the creation of 20,000 microenterprises generating over 84,000 jobs; and the building or remodeling of over 194,000 school facilities. Other projects have increased access to health care and education. The final bill for the project announced during the Fifth Solidarity Week in September 1994 reached close to U.S.$14 billion. See Victor Ballinas, "Se Realizaron más de 500,000 Obras," passim.

10

Redefining the State's Social Policies: The Case of Venezuela

Luis Gómez Calcaño

In recent years, in response to severe economic crises and conditions imposed by international financial institutions, the Venezuelan state made profound changes in its policies, moving away from its traditionally strong interventionist orientation. On the economic level, this meant diminishing the reach of state regulation and implementing an ambitious program of privatization; on the social level, it meant substituting general subsidies for more specific ones. Not surprisingly, the reforms created strong political tensions and led in some instances to violent social protests. The case of Venezuela, then, illustrates the difficulties of adopting a new market-centered economic model, especially in the context of a state-society relationship in which the state is expected to take a central role in matters of social development and at a time when the economy is burdened by large external debt.

Antecedents: The Financier-Distributor State

A distinctive characteristic of the Venezuelan state is the relative abundance of its resources, derived largely from taxes on petroleum exports. This meant that for years the battle over how state resources were distributed took the form of a negotiation, at times conflictual, between representatives of the state and the international companies that extracted and exported petroleum. The continual increase in the level of taxation on these companies allowed the Venezuelan state to appropriate a significant portion of petroleum profits, which it subsequently distributed for domestic development purposes.[1]

Thus, in contrast with a "normal" capitalist state, which must extract resources from its own economic actors, the Venezuelan state could use petroleum income to create infrastructure, offer public services, and, in general, promote the process of development. Petroleum income, then, was the source for modernizing all sectors. First, import-substitution industrialization was promoted, through easy credit and tariff protection, to strengthen a modern entrepreneurial sector, though it was still dependent on state protection. Second, the state undertook directly the creation of basic industries in the hydroelectric, iron and steel, and petrochemical sectors. And finally, the state promoted social mobility by expanding education and opening other channels for social integration. With greater or lesser emphasis, depending upon the administration in power, modernization of agriculture, urban development, labor unions, and the like were supported with petroleum revenues.

Paradoxically, the abundance of petroleum resources was simultaneously a stimulus and an impediment to development. On the one hand, it allowed Venezuela to build a productive infrastructure and modern services; on the other, it produced a chronic overvaluation of currency, which made imports more attractive. This, in turn, produced an oil industry highly cost inefficient, overprotected, and incapable of competing in the international market. Because of its highly technological nature, it was also labor unintensive and did not create employment for those who were leaving the unprofitable agricultural sector and migrating to urban centers. Their numbers swelled the ranks of the informal sector.

Despite the effort to develop a modern and self-sustaining economy, the result of policies carried out from the 1930s to the 1980s had the opposite effect: an economy that achieved high growth rates (especially in the 1960s and 1970s) but was extremely dependent on petroleum revenue. In addition, the growth of the import-substitution industry had reached its limits, and its contribution to employment was not sufficient to absorb the expanding labor force. Entrepreneurs depended on state intervention, through fixed prices and other protections, to invest and to make their investments profitable. And despite the distributive functions of the state, income inequalities continued to be severe.

The distorted nature of the development process meant that the role of the state continued to be central; rather than moving to the background, relinquishing the leading role to social actors in a modern industrial state, the state continued to perform a protective and distributive role. Even today, public expenses as a percentage of the gross internal product are comparatively high in Venezuela in relation to similarly developed Latin American nations, although there are several that exceed it.[2]

State action also contributed to legitimizing the political order, characterized as "a populist system of reconciliation."[3] A long struggle to establish democratic institutions culminated in 1958 with the formation of a coalition government among the three leading parties. In subsequent years, the parties became indispensable mediators between social actors. The two great centrist parties, Acción Democrática (AD) and the Social-Christian Party (COPEI), gradually achieved hegemony over the unions and established cooperative links with business, the military, and the Catholic Church.[4] This system of negotiation and reconciliation eased social conflicts through the close control of the parties over the public sectors when in power and through the patronage and distribution of state resources.

One of the regime's priorities in 1958 was social policy to address high rates of population growth and urbanization, which had stimulated an incessant demand for additional urban services—clean water, sanitation, housing, education, health, and transportation. The needs of the migrants, always unsatisfied, were used by the parties as a means to establish networks of co-optation and patronage. The potential for conflict these demands created was held in check by repressive measures but also, to a significant degree, because of the considerable capacity of the state to distribute public and private goods.

In the first years of the democratic government, social expenditures occupied a prominent place in the state budget. The state was, at the same time, an important source of public employment, especially in education and health services. Access to public jobs was normally controlled by membership in one of the major political parties, which also control the public employee unions. Social policy thus served in two ways to reinforce the role of the parties: by satisfying, if only partially, the demands of the people and by offering work to the clients of the parties.[5]

Nevertheless, these public services, which in the beginning responded adequately to meet social needs, gradually lost a great deal of their effectiveness. The predominance of the system of patronage and of party control over the functioning of social services produced an increasingly serious deterioration of this sector.[6] In consequence, Venezuela ranks lower in measures of public health and education than countries of the Southern Cone, even though its level of social expenditures per capita is one of the highest in the region.[7]

At the same time the social services sector was becoming more inefficient, social expenditures were growing. Increases were covered for many years by petroleum income, but the structural adjustments required after 1982 because of a decrease in petroleum income and the burden of external indebtedness exerted pressures to stop the rate of growth in social expenditures in real terms. Measures to do so aggravated the chronic problems of this sector, which eventually caused the government to conclude that a total reorganization was required to rationalize social expenditures. The Comisión Presidencial para la Reforma del Estado (COPRE), created in 1984, advanced some diagnoses and proposals along these lines, but it was only after 1989, as part of the program of adjustment and restructuring designated "The Great Turnaround" by the government of Carlos Andrés Pérez, that an attempt was undertaken to redefine radically the social policy of the Venezuelan state.

The Structural Adjustment Program Under Pérez

At the beginning of 1989, the balance of payments situation was critical: International reserves had fallen to minimal levels, there were difficulties in paying external debt, and the fiscal deficit was substantial. A severe adjustment was necessary in order to balance macroeconomic variables, and the Pérez government contacted the International Monetary Fund (IMF) for support. The adjustment program arranged with the IMF was not limited to temporary measures; it aspired at the same time to initiate a "great turnaround" in the Venezuelan economy, from statism to the primacy of the market.[8]

The priorities of the adjustment program were rigidly defined in the letter of intent presented to the IMF. The fundamental objectives to be pursued in the medium term were to strengthen internal savings; to promote the investment of foreign capital; and to diversify the economy through a process of adjustment and liberalization that would bring about a reduction in macroeconomic imbalances, increase economic efficiency, and reinforce the strategy of development.[9] The initial adjustment measures included freeing control over most prices and interest rates; gradually reducing imports and stimulating exports; allowing the rate of exchange to float freely, which meant a devaluation of the bolívar; and increasing the price of fuel.

Toward the goal of eliminating the public sector deficit in the first two years of the program an attempt was made to restrict some classes of expenditures, including social priorities. It was established that subsidies for basic foods would not exceed the limit of 1.2 percent of the gross national product in 1989 and would be progressively eliminated between 1990 and 1991. The direct transfers foreseen in the social program would reach 0.74 percent of the gross national product. In addition, public investments were intended to consume only 11 percent of GNP while financial losses incurred from commitments to pay private external debt would reach 4 percent of GNP.[10] The government openly promised to carry out a "prudent income policy, which would contribute to strengthening competitiveness, raising the level of employment, and reducing inflationary pressures," offering its employees wage increases clearly less than the rate of inflation predicted for 1989 and refusing to intervene in fixing wages in the private sector, with the exception of the minimum wage.[11]

The adjustment program was scarcely in progress when riots and looting erupted in Caracas and other cities at the end of February of 1989, initially as a response to an increase in the price of urban transport. This was also a reaction, however, to deteriorating living conditions among the popular sectors and demonstrated to the authorities that the adjustment initiatives, even if they were inevitable, would have a social and political impact that could threaten the stability of the regime.

The adjustment program conflicted with the logic of the relationship predominating until then between state, party, and civil society; but the central actors and institutions did not succeed in adapting themselves to the demands of the program with the necessary speed. The difference in the rhythms of change exacerbated conflicts among the actors, and especially between each actor and the state. The points of anchorage that until then had oriented demands and negotiations lost a good deal of their meaning and effectiveness. This was not an unforeseen consequence but a predictable effect, given that the adjustment program was attempting not only to rebalance macroeconomic variables in the short term but also to establish the bases for a structural transformation in the Venezuelan economy, the goal of which was to increase the competitiveness and the export capability of industry; reduce the intervention of the state in economic life; and, in a more general sense, create conditions that allowed all markets—in goods and services, in capital, and in labor—to operate freely and become the dynamic center of the economy, assuming the former responsibilities of the state.

The agents propelling the reforms were found as much within the state as in civil society; encouraged by the example of the economic policies recently adopted by other countries in the region, they undertook the task of changing the terms of the debate over the orientation of the process of national development. In the new orientation development was interpreted in terms of an opposition between the state and the market or between the state and civil society, depending upon whether economics or politics was emphasized. Social problems were assimilated, in a direct or indirect way, under this opposition. The image of an "omnipotent" state confronting an oppressed civil society finally became a commonplace of daily discourse.

The pervasiveness of antistatist discourse could help explain the fact that the Pérez government so faithfully accepted the orthodoxy implied by the program of adjustment. It is certain that this program was, in actuality, imposed by the IMF as a precondition for offering indispensable credits. But a climate of opinion and internal political and technical agents had now taken over the terrain to make the execution of the program viable. Their adversaries, in turn, found it difficult to present the state in a positive light when it seemed, after many years of ineffective initiatives, to be responsible for the crisis.

The absence of an organized response to the adjustment program and of coherent alternative discourses favored its rapid implementation but also stimulated a violent reaction. The riots of February 1989 by unorganized masses in the streets revealed the unrepresentative nature of the unions and parties. In effect, neither was capable of negotiating with the government over methods of applying adjustment policies. They watched the confrontations between the rioters and the authorities like helpless spectators. Despite their intentions to organize resistance to the adjustment program, the unions and the parties seemed to have lost their capacity to direct the masses politically. Nevertheless, they tried to maintain control over their clientelist networks, which allowed them at least to keep up their ranks and organization.

The adjustment program encountered numerous obstacles that impeded its coherent application. In particular, the lack of coordination of reforms between the government and congress caused the fiscal deficit to grow, which maintained high levels of inflation. In addition, the oligopolistic character of the principal markets prevented competition, and the expected benefits of the opening of the economy, such as increased competition and lower inflation, never materialized.[12] The concentration of income allowed a few to maintain an luxurious lifestyle, in biting contrast with the austerity imposed elsewhere.[13] Finally, Peréz himself, along with his advisors, was accused of corruption, which diminished his authority to impose the sacrifices demanded by the program and caused his downfall in May 1993.

The Guidelines for Change in Social Policy

The living conditions of the people had gradually been deteriorating during previous years, but the first year of the Peréz government marked a brutal decline: Average inflation was 84.5 percent in 1989, rising to 125.8 percent in that same year in the food and beverage sector—which affected 92.3 percent of the lower-income population—while wages increased on the average only 40 percent.[14] Real wages for 1990 were 50.2 percent less than in 1978, approximating where levels had been at the end of the 1940s.[15] The level of unemployment increased from 6.9 percent in 1989 to 10 percent in 1990, and the proportion of workers in the informal sector increased from 38.1 percent to 41.3 percent over the same period.[16]

It was necessary, therefore, to put into effect compensatory policies that could lessen this impact. But at the same time, it was known that the state bureaucracies charged with carrying out social policy were inefficient, that funds were frequently diverted, and that often beneficiaries did not receive the services to which they were entitled.[17] As a result, the government, advised by international institutions such as the World Bank, began to design programs and policies intended to compensate directly the sectors with the least resources, avoiding general subsidies that were considered more costly and inefficient.

The social policies initiated in 1989 were intended as a rationalization of expenditures rather than as a retreat of the state. In the first two years social expenditures were reduced in relative terms, from 9 percent of GNP to 6.7 percent between 1980 and 1990.[18] Nevertheless, this situation was reversed after 1991, and social expenditures would increase until 1993, as much in relative terms as in real per capita expenditures.[19] In fact, after 1989, social policy expenditures absorbed an important proportion of the funds contributed by international institutions to assist the adjustment and restructuring program.[20]

Paradoxically, it was not only the poorest sectors that benefited from state attention. The middle class used its influence to demand compensatory measures as well. The most notorious instance was the Law for the Protection of the Mortgage Debtor, which favored the middle and upper classes because it subsidized the difference between the previous and new interest rates. In the same way, the middle and upper classes influenced the reform of the income tax laws to their advantage.[21] And the price of gasoline, one of the lowest in the world, was only slightly increased, which meant that a highly regressive subsidy was maintained. Despite the apparent influence of antistatist ideologies, then, the demands for the state to continue subsidizing actors with the power to exert pressure were successful.

Where the state did withdraw to some degree is in the transfer of responsibility for the administration of some state programs to organized groups in civil society. I will therefore look in some detail at programs that attempted to put this new arrangement into practice.

The Principal Programs of Social Policy

Compensation policy was based on the necessity of supplementing the income of the poorest sectors during a period of transition until growth stimulated by the success of the total program would make compensation unnecessary. Special attention was paid to the most vulnerable sectors, especially children, and attempts were made to create new and more efficient methods for distributing benefits.

The immediate measures were moderate wage increases and decrees protecting job stability, enforced until December 1989, followed by unemployment insurance and the Plan de Empleo y Inversión Social (Plan of Employment and Social Investment). Under the unemployment insurance program benefits were offered to those without work for the first time in Venezuela; nevertheless, it reached only workers in the formal sector already covered by social security. The second program, however, was meant to create public jobs for unskilled workers, especially in construction, maintenance, and services. In this sense, it was linked to traditional state policies intended to compensate for the inability of the private sector to absorb labor.[22]

To replace indirect subsidies on a great number of foodstuffs, mechanisms for direct transfer to the most vulnerable sectors were created. The most important, as much for the resources allocated as for the size of the population covered, was the "food grant," which offered poor families a subsidy for each school-age child. Equivalent in 1992 to U.S.$8 per child per month, it was distributed through the banking system and established the beneficiaries through the use of information supplied by the schools. Although it was a very large program, with 2,500,000 beneficiaries in 1991, many of the poorest families were excluded because they could not send their children to school.[23]

Maternal Infant Care (PAMI), directed to children under six years and to pregnant and nursing mothers in the poorest groups, covered 650,000 women and 1,848,000 children in 1991. The program consisted of giving food (principally powdered milk) to mothers and children who came for medical attention at one of the traveling primary care units of the Ministry of Health and Social Welfare. The program was complemented by the Plan of Mass Extention of the Daily Care Homes.[24]

Other programs implemented were the Program of Aid to the Informal Economy, which promoted economic activities emerging in the poor sectors, the Program of Local Social Investment, dedicated to investment in the physical infrastructure of basic services, and the Program of Sociocultural Participation, intended to compensate for the lack of education and access to information in the poorest areas.[25]

The Executive Institutions of Social Policy

Traditionally, social policy was carried out in a scattered way by various ministries (health and social welfare, education) and by ad hoc organizations of the decentralized administration (The Venezuelan Institute for Social Security, The National Institute for Nutrition, etc.). In 1979, President Luis Herrera created a State Ministry for the Participation of Women in Development. But the technical assistance team of the Ministry of State was growing and gradually becoming institutionalized until, finally, it became the Ministry of the Family. The Pérez government decided to give this ministry the role of coordinator for all social policy and to convert it into the Ministry of Social Development.[26] At the same time, a number of civil organizations started functioning parallel to this existing social network to take charge of some of the strategic tasks involved in achieving the desired reorientation.[27]

The new programs only represented a fraction of the total expenditures on social policy, still concentrated in the large ministries (health and education) and other institutions charged with the implementation of traditional social policies. Two of the most important programs, those for food aid and maternal-infant care, remained dependent upon the those ministries to carry out their activities.[28]

The compensation programs could only begin operation at the end of 1989, owing to the lack of institutional experience with this type of program. This meant that their impact would only be felt in the following years, as a partial compensation for the drop in income of the poorest sectors. And although the resources allotted to these programs were nominally increasing, the high rates of inflation over this period forced the rapid initial growth of coverage to slow down.[29]

Ironically—and conforming to the populist tradition—programs of a compensatory nature, like food aid and donations of equipment to schools, absorbed 68 percent of the total resources of the antipoverty program between 1989 and 1992, while the programs of "compensatory investment," that is, those intended to attack the most structural causes of poverty, only absorbed 32 percent of the resources.[30]

The Decentralization of Social Policies

One of the most significant changes in social policies in the 1990s has been the move to decentralize some services as part of a more general process of decentralization impelled by COPRE and endorsed by political actors at the regional level.[31] The first step was the approval of a law permitting state governors to be elected by direct vote instead of being appointed or removed by the president. In December 1989 the first elections took place. Various winners belonged to coalitions or parties of the opposition. At the same time, a decentralization law was promulgated to regulate the transfer of powers and resources to the states.[32] Some of the most important and populous states asked that health services be transferred because of their particularly critical health needs. The process was hampered, however, by the existence of a previous, extremely centralizing, law that gave the Ministry of Health authority to organize all services. The ministry resisted yielding control over any of its resources.[33]

Nevertheless, some governors insisted on the transfer, finally achieving at the end of 1992 approval by the senate for the transfer of health services to six of the twenty-two states. The planned objectives of the decentralization consisted of:

Luis Gómez Calcaño

- improving the physical infrastructure in health;
- incorporating organized civil society into the different phases of the administrative process;
- educating and training health sector workers and improving administration;
- training in the management of public health programs and hospital administration (in some states);
- developing information systems to optimize decision making;
- decentralizing operations to the subregional and local levels.[34]

In spite of the difficulties that delayed formal approval of the agreements, the states achieved some positive results: Hospital administration and the quality of medical care improved and the gradual incorporation the civil associations into the administration of health services got underway. It should be noted, however, that positive results were obtained only in the most dynamic and relatively prosperous states; the majority of governors had not even asked for the transfer of responsibility in this field.

Decentralization of Education

In 1991 the Ministry of Education defined a strategy to eliminate serious operational inefficiencies. One reform, around which a wide consensus existed, was to decentralize public education. Although the process of decentralization has been much slower here than in health, pilot programs to improve basic schooling have been put in place on a regional level in the states of Bolívar and Mérida. At the same time, COPRE coordinated a program to strengthen the capacity of the states to participate in the process of decentralization.[35]

The Role of Nongovernmental Organizations (NGOs)

The inefficiency of overcentralized services and the partial privatization of services in order to improve the quality of delivery eventually led the government to establish links with social organizations, encouraging their participation in some programs. The program of daily home care, for example, depended upon the Children's Foundation, a semipublic organization that by law is headed by the spouse of the President of the Republic. But it was also connected to the Center for Service for Popular Action (Centro al Servicio de la Acción Popular, CESAP), a nongovernmental organization that had extensive experience in promoting and advising organizations with a base in the popular sectors. The program of aid to the informal economy was also supported by nongovernmental organizations in the areas of credit, training, and technical assistance. One of the cases in which this type of association has succeeded is described below.

Multihouseholds

"Multihouseholds" are an extension of the "daily care homes" that had been used since the 1970s as a means to look after children of low-income working mothers. The original program consisted of a mother in the community taking responsibility, in her own home, for the daily care of five children; she received training and technical assistance as well as a subsidy from the Children's Foundation. The multihouseholds, which were designed by the Ministry of the Family in consultation with CESAP, put together a larger number of children in places dedicated for that purpose, but the activity continues to be carried out by nonworking mothers. An evaluation of the program noted several positive consequences of the participation of civic organizations:

- the majority of the organizers are community leaders;
- they choose the "care mothers" based on their prior knowledge of each one of them;
- the multihouseholds stimulate other forms of community organization;
- health becomes a priority concern of the community;
- the balanced meals offered in the multihouseholds contribute to the fight against malnutrition and improve family dietary habits.

The principal obstacle the study found is a lack of trust within the community, which generates resistance to participation in the activities and reduces the number of children attending.[36] The program of multihouseholds complemented that of daily care homes and at a lower cost per child. An average number of 130,000 children participated annually between 1989 and 1992.[37]

Aid to the Informal Economy

This program, directed to production and distribution activities, aims to build upon the initiatives those in the poor sectors have taken to confront poverty and socioeconomic exclusion. The growth of the informal sector during the 1980s forced the state to formulate policies specifically for it. The interest of the state in small businesses in the informal sector has been interpreted by a member of the team that formulated this policy in terms of the interconnection of a number of economic and social processes:[38]

1. The informal economy has developed as a survival strategy in the face of employment uncertainty in the formal sector.
2. Small businesses in this sector contribute in a particular way to meeting the needs of the poor.
3. The growth of small enterprises represents an alternative in decentralizing the processes of production.
4. Many small businesses play an important role in bringing down the cost of decentralizing production in big enterprises, which subcontract to them those tasks that require less skilled labor and that are organized outside the control of institutions in the formal economy.
5. Small businesses and microenterprises are often tied to big businesses, without passing through the marketplace; the dependency this creates frequently results in an "overexploitation" of the work force.

On the basis of this interpretation, the following central guidelines for policies regarding the informal economy were proposed:[39]

1. to define the role of the informal economy in the model of development being planned;
2. to provide aid to the informal economy "as a state policy through which the problem of providing employment becomes a mechanism for linking social policy with economic policy";[40]
3. to determine prerogatives and mechanisms to protect small businesses;
4. to increase the operating capacity of the intermediary organizations of the state in order to enable them to give technical assistance in the areas of commercializing and marketing articles produced by microentrepreneurs in the informal sector so as to avoid "overexploitation";
5. to amplify the proposals of the Urban Communities for Production and to make optimal use of the labor force while also creating guarantees for protection of households and families;
6. to extend the benefits of social security to workers in the informal sector and to establish a norm that protects domestic workers.

Since the 1970s, some private organizations and foundations had proposed to provide advice, credit, and training to small businesses in the informal sector. After 1990, formal agreements were established with the Ministry of the Family, which increased the resources available to aid their work.[41] A special unit of CESAP, the AUGE (Sector of Aid to Units of Economic Management), for example, began to provide start-up businesses training in accounting, cost evaluation, and marketing and to offer credit for equipment or working capital.[42] The unit was also charged with supervising the appropriate use of credit and making recommendations for overcoming the special difficulties small businesses face.[43]

Consumer fairs, which had developed earlier as a branch of the cooperative movement in various cities, are another example of how the government has linked social policy with social organizations. The weekly fairs sell vegetables and other provisions at discounted prices, made possible because of the large amount of volunteer labor supplied by the members of local cooperatives and because of flexible management techniques. One study concluded that the fairs generate large savings for their participants, and in some cities a high percentage of the population attends. Although the fairs are held in numerous cities, they have only been successful in some, especially in intermediate-sized cities in which private enterprise has left some niches undeveloped. One reason for the success of the fairs is an attitude of "militancy" among the fair promoters because they view their work as activism not merely labor. Another is the development of "a permanent link with cooperative producers and other self-managing productive enterprises." Links to state organizations have also been created as some directors of cooperative and similar organizations become members of the boards of directors of financial institutions.[44]

Tensions over Social Policy

This new relationship between the state and social organizations provoked some tensions as service organizations feared that their role might be mistaken for that of simple agents of the government. Another risk was that by concentrating on social programs with a purely pragmatic focus these service organizations might pay less attention to long-term projects designed to effect profound sociopolitical and cultural change.[45] At the same time, however, and for the first time in many years, there appeared the possibility of organizing and executing social policies through mechanisms other than the traditional ones, which had always been tightly controlled by the political parties.

The manner in which social policy was put into practice also created tensions between the government and Acción Democrática. Program implementation was placed, at least at the highest levels, in the hands of independent professionals and technicians, some of whom were linked to international organizations such as the World Bank and who were more interested in efficiently meeting goals than in perpetuating the traditional practices of the patronage system. The participation of social movements and organizations in the distribution of subsidies also intensified competition between party and nonparty groups because both gained legitimacy through their role as intermediaries with the state.[46]

Acción Democrática constantly pushed for greater influence in the execution of social policies,[47] and they succeeded at the beginning of 1992 in placing a party faithful at the head of the Ministry of the Family, with the intention of influencing social policy to their advantage. Shortly afterward, however, following the failed coup d'etat in February 1992, Pérez named a politically independent minister. As Navarro has noted, this decision was influenced by a new alliance emerging between NGOs involved in social programs and various ministers who feared that a major party influence might negatively affect the efficacy of those programs.[48]

But this new alliance had two weak points. First, the new programs did not have a permanent institutional place in the governmental structure, and their administration was handled by ad hoc institutional bodies such as foundations. This weakened their continuity and was disadvantageous for the stability of their budgets, which had to be renewed each year by congress, without benefit of the budgetary inertia of the central administration and under the suspicious gaze of traditional politicians who saw them as competitors.[49] Second, the new social programs had fragile sources of support. As long as the parties depend on patronage, maintaining monopoly control over the distribution of goods and favors is their primary motivation. Only if the organizations of civil society have autonomy—being associated with but not subordinated to sectors of the state that have a more universalist vision of social policies—will there be a permanent basis for the reorientation of these policies. Presently, experiments in forms of nonpatronage cooperation lack sufficient institutionalization, which makes them vulnerable to political changes like the replacement of a minister or the alteration of their budget by congress.

Evaluating Changes in Social Policies

The reorientation of Venezuelan social policy in the last five years has been the subject of various evaluations. For analysts who tend to favor the restructuring of society around the market and advocate a corresponding diminution of the power of the state, changes in social policies have been a step in the right direction but are not sufficient to overcome the structural problems of the social sector.

Márquez, for example, shows that in recent years social expenditures as a proportion of total expenditures have not been reduced.[50] The growth in social expenditures after 1989 was entirely due to funding for compensation programs; expenditures in the traditional social sectors like health and education stayed the same. The effort was insufficient however. Although more resources were allocated to programs of assistance to the poor than at any other time in Venezuela, they were not able to make up for the loss of income resulting from the elimination of subsidies and the lowering of real wages.

For Márquez, the danger of paying too much attention to these programs is that they might seem like "true social policy," when they are, in the best of cases, only temporary measures. This allows one to ignore the essential problem, that of the extreme inefficiency of traditional social services controlled by the unions and other internal power groups.[51] Márquez proposes incorporating the discipline of market criteria in social policy, demanding measurable results; transferring authority for problem solving to local governments; and introducing experimentation and diversity in the production and financing of and access to social services.[52]

Navarro contrasts the relative clarity of ideas in the commercial, fiscal, and monetary aspects of the adjustment program with its failure to take fully into account the fundamental problems of the social sector.[53] The positive elements of adjustment policies include the use of private contractors, their insulation from political pressures, and the greater participation of the community. But these were rather isolated experiences and were diminished by the lack of an instrument to regulate cooperation between the state and the NGOs. Among the most significant obstacles to implementing the necessary structural reforms are the actions by the unions of public employees against decentralization of the public sector, the attempts to redistribute the health and education budgets; and the efforts to reorganize these two sectors.[54]

Those more critical of restructuring on the basis of market criteria interpret recent social policy as a turn toward traditional ways to provide aid to the poor, which has only partially compensated for the impoverishing effects of economic adjustment. The adjustment program casts aside the universalist conception of the social state, according to which the objective of social policy is to guarantee minimal conditions of well being for all. In its place, actions taken on behalf of the most vulnerable sectors merely fight the effects, but not the causes, of poverty. The adjustment program initiated in 1989 had among its most immediate effects a reduction in employment and in real wages along with an increase in inflation. The combination caused the potential beneficiaries of compensation programs to continuously increase in number, seriously compromising the capacity of the state to fulfill the planned goals for coverage and efficiency.[55]

Cartaya and D'Elía argue that the plan to combat poverty may have succeeded in temporarily containing urgent problems but that it runs the risk of being confused with true social policy.[56] The focus on mitigating the costs of the adjustment deepens the separation between economic and social policy and does not permit one to perceive the role of market forces in causing poverty; the data show that the "true social policy," defined as having an impact on the life of the poor, was economic policy.

The principal weakness of social policy, then, is the absence of an integrated view of the social and the economic spheres that takes into account, for example, the effects of restructuring the economy on the structure of demand for labor. An integrated view would have to respond to problems of financing social security and professional training, tasks related to the more general model of redefining the respective roles of the public and private sectors. Finally, they underscore that institutional weakness is one of the central factors in the deterioration of the social situation. For that reason, the reform of social policy is part of a larger reform of the state that incorporates other sectors such as management, the union movement, and civil society, "in order to achieve greater equity by increasing the political base of support and favoring the creation of pressure groups that would serve as a counterweight to traditional interests."[57]

In 1992 a team from COPRE evaluated social policy. Positive aspects were deemed to be a coherent design for programs to eradicate poverty; a definition of poverty stated in sociocultural as well as economic terms; the emphasis on concentrating programs on clearly defined objectives, using universalist criteria, and eliminating the structures of corruption and clientelism; the intention to create a social safety net and to promote the greater participation of civil society; and the rapidity with which coverage of some programs was broadened and others, like the daily care homes, were consolidated.[58]

Negative aspects included not having succeeded in designing a truly integrated plan for social development; the absence of a "strong and differentiated" institutional space for the definition and implementation of social policy, reflected in the delay in the creation of the Ministry of Social Development; the insufficient linkage between economic and social policies and the subordination of social policy to economic policy, evident in the marginal position of cultural and educational programs; the lack of differentiation between the social policy of the state and that of the government; the difficulty in maintaining programs on course due to the increase in the beneficiary population as an effect of economic adjustment; the diminution of the compensatory effect of programs based on monetary transfers and the conversion of temporary into permanent transfers, given their "high social and political sensitivity"; the insufficient coverage of programs tied to schools, which excludes many of the neediest families; the continuous deterioration in the quality of traditional services in education and health; and insufficient progress in defining procedures for the participation of civil society.[59]

The evaluation concluded by recommending the institutional strengthening of the social sector in order that social policy not continue to be subordinated to economic policy but become part of an integrated and well-coordinated effort.

Conclusions: Prospects for Social Policies in Coming Years

The studies tend to agree on several important points; perhaps the most important concerns the growing divergence in the directions economic policy and social policy have taken. At first glance, one cannot accuse the state of trying to evade its social responsibilities: It dedicated significant resources and efforts to designing and improving social policy, and especially to compensation programs. But at the same time, the model of the state-society relationship that the adjustment program promoted implied a certain delegitimation of state action. It attempted to deal with this tension by designing a "new" social policy, new as much in its objectives as in its channels of execution. It would be a question of defining public action based on private sector criteria, such as good management, effectiveness in cost-benefit terms, and universalist criteria in the selection of beneficiaries.

But this policy was not backed up by the organizational bases or sufficient internal resources to impose a global reorientation of traditional social policy. The new policy was, therefore, superimposed on the old policy, in an uncomfortable coexistence. Only in some cases (for example, food aid) were the organizations of the traditional and the newly created sectors able to interconnect. Meanwhile, the resistance of functionaries in the central bureaucracy and of political patrons in the ministries impeded to a great degree the necessary structural reforms.

The reorientation of social policy was also hindered by the shallowness of the "antistatism" the adjustment program tried to propel. Venezuelan political culture, shaped by a half century of redistribution of profits by the state, has far from overcome this model. Its tenacity is evident in the permanence of numerous subsidies and privileges, especially among groups with political clout. In addition, the marked character of the most visible social policies of traditional assistance contributed to reinforcing, not diminishing, dependence on a state perceived as the sole protector against market forces.

A notable fact in Venezuelan politics in recent years has been the relative passivity of the organized labor movement. Beyond defending the corporate interests of its affiliates, especially in the public sector, the movement has not been able to present viable alternatives for the reorganization of social security or for the defense of employment in the formal sector. Similarly, their capacity as a pressure group has been eroded by spontaneous mobilizations that developed outside union control. As a result, their role in the adjustment process has been relatively marginal.[60]

At the same time, key actors in the organizations of civil society have not yet achieved a sufficient political presence. Although many have been associated with the state in the new programs and aspire to play a more active role, they have not gained recognition by the state for the maturity and institutional stability necessary to permit them to represent the popular sectors, the principal potential beneficiaries of social policy. An additional factor to be reckoned with is the memory of the popular uprising of February 1989. Since then, economic and social policies have oscillated between technocratic recommendations for rigor in the adjustment process and the necessity of making concessions to avoid a new social explosion. This has sent contradictory signals to all involved: On one hand, there is an attempt to rationalize and modernize state action; on the other, the state maintains itself as the prisoner of its own clientele. In this manner, the burden of adjustment, which in principle the entire group of social actors must share, is evaded or at least weakened by those who are in the clientelist networks or who can exert pressure autonomously.

The fact is that neither the structural adjustment program under Pérez nor the heterodox program of the present government of Rafael Caldera has succeeded in reversing or even slowing the growth of critical poverty. The compensatory social programs, which were supposed to be temporary, have become permanent because the expected reactivation of the economy and of employment has never materialized. Their weight falls upon the already overloaded state budget, adversely affecting programs in the social sector.

Caldera's government, begun in February 1994, maintained a critical attitude toward the economic and social policies of his predecessor. Nevertheless, he has been unable to introduce significant changes either in the structure or the functioning of the social sector. Although the project of the IX Plan de la Nación gives first priority to the social sector, and within this to education, the concrete measures it proposes are not significantly different from those established by the previous government. Over the long term it proposes the creation of a network of social work institutions to be directed by community organizations with autonomous decision-making powers. In the short term, it affirms that "one must continue putting the focus on vulnerable groups."[61] This implies the continuation of programs like PAMI, the multihouseholds, and other nutritional programs.

Nevertheless, the continuity of this policy becomes increasingly compromised by the fiscal crisis that is deepening in Venezuela. The financial crisis of 1994, which led to the forced takeover by the state of numerous insolvent banks, compelled the state to compensate depositors, which produced excess liquidity and a violent acceleration of inflation. The government also instituted emergency economic measures, such as price and exchange rate controls, which produced uncertainty in the economy and discouraged new investment. In addition, the rigidity of the fiscal budget and the weight of servicing the external debt have further hampered economic growth. In 1995 the debt service amounted to 21.4 percent of the value of exports of goods and services.[62]

All this poses a challenge to the Venezuelan government's traditional way of taking action, which is based on budgetary inertia. There are various options: Either the deficit can be financed through monetary means, aggravating inflationary tendencies; or taxes can be significantly increased; or public expenditures can be severely adjusted, including those dedicated to the social sector. Any of these measures will have political costs; for this reason the government thus far has tried to use a combination of strategies without expressing a decided preference for any of them. Previous governments issued currency and devalued the bolívar to finance the deficit and compensate for the decrease in petroleum profits. But the cost of this strategy, especially for the poor, is increasingly evident. The current government has made efforts to increase internal revenue, but they are necessarily limited in the present stagnating economy and face resistance by privileged groups. For this reason, reducing public expenditures in real terms becomes an option the government can no longer delay, especially as it is recommended by international financial experts and even demanded by opinion leaders in the private sector.

There is no doubt about the inefficient nature of public spending in Venezuela and the inflationary risks of the fiscal deficit. Nevertheless, the state appears trapped in a blind alley: At the moment when austerity measures may produce the desired effect of reducing inflation and reviving the economy, the interruption in or diminution of compensatory policies (which until now have been the only ones to ameliorate the deterioration of living conditions among the poorest groups) could lead to a desperate or even violent situation.[63] Now, as parties and the political establishment in general have lost much of their credibility, a worsening of conditions would certainly contribute to greater political and social instability.

We have seen that even at the highest level of real expenditures, social policy has been relatively ineffective in Venezuela in recent years, compared both with other countries and with earlier periods (especially between the decades of the 1930s and 1960s). Most studies argue that the problem is not in the amount of resources committed but rather in the way they are managed, which, in turn, is a function of the way power was distributed among actors in the initial stages of democratization. As this political-institutional arrangement has lost its functionality and legitimacy, the social policies that it inspired have lost force.

The financier state, highly centralized and legitimized by strong parties managing extensive clientelist networks, presided over a social policy of growing expenditures with few constraints, which at the time satisfied popular demands and corporatist interests. Now, the financial maneuvering room of the state is strongly diminished: It is under pressure to decentralize, it has difficulty fulfilling its basic functions, and the parties that sustained it over the years are losing legitimacy.

An effective social policy must be integrated into the political process of state reform, which requires that the actors directly involved—those providing and using services, managers, and financiers—have a more direct role in decision making and in the organization of the sector. Beyond schemes for simple privatization or delegation of authority, it means institutionally reinforcing the capacity of social actors to supervise and monitor organizations responsible for social policy, making them accountable and capable of confronting the problems of inefficiency, inequity, and inadequate coverage in the provision of social services.[64]

Nevertheless, reforms in the social sector in themselves are insufficient to solve these problems because they are linked to the more general process of transformation of the economy and the state. Important issues remain: the restructuring of the productive sectors and the creation of employment; the redistribution of resources between the central government and the regional and local bodies; and the redefinition of the role of the state in a more restricted sense. The creation of a state based upon a productive society, with greater regional autonomy, modern political parties, and more decision-making responsibility for social actors continues to be far from assured.

Notes

1. Bernard Mommer, "La Economía Venezolana: De la Siembra del Petroleo a la Enfermedad Holandesa," *Cuadernos del CENDES,* no. 8, 1988. pp. 35–56; Ramon Espinasa and Berhard Mommer, "La Política Petrolera Venezolana en el Largo Plazo," *Cuadernos del Cendes,* no. 15–16, 1991, pp. 25–49; Miriam Kornblith and Thais Maingón, *Estado y Gasto Público en Venezuela, 1936–1980* (Caracas: Ediciones de la Biblioteca, Universidad Central de Venezuela, 1985).

2. Between 1989 and 1994, total public expenditures as a percent of GNP fluctuated between 20.8 and 24.8, exceeded only by spending in Brazil and Chile among comparable countries. See Banco Interamericano de Desarrollo, *Progreso Económico y Social en América Latina: Informe 1993* (Washington, D.C.: Banco Interamericano de Desarrollo, 1993), p. 302.

3. Juan Carlos Rey, *El Futuro de la Democracia en Venezuela* (Caracas: IDEA: 1989), p. 14.

4. Eduardo Arroyo Talavera, *Elecciones y Negociaciones: Los Limites de la Democracia Venezolana* (Caracas: Fondo Editorial Conicit-Pomaire, 1988); Juan Carlos Rey, *El Futuro de la Democracia en Venezuela,* passim; Margarita López Maya and Luís Gómez Calcaño, "Desarrollo y Hegemonía en la Sociedad Venezolana: 1958 a 1985," in Margarita López Mayo, Luís Gómez Calcano, and Thaís Maingón, eds., *De Punto Fijo al Pacto Social* (Caracas: Fondo Editorial Acta Científica Venezolana, 1989) pp. 13–124.

5. In spite of the intention to reduce the role of the state, the ministries employ more than two-thirds of the personnel and absorb two-thirds of the payroll of the central government. See *Resumen Ley de Presupuesto* (Caracas: Oficina Central de Presupuesto, 1993).

6. A good general evaluation of social policies in Venezuela has been made by researchers at the Instituto de Investigaciones Económicas y Sociales of the Universidad Católica Andrés Bello. See their *La Capacidad Compensatoria de los Programas Sociales* (Caracas: ILES/UCAB Colección Temas de Coyuntura No. 24, 1991), pp. 7–12. Evaluations of and proposals for the health sector are discussed in Thaís Maingón, *Proposiciones para una Política de Salud y Nutrición para Venezuela: Agenda Social de los 90* (Caracas: ILDIS, 1993). Studies of social security are presented in Xiomara Rausseo, *Sector: Seguridad Social, Agenda Social de los 90* (Caracas: ILDIS, 1993). A very complete evaluation of the plan to combat poverty is included in Vanessa Cartaya and Yolanda d'Elía, *Pobreza en Venezuela: Realidad y Políticas* (Caracas: CESAP-CISOR, 1991).

7. *Informe sobre Desarrollo Humano* (Mexico, D.F.: Programa de las Naciones Unidas para el Desarrollo/Fondo de Cultura Económica, 1994), pp. 145–7; *Panorama Social de América Latina* (Santiago: Comisión Económica para América Latina y el Caribe, 1994), p. 162.

8. For critical studies of the process, see, among others, Hector Valecillos, *El Reajuste Liberal en Venezuela* (Caracas: Monte Avila, 1992); and Edgardo Lander, "El Impacto del Ajuste Neoliberal en Venezuela, 1989–1993," paper presented at the XVIII International Congress of the Latin American Studies Association, Atlanta, March 1994. Moises Naím combines his testimony as an ex-minister with a favorable sociopolitical analysis of the adjustment program in *Paper Tigers and Minotaurs* (Washington, D.C.: The Carnegie Endowment for International Peace, 1993).

9. See the letter of intent presented to the International Monetary Fund, "Memorandum de Política Económica que Presenta el Gobierno de Venezuela," *Cuadernos del CENDES,* no. 10, 1989, pp. 140–9.

10. Subsidizing private external debt was agreed to by the government of Luis Herrera Campins in response to strong managerial pressure brought to bear because of the danger of bankruptcy of hundreds of companies and the consequent increase in unemployment. The subsidy to exchange risk was, to say the least, unusual (and was not recommended by the International Monetary Fund), but it was ratified with modifications, owing to the worsening of the exchange situation, by the governments of Luschini and Pérez. An analysis of the process of approval and implementation is found in Thais Maingón, "La Deuda Privada Externa: Un Analísis Sociopolítico," in Margarita López Mayo, Luís Gómez Calcano, and Thaís Maingón, eds., *De Punto Fijo al Pacto,* passim.

11. "Memorandum de Política Económica," pp. 145–6.

12. Moises Naim, *Paper Tigers and Minotaurs,* passim.

13. Edgardo Lander, "El Impacto del Ajuste Neoliberal," passim.

14. Miguel I. Purroy, "Los Equilibrios Inestables," *SIC,* no. 522, 1990, pp. 52–9.

15. Asdrubal Baptista, "La Cuestión de los Salarios en Venezuela," *SIC,* no. 534, 1991, pp. 187–9. Baptista shows, starting with a study of the relation between salaries, productivity, and investment over the past forty years, that the compression of salaries has become the fundamental source of accumulation in the non-petroleum economy to compensate for the reduction of petroleum income.

16. Vanessa Cartaya and Yolanda D'Elía, *Pobreza en Venezuela,* p. 112.

17. Navarro reports that the Ministry of Health and Social Assistance dedicated 42.7 percent of its budget to operations and maintenance in 1980 but only 22 percent in 1988. Juan Carlos Navarro, *Reforming Social Policy in Venezuela* (Washington, D.C.: Inter-American Development Bank, 1994), p. 15.

18. *Panorama Social de América Latina,* p. 102.

19. Nelson Croce and Mabel M. de Croce, *Indicadores del Gasto Social, Macroeconomia, Eficiencia y Desempeño* (Caracas: Sistema de Información Gerencial para el Sector Social, 1994); *Resumen Ley de Presupuesto,* p. 85.

20. Between 1989 and 1992 the World Bank and the Interamerican Development Bank contributed 773.5 million dollars to various social programs, which represents a 46.62 percent of the total financing of those programs. See the presentation on the Venezuelan case at the Third Regional Conference on Poverty in Latin America and the Caribbean, Santiago, November 1992 as reorted in *Actividades de los Gobiernos de América Latina y el Caribe para la Superación de la Pobreza, Respuesta del Gobierno de Venezuela* (Caracas: CORDIPLAN, 1992).

21. Juan Carlos Navarro, *Reforming Social Policy in Venezuela,* pp. 31–2.

22. *Actividades de los Gobiernos,* passim.

23. Ibid., p. 7. For an evaluative study of the program, see Boris Lima, "Focalización de Programas Masivos: El Caso Venezolano de la Beca Alimentaria," paper presented at the Third Regional Conference on Poverty in Latin America and the Caribbean, Santiago, November 1992.

24. *Actividades de los Gobiernos,* p. 8. These programs form part of the Project of Social Development (PDS), technically aided and partially financed by the World Bank. PDS includes a wide range of programs organized into four areas: improvement of maternal-infant health services; preschool education; institutional development of the private sector; and information, communication, and education. For a detailed discussion of the project, see Marino González, "De la Compensación al Largo Plazo," *SIC,* no. 535, 1991, pp. 201–4; *Venezuela Poverty Study* (Washington D.C.: World Bank, 1991).

25. *La Capacidad Compensatoria de los Programas Sociales,* pp. 16–9.

26. This transformation was not achieved in the presidential term of Pérez, but it is forecasted in the plans of the Caldera government.

27. Some of the most important of these organizations were the School of Social Management Foundation, whose objective is the formation of plans for the executive institutions of social policy; the Fund for Social Investment of

Venezuela, directed to financing social programs; and the PAMI Foundation, charged with coordinating the execution of the maternal-infant program. See Vanessa Cartaya and Yolanda d'Elía, *Pobreza en Venezuela*, pp. 154–5.

28. *La Capacidad Compensatoria de los Programas Sociales*, pp. 39–40.

29. *Seguimiento de la Ejecución Física y Financiera de los Programas Sociales Compensatorios* (Caracas: Consejo Nacional para Supervisión y Seguimiento de los Programas Sociales del Ejecutivo Nacional, 1994).

30. Ibid., pp. 23–4.

31. *Avances del Proceso de Descentralización en Venezuela*. (Caracas: Comisión Presidencial para la Reforma del Estado, 1992).

32. Ibid.

33. Adela Arrieche, H. Nunez, and Y. Sanguino, *Evaluación de las Experiencias de Descentralización y Desconcentración del Sector Salud en Venezuela* (Caracas: FUDECO-FAUS-ILDIS, 1993), p. 27.

34. Ibid., p. 36.

35. Gabriela Bronfenmajer, R. Casanova, and R. Pucci, "Inovaciones, Reformas, y Consensos en la Educación Superior Venezolana," *Cuadernos del CENDES*, no. 21, 1993, pp. 137–93.

36. Betulio Bravo, "Centros Comunitarios de Atención al Niño (Los Multihogares)," *Juntos*, vol. 2, no. 10, 1992, p. 35.

37. *Seguimiento de la Ejecución Física y Financiera de los Programas Sociales Compensatorios*, p. 18.

38. Mauricio Iranzo, "El Apoyo a la Economía Popular como Política del Estado," *SIC*, no. 548, 1992, p. 361.

39. Ibid., pp. 360–2.

40. Ibid., p. 362.

41. The agreement also included an ad hoc organization of the ministry, the Fund of Cooperation and Financing of Associated Businesses Foundation (FONCOFIN). See Leonardo Pizani, "Una Gestión Económica y Social por los Pequeños Empresarios (Balance de AUGE)," *Juntos*, vol. 1, no. 4, pp. 42–3.

42. Ibid., p. 43.

43. The program of aid to the informal economy includes not only small businesses but also collective organizations for agricultural and artesanal production and commercialization. Freites describes the program for the state of Lara, exceptionally rich in communal experiments: Seven private and public intermediary organizations participate, among them some linked to the Catholic Church, which offered aid to more than 1,400 economic enterprises in 1990–91. See Nelson Freites, "Economia Popular en Lara: Expresiones, Relaciones y Significados," *SIC*, no. 548, 1992, pp. 350–2.

44. Alberto Rodríguez and Claudia Peña, *Evaluación del Impacto de las Ferias de Consumo Popular: Sistematización de sus Claves de Exito* (Caracas: Fundación Escuela de Gerencia Social, 1991), pp. 9–28.

45. Two articles that appeared when the collaborative programs were initiated indicate the terms of the discussion. Both take into account the skepticism that collaborating closely with the government provokes, but they ultimately come

down in favor of this arrangement to the extent of proposing going beyond the role of simple executors of state policy to participating formally in the conception of social policies. See Jose Luis López, "Política Social y Sociedad Civil en la Encrucijada," *Juntos,* vol. 2, no. 9, 1991, pp. 30–2; and Domingo Méndez Rivero, "Utopia, Política Social y Organizaciones No-Gubernamentales," *Juntos,* vol. 2, no. 9, 1991, pp. 36–8. More recently, the same authors have deepened the debate over the issue. See Domingo Mendez Rivero, "FONCOFIN, la Sociedad Civil y los Gobiernos Locales," *SIC,* no. 548, 1992, pp. 356–9; and Jose Luis López, "Las Organizaciones No-Gobernamentales de Desarrollo, sus Desafios: Pobreza y Democracia," paper presented at the conference "Participación de la Sociedad Civil en Programas Sociales," Caracas, April 1995. A similar view based on the experience of the consumer fairs is presented in Gustavo Salas, *La Participación Ciudadara en el Diseño y Gestión de Programas Social,* 1991.

46. An exemplary case of this type of competition is described in Carolina de Oteiza, "La Lucha de una Comunidad por la Leche Popular," *SIC,* no. 520, 1989, pp. 458–9.

47. The pressures on the ministers exerted by the party are described in "AD Presiona al Gobierno," *SIC,* no. 531, 1991, p. 40.

48. Juan Carlos Navarro, *Reforming Social Policy in Venezuela,* p. 36.

49. José Luís López calls this a "backward" mentality because incorporating civil society in decisions to solve national programs relieves the burden on the state. See "Instalado Puente entre el Estado y la Sociedad Civil," *Juntos,* vol. 13, 1992, p. 17.

50. Gustavo Márquez, "Pobreza y Política Social," paper presented at the symposium "Los Pobres: La Mayoría Desaprovechada," Caracas, IESA-CORPOVEN, 1992.

51. For example, when it dealt with expanding the coverage of the mother-infant care program to the national level, the Ministry of Health imposed conditions that destroyed the efficiency of the program. See Ibid., pp. 17–8.

52. Ibid., p. 19.

53. Juan Carlos Navarro, *Reforming Social Party in Venezuela,* p. 38.

54. Ibid., pp. 39–40.

55. Hector Valecillos, *El Reajuste Neoliberal en Venezuela,* pp. 179–209.

56. Vanessa Cartaya and Yolanda D'Elía, *Pobreza en Venezuela,* p. 191.

57. Ibid., pp. 192–7.

58. Elena Estaba, A. Caraballo, F. Lara and F. J. Velasco, *La COPRE y el Desarrollo Social: Balance de la Política Social del Estado Venezolano en el Periodo 1989–1992* (Caracas: COPRE, 1992), pp. 22–3.

59. Ibid., pp. 24–8.

60. Hector Valecillos, *El Reajuste Neoliberal en Venezuela,* pp. 26–7.

61. *Un Proyecto de Pais: Venezuela en Consenso* (Carracas: CORDIPLAN, 1995), pp. 153–4.

62. Inter-American Development Bank, *Economic and Social Progress in Latin America, 1996 Report* (Washington, D.C.: IADB, 1996), p. 400.

63. Although it is difficult to document, the perception transmitted by the media and shared by public opinion is that levels of violence, of drug consump-

tion and trafficking, and of other forms of social decay—especially, but not exclusively, among the poorest sectors—have increased significantly in Venezuela in the last decade.

64. For a comparison of recent recommendations for social policy reform in Latin America, see Thais Maingón, "Neoliberalismo, Política Social y Nuevo Rol del Estado en America Latina," *Cuadernos del CENDES*, no. 23, 1993, pp. 73–93.

11

"Popular Deluge," the Informal Sector, Political Independents, and the State in Peru

Julio Cotler

Since the 1930s and, more intensely, since the 1950s, the processes of modernization associated with the spread of capitalism undermined the traditional bases of political power in Peru and contributed to the emergence of new social actors and the expansion of political participation. This led to the growth of several populist movements whose goal was to reduce the concentration of wealth, break down the ethnic-hierarchical divisions inherited from the colonial past, and open channels for accommodating the socioeconomic demands of the popular classes within the state apparatus. To this end, the state had to be strengthened sufficiently to represent the interests and aspirations of indigenous peoples, mestizos, and "provincials" in the regional backwaters against the exclusionary interests of native and foreign property owners—that is, the *blanquitos,* or "whites." In the populist political scheme the state was the prime mover; civil society was perceived as an undifferentiated social aggregate with little capacity to articulate itself, identify its national interests, or formulate its political objectives.

These movements were led by dominant figures who maintained a patrimonial relationship with their followers and who formulated ideologies that combined nationalist, revolutionary, and statist objectives in varying degrees. Their agendas managed to incorporate the interests of both the popular classes and the established middle sectors while excluding sectors to the political right and left who did not share their positions. This resulted in repeated sociopolitical confrontations, which intensified as a result of economic crises and contributed to a weakening of state institutions and a failure of governance that opened the door to military coups.

In Peru, the "Revolutionary Government of the Armed Forces" that ruled for twelve years (1968–1980) called for profound populist-inspired transformations in all social realms. This propelled an unusual political mobilization that overwhelmed state institutions and contributed to aggravating the economic crisis of the mid-1970s. Consequently, the constitutional regime installed in 1980 inherited an economic and political legacy fraught with strong contradictions and characterized by José Matos Mar as a *desborde popular,* or "popular deluge"—a dramatic rise in indigenous organizations and initiatives challenging legal channels and norms, particularly during a period of economic and political turmoil.[1]

The patrimonial character of the populist leaders encouraged political sectarism. Clientelism, patronage, and the distribution of sinecures fostered corruption and rent-seeking as corporatist practices emphasized centralism and the redistributive functions of the state. The profound ethnic, social, and regional inequalities, along with the high expectations of the emerging social sectors, reinforced political behaviors and attitudes that led to multiple and insurmountable conflicts. These inequalities proved so deeply rooted that they were addressed even when it became evident that they were contributing to the general instability of the social and political order.[2]

The Informal Sector

Under these conditions, the popular classes flooded government agencies with demands and protests, expressing their relative independence from their original populist patrons while promising that they were prepared to defend their demands "to the ultimate consequences." The governments of the past decade had addressed their demands at the price of runaway inflation. The external debt crisis of 1982 exacerbated the crisis, increasing inflation and underemployment. The result was an explosive growth in the number of people involved in unregulated and poorly productive activities outside the formal economy and articulated in the family, ethnic, and regional networks—that is, the informal sector.[3]

The populist and left-wing organizations initially did not know how to deal with this unusual situation, which weakened their bonds with popular sectors and contributed to extreme electoral volatility as the electorate grew from 4.5 to 9 million.[4] The rise and expansion of subversive terrorist movements further undermined political parties and social organizations. This worked to give almost complete autonomy to the armed forces, who became increasingly involved in human rights violations. As trafficking in illegal narcotics attracted large numbers of peasants and indigenous people, the precarious institutional bases of the police and the judiciary eroded further. Thus, at the end of the last decade, the continual worsening of the political crisis brought the traditionally weak government close to total collapse. No less could have been expected. The growing inability of state institutions to handle the simultaneous problems of inflation, terrorism, and drug trafficking produced massive disenchantment with the established political identities.

The "popular deluge" came to be perceived as an undifferentiated ensemble of individual and collective initiatives coming out of informal and illegal activities that while ignoring the basic rules and norms or their trade or sector were undermining the official institutional framework. These activities generated a subculture that encouraged "free-riding" and became associated with the "informalization" of society and disaffection from political and economic institutions. As a result, at the end of the 1980s institutional disarray and lack of political legitimacy were the norm.

For many analysts the growth of the informal sector was directly related to the economic crisis. Hernando de Soto and Mario Vargas Llosa in the 1990 preelectoral campaign proclaimed, however, that it was an integral part of the new social structure and that it expressed liberal aspirations of an antipopulist and antimercantilist avantgarde. Events would later prove their analysis at least partially right. Informal economic activity expanded because of sharply increasing rates of unemployment and decreasing real income, but it also expanded because it responded to desire for autonomy and upward social mobility into the ranks of independent entrepreneurs.[5] In the same vein, it has been argued that migrants in Lima, heirs to a work ethic that grants a critical importance to individual effort and the idea of progress, have developed a strategy for informal participation in the low-income market using the support of family and regional networks that are active in certain branches of economic activity.[6]

Contrary to what might be expected, the informal sector activities would absorb economic and political tensions in the face of subversive movements, which explains their ruthless attitude toward peasants, urban popular leaders, and women's organizations. At the same time and for the same reasons, as the informal sector became a refuge for the poor, it functioned as a safety valve, neutralizing social struggles. This was even the case after 1990 when the government implemented a stabilization policy that had disastrous consequences for the living conditions of the poor. The attitudes and actions of those in the informal sector belied their supposed tendency to support subversive movements and engage in mercantilist practices. The idea "aren't we all businessmen?" seems to have captured the popular imagination and supported the idea of the microenterprise as *the* means to achieve equality of opportunity for the poor. In this view, the growth of the informal sector was part and parcel of the process of democratization. In addition, the informal sector would give rise to political independents and the formation of an "authentic" civil society that functioned on the basis of market criteria and was accompanied by a depoliticization of economic decision making.

The Independents

The delegitimization of politics created the conditions for the rise of the independents—outsiders to formal political parties—as important political actors, and in the presidential election of 1990 both candidates—Vargas Llosa and Alberto Fujimori—were independents. In the midst of a severe economic and social crisis, this political realignment permitted the elected government to change strategy abruptly and adopt a neoliberal course that aggravated the decline of traditional social and political actors but elevated the importance of the independents.

In spite of the fact that the populist and leftist political parties, as well as various ethnic, social, and religious-based movements, had supported Fujimori's platform, he could ignore them because they had lost power and prestige.[7] Instead, he associated himself with the "de facto powers," convinced that the only realistic solution to getting the country back on its feet was to secure order and public safety forcefully and to introduce, via technocratic means, neoliberal measures to reorganize the economy. To some observers it was reminiscent of Hobbes's approach to political dilemmas. It explains why Fujimori adopted the authoritarian solutions proposed by the armed forces—particularly the intelligence services—and appropriated the neoliberal platform of his opponent. This change in position gave him the support of the followers of his defeated opponent, the international financial community, the entrepreneurial class, the media, and the rightist wing of the church.[8] Their support was critical in achieving the reintegration of the country into international economic and financial circuits.

This unusual coalition allowed Fujimori to stamp his government with an explicit antipolitical character that permitted the military and the state bureaucracy—along with the advisors of the multilateral organizations—to use broad powers to tackle both subversion and inflation, ignoring public opinion and the political positions of the parties. The president decided to act first and to inform himself afterward. Most government decisions were taken behind closed doors.

Nevertheless, political parties and popular organizations continued to restrain presidential decision making, to investigate government actions, and to mobilize sporadic acts of protest in spite of their divisions and lack of credibility. In response, the military intelligence services—as in the years of the military regime—launched successful "psychosocial" campaigns to discredit traditional politics: successive accusations of corruption and profiteering, charges of complicity with subversive movements, and the like. In addition, government opponents were blamed for impoverishing and failing to protect the popular classes, who were powerless when confronted with a judicial system populated by judges whom Fujimori described as "jackals." The campaigns also aimed to underscore the virtues of the managerial and pragmatic style of Fujimori, to gain public support for his authoritarian methods, and to emphasize his effectiveness in getting things done, no matter the means.

His triumph over subversive movements and the success of his economic stabilization policies, despite their costs, reinforced popular support for Fujimori,[9] as did his pragmatism, which shared a strong affinity with methods and practices in the informal sector. The latter gained legitimacy, which, in combination with the antipolitical character of the independents, further deepened the lack of respect for existing norms and institutions. Finally, the considerable social distance between the president and the traditional social and political elites also contributed to reinforcing his social and cultural identification with the popular classes, who regarded him as the political representative of their multifaceted aspirations,[10] thus further distancing themselves from the traditional political parties that were losing credibility and capacity to mobilize at every turn.

Against this background, Fujimori and the military staged the "semicoup" in April 1992 that was devised to end "traditional" politics and install a "direct democracy" that would confer absolute powers on the presidency. This action by the president, with support of the military, was approved by the majority in a plebiscite. Negative reactions by other governments, multilateral organizations, and human rights organizations interfered with Fujimori's and the military's plans in the short term but produced unexpected results later on.

Paradoxically, the international economic pressures aimed at promoting democracy and respect for human rights created the conditions for an electoral legitimization of Fujimori's rule and a reinforcement of his authoritarianism. The president agreed to call elections for a Democratic Constitutional Congress in 1992 in reaction to these pressures, but following this decision, the divisions among politicians intensified to such a degree that they were not even able to agree on those minimal accords that would have upheld constitutional conditions. Antipolitical party sentiments among the citizenry skyrocketed. Aided by the machinery of the state—controlled by the military intelligence services—and the media, independents supporting Fujimori easily triumphed. As was to be expected, the tractable majority in congress put forward an extremely presidentialist constitution that even permits the president to run for more than one term.

Despite the vast resources of the government and the absence of political party participation, however, the 1993 referendum to ratify the constitution was passed by only a narrow margin. This revealed the unsteadiness of the independents' support for Fujimori. With his sight on reelection in 1995, Fujimori began a tireless campaign of visits, donations, and social spending across the vast geography of poverty. The generous support of international financial organizations, in addition to a discourse that underscored his social identification with the "marginal" population, allowed him to create a direct relationship with the masses and to strengthen his personal style of government, reminiscent of the old populist ways.[11]

The promise of a bright economic future, which abundant foreign investment and the high rates of economic growth would insure, and the appointment of technocrats and independent entrepreneurs to positions of public responsibility also contributed to the indisputable electoral triumph of Fujimori. The lackluster image projected by his rival, former United Nations Secretary General Javier Pérez de Cuellar, and his association with politicians identified with the traditional political party structure aided Fujimori's success.

The public support for Fujimori expressed in three electoral events and the legitimization of his rule by a docile congressional majority, coupled with the "pragmatic" use of his special powers, silenced international protest. The president's effectiveness in tackling the country's difficult economic problems, together with the recognition that there were few alternatives, the successful reduction in human rights violations, and the vigorous attack on the illegal drug trade were all factors contributing to the normalization of Peru's international relations.[12] Thus, Fujimori's defeat of Vargas Llosa in 1990 and of Pérez de Cuellar in 1995, the two most internationally recognized Peruvians, consolidated the belief that Fujimori represented both the informal and independent sectors, at the same time he attended diligently to the interests of foreign investment.

The Problems of Institutionalization

The decline in traditional political parties and the emergence of the independents as a political force created conditions that Fujimori took advantage of to form a broad coalition, to eliminate the weak opposition, and to turn around the depressed conditions that existed in almost every sphere of civil society. He concentrated the state's resources and adopted a clear technocratic and antipolitical style, actions that were justified by reference to the country's exceptional circumstances. The population's approval of the president's effectiveness in getting things done and his support from the informal sector and independent majorities consecrated Fujimori as the personification of the government and the state. This allowed Fujimori to deepen his relationship with the popular classes and assume a series of providential postures in a classical populist style.[13]

This authoritarian style is no longer justified, however. The continuation of authoritarian practices is creating situations that can endanger the precarious stability that has been reached and adversely influence the future governability of the country, as critics and supporters of the government alike have noted. With subversion defeated, inflation in check, drug trafficking sharply curtailed, and the opposition neutralized, it makes little sense for the president to continue to concentrate political power in his own hands, to refuse to consider public debates or to hear opinions against his own, and to refuse to account for the actions of the secret services managed by his most trusted collaborators.

In addition, the series of reforms hastily decreed, and often approved by the subordinate legislative majority in spite of their anticonstitutional nature, are unjustifiable. Many of these reforms are designed to put the judiciary under the control of the executive and threaten the legal rights of persons and enterprises. The systematic blockage of the entrance into politics of "independents" who are not a part of the group devoted to Fujimori and the attacks on the remnants of working class organizations while employers associations are carefully cultivated, are, equally, manifestations of the antidemocratic course the regime has taken.

This explains why even radical liberals oppose government "informality" and lack of bureaucratic rules, fed by the president's intolerance and abuse of power, and why they insist that both the development of a market economy and the establishment of the rule of law are indispensable prerequisites to correct chronic instability. In other words, these critiques not only question the government's procedures but also challenge their political efficacy over the longer term. Just as the government of the armed forces almost thirty years ago worked to "democratize" society through authoritarian means and unintentionally produced a "popular deluge" as a result, the current government's attempt to modernize the country by similar means could bring about similar consequences.

However, the government's ideologues and its allies maintain that an extreme presidentialist regime is necessary for a quick and effective general restructuring of civil society and the state within the next ten to fifteen years. In this manner, rapid and sustained economic growth would be assured on the basis of the free market and the influx of foreign investment, creating conditions indispensable for a complete restructuring of the political system. These ideologues and allies, with varying doses of pragmatism and cynicism, justify the concentration of power in the hands of the executive and its domination over the judiciary and legislative branches of government, defending the actions by Fujimori and his secret service aides to prevent the emergence of contenders who could obstruct their designs. In the same way, they excuse the government for its overriding attention to foreign investment at the same time it displays indifference or hostility toward any domestic proposals or demands that do not suit its agenda.

This vision for the future contains some well known and, at the same time, controversial assumptions: first, that unlimited freedom for market forces and unrestricted economic growth are necessary—if not sufficient—conditions for the development of a democratic system in an indeterminate future; and second, that an authoritarian regime is necessary for an extended period. This strategy, which points to Singapore as a model for Peru, has—as the major objective—the reconstruction of Peru along the lines of an Asian tiger.[14] It follows the recommendations of multilateral organizations concerning the need for technocratic institutions involved in economic decision making to operate autonomously from the political and social influences flowing from rent-seeking interests. One can conclude that the regime's authoritarianism is not unrelated to the type of reform program or the political project of national reconstruction being implemented. In fact, the technocratic, antipolitical character of the government appears to create ideal conditions for carrying out these reforms, and even more so in the absence of an organized opposition. Thus, Schuldt concludes that the economic problems the government may encounter will not threaten its overall program.[15]

Nonetheless, this personal concentration of power may be self-defeating and may actually frustrate the realization of the government's objectives. First, excluding independents from the political process has caused desertions among the president's ranks, turning then not just into opponents but, rather, declared enemies of the president's personalized regime. This may lead to new forms of political turbulence and strongman (*caudillista*) confrontations with competitors for power like those prevalent in the 1980s. In the last municipal elections in Lima, for example, the candidate endorsed by the president was defeated by an independent candidate in spite of having ample governmental resources at his disposal. Apparently the electorate, while approving Fujimori's rule, sought to limit the reach of his influence. In response, however, the president has systematically reduced the contributions to the municipality's budget, thus limiting the political effects of the electoral outcome. These actions have generated widespread criticism among the general population, where support of the new mayor runs high.

Second, the personal control of public administration undermines its efficiency. To the extent that executive positions are assigned based on the president's personal trust and their performance is evaluated by his personal measures, these positions are unstable in that they cannot and do not comply with universally accepted bureaucratic standards.

Third, concentration of power is a dubious process in the face of "adjustment fatigue," as technocrats euphemistically call the unanswered protests over the failure to find solutions to social needs and demands. In addition, the lack of government attention to criticism by national industrialists of particular economic policies could severely undermine the industrial sector's stability, with grave political consequences. Similarly, the government's lack of interest in majority opinions opposing privatization of public enterprises and its contempt for the repeated critiques of the negative consequences of its economic program, especially high unemployment and low incomes, could lead to similar developments in other economic sectors. In fact, the reforms decreed by the executive have promoted a sense of acute social and economic insecurity and powerlessness within the informal and independent sectors. It comes as no surprise that demands for government intervention on their behalf abound.[16]

The absence of a political agenda that attempts to address these issues meaningfully reduces the possibility for the informal sector to articulate its interests in any organized manner. This explains why this sector operates so pragmatically, with clearly opportunistic biases regarding the need for "formalization" and regulation of its activities within a clearly defined legal context. Their local leaders are effective only to the extent that they submit or appear to adapt themselves to the ukases of central authority.

Strangely enough, none of this appears to incommode the government, at least not on the short term. The combined effects of the legacy of economic and political chaos of the past decade and the neoliberal strategy that followed have frustrated the articulation of interests and autonomous political representation; and, of course, the government has actively taken measures to prevent it.

The lack of institutional means connecting civil society and the state may result in an accumulation of frustrations and a new "popular deluge." A further spread of the informal practices of the independents will threaten the already weak social cohesion of Peru. Thus, in spite of the discrediting of the political parties, a fear exists that a populist leader—such as former president Alan García—might regain popular favor and reverse the gains of technocratic liberalism or, worse, that the subversive movements might resurface with force. That the government has managed to stimulate the growth of the economy and promote a series of public welfare measures has not reduced these fears—most certainly not after the guerrilla attack on the Japanese embassy and the subsequent hostage crises that erupted at the end of 1996—and has intensified the demands for the institutionalization of democratic forms and procedures. These would include the consolidation of citizenship, attention to social demands, eradication of the discretionary character of presidential politics, and ending the political opportunism of the independents. In this manner, Peru would evolve from its present technocratic liberalism toward the liberal-democratic option.

Notes

1. José Matos Mar, *Desborde Popular y Crisis del Estado: El Nuevo Rostro del Perú en la Década de 1980* (Lima: Instituto de Estudios Peruanos, 1984).

2. Julio Cotler, "Political Parties and the Problems of Democratic Consolidation in Peru," in Scott Mainwaring and Timothy R. Scully, eds., *Building Democratic Institutions: Party Systems in Latin America* (Stanford: Stanford University Press 1995), pp. 323–53.

3. In 1981 the informal sector represented 39.3 percent of the employed population of Lima. This proportion increased to 51.1 percent in 1991 and stabilized around 53 percent over the next two years. *Los Rasgos Esenciales de la Problematica de los Estratos no Organizados de la Economía* (Lima: Ministerio de Trabajo y Previsión Social, Dirección General del Empleo, Documentos de Trabajo. Serie: Apuntes No. 8, 1983), figure 1, p. 26. See also Francisco Verdera V., *Propuestas de Redefinición de la Medición del Subempleo y el Desempleo y de Nuevos Indicadores sobre la Situación Ocupacional en Lima* (Lima: Organización Internacional del Trabajo, Equipo Técnico Multidisciplinario para los Países del Area Andina, 1995), figure 8, p. 54.

4. Between 1978 and 1990, Peru had the highest electoral volatility among twelve Latin American countries, topped only by the presidential election in Brazil. See Scott Mainwaring and Timothy R. Scully, *Building Democratic Institutions*, Table 1.1, p. 8.

5. Romeo Grompone, *Talleristas y Vendedores Ambulantes en Lima* (Lima: Desco, 1985).

6. Norma Adams and Nestor Valdivia, *Los Otros Empresarios: Etica de Migrantes y Formación de Empresas en Lima* (Lima: Instituto de Estudios Peruanos, 1991); Jurgen Golte and Norma Adams, *Los Caballos de Troya de los Invasores: Estrategias Campesinas en la Conquista de la Gran Lima* (Lima: Instituto de Estudios Peruanos, 1990); Carlos Ivan Degregori, "Del Mito de Inkarri al Mito del Progreso: Poblaciones Andinas, Cultura e Identidad Nacional," *Socialismo y Participación*, no. 36, 1986, pp. 49–56.

7. Carlos Ivan Degregori and Romeo Grompone, *Elecciones 1990: Demonios y Redentores en el Nuevo Perú. Una Tragedia en dos Vueltas* (Lima: Instituto de Estudios Peruanos, 1991).

8. Julio Cotler, "Crisis Politica, Outsiders y Autoritarismo Plebiscitario: el Fujimorismo," in *Política y Sociedad en el Perú: Cambios y Continuidades* (Lima: Instituto de Estudios Peruanos, 1994), pp. 165–228.

9. Julio Carrión, "The 'Support Gap' for Democracy in Peru: Mass Public Opinion toward Fujimori's Self-Coup: Implications for Democratic Theory,"

paper presented at the XVIII International Congress of the Latin American Studies Association, Atlanta, March 1994. See also Mario F. Novarro, "Democracia y Reformas Estructurales: Explicaciones de la Tolerancia Popular al Ajuste Económico," *Desarrollo Económico,* vol. 35, no. 139, 1995, pp. 443–65.

10. Guillermo O'Donnell, "¿Democracia Delegativa?" *Cuadernos del CLAEH,* No. 61, 1993, pp. 5–20.

11. Romeo Grompone y Carlos Mejia, *Nuevos Tiempos, Nueva Política: El Fin de un Ciclo Partidario* (Lima: Instituto de Estudios Peruanos, 1995).

12. Julio Cotler, *Drogas, Derechos Humanos y Economía. La Internacionalización de la Política: El Caso Peruano* (Lima: Institute de Estudios Peruanos, in press).

13. In the article "Firm hand on the popular pulse," which has the suggestive subtitle "Peru's president is making a success of running the country like a company," Sally Bowen tells us that "Perhaps the most frequent criticism of Mr. Fujimori's style of government is his disinclination to build institutions.... What, then, will become of Peru if the presidential helicopter crashes or an assassin's bullet find its target? . . . 'Don't worry,' jokes Mr. Fujimori, with all the confidence of a born survivor. 'I'll go on managing Peru from heaven.'" *Financial Times,* May 10, 1995.

14. See the interview of Victor Joy Way in *Revista SI,* April 1, 1996.

15. Jurgen Schuldt, *La Enfermedad Holandesa y Otros Virus de la Economía Peruana* (Lima: Universidad del Pacifico, 1994).

16. *A la Intemperie: Percepción sobre los Derechos Humanos* (Lima: Coordinadora de Derechos Humanos, 1996).

12

NGOs, the State, and the Development Process: The Dilemmas of Institutionalization

David Lehmann and Anthony Bebbington

During the prolonged period of military rule and fiscal collapse that, to a greater or lesser extent, afflicted many countries in Latin America, voluntary organizations of the most varied kind flourished, particularly nongovernmental organizations, or NGOs. Once an innocuous acronym awarded by the UN to well-heeled international interest groups entitled to attend and address its meetings, this term has come imperceptibly to mean something quite different in the language of the international development community. It has lost its quasi-legal significance and has gained a multitude of connotations and associations, to the point where to talk of "the NGOs" is to evoke activism, technocracy, competition, commitment, populism, development, and participation. To emphasize the dissonance would not be in the least inappropriate because if there is one thing NGOs are noted for, it is the amount of noise they make and the number and force of their opinions. In that, but only that, they carry on the tradition of those well-established international bodies (the International Trade Union Confederations, the International Chambers of Commerce, and the like) whose role at the UN is exclusively to speak, since they have voice but no vote.

The NGOs in civil society also have voice but no vote, but unlike their distinguished establishment counterparts, they have not much money either; it is therefore surprising that they have acquired such a high profile—expressed notoriously in the jamborees organized by and for them on the margins[1] of recent major international conferences on women (in Nairobi in 1985 and Beijing in 1995), on population (in Cairo in 1994) and on the environment (in Rio de Janeiro in 1992). The reason in part is that they have acquired the profile by force of their collective exis-

251

tence rather than as individual organizations. The term NGOs no longer has any coherent meaning at all if it is taken to refer to individual organizations; rather it refers to them in the plural, as a collectivity. Its frequent usage as a collective noun tells us that in some sense those who speak of NGOs know that they are dealing with a movement. The term has lost much of its literal significance; that is, to say that this is a set of "nongovernmental" entities tells us almost nothing about what they really do and less about the activities of those bodies to which we know, in using the term, we are referring. When Sub-Comandante Marcos, master of the art of style over substance, addressed one his many messages during the Chiapas uprising *"desde alguna parte de las montañas del sur de México"* to *"las ONG,"* he presumably had in mind a collectivity not a set of disparate discrete institutions, agencies, offices, and ginger groups. And the same could be said of Mexican officials who occasionally denounce NGOs on account of their purported manipulation of the human rights issue for political purposes, with the warning that soon their bluff will be called.

What we are witnessing here above all is a subculture and a movement, or at least part of a movement. We can thus neatly evade the question "what is an NGO?" and, given the eloquence of Joe Foweraker's discussion in this volume, we can also sidestep the question "what is a movement?"

To begin, we must focus on NGOs as part of a movement but one marked by its international, even cosmopolitan, character. In this way we overcome the difficulties posed by NGO reliance on international charitable and to some extent official funding because we place them in a context where they are a part of something larger, of which they are only one dimension, and which includes those very international agencies that fund the domestic NGOs in recipient countries. An additional advantage of this perspective is that NGOs can be seen to have characteristics and variations that go back to their role as bearers of a range of basic social values. By describing them as part of a movement we avoid doubts about the legitimacy or appropriateness of their "dependence" on "money from abroad" because in this conception the opposition between "home" and "abroad" becomes secondary, and the funding agencies are part of the same movement in any case.

A further corollary is that NGO activists and managers are political animals: They deal to some extent in ideals, in nonmaterial results, and they obtain their funding on the basis of proposals and projects rather than on a commercial basis. They have developed a method for selling themselves and a language in which to do it—much as a politician will "sell" himself or herself. This must be seen in the context of an international network of people and institutions in which money is in search of projects, and project managers are in search of money—yet the two cannot be brought together by conventional market mechanisms because the ideals they represent are quintessentially antimarket and humanitarian. The movement also deals in the coinage of policy: Influencing governments is an important part of its agenda because the NGO phenomenon is to some extent a movement of ideas. In short, there is less to be gained from asking "what is the essence of NGOs?" than from locating the NGO movement within a worldwide participatory, alternative movement.

NGOs in an International Context

The international context we propose is that of the rise of a historical subject, a historical project, and a new system of historical action, more or less in conformity with the schema outlined by Alain Touraine in numerous works on social movements.[2] In Touraine's conception, which seen from the perspective of today cannot but appear rooted in both time and space, the historical subject was the working class, the project was social democracy, and the system of action was organized capitalism in its triumphant phase. The NGOs fit into a different social movement but one that nonetheless does fit Touraine's demanding and admittedly somewhat ethnocentric requirements.

The historical subject in this case is a vast network of individuals and groups sharing in a global movement of dissidence, of nongovernmental spokespeople and agencies, of interest and "cause-oriented" groups. As a network, it cannot be neatly categorized (as "the industrial working class" had been), and it does not neatly fit into the dynamics of a "system of historical action," such as the capitalist mode of production. Yet this network is identifiable by its insertion in the international development policy community as the bearer of policy interventions emanating from civil society. By civil society is meant here the cause-oriented associations, charities, pressure groups, and agencies that arise on the margins of official policymaking and resource allocation yet have managed to acquire a certain legitimacy as representatives of not necessarily, or even in the least, a significant body of opinion but rather the "conscience," not infrequently the guilty conscience. Free of the shackles of procedure and convention, the network and its members are concerned with issues of political, ideological, and moral substance to a far greater extent than official institutions and political parties can be, constrained as these are by procedure, by electoral considerations, and by the niceties and calculations of international political exchange. They are also somewhat different from institutionalized pressure groups because the latter are beholden to their constituents and held to a tight brief by them, whereas cause-oriented groups are beholden to none but themselves. Thus we have the rise of a cosmopolitan, opinion-influencing intelligentsia. Today, this international network of civil society is an established part of the policy community not only in the sense that its activists debate in the same fora as government and partisan representatives but also in that they are incorporated into the policy formulation and implementation process through consultations with the major development institutions.

Thirty years ago this network barely existed at the international level. Now it is an established participant in extremely important processes, in an uneasy but intensifying partnership with counterparts in the international financial institutions and in government. The economic policies, and increasingly the environmental and social policies, of most countries in the world are shaped in debates and negotiations that take place among a global intellectual elite employed partly by the World Bank and similar institutions and trained in the economic departments of a small set of universities, principally in the United States and to a lesser extent in Europe. This is a network of like-minded people who, even if they are ministers, behave like technocrats serving political masters,[3] and it is with this international policymaking technocracy that the NGO network has entered into a cooperative relationship. Technocrats will not be part of a movement; they are confined to particular arenas—those of their institutions or their office, the single level of their professional competence. The NGOs are part of a movement because they operate at many different levels and in many different arenas: working in fields and factories, providing health care or education, managing programs of technical assistance to farmers, running documentation centers, and so on. They mobilize the intelligentsia, they mobilize public opinion, their networks penetrate the media and the nooks and crannies of the world of education and research, and they are unconstrained by allegiance to party or state. NGOs present themselves as "value-driven" and justify their existence primarily in terms of ideals and only secondarily in terms of expertise or professionalism. They are able, at the same time, to mobilize expertise, to develop projects and manage them—that is, to put their ideals into practice with means of their own or at least means raised by their own efforts, in contrast with political parties, which can only "apply" their ideas through the cumbersome and often resistant machinery of the state.

Although to say NGOs operate at the level of a "system of historical action" may be somewhat too grand, it is true that they operate domestically and internationally within a development policy community that itself is a powerful determinant of the content of government policy across the globe. They are also bearers and to some extent creators of a historical project or projects. A historical project is much more than an ideological slogan. It need only be recalled that social democracy itself has been less a single ideology than a wide-ranging intellectual and institutional apparatus for the production of a historical agenda for thought and action: Universities, government agencies, political parties, the trade union movement have been and often still are fora for the production of all manner of agendas, and although they may share in the broad social democratic subculture, they vary enormously in content and direction.

Today we observe another subculture, among whose many contrasts with social democracy are its global and cosmopolitan character, its reliance on networks more than institutionalized mechanisms, and its uneasy attitude about state power, but that shares the pervasiveness and the multiple levels of intervention of social democracy. Through innumerable think-tanks—small and large, official and unofficial—seminars and conferences, university courses and departments, we observe a wide range of dissidence surrounding issues of human rights, political inclusion, the environment, and gender. In this context NGOs collectively are a major player and even set agendas—often conflicting agendas but influential ones nevertheless—and they are influential because they are able to invoke civil society in their support. This invocation may not always be justified or successful, but having this extra "voice" sets them apart within the international development system. Certain ideas taken to be characteristic of the NGO movement make it easy to idealize and to mistake the part for whole. We tend to assume that all NGOs are committed to "alternative" development strategies, to autochthony and authenticity, to respect for the environment and for tradition. But as with social democracy, within the global movement for alternative development there are a wide range of voices. NGO advocates of the poor coexist with those whose priority is greater efficiency or simply more money to be channeled to the development cause. Many specialize in particular areas of concern—children, health, the environment, education. Some act as pressure groups, others are more project-oriented; some primarily subsidize popular movements and train their leaders; some are concerned with encouraging participation, others more with results. The list of activities and issues is endless and subject to changes in fashion, priorities, or circumstances, but the method of action of the NGOs is here to stay, and it is on account of their method rather than the substance of their views, claims, prejudices, philosophies, or achievements that NGOs merit attention.

As an NGO develops it creates networks, and, if successful, innumerable networks. While some of its leaders travel the world attending conferences and courting donors, others lobby governments and parliaments on behalf of particular causes. The organization itself will have contacts with organizations representing small communities, poor communities, indigenous groups, and farmers' or workers' groups. Representatives may even testify before congressional committees. The NGOs and grassroots support organizations (GSOs)[4] create for themselves a ubiquitous presence in linking disparate decision-making bodies to a worldwide archipelago of popular or grass-roots voices. This is not to say that the problems of poverty are thus solved or that in the midst of this feverish movement and agitation there are not personal ambitions, power struggles, ideological and political rivalries, and pursuit of resources. But this pattern is distinctive because these contacts are not mediated by an apparatus of formal representation, as in trade unions or established interest groups, or by political clientelism but rather by networks that cut across those social boundaries that in politics and in the distribution of income and wealth are so central and decisive—namely, those of nation, ethnic group, class, and gender.

It is difficult to understate the importance of this fluidity and network-based interaction in characterizing NGOs and defining their distinctiveness. Trade unions are established for particular purposes, for example, and much as their leaders may take up political positions and contribute to ideological debates, their procedures, their structures of representation, and their priorities are defined by the interests they exist to serve. Were it otherwise, they would lose legitimacy and the support of their members. Political parties are likewise hierarchical apparatuses organized to raise money to win elections and not infrequently to distribute the fruits of power to their members and constituencies. But NGOs can shift priorities and change their structures according to changing circumstances and leadership; they may receive funding from one kind of source but work on behalf of another; they rarely have wealth of their own so their only "capital" is in their staff and volunteer activists and the legitimacy they command among a wide range of constituencies: They deal not only with the people whose needs they seek to serve but also with the politicians whose decisions they seek to influence, with international agencies, and not least with public opinion. This fluidity—this ability to be involved in a variety of spheres and at a variety of levels of the social system and the power structure—is a central feature of NGOs. They range in their contacts from local church-based organizations to the World Bank, they make transnational inter-NGO alliances, they combine advocacy groups in the different countries, they mobilize grass-roots groups.[5]

One of the most serious constraints on NGOs is funding, and their continuous search for financial support has colored their image in the eyes of a cosmopolitan intelligentsia who once saw in them the untainted expression of an emerging civil society. But NGOs should not be embarrassed by this nor should their critics seize upon it as a sign of moral weakness; they share this obsessive need for funding with political parties, churches and religious groups of all kinds, interest groups, academic researchers, and countless other nonprofit groups and agencies. NGOs can hardly be expected to operate with disregard for the preferences of their patrons and sponsors, while for their part patrons and sponsors must respect the autonomy of the NGOs if their own acts of charity are not to be discredited as disguised advertisement or ideological manipulation. The NGO sponsor/donor relationship is undoubtedly fraught with imbalances and potentially wasteful,[6] but these are inevitable consequences of the particular roles each plays in international politics and development decision making. To be less so, it would have to be more directive, in which case the relationship would become indistinguishable from that between a head office and a subsidiary.

Historical Conditions for the Emergence
of the NGO Community in Latin America

The method of organization is that of a cooperative partnership. NGOs do not usually set up businesses in the conventional sense, even if those involved do want to make a living out of the work they do. Rather they establish a group of professionals and a supporting staff and then go in search of funding or consultancy work. When the movement first began to flower in Latin America in the 1970s, under the shadow of military dictatorship, it was distinguished by the prominent participation of social scientists who had been expelled from university positions or whose positions had been marginalized. At first they were able to establish research institutions, supported by major international bodies such as the Ford Foundation and the Swedish Agency for Research Cooperation with Developing Countries (SAREC), as a sort of salvage operation for an endangered community. Inevitably this source of support reached its limits, and the growth of research organizations outstripped "hard" funding capacity; research organizations then began to branch into "soft money" advisory and managerial work, some of which was in development projects. As the deterioration of public finances gathered pace in the wake of the debt crises of the early 1980s, bringing about the collapse of university salaries, it was this income-generating activity that came to be a salient feature of NGOs. The "pure" research institutions became a select minority; grass-roots social movements were too weakly structured, in financial or managerial terms, to undertake development projects independently. Research centers in need of funding and grass-roots movements connected, and thus, gradually, what had begun as a salvage operation for unemployed university professors and researchers became a link between the people at the grass roots and the international development community. At first this meant the international NGOs, but more recently it has come to include, directly or indirectly, governments of donor countries and countries where the NGOs themselves operate.

NGOs and the Military Dictatorships of the 1970s

In Chile, a unique set of circumstances created a broad-based coalition of international support for erstwhile supporters of the Unidad Popular (UP) government overthrown by the 1973 military coup. The UP government had been freely elected, had abided by the rules of the political system, and its program made sense to European political observers. In contrast, the overthrow of the Argentine Peronist government in 1976, though accompanied by persecution as brutal as that in Chile, found little sympathy abroad because Peronism was so little understood. Argentine dissidents also did not take up the challenge: The hundreds of thousands, young people especially, who seemed to support a "radical left" and "revolutionary" version of Peronism and who had contributed in no small measure to the disintegration of the Peronist government over the 1972–1976 period, vanished almost overnight. They were not exiles, more expatriates, because the Argentine military government refused even to send those it regarded as subversives to trial or to allow them to leave the country: they were simply made to "disappear." Chilean exiles, in contrast, had been forced out in an attempt to cleanse the country of their influence; they spent years away, keeping alive the flames of international solidarity.

But although it is therefore not surprising that there was a far greater proliferation of international support for NGOs and GSOs in Chile than in Argentina during the period of dictatorship, it is surprising that after the military left power, the positions of the grass-roots activists in both countries began to converge. The international NGOs took the view that with the return to elected government their contribution was no longer so urgent and their local partner organizations could generate funds and resources; at the same time, governments saw in the local NGOs and GSOs useful partners in social policy.

NGOs and the Changing Role of the Church

The role of the church in the two countries also differed significantly. In Argentina, the church had been an ally of Peronism since its beginning at the end of World War II. Relations between the military and the church during the 1976–1983 period were mostly very good. Opposition priests were given no support by the hierarchy, which never spoke against atrocious human rights abuses, even when their own priests and bishops were victims.

In Chile, the church trod a careful middle road. In the 1970s the Cardinal Archbishop of Santiago, Silva Henriquez, took a strong line in defense of human rights and set up a Vicaría de la Solidaridad with the dual task of giving legal and other practical support to those who had suffered from persecution and of channeling international charitable support to innumerable projects. He even established a parallel university, the Academia de Humanismo Cristiano, which carried out research and offered postgraduate courses. But after his retirement a more moderate figure was appointed, and by the time the Pope visited the country in 1987 a palpable change was in evidence. As time passed, the church sustained a very hard line on birth control and abortion, and a return to the moralistic Christianity of old could be observed even in the activities of Comunidades Eclesiales de Base (Christian-base communities, or CEBs), which were set up to reflect a religious and political disposition that recognizes the validity and authenticity of the ideas and views of the people themselves—referred to as *basismo*.[7] After the return to electoral government in 1990, the Archbishop of Santiago dissolved the Vicaría on the grounds that the government could now handle public welfare; NGOs and GSOs, on the one hand, and political parties, on the other, pursued their own agendas with neither support nor interference from the church.

Brazil offers a different case. There, dioceses, in gentle defiance of the Vatican, have given strong support to Christian-inspired sociopolitical activities. Such activities are supported by priests but take place independently from hierarchical control. The outcome in Brazil has perhaps been the greater resilience of Catholic networks such as Catholic Workers Action (ACO) and the greater independence of the *pastorais* (pastoral missions) that minister to various disadvantaged groups.

From 1985 an apparently obscure organization entitled Association for the Diffusion of Training and Projects (ADITEPP) initiated a program of meetings aimed at strengthening local-level leadership in a wide range of local networks and community organizations, encouraging individuals to take on responsibilities in neighborhood groups and offering training courses. Thereafter, *proyectismo*, which is such a central feature of NGO life, proliferated in Brazil. Between 1983 and 1989 the Catholic Center for Religious Statistics and Social Research (CERIS), formally linked to the church hierarchy, processed over 2,000 "miniprojects" for funding by international bodies, mostly Catholic.[8] According to one survey, 70 percent of Brazilian NGOs were principally funded by agencies linked to religious bodies, or *agencias confessionais*, which more strictly means agencies of a corporate religious nature such as the German Bishops' Adveniat or Catholic World Relief.[9] Other data showed roughly one third of NGOs being "at the service of the popular movement," a term which in this context refers to organizations linked at once to the church and to the people.[10] In Brazil some of the most prominent organizations dedicated to support of popular movements were officially supported in their early stages by the church, and individuals connected with them were often priests, former priests, or members of holy orders; in addition, large numbers of their activists[11] owed their involvement to their early participation in CEBs or similar church-sponsored grass-roots organizations.[12]

Brazil is the only Southern Cone country where divisions within the church have had consequences for the actions of the church. Elsewhere they have been largely ideological disagreements with little practical effect. Although, the grass-roots, or popular, movement in Brazil has been more reliant than elsewhere on priests and members of holy orders for advice, guidance, and leadership, at the same time those priests and bishops who have remained committed to the cause of the poor have been a source of division within the hierarchy and thus have enjoyed only dwindling support from "above"—the Episcopal Conference, where the *basista* majority has been in decline since the late 1980s—and of course from Rome. Even the great voice of the poor, Dom Helder Camara, has been ineffective in changing the structure and culture of his own archdiocese to reflect his orientation towards the "people's church" or "church of the poor."[13] In short, groups and organizations agitating for change inside the church have been more successful outside than in.

The Dilemma of Institutionalization:
NGOs Between *Basismo* and Technocracy

In the years since the military left power, the relationship between the state, the NGOs and GSOs, and grassrroots activism has become more complex. In Chile the postmilitary government was staffed to some extent by people from the NGO sector, especially in the field of social policy, so it was not surprising that this produced something like a partnership between NGOs and the state. The NGOs need contracts and the state has work for them, especially in view of the absence of any prospect of a revived welfare state; thus, circumstances are ripe for a moderate technocratic framework where the political content of NGO action is significantly reduced.

The situation in Argentina seems little different. There has been, if anything, a more dramatic shift toward neoliberal policies, and here too the radical intelligentsia of yesterday is adapting itself in as constructive a way as possible. Activists in the *movimiento villist*, Argentina's popular movement, have found their way not into NGOs but into local government where they are supporting efforts at communal self-management.

In both countries, then, some sort of convergence has occurred between neoliberalism and the tradition of grass-roots mobilization, and it takes the form of a nascent partnership that may or may not go far but does not seem for the time being to place a strong emphasis on popular mobilization. The language of the international alternative development subculture is still there, but it has become domesticated, it has lost its dissident edge, and in Chile it has also lost the element of Catholic *basismo*. In an unexpected convergence, the antistatism of neoliberalism has found a partner in the *basista* hostility to bureaucracy cultivated by the NGO movement. The grass-roots organizations, for their part, tend in these circumstances to resemble clients more than partners—passive recipients of credit schemes or technical assistance or training programs—rather than mobilized forces for change.

Brazil continues to exhibit a different pattern. For all the trials, tribulations, and crises of the 1980s and early 1990s the country has experienced neither the institutional disintegration of Argentina nor the extremes of neoliberal reform of Chile. Despite all the problems that beset the Brazilian state apparatus, it still, for example, honors its obligation to pensioners, unlike Argentina, which has more or less legally disavowed that obligation. And there has never been any question that the Brazilian church might create a parallel welfare state to rescue those marginalized by the dismantling of public welfare, as happened in Chile in the 1970s and 1980s. In Brazil the NGOs and GSOs do not find a ready partner in state institutions, and as a result they may be forced to continue to rely on international donations more than their Chilean counterparts, but they may also preserve more *basismo*. Projects continue to be small; they look less like consultancy or subcontracting, which is the effective content of partnership with the state; and the method continues to count for more than the product or outcome.

Brazilian NGOs are distinctive in other ways, which may contribute to their more political, less commercial or practical agenda. Although clientelism in the sense of political parties doling out individual favors, especially jobs, is common throughout the region, in Brazil, clientelistic relationships and personal dependency are embedded in elaborate networks of kinship and in employment relations, especially in the countryside. The discourse of the *movimento popular* in Brazil uses the term *assistencialismo* to describe these relationships as well as political clientelism more generally, and it is striking to observe how pervasive the anti-*assistencialista* discourse is in those circles. Yet because this is the country with the most advanced industrial base and the most sophisticated managerial and technocratic elite in the region (except perhaps for Chile), it is not entirely surprising to find that on occasion even the state attempts to reform the system. In a notable instance, a government bureaucracy has used deft techniques to encourage participation in and monitoring of a health program "from below" and has sent professionals to villages to work in preventive care and health education.[14] Here the state itself learned from the NGO movement. Of course, it was able to marshall infinitely more resources than NGOs command, but with unusual political will and capacity it has apparently instituted an effective anticlientelistic mechanism at the core of the program.[15]

This vignette illustrates a surprising instance of anticlientelistic mobilization within the state apparatus but, paradoxically, it occurred in the absence of NGOs from a program that should have been tailor-made for them. In Brazil more generally, partly no doubt on account of the sheer size of the state, NGOs have found little vocation in making partnerships with a government that would inevitably dwarf them; at the same time, they have maintained a more independent stance with greater commitment to grass-roots activism and are more preoccupied with the method of participatory management than with the substance of particular projects.

In Brazil NGO hostility to clientelism is directly tied to a core feature of the political culture and reflects the multilevel character of their intervention: Brazilian NGOs have been more receptive than their counterparts elsewhere in the Southern Cone to direct involvement in partisan politics. The *basista* church, including both committed priests and activists in related social movements, played an important role in the formation of the Workers' Party (PT) in the early 1980s and also in broadening the party's electoral appeal, enabling it to expand its support beyond its core in the industrial and manufacturing centers of São Paulo to the urban middle class and the peasantry. It was less successful in penetrating the less organized sectors of urban society, where the old ghosts of populism still hold sway.[16] The party has had shifting and volatile fortunes, doing well in municipal elections in several major cities but badly in national congressional elections. Many activists in the NGO fraternity make little secret of their sympathy and support for the PT and even for particular factions within it, and although we cannot know their number or the extent of their influence, the significant point is that the culture of NGOs in Brazil does not frown upon partisan political commitment. In Chile, on the other hand, the political involvement of NGOs ended with the referendum of 1989, when the people voted not to allow Augusto Pinochet to remain in office and many NGOs placed their staff and their expertise at the service of the referundum campaign against his candidacy for reelection. Now that the period of military rule is over, NGOs— somewhat in the manner of charitiable organizations in Europe and North America—keep their political preferences to themselves.

The Brazilian NGOs, less reliant than elsewhere on consultancies and partnerships with politically sensitive national and international organizations, have on occasion taken up high-profile campaigns single-handedly, such as the cause of Chico Mendes and the rubber-tappers of Amazonia, the issue of violence in Rio de Janeiro, and the Campaign against Hunger. Some critics claim, controversially, that the NGOs may even have endangered Chico Mendes's life by exposing the land-grabbers of the state of Acre to the spotlight of international media attention. In the campaigns against violence and hunger, NGOs take on the leadership of nonpartisan but nevertheless political campaigns in which they manage on the one hand to gain the support of large corporations, while on the other hand they propagate the message that to confront the questions of hunger and violence society must change—charitable works and good will are not enough. So we see that in Brazil the discourse of protest, dissent, and popular mobilization, with its strong *basista* emphasis, now finds a counterpoint in a different discourse in the NGO movement, directed toward the big issues—a reaction to a postauthoritarian but not yet fully democratic polity in which citizenship remains a privilege more than a right and the construction of civil society faces serious obstacles in clientelistic politics and corruption, especially in institutions concerned with basic freedoms, namely the judiciary and the police. The transition to the world of commericial/consultancy/subcontracting partnerships is not easily made. Brazilian NGOs are concerned more than those elsewhere in the Southern Cone with keeping alive big political questions, but they concentrate on ones that command consensus and do not necessarily provoke partisan responses—namely, citizenship, hunger, and violence.

Thus far we have observed that in a country like Chile the issue of postauthoritarian-era democracy is accepted as resolved in its broad outlines, so that even if much remains yet to be done, there are few forces in society that question the adequacy of the prevailing institutions and political culture to do it. In Brazil, however, there are powerful voices urging that the institutions and the political culture are far from acceptable. Rather than bowing to the neoliberal agenda, many NGOs even adopt novel methods of mobilizing opinion, while raising money from big corporations and cooperating with state and federal government—not now as consultants or subcontractors but on an equal footing, legitimated by the public opinion they have rallied to their support.

In Mexico the issue of democracy and authoritarianism remains, at a very deep and unhappy level, unresolved. The Mexican Partido Revolucionario Institucional (PRI) has been in power for so long that despite, or even because of, recent economic and political crises, it is difficult for the millions whose livelihood depends on the party's infinitely intricate and elaborate patronage system even to imagine an alternative in power.[17] The party has decades of experience in the arts of co-optation and repression, and there are few political opinions that cannot find a niche in its ample architecture. Thus the politial space NGOs opened in Brazil has been less easy to find in Mexico. The Solidaridad program created by Carlos Salinas set out to combat, undermine, or merely replace those political habits regarded by the modernizing and enlightened intelligentsia on all sides as "traditional" forms of clientelism. It operates outside the traditional patronage system, employing technocratic staff to allocate and manage its very substantial funds, thus deepening the process of centralization of patronage and power. Yet those who would dismiss Solidaridad as "merely" a modernization and centralization of patronage are rushing too hastily to judgment and are also being too judgmental, for the program has borrowed more than one tactic from the NGO culture. Among these is the *proyecto*—together with the idea, taken from the earliest experiments in what was once known as "community development," that the state's contribution of capital should be complemented by local input of labor. We also observe in Solidaridad a concern with autonomy vis-à-vis the state apparatus, which indicates that there are elements within the official circles who can keep independent of the PRI, the state governors, and municipal authorities and who encourage civil society to produce a leadership capable of being interlocutors with the state. Thus the Instituto Nacional Indigenista (INI), since 1990, has stimulated the creation of some 100 leadership councils (*consejos directivos*) out of local indigenous organizations, some of which had broad-based memberships and politically active leaders; the INI staff were able to protect them from the pressures of the established clientelistic networks. These councils manage the disbursement and operational aspects of funds, though admittedly not the decision to disburse, and even in Chiapas, which has the most authoritarian of the state power structures, have been able to maintain a degree of freedom.[18] On a broader front, Mexico since the 1980s has seen a growth in *concertación social*, whereby "state managers ... demonstrate a limited but still unprecedented willingness to cede legitimacy to autonomous citizens' groups by establishing both formal and informal ... agreements," a pattern that became particularly prevalent in the wake of the 1985 earthquake in Mexico City.[19] Once again, then, we find the putative space that NGOs would regard as their own being occupied by the state—or more precisely, in the Mexican case, by semi-autonomous factions and institutions within a sprawling multifaceted state apparatus.

NGOs and Their Changing Role in the Development Process

So far we have concentrated on NGOs as sociopolitical actors, exploring the extent to which they can be described as bearers of certain values and also how, through their distinct mode of operation and their insertion in a worldwide social movement, they are positioned to disseminate those values throughout society. But there have also been frequent allusions to the more mundane activities whereby NGOs thrive and take part in the business of development as partners, consultants, subcontractors, and the like, and it is to this domain that we now turn.

A large number of NGOs and GSOs over time slipped—in some cases reluctantly—into a range of partnership relations with the official development community at both national and international levels.[20] Once they became involved in the world of project management, they had to take on staff and develop administrative capacity, so the momentum became self-perpetuating. Some have become large-scale institutions, such as Centro de Estudios y Promoción del Desarollo (DESCO) in Peru, or Grupo de Investigación Agraria (GIA) in Chile, with a wide-ranging capacity to carry out research, publish, operate documentation centers, manage projects, influence policy debates, and so on. These have a self-sustaining capacity. But others—smaller, more specialized, and perhaps above all more narrowly dependent on funding from one or two international NGOs—have become vulnerable to changing priorities in the international development community; they may find that from one year to the next an agency simply abandons them as fashions change. In these circumstances their role as well as the content of their actions begin imperceptibly to change: Where at first their proposals responded to demand from the grass roots, now NGOs must persuade their constituency that a particular project is suitable to them, uncomfortably aware that this may simply be because the trend in funding has changed.

NGOs also find that they gradually lose their "oppositional" legitimacy. As they cooperate with official development institutions, it becomes more difficult to claim they are offering an alternative to the prevailing models. Their success lies in the adoption by the international official development community of what were once considered dissident ideas. NGOs themselves, now high on the agenda of the official institutions, find themselves the object of those institutions' persistent solicitations—so what can they offer that is different?

Their success also represents a constraint that arises from the narrowing of the NGOs's field of action. During the years of political persecution under authoritarian regimes, a project could be presented and indeed experienced as a contribution to a broader process of political change and humanitarian concern. But as persecution, finally, died down, funding eroded and the "business side" of the projects became more consuming. The result is that today a certain sort of NGO is experiencing a crisis of legitimacy, of financial survival, and indeed of ideology.[21] Their legitimacy is in question because processes of democratization of varying depth and sustainability have led state apparatuses to take over—or recapture—their developmental role, while technocratic elements within the state, bypassing established clientelistic relationships as distasteful to them as to the *basistas*, have also adopted NGO-style methods in the management of projects and social welfare programs. One asks, then, why NGOs need to continue in operation when their resources are so much more at risk and even less reliable than those of the state. NGOs' financial survival is at issue because their projects are strong on capital but weak on supplying the essential maintenance income to provide schools with teachers, hospitals with doctors and nurses, rural credit programs with agronomists, and so on. And their ideological identity as embodiments of a democratic project is at stake because in an increasingly democratic culture questions are raised about accountability; because NGOs are not elected and yet claim to speak on behalf of a constituency, people at the grass roots will begin to ask who is operating in whose interest.

Yet it would be unjust to leap to the claim that somehow NGOs are "undemocratic." Like any other charitable body they emerge from a process of opinion formation and interest agglomeration among a particular coalition or collectivity. Their legitimacy does not rest on any majoritarian or electoral criterion of representation but rather on a claim to representativeness that is the result of the interplay between intense interaction with their constituency and the skillful handling of public relations, image, and presentation. It can only be established by repeated affirmation through communication with their constituency and through tangible expressions of support from it, as well as through reasonably successful propagation of their message or of the worthiness of their cause in the wider national and international sphere. Paradoxically, then, they need to be in more regular and intense consultation with their base than do political parties. Does not empirical research repeatedly show that public opinion views parties with notorious cynicism, deploring the contrast between their assiduous attentions at election time with their contemptful disinterest and neglect in their supporters during the long years between elections?[22] Indeed, NGOs can gain symbolic support through the multilevel contacts that set them apart from other types of organizations; that is, they are able to represent themselves as enjoying grass-roots support through the material support received from higher levels in the developmental hierarchy, namely, from institutions of the state or international organizations. In this way they can persuade the wider world that they have grass-roots support even when they are neglecting that aspect of their work. In short, advertising and marketing are central features of the NGO survival plan.

It is evident that legitmacy can also be lost. NGOs are vulnerable to competition from one another, each selling a different cause or a different version of a similar cause, and from the state. They stand in relation to institutional politics in a similar way as informal economic activities to formal ones: The NGO sector, like the informal sector, is characterized by ease of entry but also by greater insecurity.

NGOs also face criticism that calls in question their much-praised efficiency. Putting hitherto-received opinions to the test, recent studies in the Peruvian and Bolivian Andes and in Chile that showed a negative rate of return in the former case and a "zero impact" on peasant families in the latter are doubtless open to question on methodological and other grounds, but they do raise the question of the financial survival of NGOs now that they regard their efficiency as a "selling point."[23] The measurement of efficiency is a difficult issue because NGO objectives are not the same as those of a government project—which looks to some sort of social benefit measured in "cost-benefit" terms—or to those of a private business: NGOs may legitimately defend their work on grounds of its experimental character in that they may be testing new approaches or methods in the hope that, if they prove effective, others, such as government agencies, may take them up. They may also legitimately claim to be charitable bodies whose job is precisely to give resources to worthwhile causes or institutions, not to lend on a commercial basis. Nevertheless, there are questions of efficiency to be asked, such as the alternative uses to which resources could be put, and questions about the assumption that because, compared to other available agencies, NGOs are quite cheap, they are therefore more efficient. Observers might be forgiven for thinking that if NGOs used more experienced or professional, if more expensive, staff they might achieve better results; but on the other hand, it can be reasonably argued that the very idealism and commitment of their staff constitutes part of their contribution and that to shift to a pure managerial mode would undermine the cause of NGOs, especially of the "alternativists" and "dissidents" among them.

Another criticism concerns the salaries of local NGO staff or their way of life. This is hardly surprising: NGO professionals may not earn the same as similarly qualified staff of a multinational corporation, but they do have a reasonable middle-class standard of living and may even live marginally better than the university professors whose pay has collapsed in most countries of the region. But compared to the dispossessed whose needs they profess to be serving, they are well off. The real problem is not the income gap between the NGO intermediaries and their grass-roots clientele but rather its lateral effect, namely that it creates a social distance between beneficiaries and NGO personnel and, conversely, expresses an intimacy between the latter and representatives of international agencies in the eyes of potential beneficiaries. These power relationships are real and can only be overcome by competition among NGOs, which in turn would lead them to become more commercial and less altruistic. Now NGO resources are generally allocated on a nonmarket basis, so there is a danger that as intermediaries they may use their position to manipulate the choices of their clientele or to monopolize control over resources being made available by certain agencies or to certain constituencies or types of beneficiary. To some extent, this must be an inevitable outcome: International agencies need to disburse funds, they need information and expertise, and they are evidently precluded from using a market mechanism to solve the problem; so discretion, expertise, and trust count for a great deal in this rather small and occasionally incestuous world.

A Final Comment

This element of trust can also take on a political or ideological character, leading to charges of "ideological clientelism." Western European and North American agencies and their officers not infrequently have their pet ideas, their pet theories, and their pet partners. At the same time, in the recipient community of NGOs and grass-roots organizations there is no shortage of people ready to pander to these more or less illusory projections of the idealized. In the literature of the dissident development community, for example, we read of disappearing cultures, of peoples deprived of age-old practices and rituals, wrenched into a competitive and destructive world of mass production and commoditized labor. From this community come those who would save disappearing cultures, in a spirit that runs very deep in the culture of the post-Enlightenment intelligentsia. They are heirs to ideas of authenticity, of faithfulness to the roots of a civilization, of heritage that are inescapable features of European culture. The culture of NGOs is indissolubly linked in Latin America to the projection of a certain image of the people, whose purported innocence can bring about a rebirth of a patriotic ideal.[24] Those who find themselves the object of NGO causes respond to some extent with complicity, by entering the game and playing the part assigned to them. But there may come a point where the client, or perhaps their newly matured leadership, perceive decreasing returns in the manipulation of ideas of authenticity and alternativeness. In doing so, they may be said to be bearing witness to the success of the NGOs, whose ideal of autonomy has finally been achieved, not always in a manner that would satisfy their amour propre but certainly in a manner that should offer them arguments against even their most high-minded detractors.

Notes

1. In reality these have been the center because the official parts of the meetings have been so disappointing and irrelevant, dominated as they invariably are by extraneous political and diplomatic considerations.

2. See Alain Touraine, *Production de la Société* (Paris: Editions du Seuil, 1973). On Latin America, see his *Actores Sociales y Sistemas Políticos en América Latina*

(Santiago: Programa del Empleo para América Latina y el Caribe [PREALC], 1987).

3. I refer here to the now standard appointment to ministerial positions of economists who, having no electoral past and aspiring to no electoral future, therefore have no independent political base. Examples include almost every Brazilian minister of finance from 1980 to 1993, excepting Delfim Neto and Fernando Henrique Cardoso, and most Mexican ministers of finance.

4. Grass-roots support organizations is a term coined by Thomas Carroll to describe NGOs in developing or recipient countries whose role is to provide support of various kinds—organizational, financial, or political—for grass-roots organizations. They have neither substantial resources nor a grass-roots organization of their own, hence their crucial but intermediary role. Thomas Carroll, *Intermediary NGOs: The Supporting Link in Grassroots Development* (West Hartford, CT: Kumarian Press, 1992).

5. Jane Covey, "Accountability and Effectiveness in NGO Policy Alliances," *Journal of International Development,* VII, 6, 1995, pp. 856–67.

6. For a passionate and doubtless partial view, but nevertheless one from within the system, see J. Perera, "In Unequal Dialogue with Donors: The Experience of the Sarvodaya Shamardana Movement," *Journal of International Development,* VII, 6, 1995, pp. 869–78.

7. See John W. Swope, "The Production, Recontextualization and Popular Transmission of Religious Discourse: A Case of Liberation Theology and Basic Christian Communities in Santiago, Chile" (Ph.D. dissertation, Institute of Education, University of London, 1992).

8. Ana Maria Doimo, *A Voz e a Vez do Popular: Movimentos Sociais e Participação Política no Brasil pós–70* (Rio de Janeiro: Relume Dumara, 1995) p. 158.

9. Ruben Cesar Fernandes and Leandro P. Carneiro, *As ONGs Anos 90: A Opinião Dos Dirigentes Brasileiros* (Rio de Janeiro: ISER, 1991).

10. Leilah Landim, ed., *Sem Fins Lucrativos: As Organizações Não-Governamentais no Brasil* (Rio de Janeiro: ISER, 1988).

11. Cesar Fernandes and Leandro P. Carneiro, *As ONGs Años 90,* passim.

12. Ana María Doimo, *A Voz e a Vez do Popular,* pp. 162–4.

13. Richard Marin, *Dom Helder Camara: Les Puissants et les Pauvres. Pour une Histoire de l'Eglise des Pauvres dans le Nordeste Brésilien (1955–1985)* (Paris: Les Editions de l'Atelier/Editions Ouvrières, 1995).

14. J. Tendler and S. Freedheim, "Trust in a Rent-Seeking World: Health and Government Transformed in Northeast Brazil," *World Development,* 22, 12, 1994, pp. 1771–91.

15. In contrast, a movement of health professionals that attempted the gargantuan task of refocusing the entire national health system of Brazil and reducing its vulnerability to graft was sadly unsuccessful. See K. Weyland, "Social Movements and the State: The Politics of Health Reform in Brazil," *World Development,* 23, 10, 1995, pp. 1699–1712.

16. Geert Banck, "Cultural Dilemmas behind Strategy: Brazilian Neighbourhood Movements and Catholic Discourse," *European Journal of Development Research,* 2, 1, 1990, pp. 65–88; Maria D'Alva Kinzo, "The 1989 Presidential Election:

Electoral Behaviour in a Brazilian City," *Journal of Latin American Studies*, 23, 2, 1993, pp. 320–46.

17. One recalls the fear of the unknown that prevailed in France at the prospect of regime change during the period of uninterrupted Gaullist government from 1958 to 1971 when finally François Mitterrand won the presidential election. Until then a large portion of the electorate believed that the arrival of the opposition in power would be a fulfillment of Charles de Gaulle's dictum "après moi le déluge." In the event, of course, it was nothing of the kind. Perhaps in Mexico the same would happen.

18. Jonathan Fox, "Targeting the Poorest: The Role of the National Indigenous Institute in Mexico's Solidarity Program," in Wayne A. Cornelius, Ann L. Craig, and Jonathan Fox, eds., *Transforming State-Society Relations in Mexico: The National Solidarity Strategy* (La Jolla: Center for U.S.-Mexican Studies, University of California, San Diego, 1994), pp. 166–87. The preface to this volume is dated 31 December 1993, the day before the Zapatista uprising in Chiapas, and Fox's account of the degree of autonomy achieved by indigenous organizations in that state in the face of opposition by the political authorities is prescient.

19. Ibid., p. 183

20. John Farrington and Anthony Bebbington, with Kate Wellard and David J. Lewis, *Reluctant Partners? Non-Governmental Organizations, the State and Agricultural Development* (New York: Routledge, 1993). Anthony Bebbington and Graham Thiele, with Penelope Davis, Martin Prager and Hernando Riveros, *Non-Governmental Organizations and the State in Latin America: Rethinking Roles in Sustainable Agricultural Development* (New York: Routledge, 1993).

21. This point has been elaborated in Anthony Bebbington, *Crisis y Caminos: Reflexiones Heréticas sobre las ONG, el Estado y un Desarrollo Rural Sustentable en América Latina* (La Paz: NOGUB-Cotesu, 1995).

22. See, for example, David Lehmann, "Modernity and Loneliness: Popular Culture in Quito and Guadalajara," *European Journal of Development Research*, II, 1, 1990, pp. 37–64.

23. N. van Niekerk, *El Desarrollo Rural en los Andes* (Leiden: University of Leiden Studies in Development, 1994); R. Lopez, "Determinants of Rural Poverty: A Quantitative Analysis for Chile" (Washington, D.C.: World Bank, 1995), manuscript.

24. This is elaborated at length in David Lehmann, *Struggle for the Spirit: Religious Transformation and Popular Culture in Brazil and Latin America* (Oxford: Polity Press, 1996).

13

Social Movements and Citizenship Rights in Latin America

Joe Foweraker

This chapter analyzes the relationship between social movement activity and the achievement of citizenship rights in contemporary Latin America. Social movements arise within civil society, but the core rights of citizenship must ultimately be granted and guaranteed by the state.[1] The relationship between movements and rights must therefore be examined in the broader and interactive context of state and civil society. But the passage from social mobilization to citizenship rights can be both direct and indirect. On the one hand, social movements may claim rights directly from the state and its apparatuses. On the other, they may seek more indirect influence within political society, where the formal struggle for public power and political rule takes place. In contemporary Latin America the latter route will necessarily focus on the role of social movements in the political transitions from authoritarian to democratic rule. Thus, once the relationship between movements and rights has been established, the chapter will consider the role of social movements in both civil and political societies and go on to argue for the key role of rights struggles in projecting social movements from civil into political society. This prepares the ground for an inquiry into the (direct) impact of social movements on the state and their (indirect) influence on democratic transitions. The subsequent decline of social movements is then examined, and the reasons for it debated, before illustrating both the rise and decline of the movements with a discussion of women's mobilization in the continent. The argument concludes with an assessment of social movements and citizenship rights in the newly democratic polities of Latin America and the possible future role of social movements in further expanding those rights.

Social Movements and Citizenship Rights

It is widely observed that just as social movements in Latin America must struggle to get their demands met, so these demands have increasingly been stated in terms of rights. Where authoritarian regimes compressed the public sphere, social movements asserted their right to expand it. "The suppression of some traditional rights produced a redefinition and expansion of the understanding of rights . . . to reconquer rights which traditionally existed and to fight for new rights."[2] Where state policies excluded the popular sectors and denied them a voice, social movements mounted "a struggle for equal rights, justice . . . and the recognition of a minimum threshold of rights associated with belonging to and inclusion in the social system."[3] The struggle for rights demonstrates that "while the state is the agency of the legalization of rights, it is neither their source nor the basis of their validity. Rights begin as claims asserted by groups and individuals in the public spaces of an emerging civil society";[4] and, in this sense, political rights are positive rights of equal participation rather than freedoms or liberties.

The assertion of the political right to participate is an assertion of citizenship. These "struggles from below, in which subordinate social sectors redefine their identities and their rights" are "an attempt to widen their space for action and extend the boundaries of their social and political citizenship."[5] In small popular church communities "individuals are being citizens and are also exercising a right which they cannot take for granted, namely that of assembly."[6] In entering the public sphere for the first time women are demanding recognition of their rights as citizens (and rejecting representation by men, whether as spouses, neighborhood leaders, or politicians).[7] In the countryside rural cooperatives "bolster citizenship . . . by creating rights and an awareness of rights among members," and even struggles over land are mainly "founded on an objection to violations of rights."[8] In their majority demands for rights are demands for fair dealing by the authorities, and this is what spurs social movements to "oppose corruption and favor transparency . . . oppose arbitrariness and favor due process."[9] The result has been to place "the theme of citizenship—that is, of the human and civil rights of persons— at the forefront of popular movements, avoiding the assumption of earlier radicalisms that there could be no citizenship without a total transformation of society."[10] Citizenship, in short, must be achieved in the here and now: "Now we demand what we deserve, what corresponds to us as citizens of this country. We demand what is legally ours. We demand our rights."[11]

The struggle for rights has more than a merely rhetorical impact. The insistence on the rights of free speech and assembly is a precondition of the kind of collective (and democratic) decision making that educates citizens. The "affirmation of the right to specificity and difference" by women or ethnic groups[12] is a precondition of plural and democratic society. In other words, "the practice of rights and the corresponding forms of social learning help . . . to establish a political culture that values societal self-organization."[13] But social movements also press to put rights (labor rights, land rights, human rights) on the active political agenda, and it is the denial or abuse of these rights that produces political antagonism.[14] The exercise of rights challenges the political order and, in authoritarian conditions, even expressive collective action can amount to a claim on citizenship. Social movements seek to enter the political stage and also to rewrite the political script.[15]

Social Movements in Civil and Political Societies

The most comprehensive theoretical account of modern social movements has asserted that the condition of possibility for their emergence is "the differentiated structure of modern civil society: legality, publicity, rights (to assemble, associate, and communicate free from external regulation), and the principles of democratic legitimacy."[16] But in Latin America, on the contrary, these movements mainly arose under authoritarian regimes and in far more constricted civil and political conditions. They did not therefore derive from democratic principles but may have contributed to create them through encouraging political transitions from authoritarian to democratic regimes. There is no doubt that massive increases in social mobilization coincided with democratic transitions in countries like Brazil, Uruguay, and Chile, but the precise role of social movements in these transitions remains untheorized and unclear.

Harsh authoritarian regimes can easily quash social mobilization, but it has been suggested that the process of liberalization may catalyze increasing opposition and a "resurrection of civil society."[17] The implications of this "resurrection" remain unclear, and more recent contributions to the large literature on democratic transitions have failed to clarify the role of social movements and their links with other political actors in the transition process.[18] Hence the movements tend to be seen in uniform teleological terms as progressing inexorably from daily resistance to political protest to democratic project. This successfully avoids both the variety of democratic transitions[19] and the complexities of civil society, often with banal results: "Where popular leaders are committed to democracy and enjoy broad legitimacy in their organizations and movements, prospects for democracy are better."[20]

One way forward is to broaden the focus. The literature on social movements in Latin America has correctly emphasized their relation to the state. But the study of democratic transitions must focus first on the "institutional make-up and internal articulation of civil society itself," before exploring the "channels of influence between civil and political society and between both and the state."[21] In other words, the contribution of social movements to the defense of community and the formation of identity in civil society must be linked to the strategic choices and political projects that are capable of shaping political society. In a democratizing setting the latter is the arena in which the polity specifically arranges itself for political contestation to gain control over public power and the state apparatus and will therefore include constitutional provisions, electoral rules, political party programs, party alliances, and, finally, legislative procedure. But in what ways can civil society contribute to the constitution or reconstitution of this arena?

Social movements are always rooted in social networks of family, community, and face-to-face groups. Insofar as they articulate the felt needs and proper demands of such networks they develop a kind of civic legitimacy or "recognized right to exist."[22] This "freedom of political identification" from being "nullified or even determined solely by the authority of the national State" is something that "democracy alone realizes,"[23] and civil society is the cradle of such collective identities. At the same time, these identities are not passive and indistinct parts of mass society but active and diverse groups that have specific political objectives and make specific demands about wages, houses, land, professional privileges, human rights, legal inequalities, and fair elections. In short, they all contribute to the kind of civic and political associationalism that is essential to political education and contestation. On the one hand, they act as schools of democracy in the form of intellectual caucuses, popular assemblies, demonstrations, sit-ins, and negotiations with political authorities. On the other, they monitor government policies and initiatives and protest when rules are infringed or promises broken. In doing so they seek to restore the public sphere and reclaim this space from authoritarian constraints and controls. Hence, the vindication of this public sphere is not pursued as a means to power but as an end in itself, as a sphere of freedom where political society can decide its own rules.[24]

Social movements therefore have a role to play in reconstituting the conditions for the unimpeded operation of political society. The precise role will vary with the nature of the authoritarian regime. For example, it is argued that the Argentine military government atomized, depoliticized, and privatized civil society while reducing and rigorously controlling the public sphere; whereas civil society seemed to survive authoritarian rule in Brazil with a proliferation of urban social movements, professional associations, and popular church communities. Moreover, the state itself can often promote social movements, wittingly or unwittingly, with unpredictable political results. Civil society will therefore suffer different constraints and enjoy different degrees of freedom under different regimes, and, consequently, social movement strategy will vary too. Just as negotiation with the state may be justified, despite the risks of co-optation, so may alliances with political parties, despite their expediency and their preoccupation with political power.

Rights Struggles Within Political Society

Yet the main bridge from civil to political society is constructed by what most social movements under authoritarian regimes have in common, which is the discovery, vindication, defense, and expansion of rights. Accordingly, it is argued that the political education and associationalism implicit in social movement activity generate new political demands that add up to a struggle for popular citizenship: Social and economic demands meet the kind of political constraints that then generate an insistence on political rights (or on the political conditions for getting the original demands met); or social mobilization provokes the kind of political repression that obliges the movements to defend and expand their fundamental rights. But whatever the mechanism that translates petitions into demands and favors into rights, *this is the essential step in the projection of social movements into political society.*

There are potential problems with this interpretation. First, it is too naive and optimistic to assume "an automatic and more or less direct path between the insistence on the right to running water, voting for the opposition and the demand for a change of political regime; and from the community movement, to the trade union movement, to the political party."[25] Second, social movements tend to pursue social rights that are more strictly political entitlements than political rights and that may therefore create not political citizens but political dependents or clients. In other words, social movements aspire to citizenship in the Parsonian sense of equal conditions of participation in the societal community rather than in the state.[26] It then remains moot whether the struggle for social rights finally contributes directly or indirectly to the achievement of the core rights of political citizenship such as speech, belief, association, assembly, and individual security, as well as substantive and procedural equality before the law.

This debate has a special resonance in Latin America where, historically, the co-optation of the labor movement into a clientelistic and corporative framework led to a political trade-off of the political rights of citizenship for the social rights of citizenship (for restricted and privileged sectors of the population). This inevitably undercut any sense of universal rights and promoted in their place a set of social benefits in the form of legal privileges and political prerogatives.[27] There is no doubt that both sets of rights (political and social) can be effective in mediating between civil society and the modern bureaucratic state; but the struggle for social rights may be less effective in advancing the democratic agenda under patrimonial, clientelistic, and authoritarian regimes. The key question then becomes whether the specific demands of social movements are satisfied through these particularistic power relations or transformed into more general demands for broader-based and political rights.[28]

The answer to this question will depend on both place and period. Social rights may play a different role in closely controlled corporatist institutions and in the highly clientelistic and corporatized systems of countries like Mexico and Brazil. The political cultures of Chile and Uruguay, on the other hand, were both less corporatized and somewhat more sensitive to the universal rights of citizenship. But even in Mexico and Brazil, where the extension of benefits had come at the expense of rights, the labor movements of the 1970s and 1980s put labor rights back onto the political agenda; while the corporatist co-optation of labor created an institutional context that favored the growth of these movements.[29] In Mexico, powerful movements within state-chartered corporations shook the foundations of the political system. In Brazil, the "new unionism" of the late 1970s insisted that the workers themselves should decide their own forms of organization, while the chaotic strikes of 1979 seemed inspired by an assertion of rights rather than a demand for concessions.[30] Direct bargaining between employers and "authentic" labor leaders bypassed the corporatist controls of the state, hence securing the de facto right to strike and challenging the core of the exclusionary labour system. State repression only accelerated the collapse of legal constraints, thereby "freeing" labor for fuller citizenship: How could workers be citizens of the nation when they were less (or more) than citizens in labor relations?

Social Mobilization, Rights Struggles, and the State

In laying claim to rights, social movements have to mobilize. This mobilization can appear cyclical, and the movements themselves discontinuous. Immediate demands can be satisfied. The costs of mobilization are high. Alliances are hard to achieve. But the discontinuity may be more apparent than real, with new movements emerging from old ones and old movements building a collective memory of victories and defeats. Moreover the social needs that drive the movements are not temporary, and the rights they claim are not conjunctural. In Brazil the wide range of new movements that emerged in the late 1970s focused on everything from the cost of living to gender and race issues, and they mobilized poor neighborhoods, squatter settlements and working class communities.

The new urban middle class was also important in this associational impulse[31] and the middle class and the popular sectors achieved a temporary alliance during the campaign for direct elections (*diretas já*) in 1984; but the alliance was precariously constructed around one single demand and dissolved immediately after the congressional vote was lost on the 25th April. The campaign clearly expressed a popular search for a lasting democratic solution, but it also revealed the volatility of popular protest and the difficulty of sustaining high degrees of mobilization. Similarly in Chile, middle class and popular sectors mobilized together during 1983, but the different groups lacked any principle of unity beyond "Democracy Now," and so did not conceive a "set of intermediate goals that could maintain a high level of mobilization and force negotiation with the regime."[32] Hence the mobilization subsided and returned to recurrent agitation by the most militant groups, with the struggle for democracy condemned to mobilization without political strategy. An analogous story could be told of Cárdenas's campaign for the presidency of Mexico or of the massive mobilization inspired by the Democratic National Front before and after the elections of July 1988.[33] The political capital generated by this upsurge of popular energy then dissipated in the absence of a negotiating strategy (or was squandered by the refusal to negotiate with the incumbent regime).

Social movements mobilize to press their demands, but mobilization entails negotiation with state agencies and political authorities if these demands are to be won. Hence the movements are not progressive in the sense of being intransigent. Still less are they radical democrats yearning for an egalitarian democracy.[34] They insist on autonomy not as an absolute value but as a precondition of effective negotiation. Thus, urban social movements in Brazil mobilized "originally in confrontation with the state in the attempt to open space for underrepresented interests, or to assure entrance of new groups into the political arena."[35] New councils were set up to channel their demands, and these certainly appeared more accessible than the old clientelistic networks; but it is difficult to decide if this was participation in decision-making or a new form of co-optation. The lesson is that long-term mobilization involves permanent negotiation, and the process of putting and negotiating demands may itself disseminate a sense of rights and the idea of citizenship. On the other hand, it will be argued below, social movements rarely have direct access to the negotiations that underpin democratic transitions.

Once negotiation is routinized, the state looks less like an enemy of the social movements. In Brazil, at least, the centralizing and developmentalist state carried through administrative reforms and improved the reach and delivery of public services. Because the military governments continued to compete for the popular vote, they kept negotiations open and sometimes made concessions. The Figueiredo government (1979–85) began to expand popular housing projects and implemented a wage policy that actually favored the poorest of the workers (before the crisis of 1982 put a stop to these popular policies). In themselves these changes cannot demonstrate a greater commitment to popular participation, let alone democracy. They may simply indicate the growing ability of the state to absorb popular demands. But the relationship between state and social movements is certainly more complex than simple confrontation.

Nonetheless, there are still severe limits to what social movements can achieve through the combination of mobilization and negotiation. First, there are the enduring problems created by populism and clientelism. On the one hand, the apparatuses of the authoritarian state continued to use these well-tried mechanisms of co-optation and control. Despite the multiplication of "autonomous" urban social movements in Mexico in the late 1970s and early 1980s and the national alliance strategy of the CONAMUP (National Coordinating Committee of Urban Popular Movements), the majority of popular organizations in the city continued to be managed and manipulated by the CNOP (National Confederation of Popular Organizations), one of the three main state-chartered union corporations run by the ruling party, the PRI (Institutional Revolutionary Party). On the other, the same mechanisms are reproduced through the projection of social movements into political society and their initial imbrication with political parties. Social movements fielded candidates in the more urban areas of Brazil for the 1982 elections, but the clientelistic ties to party machines either divided and demobilized the movements or led to the creation of parallel and more conservative popular organizations.

Secondly, the strategy of mobilization and negotiation can only be successful where government itself (or the public administration) is prepared to negotiate. Despite the almost monthly demonstrations launched by popular organizations in Chile during the wave of protest of 1983, the military government survived the crisis and proceeded "according to the institutional design and timetable set forth in the constitution."[36] Any concessions it made were informal and reversible. Moreover, as confrontation replaced negotiation, it raised the profile of the most radical and violent protesters (students and urban youth) and isolated them from other popular sectors, making mass-based mobilization more difficult. Ultimately thousands of troops were deployed on the streets of Santiago, and thousands of protesters detained. In Argentina, on the other hand, the military government preempted popular protest by evicting hundreds of thousands of squatters (*villeros*) from the shanty towns of Buenos Aires; and neighborhood councils could do nothing to prevent the continual violence except file judicial complaints.[37] When the punitive tax hikes of 1982 finally provoked widespread unrest, the government again refused to negotiate. In neither case did popular protest by social movements succeed in shaking the confidence of the military regime.

Even in the limiting case of Argentina, however, it has been argued that social movements did play a role in democratizing political culture, developing community and self-government, and revitalizing local politics.[38] In short, it is recognized that social movements do have a role "in the creation of at least the foundations of new democratic cultures."[39] But most commentators are skeptical of the impact of social movements on democratic transitions and instead emphasize the salience of elite actors and political pacts in this process.[40] Social movements may practice democracy (in some degree at some times), and social mobilization may encourage more democratic social relations, but it remains difficult and often impossible to institutionalize these effects or to achieve institutional guarantees for popular participation. Social movements tend to express specific and transitory demands, and their objectives change, either because of internal disputes and factionalism or because of state initiatives. Hence, widespread mobilization by social movements may find little institutional response, and "scholars should acknowledge just how limited their short-term impact really is."[41]

Social Movements and Democratic Transitions

There are reasons to take issue with this conclusion. First, the analysts tend to have a formal view of the linkages between social movements and political institutions. They ignore the longer-term impact of mobilization and demand-making on the broad contours of the legal-institutional terrain linking civil society to the state; and close empirical study can demonstrate in some detail the success of social movements in reconfiguring this terrain.[42] In short, social movements are capable of disputing state policies and catalyzing institutional reforms.[43] Second, the analysts are too pessimistic regarding the projection of social movements into political society. For democratic transition to occur there must be the differentiation of a political element capable of strategic consideration, and the partial co-optation or institutionalization of social movements may be a proper price to pay for the emergence of agile political actors that can negotiate with incumbent regimes. The Chilean process finally came close to this model, and the Mexican process may yet get there. Third, even if it is agreed that the governing bloc must decompose before the transition can come about, social movements may still be important in widening the breach: "Without some initial cracks in the authoritarian coalitions their impact was limited, but once such cracks appeared they bolstered the efforts to oust autocratic governments."[44]There is no doubt that the direct elections campaign of 1984 in Brazil succeeded in bringing the transition forward if not in actually bringing it about. Finally, it may be prudent to reject the characterization of democratic transition as a once-off historical event: Social movements have only recently begun to insist on the rights of citizenship, and democratic transitions themselves may have some way to go.

Nonetheless, it is undeniable that, at the moment of transition itself, social movements are obliged to approach political society in order to project their goals into the world of party programs, political bargaining, and elections. Because it is the political parties that are the natural focal point for negotiated transition, the impact of the movements will be closely conditioned by the form and timing of their insertion into the party system. For this reason the role of the movements varies considerably from case to case. In Uruguay political parties had continued strong and the party system remained stable, and it was the parties that took control of the transition process. Social movements had played an important but limited and conjunctural role in creating the conditions for transition, and very few survived the transition itself.[45] In Argentina, very differently, the political parties were strong but the party system had never been successfully institutionalized, and the existence of "strong subcultures in a weak system" produced an "anarchic corporatism" and violent clashes between the contending social forces.[46] The weakness of political society meant that social movements could achieve little political purchase on the transition, and social mobilization fell far short of precipitating this transition. In Chile, on the other hand, the party system and its links with social movements had always been central to the political system overall. Political parties were suppressed, but party activists continued to play a key role in stimulating new forms of social mobilization. But the very strength of party tradition and organization meant that the parties tended to lose touch with this mobilization at critical moments,[47] while partisan divisions fragmented the opposition to the regime from the mid-1980s.[48] In these circumstances both parties and movements tended to remain preoccupied with short-term survival tactics and fleeting political alliances, so that the movements' engagement with political society could do little to develop a coherent strategy of democratic transition until the "constitutional moment" of the plebiscite.

The diversity and complexity of the transition process invalidates the simple, dichotomous scheme that separates the democratic struggles of the advanced world from the popular struggles of Latin America. According to Laclau and Mouffe, the diversity of social antagonisms in "central" countries encourages the multiplication of democratic struggles but prevents them from constituting a "people." In Latin America, on the contrary, "the predominance of brutal and centralized forms of domina-

tion tends from the beginning to endow the popular struggle with a centre, with a single and clearly defined enemy," and the diversity of democratic struggles is reduced to a single antagonism between the "principle
of domination" vested in the state and the "people." In short, this is not
democratic struggle at all but popular struggle where "discourses ten-
dentially construct the division of a single social space into two opposing
fields";[49] and an insistence on "autonomy" from the authoritarian state
converts all social movements into an uncomplicated oppositional identity that determines their strategic choices.

But nothing in this approach captures the various motives for social
mobilization, the diverse modes of identity formation, or, above all, the
complexities of strategic calculation (especially with regard to political
party alliances) that characterize popular struggle in Latin America. It is
suggested that in the modern or "hegemonic form of politics," in Western
Europe, for example, the frontiers between antagonistic social forces are
inherently unstable and porous; but there is no recognition that under the
authoritarian regimes of Latin America the frontiers between civil society
and the state are equally unstable, "negotiated," and subject to the outcomes of strategic success and failure. The result is a fundamental mis-
reading that ignores both the diversity of social movements and of democratic struggles (not to mention the political and cultural differences
marking the legal-institutional terrain conjoining state and civil society in
different countries) and their strategic coalescence around recurrent demands for universal rights.

Democratic Transitions and Social Movement Decline

At the moment of regime crisis, social mobilization can make a difference
to the fact and the outcome of democratic transition. The impetus of mobilization can open or widen breaches in the dominant coalition as well
as influence the strategic calculations of elite actors in the economy and
the state. If the crisis continues, repression becomes more difficult, and
social movements may perceive new opportunities for winning their political demands. For a time mobilization becomes more important than
sustained organization. But the movements begin to lose impetus once
negotiations begin with the incumbent regime, and parties or proto-par-
ties begin to move to center stage. Broad alliances between movements
become less likely with the shift from economic corporate goals to party
political and electoral objectives. In the model of "transition through
transaction,"[50] authoritarian elites manage to retain inside influence over
the state apparatuses, and the process of compromise and pacts leads to
strong institutional continuities. Administrative cadres are often un-
changed and the executive remains predominant over a weak and unsta-

ble party system. Because social movements were unsuccessful in institutionalizing the degrees of representation achieved through mobilization and negotiation, they are now sidelined from policymaking and removed from the centers of power. Their uncertain connection with
political parties means that they have no realistic hope of defining the political agenda (while the parties lack insertion in social movement "constituencies"). In short, with the transition to a democratic set of rules, social movements begin to decline.

The economic crisis that closely accompanied recent democratic
transitions in Latin America meant that social movements mainly
failed to influence the distribution of real resources in their favor. This
effect was reinforced by the austerity programs promoted by the International Monetary Fund and the foreign banks, while neoliberal economic reforms in general responded to a conception of civil society as
a market economy of atomized individuals and not as a social arena for
collective political action. The lack of any effective link with political
parties meant that the movements were drawn into the sphere of the
state, where they were again subject to populist maneuvers and clientelist tactics. In Brazil, especially, the movements' attempts to secure
corporative protection in the new constitution led to new forms of corporatist control. Political elites jockeyed for position, the executive
tried to buy support in congress, politicians tried to buy a new electorate, and all this catalyzed clientelism and promoted the comeback of
populist politicians. Moreover, because parties were poorly entrenched
and unattached to large constituencies, they could not act as brokers in
distributional conflicts, and so the problem of corruption could spread
unimpeded.

Above all, with the transition to democracy, the struggle for citizenship
moves to the constitutional sphere, and social movements lose their pre-
eminent role as defenders and promoters of legal and political rights.
Every state administration that is organized through bureaucratic power
relations will seek to institutionalize positive law and so create "subjects
capable of political obligation, and later the rights of citizens";[51] and a
newly democratic regime will seek to build its legitimacy by insisting on
these rights. In other words, "citizenship" becomes an identity that is de-
fended and disseminated by the state against all class and regional differences and against the specific identities and claims of social movements.[52] But social movements had often pressed for citizenship rights
and challenged social and political institutions to see these rights en-
shrined in law and put into practice. Insofar as this occurs through democratic transition, many of their demands are met, and their political
energy begins to dissipate. "Successful social movements inevitably lose
their reason for being."[53]

Social Movements and Political Society Revisited

Under authoritarian regimes civil society itself had become politicized, partly because of the total or partial suppression of the main actors of political society. With the advent of democracy, civil and political societies are more clearly differentiated, and social movements must learn new rules of the political game. But it is suggested that the movements "emerged in an authoritarian situation which continues to define their approach to politics," and that they are unable to adapt the confrontational tactics of the transition period to the strategies of negotiation and compromise necessitated by the new democratic status quo.[54] In other words "these movements and these protagonists have not learnt how to deal with a democratic scenario and have little historical memory of how to do so."[55]

These observations are redolent of Laclau and Mouffe's approach and probably mistake the kind of political learning achieved by social movements under authoritarianism. But there is little doubt that social movements multiply during democratic transition as do the direct channels to the state apparatus. Yet different parts of the state apparatus can be either receptive or repressive, and social movements can insist on their autonomy or accept clientelism, depending on the circumstances. The relationship with the state remains ambiguous, and the process of political representation is tortuous, unpredictable, and reversible. For the social movements, post-transition political society becomes what the Brazilians call a *jôgo surdo*, a "dance of the deaf." The rules may be new but they are not clear (and they vary according to local and regional context). Most popular leaders would therefore need no convincing that "the process of establishing a democracy is a process of institutionalizing uncertainty."[56]

The difficulties that social movements may encounter in political society are compounded by political parties. There is no natural affinity between the local, regional, or corporate demands of social movements and the national programs of political parties. While parties seek to secure power through forms of territorial representation, social movements continue to press for material benefits and "substantive" democracy through direct participation.[57] Local leaders may well view party militants with suspicion and seek to bypass the parties by a direct approach to municipal authorities and government agencies. Parties, on the other hand, may try to attract local leaders, but they soon discover that it is not easy to take the local out of the leader. It can be argued that in an ideal world social movements should move beyond their local context and promote the formation of a civic culture, but, in the case of Brazil, their successful insertion into the Workers' Party (PT) retarded the party's elaboration of a national and popular program.

As democratic transition proceeds, political parties reemerge and begin to compete for popular support among social movements, not least because their bargaining power depends on this support in some degree. At the same time, some social movement activists will seek political party affiliation to advance their own careers. Social movements cannot therefore escape the increasing salience of partisan politics in a more open political society, and "the democratization process they help encourage creates the conditions for internal division and competition."[58] As a result, conflicts arise both within the movements and between movements and political parties; and movements and parties draw further apart and closer together in a fluctuating rhythm. In Argentina the transition to democracy created greater space for legal action, accentuatuating the divisions between different urban social movements. In Bolivia the advent of democratic government in October 1982 seemed to catalyze factional strife within the rural movements. In Brazil the New Republic reinforced the heterogeneity of the social movements and left them increasingly isolated.

The democratic transitions of Latin America have depended on covert and exclusionary pacts between parties that are elitist, hierarchical, and socially conservative. Their most likely outcome is therefore a restricted democracy where social movements are isolated, repressed, or marginalized. But the real result varies according to the political culture. The strong state apparatuses and highly developed party systems of Chile and Uruguay appeared to displace social movements and leave them diminished. Social movements sought institutional expression in parties, unions, and nongovernmental organizations (NGOs) and could not easily contest the broad consensus that supported the traditional democratic way of life. In Argentina, on the other hand, the movements tended to suffer not from democratic but from "deeply entrenched authoritarian traditions,"[59] and despite some influence on party platforms for the 1983 elections, they failed to secure more permanent forms of representation and rapidly lost ground. In Brazil social movements found a real voice in the authentically new Workers' Party, and they mobilized to give the party a mass character. Rather than reemerging from authoritarian rule, the Workers' Party transformed itself in response to popular struggle under authoritarian rule and may yet serve as the centerpiece of an electoral coalition that controls national government.

During democratic transitions political parties have done what was necessary to prevent authoritarian reversals. The very fact of elections implies negotiations between opposition parties and the incumbent regime, often leading to a more than representative share of the vote for parties close to the regime. To achieve such a result, social movements have to be controlled and demobilized. In Brazil the presence of the

Workers' Party encouraged many movements to participate in the elections of 1982 and in the campaign for direct presidential elections of 1984. But regional opposition victories in 1982 and the diversions of the national campaign of 1984 both tended to demobilize the movements as vehicles for community or sectoral demands. Even in Brazil, therefore, social movements risked demobilization if they participated in party politics.[60] In Chile the more moderate movements were rapidly drawn into political society as soon as a date had been set for the constitutional plebiscite, and grass-roots mobilization only lasted as long as the plebiscitary and electoral campaigns themselves. Participation rates dropped dramatically after March 1990, indicating that social movements were likely to be permanently demobilized by the return to democratic politics.

Despite this recent evidence, the historical record has tended to show that electoral politics legitimates other forms of association and protest by providing legal protections. The rights to organize, recruit, speak, assemble, publicize, and demonstrate are essential to multiparty systems with universal suffrage; and it is difficult for governments to withhold these rights from other social actors, even in elite or restricted democracies. In this way, "state toleration or promotion of various sorts of electoral association . . . provide a warrant and a model for the action of associations that are quasi-electoral, semielectoral or even nonelectoral."[61] In Latin America, too, it is not impossible that the entrenchment of electoral politics will finally favor the spread of social movements (and the character of social movements might change as a result). There is little doubt that, even in the Southern Cone, democratic transitions have already helped to rebuild the labor movement. Outside the Southern Cone, social movements have challenged the political parties' monopoly of representation in two of the continent's more resilient democracies, Colombia and Venezuela. The different regional movements grouped within the Democratic Alliance M-19 in Colombia fleetingly gained a national profile in the general elections of May 1990 in their continuing attempt to fill the void created by the violence and corruption of the two major parties; and in both Colombia and Venezuela social movements have sought to deepen and expand the democratic arrangements forged through the elite pacts of the 1950s. It is not inconceivable that they may play a similar role in Brazil or the Southern Cone countries in years to come.

Democratic Transitions and Women's Mobilization

The military and authoritarian regimes of Latin America had a specific impact on women. First, women were relegated to the private sphere. Despite their increasing participation in the labor market and their educational attainments, they were confined to the home. The governments of Chile and Argentina even maintained the *potestad marital* that gave men full control over the person and property of their spouses. In the public sphere, laws, employment programs, jobs, and pay scales all prejudiced women; and women played almost no part in government itself. Second, their families were assaulted by intimidation, torture, and disappearances, and women themselves were subjected to sexual torture, with family ties manipulated to increase its effectiveness. Third, economic crisis and austerity policies threatened the survival of poor families on the urban periphery and thus mobilized women to defend their livelihoods. In short, by reinforcing the authoritarian culture of the family, fusing the questions of women's rights and human rights, and raising the stakes of economic survival, the military governments effectively politicized the private sphere, mobilized women for social action, and stimulated them to join the civilian opposition. Hence, the women's movements were "shaped from the beginning by their role in opposition to the military dictatorships. Ironically, military authoritarian rule, which intentionally depoliticized men and restricted the rights of 'citizens,' had the unintended consequence of mobilizing marginal and normally apolitical women."[62] The conditions of military rule catalyzed three main kinds of women's organization. Initially the most visible were the human rights groups that protested the detentions, torture, and disappearances. At the core of organizations like the Permanent Assembly for Human Rights and the Families of the Detained and Disappeared in Argentina, for example, were the relatives of those who had suffered at the hands of the regimes. In some cases their activism grew out of their work in the popular church and therefore received some support from the church (but not in Argentina). Less visible were the properly feminist groups that recruited middle-class professionals and women on the left who were frustrated by the failure of left-wing parties to take women's issues seriously. Their numbers and their ideas multiplied with the return of exiles from Europe and North America, and they began to provide legal aid, counselling, and education to torture victims, women's groups, and the broader opposition. Finally, there were the associations of poor urban women who were forced to respond to the removal of state benefits and subsidies and to the lack of basic services. They set up communal kitchens, infant feeding centers, and neighborhood workshops and attracted support from international agencies and the church. It was the question of economic survival that shaped the social agenda of the women's movement and, crucially, gave it a mass base.

In Chile the government thought of women as dedicated to abnegation and service and therefore its "natural" allies.[63] Its grand women's organizations set out to build discipline and civil allegiance. But increasing poverty and destitution encouraged a different kind of participation. The church fostered community struggles, the left organized neighborhood associations, and the existing network of mothers' centers were turned to the opposition's own purposes. The result was an explosion of female organizations, with more than a thousand Popular Economic Organizations in Greater Santiago by 1985. The women's groups were distinguished by their capacity to act in unity and to mobilize independently of the political parties, witnessed in the massive demonstration of Women for Life in December 1983.[64] This mobilizational capacity gave women a high profile during the democratic transition. At the moment of the plebiscite a Women's Command coordinated the attempts of party activists to reach women voters, and, for the first time, the campaign projected women's issues into the struggles of political society. Despite the traditionally conservative pattern of female voting in Chile, 52 percent of women voted against the prolongation of the Pinochet dictatorship.

In Brazil, too, the church urged women to join community struggles, left-wing parties placed female militants on the urban periphery to mobilize, and the military itself allowed women the leeway to organize because it did not view them as "political."[65] As the regime liberalized, women's mobilization grew. In Argentina, on the other hand, the church gave tacit support to the military, the left was decimated in the "Dirty War" (the name given to the military regime's assault on civil society), and women's militancy was reduced to and concentrated in the human rights organizations (which explains both their high profile and their isolation). But even in Argentina housewives's movements spread across the urban periphery during the latter months of 1982 (the so-called *vecinazos*), and, at the time of the transition, "each of the parties rushed to constitute its own women's front"[66] in order to win the women's vote. Alfonsín's Radical Civic Union took the Madres' slogan, "We are life," as the leitmotif of its own campaign, and its success was partly owing to the women's overwhelming support.

Women's mobilization may serve as a litmus test for the fate of social movements following democratic transitions. In Argentina the human rights groups were disappointed by the failure to pursue the perpetrators of the "Dirty War," and the creation of a National Women's Agency in the Ministry of Social Security was widely seen as a palliative measure. More positively, the Argentine version of *potestad marital* was modified, divorce was legalized, child care facilities were extended, contraception was made available, and domestic violence against women became a widely debated public issue. But party leaders did not fulfill campaign promises, and women's political careers were largely confined to government programs like the National Food Program and the National Literacy Campaign. Overall, women failed to achieve a higher profile in political society.

In Brazil a National Council on Women's Rights was established following the transition of 1985, but very few women were elected to parliaments at state or federal levels, women's demands found only a faint reflection in the constitution, and women's mobilization declined. In a typical trajectory for social movements, women were removed from decision-making arenas where (male-dominated) party and interest group politics took over; and as women's groups also changed tactics to pressure group politics, they increasingly courted co-optation and division.[67]The only other mass-based movement in Chile also ran increased risks of co-optation, but this time by political parties rather than the state apparatus itself. The (male-dominated) parties set up women's sections that were mere appendices of the power structure, and so the principled adhesion to sexual equality was never put into practice. Very few women were elected in the first elections of the transition and thus had no significant place in either legislature or executive.[68] It is therefore not surprising that in Uruguay, where the movement had nothing like the impetus achieved in Chile and Brazil, not one woman was elected to the national legislature in 1985. In sum, it must be concluded that, despite some not unimportant policy changes, "the political representation of women ... has not improved substantially": Nowhere did women's mobilization secure greater power or institutionalized participation of an enduring kind.[69]

The Fate of Social Movements and the Democratic Future

On the evidence of recent democratic transitions in Latin America, it is clear that "social movements are unlikely to radically transform large structures of domination or dramatically expand elite democracies, certainly not in the short run."[70] But they may still have an important role to play in democratizing social relations and in mediating between local communities and political systems, thus strengthening the connection between civil society and institutional politics. The decline of the movements that follows democratic transition need not therefore mean the end of their political potential. New collective identities have been created. Civil society has been discovered and transformed. Politics is more plural. Democracy is now valued as an end in itself.

However, this optimistic view depends on arguments of *longue durée.* The political impact of social movements is understood to be gradual and cumulative. State agencies and political parties slowly come to recognize the movements as legitimate players on the political scene and engage in dialogue with them. Social movements at the grass roots continue to search for ways to express and represent popular demands. And the many small contests and conflicts can and do add up to a more comprehensive challenge to traditional political practices. My own work on Spain and Mexico[71] tends to support the argument that social movements are successful in changing popular perceptions, institutional cultures, and political practices, even if these changes are unlikely to be sudden or dramatic. But doubts remain. On the one hand, it seems important to distinguish between the myriad forms of cultural and political resistance at the local level (that have characterized popular culture since time immemorial) and contemporary social movements that aspire to make some impact on the political system overall. On the other, it is important for the shorter term to decide whether social movements act to deepen and defend precarious democratic arrangements or to increase the threat of authoritarian reversal. More concretely, can social movements strengthen democracy "while simultaneously challenging the exclusionary mechanisms of specific democratic institutions"?[72]

The question of exclusion is crucial to an appreciation of the relationship between social movements and democracy in contemporary Latin America. Indeed, the critique of current democratic arrangements as being "elitist and unconnected with the lived experience of the mass of the population" has been characterized as the "social movements perspective."[73] At present the clear predominance of elite over popular democracy is expressed in the strong adherence to neoliberal economic policies: Only a neoliberal strategy can lead to the successful consolidation of democracy because the social democratic path is "hopelessly overoptimistic given the weak productive base."[74] But the problem with the neoliberal approach is that "what can be consolidated by these means would seem to exclude many of the features commonly associated with full liberal democracy (high participation, authentic political choice, extensive citizenship rights)."[75] In other words, this exclusionary model leads to "a very partial form of democratic politics—a form of politics in which the involvement of some bears a direct relation to the limited or non-participation of others."[76]

This partial form of democracy has been called the second-best outcome for the countries of Latin America. "Reformist, populist or socialist projects had been attempted and had failed; reactionary authoritarian projects had also been attempted and had also failed."[77] The result was "democracy by default"—or political systems that fail to consolidate or institutionalize democracy and that "will not conform neatly to any of our theoretical or practical models of authoritarian and democratic regimes." In short, there will be democratic advance and authoritarian retreat but not "a nice neat linear movement from one clear-cut regime type (authoritarian) to some other type (democratic)."[78] However, the limitations on democracy and, consequently, the indeterminacy of regime type, will vary from country to country:

> restrictions on national sovereignty; curtailment of political choice by market mechanisms; façade arrangements intended to project an external image of pluralism without disturbing traditional power relations; the persistence of undemocratic structures in rural areas; policy paralysis derived from fiscal crisis; misguided design of institutional arrangements; a fragmented civil society incapable of generating legitimacy or social consensus.[79]

All these and further limitations are possible, in any combination. Although there is some evidence that these partial democracies are having some success in subordinating the armed forces to the rule of law, their lack of institutionalization is seen most flagrantly in their highly presidentialist forms of government and the rapid resort to arbitrary decision making. This style of governance has been called "delegative democracy" or "democratic Caesarism" and is typical of these "hybrid regimes that . . . give the executive quasi-authoritarian power in times of crisis." What then matters is not the institutional form of political participation but access to the executive; and, whatever the specific configuration of the "hybrid regime," what remains constant is "the inclination . . . to capture executive sources of benefits that flow more as patronage and privileges than as universal rights."[80] In short, the partial democracies of Latin America merely pay lip service to liberal values and democratic rights and continue to practice the politics of populism and clientelism. What is then required is "a thorough examination of the relation between formal rights and actual rights, between commitments to treat citizens as free and equal and practices which do neither sufficiently."[81] What this examination will reveal is that social movements still have a vital and specific role to play in securing democratic government. Whereas elite actors, party leaders, and pressure groups target the executive and "usually operate through parties and legislatures only to defend achieved privileges,"[82] social movements will continue to press for more popular participation in decision making and a more positive application of democratic rights. Above all, social movements will mobilize to close the gap between the rhetoric and reality of citizenship, between the promise and the practice of democratic rights. Indeed, in the present context of partial democracy the best working definition of a social movement is a popular organization that can make plausible claims to exercise a perceptible impact on the extension and exercise of the rights of citizenship.

Notes

1. The core rights of citizenship are understood to be both civil and political. Civil rights are those necessary to individual freedom and are associated most directly with the rule of law and the system of courts. Political rights ensure participation in the exercise of political rule and are associated with election and parliamentary institutions of different kinds.

2. Scott Mainwaring and Eduardo Viola, "New Social Movements, Political Culture and Democracy: Brazil and Argentina in the 1980s," *Telos*, no. 61, 1984, p. 33.

3. Elizabeth Jelin, "Citizenship and Identity: Final Reflections," in Elizabeth Jelin, ed., *Women and Social Change in Latin America* (London: Zed Books, 1990), p. 206.

4. Jean Cohen and Andrew Arato, *Civil Society and Political Theory* (Cambridge, MA: MIT Press, 1992), p. 446.

5. Elizabeth Jelin, "Introduction," in Jelin, ed., *Women and Social Change in Latin America*, p. 5.

6. David Lehmann, *Democracy and Development in Latin America: Economics, Politics and Religion in the Post-War Period* (Philadelphia: Temple University Press, 1990), p. 153.

7. Helen Safa, "Women's Social Movements in Latin America," *Gender and Society*, vol. 4, no. 3, 1990, pp. 354–69.

8. Lehman, *Democracy and Development in Latin America*, p. 163.

9. Ibid., p. 151.

10. Ibid., p. 147.

11. Cathy Schneider reports this assertion of the president of a democratically elected neighborhood council in Yungay, one of the urban districts of Santiago de Chile organized by the Chilean Communist Party, in "Radical Opposition Parties and Squatters Movements in Pinochet's Chile," in Arturo Escobar and Sonia E. Alvarez, eds., *The Making of Social Movements in Latin America: Identity, Strategy, and Democracy* (Boulder: Westview, 1992), pp. 260–75.

12. Jelin, "Citizenship and Identity," p. 206.

13. Cohen and Arato, *Civil Society and Political Theory*, p. 440.

14. Chantal Mouffe, "Hegemony and New Political Subjects: Toward a New Concept of Democracy," in C. Nelson and L. Grossberg, eds., *Marxism and the Interpretation of Culture* (Urbana: University of Illinois Press, 1988), p. 126.

15. "In modern civil society, rights are not only moral oughts, but also empower. Rights do not only individualize, they are also a medium of communication, association and solidarity. They do not necessarily depoliticize; they can also constitute a vital connection between private individuals and the new public and political spheres in society and state." Cohen and Arato, *Civil Society and Political Theory*, p. 297.

16. The authors go on to ask, "How else can one account for the worker's movement, civil rights movement, the women's movement, the ecology movement, regional struggles for autonomy, or any modern social movement?" Ibid., p. 295.

17. Guillermo O'Donnell and Philippe Schmitter, *Transitions from Authoritarian Rule*. Vol. 4: *Tentative Conclusions about Uncertain Democracies*. (Baltimore: Johns Hopkins University Press, 1986), p. 26 and passim.

18. Daniel Levine, "Paradigm Lost: Dependency to Democracy," *World Politics*, vol. XL, no. 3, 1988, pp. 377–94.

19. Democratic transitions express a wide variety of trajectories and outcomes. The role of social movements within them is conditioned by the specific rhythm of the "protest cycle," the shape of the political opportunity structure, and the contingencies of strategic choice. By way of example, in Chile it took a long "cycle of protest" and a rising rhythm of social mobilization to create the political conditions for the plebiscite and the eventual return to democratic government, while in Argentina mass mobilization did not occur until elections had been announced and the transition itself was almost a foregone conclusion.

20. Scott Mainwaring, "Transitions to Democracy and Democratic Consolidation: Theoretical and Comparative Issues," in Scott Mainwaring, Guillermo O'-Donnell, and J. Samuel Valenzuela, eds., *Issues in Democratic Consolidation: The New South American Democracies in Comparative Perspective* (South Bend, IN: University of Notre Dame Press, 1992), p. 310.

21. Cohen and Arato, *Civil Society and Political Theory*, p. 19.

22. Ibid., p. 48.

23. Alessandro Pizzorno, "On the Rationality of Democratic Choice," *Telos*, no. 63, 1985, p. 69.

24. Francisco Weffort argues that both the concept and reality of civil society have been very tenuous compared to the strength of state traditions and myths in Brazil. The links between civil society and democracy were weak or deformed. Democracy was always seen as a "means to power": "The instrumental conception of democracy runs through our history like a curse." The rediscovery of civil society and associationalism were therefore essential to the reconstitution of a democratic political society. "Why Democracy?" in Alfred Stepan, ed., *Democratizing Brazil* (New York: Oxford University Press, 1989), p. 334.

25. Teresa Pires de Rio Caldeira, "Women, Daily Life and Politics," in Jelin, ed., *Women and Social Change in Latin America*, p. 49; The involvement of urban movements from different regions of Brazil in municipal politics demonstrated that their main concerns were community needs and effective management, not political rights or political party programs. See Edison Nunes and Pedro Jacobi, "Movimentos Populares Urbanos, Participação e Democracia," in Machado da Silva et al., eds., *Movimentos Sociais, Minorías Etnicas e Outros Estudos* (Brasilia: Associação Nacional de Pós-Graduação e Pesquisa en Ciàncias Sociais [ANPOCS], 1983), pp. 205–26.

26. It is in this sense that the savagery of much urban speculation and exploitation makes the Latin American city "a city without citizens," or that the struggle of urban movements to defend their land and a communal living space is a struggle for "urban citizenship." See, Manuel Castells, *The City and the Grassroots* (London: Edward Arnold, 1983); A. Massolo and Lucila Diaz Ronner, "La Participación de las Mujeres en los Movimientos Sociales Urbanos," Programa Integrado de Estudios sobre la Mujer, El Colegio de México,

México, D.F., July 27, 1983. The general point is that many social movements are based on primary groups "rather than the secondary, professional and more anonymous groupings which embody a liberal image of active citizenship," and are therefore more easily subject to clientelistic control and paternalistic manipulation. Lehmann, *Democracy and Development in Latin America*, p. 154.

27. If the notion of social rights "actually contradicts the notion of citizenship, which cannot be made consistent with any form of paternalism," this was certainly true of organized labor's "quest for particular privileges." Cohen and Arato, *Civil Society and Political Theory*, p. 127; see also James M. Malloy, "The Politics of Transition in Latin America" in James M. Malloy and Mitchell A. Seligson, eds., *Authoritarians and Democrats: Regime Transition in Latin America* (Pittsburgh: University of Pittsburgh Press, 1987), p. 254. Moreover, because labor leaders secured as much or more access to social benefits under authoritarian as under democratic regimes, they did not develop a primary commitment to democracy either in principle or for its social welfarism.

28. The question is not merely rhetorical. Since welfare provision in Latin America is precarious and spotty, even social rights must often be won by recurrent mobilization, which may lead to—or be forced into—a broader political agenda.

29. Joe Foweraker, *Making Democracy in Spain: Grass-roots Struggle in the South, 1955–1975* (New York: Cambridge University Press, 1989).

30. Margaret Keck notes the massive expansion of the industrial working class in Brazil and emphasizes that most of the workers belonged to a new generation that had grown up under military rule: "The pre-1964 period was at most a childhood memory . . . these young workers were building their organizations on the basis of experience gained under the authoritarian regime." "The New Unionism in the Brazilian Transition," in Stepan, ed., *Democratizing Brazil*, p. 260, 289.

31. Renato Boschi, *A Arte de Associação: Política de Base e Democracia no Brasil* (São Paulo: Edições Vertice e IUPERJ, 1987).

32. Manuel Antonio Garretón, *The Chilean Political Process* (Boston: Unwin Hyman, 1989), p. 153.

33. Joe Foweraker, *Popular Mobilization in Mexico; The Teachers' Movement, 1977–1987* (New York: Cambridge University Press, 1993).

34. Mainwaring and Viola, "New Social Movements, Political Culture and Democracy," p. 23.

35. Renato Boschi, "Social Movements and the New Political Order in Brazil," in John D. Wirth, Edson de Oliveira Nunes, and Thomas E. Bogenschild, eds., *State and Society in Brazil* (Boulder: Westview Press, 1987), p. 184.

36. Garretón, *The Chilean Political Process*, p. 154.

37. Juan Silva and Frans Schuurman, "Neighbourhood Associations in Buenos Aires: Contradictions within Contradictions," in Frans Schuurman and Ton van Naerssen, eds., *Urban Social Movements in the Third World* (London: Routledge, 1989), pp. 45–62.

38. See Mainwaring and Viola, "New Social Movements, Political Culture and Democracy," passim; and Elizabeth Jelin, ed., *Ciudadania e Identidad: Las Mujeres*

en los Movimientos Sociales Latinoamericanos (Geneva: United Nations Research Institute for Social Development [UNRISD], 1987), passim.

39. Boschi, "Social Movements and the New Political Order in Brazil," p. 185.

40. Willem Assies, Gerrit Burgwal, and Ton Salman, *Structures of Power, Movements of Resistance: An Introduction to the Theories of Urban Movements in Latin America* (Amsterdam: Centro de Estudios y Documentación Latinoamericanos [CEDLA], 1991); John Higley and Richard Gunther, *Elites and Democratic Consolidation in Latin America and Southern Europe* (New York: Cambridge University Press, 1992).

41. Boschi, "Social Movements and the New Political Order in Brazil," p. 184.

42. See Foweraker, *Making Democracy in Spain,* passim; and Foweraker, *Popular Mobilization in Mexico,* passim; Joe Foweraker and Ann Craig, *Popular Movements and Political Change in Mexico* (Boulder: Lynne Rienner, 1990).

43. Ilse Scherer-Warren and Paulo Krischke, *Uma Revolução no Cotidiano? Os Novos Movimentos Sõciais na America do Sul* (Saõ Paulo: Brasilense, 1987).

44. Mainwaring, "Transitions to Democracy and Democratic Consolidation," p. 315.

45. The military's attempts to repress and discipline civil society did stimulate the emergence of social movements. The years between the plebiscite of 1980 and the transition of 1984 were a period of intense associationalism around specific interests but outside the framework of the state. Moreover, there is little doubt that the series of alliances that constructed the National Concentration Project (CONAPRO) contributed to reconstituting political society and filling a temporary institutional void. This process was underpinned by the labor movement that both regained its traditional autonomy and strengthened its bargaining position through the merger of the Interunion Assembly of Workers (PIT) and the National Workers' Council (CNT).

46. Renato Boschi, "Social Movements, Party Systems and Democratic Consolidations: Brazil, Uruguay and Argentina," in Diana Ethier, ed., *Democratic Transition and Consolidation in Southern Europe, Latin America and Southeast Asia* (London: Macmillan, 1990), p. 230; Guillermo O'Donnell, "Democracia en la Argentina Micro y Macro," in Oscar Oszlak, ed., *"Proceso," Crisis y Transición Democrática* (Buenos Aires: Centro Editor de América Latina, 1984), p. 24; On the other hand, civil society, at least in its "corporatist" forms, was strong, and the working class was highly organized within the Peronist (Justicialist) Party. But the military intervened repeatedly to prevent the Peronists from taking over government, and this anticonstitutional veto finally damaged the legitimacy of any elected government and reduced the civil commitment to democratic policies.

47. The huge mobilization of May 1983 and the following month had succeeded in uniting middle and popular sectors for the first time in many years. But the strength of the repression and the selective co-optation of middle-class demands had reduced mobilization to the more radical student and youth groups, especially on the urban periphery. From this moment opposition to the regime tended to split between the political party opposition and the "social" opposition of popular sector organizations. These organizations were plagued by problems of daily survival, which the traditional thinking of the parties failed to address.

48. Garretón, *The Chilean Political Process*, p. 173; Although all parties in Chile backed mobilization, they set different goals. The Christian Democrats and the "center" sought negotiation; the left parties wanted to bring down the regime. The Assembly of Civility (*Asamblea de la Civilidad*) of 1986 aimed to overcome these divisions by bringing together professional associations, labor unions, and, in principle, the popular urban sectors, as well as women's organizations and human right groups. But despite the assembly's massive mobilization of July 1986, both the opposition in general and the labor unions in particular remained divided; at the same time, political party rivalries undermined the first Unitary Congress of Urban Settlers. The student and women's movements escaped the worst of the factionalism for a time but finally came to feel its adverse effects.

49. Ernesto Laclau and Chantal Mouffe, *Hegemony and Socialist Strategy: Towards a Radical Democratic Politics* (London: Verso, 1985), p. 131.

50. Donald Share and Scott Mainwaring, "Transitions through Transaction: Democratization in Brazil and Spain," in Wayne Selcher, ed., *Political Liberalization in Brazil* (Boulder: Westview, 1986), pp. 175–215.

51. Cohen and Arato, *Civil Society and Political Theory*, p. 439.

52. Alain Touraine, *Actores Sociales y Sistemas Políticos en América Latina* (Santiago: Programa Regional del Empleo para América Latina y el Caribe [PREALC]-Oficina Internacional del Trabajo [OIT], 1987).

53. Jane Jaquette, "Conclusion: Women and the New Democratic Politics," in Jane Jaquette, ed., *The Women's Movement in Latin America: Feminism and the Transition to Democracy* (Winchester, MA: Unwin Hyman, 1989), p. 194.

54. Mainwaring and Viola, "New Social Movements, Political Culture and Democracy," p. 44; Escobar and Alvarez, eds., *The Making of Social Movements in Latin America*, passim.

55. Maria del Carmen Feijóo and Monica Gogna, "Women in the Transition to Democracy," in Jelin, ed., *Women and Social Change in Latin America*, p. 108.

56. Adam Przeworski, "Some Problems in the Study of the Transition to Democracy," in Guillermo O'Donnell, Philippe Schmitter, and Laurence Whitehead, eds., *Transitions from Authoritarian Rule: Comparative Perspectives* (Baltimore: Johns Hopkins University Press, 1986), p. 58.

57. In general "the move to electoral parties with their less intense, more inclusive, more abstract form of political identification and their lower degree of direct participation tends to devalue and replace movements and associations with their more particular, but also more intense and participatory forms of organization." Cohen and Arato, *Civil Society and Political Theory*, p. 53.

58. Mainwaring and Viola, "New Social Movements, Political Culture and Democracy," p. 44.

59. Ibid., p. 43.

60. Boschi, *A Arte de Asociação*, passim; Scherer-Warren and Krischke, *Uma Revolução no Cotidiano*, passim.

61. Charles Tilly, "Social Movements and National Politics," in William Bright and Stuart Harding, eds., *State Building and Social Movements* (Ann Arbor: University of Michigan Press, 1984), p. 311.

62. Jane Jaquette, "Introduction," in Jaquette, ed., *The Women's Movements in Latin America*, p. 5.

63. Maria E. Valenzuela, "Mujeres y Politíca: Logros y Tensiones en el Proceso de Redemocratización," *Proposiciones*, no. 18, 1990, pp. 210–32.

64. Garretón, *The Chilean Political Process*, passim; During the 1970s women had staffed various human right groups and carried out solidarity work with prisoners and their families, and in 1979 a women's committee of the Chilean Human Rights Commission was formed. By the early 1980s women were active in three major female confederations.

65. Sonia E. Alvarez, "Women's Movements and Gender Politics in the Brazilian Transition," in Jaquette, ed., *The Women's Movement in Latin America*, pp. 18–71.

66. Maria del Carmen Feijóo, "The Challenge of Constructing Civilian Peace: Women and Democracy in Argentina," in Ibid., p. 81.

67. Alvarez, "Women's Movements and Gender Politics in the Brazilian Transition," passim.

68. Patrícia M. Chuchryk, "Feminist Anti-Authoritarian Politics: The Role of Women's Organizations in the Chilean Transition to Democracy," in Jaquette, ed., *The Women's Movement in Latin America*, pp. 149–84.

69. Safa, "Women's Social Movement in Latin America," passim. Sadly, this is now true even of Nicaragua where the women's movement had made very substantial advances. Women had accounted for about 30 percent of the FSLN's armed combatants and so had a clear expectation that the revolutionary government would address their concerns. Because women also made up the great majority of poorest Nicaraguans, they did benefit considerably from the government's general welfare and reform policies (including land reform), and the government also made men legally responsible for the welfare of their families, which furthered the cause of sexual equality. But there were no constitutional or legal guarantees for these advances, and most of them have since been reversed by economic and political crisis.

70. Sonia Alvarez and Arturo Escobar, "Conclusion: Theoretical and Political Horizons of Change in Contemporary Latin American Social Movements," in Escobar and Alvarez, eds., *The Making of Social Movements in Latin America*, p. 325.

71. Foweraker, *Making Democracy in Spain*, passim; and Foweraker, *Popular Mobilization in Mexico*, passim.

72. Roberto Barros, "The Left and Democracy: Recent Debates in Latin America," *Telos*, no. 68, 1986, p. 64.

73. Laurence Whitehead, "The Alternatives to Liberal Democracy: A Latin American Perspective," *Political Studies*, vol. XL, 1992, p. 154.

74. Ibid., p. 156. Because the neoliberal approach has the clear advantage of being feasible, "the choice would be between a stunted version of liberal democracy that works, or a generous vision of social democracy that remains a mirage (the Chilean Constitution of 1980 versus the Brazilian Constitution of 1988)." Ibid., p. 154.

75. Ibid., p. 154.

76. David Held, "Democracy from City-states to a Cosmopolitan Order?" in *Political Studies*, vol. XL, 1992, p. 20.

77. Whitehead, "The Alternatives to Liberal Democracy," p. 148.

78. Malloy, "The Politics of Transition in Latin America," pp. 251–2.

79. Whitehead, "The Alternatives to Liberal Democracy," p. 158.

80. See Guillermo O'Donnell, "Delegative Democracy?," Working Paper No. 172, Helen Kellogg Institute for International Studies (South Bend, IN: University of Notre Dame, 1992); and Malloy, "The Politics of Transition in Latin America," pp. 252–7.

81. Held, "Democracy from City-states to a Cosmopolitan Order," p. 20.

82. Malloy, "The Politics of Transition in Latin America," p. 252.

About the Contributors

Anthony Bebbington, formerly with the Overseas Development Administration in London, is presently associate professor of geography, Institute of Behavioral Sciences, University of Colorado at Boulder. He is the author of *Crisis y Caminos: Reflexiones Heréticas acerca de las ONGs, el Estado y un Desarrollo Sustentable en América Latina* (1996).

Julio Cotler is professor of anthropology at San Marcos University and a researcher at the Institute of Peruvian Studies, both in Lima. He has authored and edited numerous books and articles on social and political development in Peru and other Andean countries, including *Clases, Estado y Nación en el Perú* (1978).

Joe Foweraker is professor of government, University of Essex, England. He specializes in popular political organization and state-society relations in Latin America and Europe. His publications include *The Struggle for Land: A Political Economy of the Pioneer Frontier in Brazil* (1981), *Making Democracy in Spain* (1989), *Popular Mobilization in Mexico* (1993), and *Theorizing Social Movements* (1995).

Pablo Gerchunoff, senior research associate at the Institute Torcuato di Tella in Buenos Aires has published extensively on problems of the labor market and on privatization and deregulation of the Argentinian economy.

William Glade is professor of economics at the University of Texas at Austin. He is the author and editor of many books and articles on economic development in Latin America, including *State Shrinking: A Comparative Inquiry into Privatization* (1986) and *Privatization of Public Enterprises in Latin America* (1991).

Luis Gómez Calcaño, director of the Center for Development Studies (CENDES) of the Central University of Venezuela in Caracas, has published many articles and research reports on sociopolitical development in Venezuela.

Lawrence Graham is professor of government, University of Texas at Austin. He has published extensively on issues of government in Latin America and Mediterranean Europe, including *The State and Policy Outcomes in Latin America* (1990).

David Lehmann is director of the Centre of Latin American Studies, University of Cambridge, England. His many publications in the areas of agrarian development and social movements include *Peasants, Landlords and Governments* (1974) and *Democracy and Development in Latin America* (1990).

Victoria Rodríguez is associate professor at the Lyndon B. Johnson School of Public Affairs, University of Texas at Austin. She has written widely on opposition governments and state and local governments in Mexico, including (with Peter M. Ward) *Policymaking, Politics, and Urban Governance in Chihuahua: The Experience of Recent Panista Governments* and *Political Change in Baja California:*

Democracy in the Making? (1992). Her most recent book is *Decentralization in Mexico.* Her current research interests focus the role of women in contemporary Mexican politics.

Jon Shefner is research associate in the Department of Sociology, University of California at Davis. He is involved in research on poverty programs and social movements in Mexico.

Patricio Silva, lecturer of political science at the University of Leiden, The Netherlands, has published extensively on the problems of democratization and state reform in Latin America, including *The Politics of Expertise in Latin America* (1996, with Miguel Centeno).

Peter H. Smith is professor of political science, Simón Bolívar Professor of Latin American Studies, and director of the Center for Iberian and Latin American Studies at the University of California, San Diego. He has written numerous books and articles, including *Modern Latin America* (1994, with Thomas Skidmore) and *Talons of the Eagle* (1996).

Juan Carlos Torre is senior research associate at the Institute Torcuato di Tella in Buenos Aires. He has written books and articles on the labor movement in Argentina and is presently involved in a study of the political and institutional aspects of economic reform programs in Latin America.

Menno Vellinga is professor of development studies, Faculty of Geographical Sciences, and director of the Center for Latin American and Caribbean Studies, at Utrecht University, The Netherlands. He is the author and editor of many books and articles on socioeconomic and sociopolitical aspects of development in Latin America, including *Burguesía e Industria en América Latina y Europa Meridional* (1988, with Mario Cerutti); *Industrialización, Burguesía y Clase Obrera en México* (1989); and *Social Democracy in Latin America* (1993).

Howard Wiarda is professor of political science at the University of Massachusetts and professor of national security policy at the National Defense University in Washington, D.C. He has written extensively on political developments in Latin America, including *The Democratic Revolution in Latin America* (1990) and *Politics and Social Change in Latin America* (1992).

Index